Imke Mendoza, Sandra Birzer (Eds.)
Diachronic Slavonic Syntax

Trends in Linguistics
Studies and Monographs

Editors
Chiara Gianollo
Daniël Van Olmen

Editorial Board
Walter Bisang
Tine Breban
Volker Gast
Hans Henrich Hock
Karen Lahousse
Natalia Levshina
Caterina Mauri
Heiko Narrog
Salvador Pons
Niina Ning Zhang
Amir Zeldes

Editor responsible for this volume
Chiara Gianollo

Volume 348

Diachronic Slavonic Syntax

Traces of Latin, Greek and Church Slavonic in Slavonic Syntax

Edited by
Imke Mendoza and Sandra Birzer

We would like to express our thanks to the Fritz Thyssen Foundation for funding both the conference and this volume.

Fritz Thyssen Stiftung
für Wissenschaftsförderung

ISBN 978-3-11-135325-8
e-ISBN (PDF) 978-3-11-065133-1
e-ISBN (EPUB) 978-3-11-064720-4

Library of Congress Control Number: 2021952033

Bibliographic information published by the Deutsche Nationalbibliothek
The Deutsche Nationalbibliothek lists this publication in the Deutsche Nationalbibliografie; detailed bibliographic data are available on the Internet at http://dnb.dnb.de.

© 2023 Walter de Gruyter GmbH, Berlin/Boston
This volume is text- and page-identical with the hardback published in 2022.
Typesetting: Integra Software Services Pvt. Ltd.
Printing and binding: CPI books GmbH, Leck

www.degruyter.com

Preface

The contributions of this volume are based on presentations given at the conference "Diachronic Syntax of the Slavonic Languages 3. Traces of Latin, Greek and Church Slavonic in Slavonic Syntax", which took place at the University of Salzburg on November 3–4, 2017.

We would like to express our thanks to the Fritz Thyssen Foundation for funding both the conference and this volume. We would also like to thank Nicholas Peterson, who proof-read the contributions from a native speaker's point of view, Adrian Kuqi for his help with copy-editing the volume as well as numerous colleagues for their peer review of the contributions in this volume.

Contents

Preface —— V

Glossing —— IX

Imke Mendoza and Sandra Birzer
Introduction —— 1

Part I: The influence of Latin on Slavonic vernaculars

Anna Kisiel and Piotr Sobotka
The paths of grammaticalization of North Slavonic connectors. An interface point of Slavonic, Greek and Latin —— 11

Agnieszka Słoboda
The influence of Latin on the syntax of Old Polish numerals —— 37

Pavel Kosek, Radek Čech and Olga Navrátilová
The influence of the Latin Vulgate on the word order of pronominal enclitics in the 1st edition of the Old Czech Bible —— 53

Sanja Perić Gavrančić
The *accusativus cum infinitivo* in 16th–19th century Croatian texts. Contact-induced and internally motivated syntactic change —— 81

Barbara Sonnenhauser and Marisa Eberle
Relative coordination. *Kateri-/koteri*-relatives in 18th century Slovene and Kajkavian —— 107

Part II: The influence of Greek on Church Slavonic

Anna Pichkhadze
Blocking of syntactic constructions without Greek counterparts in Church Slavonic —— 133

Jürgen Fuchsbauer
The article-like usage of the relative pronoun *iže* as an indicator of early Slavonic grammatical thinking —— 163

Simeon Dekker
Past tense usage in Old Russian performative formulae. A case study into the development of a written language of distance —— 179

Part III: The influence of Latin on Church Slavonic

Vittorio S. Tomelleri
When Church Slavonic meets Latin. Tradition vs. innovation —— 201

Ana Šimić
Non-strict negative concord proper and languages in contact. Translating Latin into Croatian Church Slavonic and Greek into Old Church Slavonic —— 233

Part IV: In lieu of a conclusion

Hanne Martine Eckhoff
First attestations. An Old Church Slavonic sampler —— 255

Index —— 303

Glossing

The glossing abbreviations used in this volume are mainly based on the Leipzig Glossing Rules (LGR). Abbreviations that are not included in LGR are listed below.

AOR	aorist
COMPV	comparative
CON	conjunction
COP	copula
GEN/ACC	syncretism of genitive and accusative for animate masculine nouns in direct object position
GRDV	gerundive
IMPERF	imperfect
INDECL	indeclinable
LF	long form (adjectives)
LPTCP	*l*-participle (used for compound verb forms)
MED	mediopassive
OPT	optative
PLUPRF	plusperfect
PRED	predicative (a non-verbal form, most often an adverb, functioning as predicate)
PTCL	particle
SUP	supine

Imke Mendoza and Sandra Birzer

Introduction

This is the second "Diachronic Slavonic Syntax" volume that focuses on the impact of language contact on syntactic change. Unlike its predecessor (Hansen, Grković-Major, and Sonnenhauser 2018), it tackles a very specific and rather narrow problem. The contributions in this volume explore the role of so-called "literacy contact" in the history of the Slavonic languages (Middle Ages to early 19th c.). The source languages involved are Greek, Latin and Church Slavonic, which served as literary languages before and during the emergence of literary varieties based on Slavonic vernaculars.

The Slavonic languages with their complex relations to Latin and Greek are a rewarding object for the study of literacy contacts from both a solely Slavonic and a typological perspective. Even though the interrelation between said literary languages and their impact on the Slavonic vernaculars has been a topic in Slavonic studies from the very beginning, only few works address this issue systematically and from a theoretical perspective. This is particularly true when it comes to the level of syntactic influence. The volume at hand aims to shed some light on the conditions and results of literacy contact in the realm of syntactic structures.

1 Literacy contact

The overwhelming majority of language contact theories model only face-to-face contact, i.e., the contact of language users in canonical communication situations. This is, however, not the only setting for language contact to happen. Another important scenario is the so-called *literacy contact*. The term was first introduced to Slavonic historical linguistics by Verkholantsev (2008: 136–137) and has been taken up and redefined by Rabus (2013).[1] He understands literacy

---

[1] Verkholantsev shaped her definition of literacy contact using Ruthenian as a case study. She suggests that the development of Ruthenian into a polyfunctional language was influenced by two phenomena, namely "a systematic linguistic process of language contact between the speakers of Belarusian/Ukrainian dialects and the Poles, which resulted in language interference, mixing, and koineization; the other – the process of literacy contact, which introduced literacy interference from Polish and Church Slavonic into the language of emerging Ruthenian writings"

Imke Mendoza, Paris-Lodron-Universität Salzburg, e-mail: imke.mendoza@plus.ac.at
Sandra Birzer, Otto-Friedrich-Universität Bamberg, e-mail: sandra.birzer@uni-bamberg.de

https://doi.org/10.1515/9783110651331-001

contact as a situation characterized "nicht durch mündliche Interaktion, sondern durch die Transmission und Rezeption sowie Übersetzung schriftlicher Texte" ['not by face-to-face interaction, but by transmission, reception and translation of written texts', translation SB & IM] (Rabus 2013: 66). Unlike face-to-face contact, literacy contact does not originate from the direct interaction of the communication participants but from the interaction of a language user with the written word. Rabus notes that there are "Situationen [gibt], in welchen sowohl die direkte Face-to-Face-Interaktion als auch literacy contact wirksam sind [. . .]. In solchen Situationen wirken also zwei Einflussebenen parallel oder zumindest gleichzeitig" ['there exist situations in which both direct face-to-face interaction and literacy contact take effect. Thus, in such situations two levels of influence operate interdependently or at least simultaneously', translation SB & IM] (Rabus 2013: 66). We will narrow our own definition even further and define literacy contact as follows: literacy contact takes place when a bilingual language user encounters instances of the conceptually written register of the source language and that encounter exerts influence on the morphosyntactic structure of the bilingual's text production in the target language.[2]

This type of language contact not only requires linguistic skills that are different from those we need for face-to-face interaction, but it also represents a different type of acquisition of the language that later might become the source language. As a rule, the target language is acquired as first language (L1), whereas the source language is usually a second language (L2) and is acquired by formal instruction. Church Slavonic as target language for Greek and Latin influence is the exception to this rule.

In a simplified scheme, one may assume that participants in face-to-face contact necessarily acquire audio-receptive and oral productive skills in L2. The acquisition process goes along with a layman's insight into phonetics / phonology, prosody and possibly into the specificities of the source language's informal, colloquial reg-

---

(Verkholantsev 2008: 137). This statement carries two assumptions we do not necessarily share. Firstly, she apparently conceives face-to-face contact and literacy contact as an opposition with the former as the systematic, regular variant of language contact, and the latter as a haphazard, unsystematic form of influence. Secondly, literacy interference seems to imply the transfer of certain literary genres, without, however, relating this process to the language structures used in or even specific for those genres. These findings can hardly be generalized, so we take Rabus' approach as point of departure.

2 This also neatly fits Rabus's observation on the perception of Church Slavonic, one of our source languages, by its bilingual users: "The external, scientific characterization of Church Slavonic as being relevant predominantly in its written form is actually in line with the internal, local characterization of the pre-modern Slavs themselves: they used to call Church Slavonic words and constructions *knižnye* 'bookish'." (Rabus 2014, 340, italics original).

isters. Typically, L2 acquisition in face-to-face-contact takes place without formal instruction.

Literacy contact, in turn, implies receptive skills in writing of the L2, and probably also productive skills. We may assume that L2 is acquired by formal instruction, especially with regard to the productive skills. This goes along with at least basic knowledge of morphology and syntax and ideally also of certain features of L2's formal, bookish registers. In addition, the language users also command a set of language skills in their respective first languages that, however, does not necessarily correlate to the skills they show for L2.[3]

Literacy contact is thus quite different from face-to-face-contact and very likely to produce different results, not least because spoken language differs from written language in many respects. The possible impact of different modes of language contact has not yet been investigated systematically, but it is reasonable to assume that the mode affects at least two areas: phonetics/phonology and syntax/morphosyntax. Literacy contact probably does not leave many traces on the phonetic/phonological level of the target language, while the transfer of complex (morpho-)syntactic constructions is presumably a common phenomenon.

1.1 Literacy contact in Slavonic

Even though Slavonic literacy contact has not been an object of research *sui generis*, it has been an issue in Slavonic linguistics from its very beginnings. As early as 1822 Dobrovský, one of the founding fathers of Slavonic linguistics as a scientific discipline, noted that Old Church Slavonic was in fact modelled after Greek: "Exempla servilis imitationis [of Greek syntactic patterns] sat obvia sunt" (1822: 610). Ever since, the literature has abounded in works on the role of Church Slavonic in the emergence of modern standard varieties, particularly Russian, the influence of Greek on Church Slavonic, and the influence of Latin on the West Slavonic and western South Slavonic varieties.

In an attempt to systemize literacy contact involving Church Slavonic, Greek and Latin one could try and use the seemingly clear-cut cultural divide between *slavia romana*, where Latin was widely used as a written or literary language, and *slavia orthodoxa*, where Church Slavonic was used for ecclesiastical purposes

---

[3] Today's heritages speakers often display a similarly unbalanced distribution of linguistic skills. They usually have a good command of the formal and bookish registers of their L2 (i.e., the majority language), whereas L1 is typically restricted to more colloquial styles.

(liturgy, bible translations, etc.).[4] (Old) Church Slavonic, in turn, was heavily influenced by Biblical Greek. The division between the Latin and the Church Slavonic / Greek spheres of influence, however, becomes somewhat blurred when we turn to later periods, where the Latin and Church Slavonic spheres could intersect. We thus find three trajectories in Slavonic literacy contact involving Church Slavonic, Latin and Greek:

i) Latin > Slavonic vernacular, ii) Greek > (Old) Church Slavonic > Slavonic vernacular, iii) Latin > Church Slavonic.[5]

In the following, we will briefly discuss these scenarios.

i) Latin > Slavonic vernacular

Like for the Germanic and Romance languages, Latin was an important contact language for West Slavonic and the western South Slavonic varieties.

Latin was the primary written language in the Middle Ages in the lands of the Bohemian Crown and in Poland (cf. e.g., Siatkowska 1992 on Polish and Czech, Dubisz 2007 on Polish). Its replacement by vernacular varieties was a slow, step-by-step process and left its imprint in the form of numerous lexical and syntactic borrowings in Czech and Polish. During this process, many Latin lexical items belonging to the realm of church and religion were first borrowed from Latin to German and then wandered eastwards: from German to Czech, form Czech to Polish and eventually from Polish to East Slavonic.

Latin also very likely had a certain impact on diatopic and diachronic varieties of Slovene and Croatian (cf. e.g., Sonnenhauser & Eberle, this volume).

ii) Greek > (Old) Church Slavonic > vernacular

Biblical Greek was the source language for Old Church Slavonic, which dates from the early 860ies and is the oldest attested Slavonic language.

---

[4] (Old) Church Slavonic is sometimes dubbed as "Latin of the East", which implies an extensive overlapping of their respective functions. This conception is, however, not quite accurate. Church Slavonic was rarely used outside ecclesiastical contexts, whereas Latin was also the language for science, law, administration and literature cf. Keipert (1987). In addition, there is a difference between the relation of Latin and the Romance languages, on the one hand, and Church Slavonic and the modern Slavonic languages, on the other hand. The Romance languages actually developed out of Latin vernaculars, whereas Church Slavonic is not the predecessor of all Slavonic languages, but rather the first written Slavonic variety which co-existed alongside the Slavonic vernaculars. – For the dichotomy *slavia romana* vs. *slavia orthodoxa* see Picchio (1991) and Tolstoj (1997).

[5] A complete picture also must include the impact of (written) German on the West Slavonic and the western South Slavonic languages at certain times and the strong influence Czech had on the Polish literary language until the 16th c. However, these relations are outside the scope of this volume.

Old Church Slavonic is the product of bilinguals who spoke Greek and a South Slavonic vernacular and, on this basis, devised a new, exclusively written Slavonic variety in order to translate from the literary register of Greek. The strong impact of Greek continued after the establishment of Old Church Slavonic.

Church Slavonic developed several so-called recensions that were characterized by certain features of the respective local vernaculars. The Church Slavonic recensions are thus the result of *in situ* contact with different Slavonic vernaculars. They served as literary languages for many Slavonic speaking communities and had an enormous impact on the development of the modern Slavonic standard languages, particularly in the East and the South. Church Slavonic thus had a twofold role. It served as target language in a contact situation with a non-Slavonic language and as source language in inner-Slavonic contact scenarios.

The earliest Church Slavonic documents are associated with the Slavonic West, e.g., the Kiev Missal (probably 10th c.)[6] and the Freising manuscripts.[7] Its strongest influence, however, Church Slavonic exerted in the languages of *slavia orthodoxa*. The impact on South Slavonic languages happened most notably in Croatia, where there is a strong tradition of Croatian Church Slavonic. There are also traces of Church Slavonic in Old Czech (Večerka 2010; Ziffer 2014), a product of the Church Slavonic tradition in the Bohemian lands from the very beginning of Slavonic literacy until the mid-14th c.

iii) Latin > Church Slavonic
Latin influence on Church Slavonic is, at least in the early documents, rather sparse. A case in point are translations from Latin such as the Kiev Missal, or possible Latin influences in the Sinai psalter (cf. Lépissier 1964; Ziffer 2014). Latin influence on Croatian Church Slavonic is detectable as of the 12th c. (Reinhart 1990). The contact between Latin and East Slavonic recensions of Church Slavonic took place in a number of translations from Latin, in particular the translations by Archbishop Gennadij and his followers (*Gennadievskij kružok*) in Velikij Novgorod in the late 15th/early 16th c. (see Tomelleri 1998; 2011 and this volume).

For reasons of space, we will not delve further into the intricacies of the different contact scenarios. Our short survey, however, has shown that a given language

---

[6] The Kiev Missal is held to be the oldest extant Old Church Slavonic manuscript. Linguistically, it is characterized by certain West Slavonic features.
[7] The Freising manuscripts (late 10th/early 11th c.), the oldest Slavonic manuscript in Latin script, share a number of features with Slovene, which is why the language used in these documents sometimes goes by the name of "Old Slovene" (Trunte 1998: 14). However, there is no tradition of Church Slavonic influence on Slovene, its further development is determined by literacy contact with Latin and German (and face-to-face contact with German).

often is part of a multi-layered contact situation with various contact languages and different contact types. This opens up some questions for further studies, such as the possible indirect influence of Latin on vernaculars via Church Slavonic (Latin > Church Slavonic > vernacular), the possible coexistence of direct and indirect Latin influence, or the competition of two source languages and its results in the target variety. Some of these issues will be addressed in the following contributions, others still await further research.

2 Literacy contact and its impact on Slavonic syntax

The volume brings together contributions that investigate syntactic structures resulting from different language contact scenarios from various and often new angles and perspectives. It is organized in four parts. Parts I – III contain contributions that deal with the aforementioned trajectories of literacy contact (part I-III) and a fourth part that is of a more general nature.

The contributions in part I study the influence of Latin on (early) Polish, Czech and pre-standard South Slavonic varieties. Anna Kisiel & Piotr Sobotka (*The paths of grammaticalization of North Slavonic connectors – An interface point of Slavonic, Greek and Latin*) and Agnieszka Słoboda (*The influence of Latin on the syntax of Old Polish numerals*) show that language contact can affect the parts of speech of a language. Kisiel & Sobotka trace the so-called pro-sentence markers in several Slavonic languages back to a Latin model and Słoboda analyses the influence of Latin on the class of numerals in Polish. Pavel Kosek, Radek Čech & Olga Navrátilová (*The influence of the Latin Vulgate on the word order of pronominal enclitics in the 1st edition of the Old Czech Bible*) and Sanja Perić Gavrančić (*Accusativus cum infinitivo in 16th–19th century Croatian texts: contact-induced and internally motivated syntactic change*) explore how language contact gives rise to additional patterns in the target languages. Barabara Sonnenhauser & Marisa Eberle analyse in their contribution *Relative coordination. Kateri-/koteri-relatives in 18th century Slovene and Kajkavian* the occurrence of certain relative strategies in Kajkavian Croatian dialects and Slovene and link their fate to the impact of Latin on these varieties.

Part II contains contributions that discuss the impact of Greek on Church Slavonic. Pichkhadze and Fuchsbauer address the traditional topos of Greek influence on Church Slavonic, albeit from new angles. Anna Pichkhadze describes in *Blocking of syntactic constructions without Greek counterparts in Church Slavonic* the "passive" aspect of language contact, i.e., how imported Greek constructions suppress genuinely Slavonic patterns. Jürgen Fuchsbauer searches in *The article-like usage of the relative pronoun iže as an indicator of early Slavonic grammatical thinking* for the language internal motivation for borrowing an idiosyncratic Greek syntactic pattern to Old Church Slavonic. Dekker's study of tense usage in the Novgorod variety of the Old Russian vernacular (*Past tense usage in Old Russian performative formulae: A case study into the development of a written language of distance*) analyses the interaction of two source languages and traces certain uses of the aorist in Old Russian back to Church Slavonic and, indirectly, to Greek.

The contributions of the third part address the influence of Latin on different redactions of Church Slavonic. Vittorio S. Tomelleri studies the possible influence of Latin on Church Slavonic in Church Slavonic translations from Latin and discusses the competition of Slavonic and Latin syntactic patterns (*When Church Slavonic meets Latin. Tradition vs. innovation*). Ana Šimić shows in *Non-strict negative concord proper and languages in contact: translating Latin into Croatian Church Slavonic and Greek into Old Church Slavonic* how a newer source language, namely Latin, neutralizes the impact of the older one, i.e., Church Slavonic.

Part IV includes only one, albeit substantial contribution. In *First attestations. An Old Church Slavonic sampler* Hanne Eckhoff reviews all the issues discussed in this volume from a strictly empirical perspective. Using Greek and Church Slavonic parallel corpus data, she provides the Greek-Church Slavonic background to the other contributions, thus offering new insights into the relation between these two languages.

References

Dobrovský, Josef. 1822. *Institutiones linguae slavicae dialecti veteris*. Vindobona: Schmid.
Dubisz, Stanisław. 2007. Wpływ łaciny na języ polski. *Poradnik językowy* 5. 3–13.
Hansen, Björn, Jasmina Grković-Major & Barbara Sonnenhauser (eds.). 2018. *Diachronic Slavonic Syntax: The Interplay Between Internal Development, Language Contact and Metalinguistic Factors*. Berlin & Boston: de Gruyter.
Keipert, Helmut. 1987. Kirchenslavisch und Latein. Über die Vergleichbarkeit zweier mittelalterlicher Kultursprachen. In Gerhard Birkfellner (ed.), *Sprache und Literatur Altrußlands*, 81–109. Münster: Aschendorff.
Lépissier, Jacques. 1964. La traduction vieux-slave du Psautier. *Revue des études slaves* 43. 59–72.
Picchio, Riccardo (1991). Slavia ortodossa e Slavia romana. In Riccardo Picchio, *Letteratura della Slavia ortodossa*, 7–82. Bari: Dedalo.
Tolstoj, Nikita I. 1997. Slavia Orthodoxa i Slavia Latina. Obščee i različnoe v literaturnojazykovoj situacii. *Voprosy jazykonznanija* 1997(2). 16–23.

Trunte, Nikolaos H. 1998. *Slavenskij jazyk. Ein praktisches Lehrbuch des Kirchenslavischen in 30 Lektionen*. Bd. 2. München: Sagner.
Reinhart, Johannes. 1990. Najstarije svjedočanstvo za utjecaj Vulgate na hrvatskoglagoljsku Bibliju. *Slovo* 39–40. 45–52.
Rabus, Achim. 2013. Die Rolle des Sprachkontakts für die slavischen (Standard-)Sprachen (unter besonderer Berücksichtigung des innerslavischen Kontakts). Habilitationsschrift, Universität Freiburg. https://www.slavistik.uni-freiburg.de/personal/univ-prof-dr-achim-rabus/RabusHabil.pdf (accessed 31 March 2021).
Rabus, Achim. 2014. Siblings in contact: the interaction of Church Slavonic and Russian. In Juliane Besters-Dilger (ed.), *Congruence in Contact-Induced Language Change: Language Families, Typological Resemblance, and Perceived Similarity*, 337–351. Berlin & Boston: de Gruyter.
Siatkowska, Ewa. 1992. Rola wpływów obcych w rozwoju języka na przykładzie wpływu łaciny na język czeski i polski. In Kwiryna Handke (ed.), *Słowiańskie pogranicza językowe*, 141–145. Warszawa: Slawistyczny Ośrodek Wydawn.
Tomelleri, Vittorio S. 1998. Zur Geschichte des westlichen Einflusses in Russland: die *Dicta Sancti Augustini*. In François Esvan (ed.), *Contributi italiani al XII Congresso internazionale degli Slavisti (Cracovia 27 Agosto-2 Settembre 1998)*, 147–181. Napoli: Assoc. Italiana degli Slavisti.
Tomelleri, Vittorio S. 2011. Latinskaja tradicija u vostočnyx slavjan (nekotorye zametki). In G.I. Ševčenko et al. (eds.), *Aktual'nye problemy filologii: antičnaja kul'tura i slavjanskij mir*, 214–224. Minsk: RIVŠ.
Večerka, Radoslav. 2010. *Staroslověnská etapa českého písemnictví*. Praha: Nakl. Lidové Noviny.
Verkholantsev, Julia. 2008. *Ruthenica Bohemica. Ruthenian Translations from Czech in the Grand Duchy of Lithuania and Poland*. Wien, Berlin & Münster: Lit.
Ziffer, Giorgio. 2014. Slavia orthodoxa und Slavia romana. In Sebastian Kempgen, Peter Kosta, Tilman Berger & Karl Gutschmitdt (eds.), *Die slavischen Sprachen / the Slavonic languages*. Halbband 2, 1308–1319. Berlin & Boston: de Gruyter.

Part I: **The influence of Latin on Slavonic vernaculars**

Anna Kisiel and Piotr Sobotka
The paths of grammaticalization of North Slavonic connectors. An interface point of Slavonic, Greek and Latin

Abstract: In this paper, we examine the historical development of Slavonic connectors derived from a preposition and a demonstrative pronoun, e.g. Pol. *zatem* 'therefore, thus' from *za tym* 'behind this'. In the first, theoretical part, we discuss the features of prosentential markers such as Pol. *to* 'this' and their place in the structure of the utterance. In the second, analytical part, we concentrate on the degree of lexicalization of the discussed elements and the conditions for their grammaticalization and pragmaticalization. We argue that the connectors in question can be divided into two basic types: *de dic*to and *de re*. Originally, the pronoun in the *de dicto* connectors played the role of a prosentential pronoun, while that in *de re* connectors acted as an anaphorical pronoun; this difference has given rise to today's distinction (albeit blurry) between linking particles and conjunctions. Linking particles based on the analyzed pattern developed much more productively in West Slavonic languages than in East Slavonic languages; we conjecture that this may be due to the influence of Latin on West Slavonic (rather than Greek on East Slavonic) as a liturgical source language.

Keywords: grammaticalization, Slavonic languages, linking particles, conjunctions, Latin influence

1 Introduction

Quite a large group of contemporary Slavonic connectors[1] can historically be seen as lexicalized compositions of a preposition and a pronoun, cf. Russ. *potom* 'then,

---

[1] By the term *connector*, we mean lexemes having a linking or connecting function as conjunctions, relators, prepositions or linking particles. In this paper, we focus on so-called linking particles as understood in Wajszczuk (1999, 2005, 2010), i.e. units that are theme-rheme sensitive, however, unlike conjunctions, do not open a left position for a syntactic component. Thus, both linking particles and conjunctions are subsets of the connectors class.

Anna Kisiel, KU Leuven, e-mail: anna.kisiel@kuleuven.be
Piotr Sobotka, Institute of Slavic Studies, Polish Academy of Sciences, Warsaw,
e-mail: p.sobotka@uw.edu.pl

https://doi.org/10.1515/9783110651331-002

afterwards', *potomu* 'that's why', Pol. *zatem* 'therefore, thus', Cz. *proto* 'therefore, because of it', Cro. *dotada* 'until then', etc. Some of these words have completely lost their connection not only with the preposition, which is quite understandable considering their non-spatiotemporal meanings, but above all with the pronoun. However, the degree of lexicalization differs between languages and units, cf. the Pol. conjunction *dlatego* 'therefore' vs the delexicalized construction of a preposition and an anaphoric pronoun *dla tego* 'this is why' in the linking function:

(1) a. Pol. *Nic   nie   zrozumiał   dlatego   poprosił   o*
        nothing not   understand.PST.3SG   so.CON   ask.PST.3SG about
        powtórzenie.
        repeating.ACC.SG
        'He did not understand anything, so he asked to repeat it.'
        (National Corpus of Polish)

vs

b.' Pol. *Kobieta   ma   brodę,   dla   tego*
        woman.NOM   have.PRS.3SG   beard.ACC   for   this.GEN
        jest   dziwniejsza   niż   inne.
        be.PRS.3SG   stranger   than   other.PL
        'The woman has a beard and for this reason ['this' ≈ as was said that she has a beard] she is stranger than the other women.'
        (cf. Glaber, *Gadki* [Tales] (1535))

vs

b." Pol. *I   dlategoć   nam   przykazał   czuć*
        and   that's_why.CON.PCTL   we.DAT.PL   order.PST.3SG   feel.INF
        o   sobie.
        about   each_other.LOC.SG
        'And that's why he told us to take care of ourselves.'
        (cf. Seklucjan, *Katechizm* [Catechism] 18)

vs

b.''' Pol. *Kościół   sam   zbudował   nawyższy.   I   dla*
          Church   himself   build.PST.3SG   God_Most_High   and   for
          tego   dziedzictwem   Bożym   ji   zową.
          this.GEN   heritage.INS   god.ADJ   it.ACC   call.PRS.3PL
          'The Church built the God Most High itself. And for this reason they call it God's legacy.'
          (cf. Seklucjan, *Wyznanie wiary* [Confession of faith] d2 7)

Of course, in the case of (1b') a special contrastive stress is required on the demonstrative pronoun. Comparison of examples (1a) and (1b') as well as (1b") shows that the original demonstrative pronoun in (1a) did not have an ostensive function, referring to an object, but rather had a discursive function, referring to something said about an object. Moreover, a comparison of examples (1b") and (1b'") of the same author shows different levels of lexicalization of the compounds *dlatego* 'that's why' and *dla tego* 'for this reason'.

The subject matter of this paper concerns originally prosentential constructions (also called prosentence anaphora) or simple words that are treated as "standing for" a whole sentence in texts as well as an oblique and predicative part of a discourse (someone's saying embedded in a discourse). These expressions are usually interpreted as pronouns anaphorizing sentences (cf. Russ. *èto*, Pol. *to*, Cz. *ten(to)*, Cro. *ovaj* etc., cf. also Table 1). Therefore, the prosentential marker must be understood in relation to a whole sentence, i.e. a predicative construction as in (2)–(3):

(2) Cz. *Nevím, co Karel píše, ale vím,*
not_know.PRS.1SG what Charles write.PRS.3SG but know.PRS.1SG
že to nikdy nebudu číst.
that it.ACC never not_be.FUT.1SG read.INF
'No matter what Charles writes, I will never read it.'
(Czech National Corpus)

(3) Russ. *Tak znaj že, čto ne budet tebe,*
So know.IMP.2SG so that not be.FUT.3SG you.DAT
pervosvjaščennik, otnyne pokoja! Ni tebe, ni
High_Priest from now peace.GEN.SG neither you.DAT nor
narodu tvoemu [...] èto ja tebe govorju.
people.DAT your.DAT this.ACC I.NOM you.DAT speak.PRS.1SG
'So you should know, High Priest, that from now on you will have no peace, neither you nor your people. This I am telling you.'
(Bulgakov, *Master and Margarita*)

Some of these expressions, especially when combined with what was originally a preposition of place (see above), have evolved into utterance modifiers (linking particles or conjunctions), as in the Old Polish example (4), where *za tym* or *zatym* (lit. 'behind this') can be interpreted both objectively (as a construction of a preposition and a pronoun standing for the previous sentence understood as 'after that [previous] sentence') and discursively (as a connector or more specifically as a linking particle with the meaning 'therefore', 'and so'). The basic structure in (4) is clear: 'Somebody$_1$ said: [content 1]; behind this (utterance) somebody$_1$ said: [content 2]'. In modern Polish, *zatem* 'therefore' is more a linking particle than an anaphoric marker. However, in older examples, like in (4), it can be assumed that the word *zatym* served two functions: anaphoric (prosentential) as well as connecting or linking. The observed univerbation of *zatym* points to the on-going process of transformation from the relative construction *za tym* into a linking particle.

(4) OPol Odpowiedziawszy *pan jego i rzekł jemu: «Sługo zły a leniwy! Wi<e>działeś, iże żnę ja, gdziem nie siał, a zbiram, czegom nie rozsypał. Tegodla miałeś polecić <moje pieniądze> kamsorom albo tem, co pieniądze przemieniają, a ja przyszedwszy zaprawdę wziąłbych me pieniądze z zyskiem»*. *A* **zatym** *rzekł swym sługam: «Weźmicie od niego funt moj i dajcież temu, ktory <dziesięć> funtow ma. Boć każdemu, ktory ma, będzie dano opwito; ktory ni ma, i to, co ma, będzie odjęto.*

'His master answered and said to him, "You bad and lazy servant! You knew that I reap where I had not sown, and I harvest what I had not strewn. Therefore, you should entrust my money to the money-changers or to those who exchange money, and if I had come I would have taken my money for a profit". *Then/therefore* he said to his servants: "Take away my pound from him and give it to the one who gets ten pounds. For to everyone who has will be given abundantly: to the one who does not have, that what he has will be also taken away".' (*Rozmyślanie Przemyskie* [The Przemyśl Meditation] 490/17)

In this article, we investigate which factors were involved in the origin and development of Slavonic depronominal connectors and particles. We discuss different Slavonic constructions with so-called prosentence markers, e.g. Ru. *potom*, Pol. *ponadto/nadto*, *poza tym*, *przy tym*, *przeto*, *zatem*, Cz. *protože*, *zato*. The shared semantic component 'that what was said in a previous utterance. . .' is one of the presumable factors of their grammaticalization. The prosentential markers comprise a "transitional" part-of-speech class that oscillates between the objective and discursive levels of the language. They operate on both the sentence structure (as compositions of prepositions and prosentence pronouns) and the utterance structure (as conjunctions or linking particles[2]). Most of these constructions can be seen as connectors embedded into a discourse. This linking function makes them an important source for Slavonic conjunctions and linking particles. In other words, they have undergone a process of grammaticalization

---

[2] The issue of prepositions and prosentential markers as a pattern for Slavonic linking particles has been noticed in Sobotka & Żabowska (2017).

and pragmaticalization, understood as a path by which conjunctions/linking particles are created from what were formerly compositions of different degrees of grammaticalization (cf. Vanhove 2010, Giacalone Ramat and Mauri 2011). This process has been especially intense in the West Slavonic languages (only a few, if any, examples of such use of prepositions and pronouns can be observed in OCS or Old East Slavonic texts). This intensity can be explained by the specific discursive potential of Czech and Polish on the one hand and the influence of Latin on the other. Next to the aforementioned semantic structure and the resulting connecting function of the expressions in question, this adds two more factors to their development. The prepositional and pronoun constructions can be found in all North Slavonic languages, however, it is mostly in Czech and Polish that they develop into *linking particles* in our understanding of the term. The semantic component referring to the act of speaking is redundant for particles that operate at an utterance level, which shows deviant example such as Pol. **zatem / poza tym, co powiedziałem* 'so / besides what I said'. Russian parallel examples like *krome togo, čto ja skazal* are not only semantically correct, but also frequently used.

The article consists of two main parts. In the first, theoretical part, we discuss the features of prosentence markers and their place in the structure of an utterance. This is accompanied by a short description of Slavonic prepositions and their functions. In this way, both elements of the compositions that later gave rise to conjunctions and linking particles are presented. In the second, analytical part, in turn, we concentrate on defining the level of lexicalization of the discussed elements and the conditions for their grammaticalization and pragmaticalization. To trace the development path of Slavonic linking particles, we consider three examples – Old Russian *potomu* 'that's why', Czech *nadto* 'moreover', Polish *zatym/zatem* 'thus' – in comparison with Latin *itaque* 'thus' and Greek *oun* 'then'. In the final part we conclude that the type of pronoun is a key factor in the grammaticalization process which brings to life two kinds of connectors: conjunctions and linking particles. The main difference in the formation of these two classes is that while conjunctions are derived from constructions with anaphoric pronouns, particles arise from these involving prosentential pronouns. To put it differently, the conjunctive compounds originally refer to an object, whereas the particle ones to an utterance. This explains the possibility of delexicalization of conjunctions. The mechanism seems to be common for all North Slavonic languages, showing different degrees of possible grammaticalization of the compounds in question. Even though these two main classes have been recognized in the literature, they seem to have no sharp boundaries. Our analyses show that they have different sources, and that conjunctions and particles differ in terms of the degree of grammaticalization of the pronoun in the original compounds.

2 Prosententialization

Prosententialization[3] (sentence pronominalization) is alongside pronominalization one of the most frequent types of anaphora.[4] Both processes can be controlled by the same device – pronouns that refer to something (or someone) previously mentioned.[5] Prosententialization is organized by the pronoun *this*[6] (or *that, it, so*) (cf. Table 1). Even though the repertory of pronominal devices is similar in most

---

[3] For a terminological discussion see Crompton (2017) and Webber (1991). In the literature, different terms have been proposed for the discussed phenomenon, e.g. 'extended reference', 'reference to fact', 'situational anaphora', 'complex anaphora', 'abstract object anaphora', 'discourse deixis', 'impure textual deixis'. We choose the term 'prosententialization' (suggested in Polański 1967) as analogous to pronominalization. Prosententialization is here defined as a mechanism of pronominal expressions referring to propositional or discursive referent.
[4] We omit in this article other (often disputable) types of anaphora that are not realized by pronouns, such as ellipsis (e.g. Panevová 1996, Saeboe 1996) or binding with particles (e.g. Grochowski 1996).
[5] This is, of course, not their only function. They are specialized in deixis, i.e. drawing the attention of an interlocutor to something defined by the situation of communication (Bühler 1934, Frei 1944, Lyons 1979, Fillmore 1997, Diessel 1999, Dixon 2003, Levinson 2006). Even though the central pronoun here *this* is sometimes called a discourse (text) deictic pronoun, deixis and anaphora should not be regarded as identical phenomena (cf. the continuum perspective on the two phenomena in Cornish (2009) and the emphasized similarity between the two: "deixis and anaphora are procedures for coordinating the speech participants' attention throughout the flow of text as produced within a given context to which they are both party function to create a joint focus of attention." (Cornish 2009: 2). As stated in Lyons (1979: 102), "anaphora presupposes that the intensional correlate of the referent should already have its place in the universe-of-discourse. Deixis does not: indeed deixis is one of the principal means open to us of putting the intensional correlates of entities into the universe-of-discourse so that we can refer to them subsequently". Pronouns, in particular *this* and *it*, can also participate in other non-anaphoric phenomena such as clefting (Fichtner 1993, Declerck 1994, Hedberg & Fadden 2007, Dufter 2009, Hartmann & Veenstra 2013, Davidse 2014) and pseudo-clefting (Higgins 1979). This range of functions shows their general high sensitivity for the theme-rheme structure, especially for indicating a theme of an utterance (cf. Geluykens 1984, Kaiser 2011).
[6] Based on the pronoun and its function, Cornish (2011) calls prosententialization a subtype of anadeixis, an intermediate phase between deixis and anaphora: "'Anadeixis' is the type of indexical reference which combines the anaphoric and deictic procedures to different degrees. That is, the indexical expressions which realize it are anaphoric to the extent that their referent is already (potentially) present in the discourse representation assumed by the speaker to be shared by speaker and addressee at the point of occurrence, and is retrieved via this reference; however, that referent is less than highly salient at the point of use, unlike the situation which prevails with canonical anaphora. And it is deictic to the extent that the speaker is having recourse to the utterance context to redirect the addressee's attention focus to a referent which, although potentially available within the discourse context at the time of utterance, is not the one to which subsequent reference would be expected to be made at that point. It is not canonically deictic, in that no totally new referent is being introduced into the discourse thereby, and not all the utterance-level parameters are being altered via this reference." (Cornish 2011: 9).

languages (cf. Lith. *tai, tas*), different languages select lexical repetition more or less frequently. Hebrew for example is among the ones choosing lexical repetition more often (Blum-Kulka 2004), whereas Slavonic languages prefer anaphora (or, less often, cataphora, cf. Bogusławski (1996)).

Table 1: Slavonic prosentence demonstratives.

Russian	Polish	Czech	Croatian
èto / to	to	to	to
tak	tak	tak	tako
ten	ten	ten(to)	ovaj
takoj	taki	takový	takav / onaj
–	tyle	tolik	toliko

Sinclair (1993) defined what we understand here by prosentantialization as a process of reclassifying a previous sentence by "demoting" it to an element of a new sentence (cf. Crompton 2017). Two different types of prosententialization were studied by Francis (1994) and Halliday and Hasan (1976) and Crompton (2017): prosententialization by a nominal phrase including a demonstrative pronoun (or at least a demonstrative pronoun accompanied by a nominal phrase that interprets the antecedent, like in (5)), or by a pronoun alone, like in (6). Crompton (2017), quoting among others Gray's (2010) study, claims that sentence-initial *this* is most likely a prosententializer (performs complex anaphora in his terms, cf. (6)), which seems to be the case also for e.g. Polish *to* 'this', *co* 'what', *tak* 'so'. This does not imply, however, that Polish prosententializers cannot occur in other positions, cf. (7). Here, we confine our research to the Slavonic prosententializer *to* 'it' not accompanied by a nominal phrase and following a preposition. In most cases this amounts to the prosententialiser taking a second position in a subordinate sentence. Although the examples in this section are restricted to Polish, the description is applicable and generalizable to other Slavonic languages.

(5) Eng. *Anthony Burgess thinks hero worship is peculiar to the British. He explains it... While* this *is an old-fashioned diagnosis...* (Francis 1994: 86)

(6) Eng. *To simplify the exposition we limit our analysis to two-person, finite, multistage games with observable actions. This also allows us to use a notation...* (Crompton 2017: 140)

(7) Pol. *Honorata nie miała swoich dzieci. Pewnie*
 Honorata not have.PST.3SG own.GEN.PL kid.GEN.PL probably
 wiele razy w życiu roniła je
 many times in life.LOC miscarry.PST.3SG they.ACC
 gdzieś w polu podczas pracy, ale
 somewhere in field.LOC during work.GEN but
 nie wiedziała o tym. Opowiadała to tak: [...]
 not know.PST.3SG about it.LOC tell.PST.3SG it.ACC so
 'Honorata didn't have kids. Probably many times in her life she miscarried while working somewhere in a field but she never knew about it. She told it like this: [...]'.
 (National Corpus of Polish)

What makes pronominalization and prosententialization different is not only the antecedent of the pronoun, but also the pronoun itself. As pointed out by Cushing (1972), the nature of a pronoun determines what the relation between the pronoun and its antecedent is. While personal pronouns can only mark pronominalization, the pronouns central for our contribution *this / it* can participate in both phenomena. Personal pronouns (3rd person) are coreferential with previously given themes (subjects), such as Peter in (8) and Asia in (9a). In Polish for example, demonstratives can potentially have the same reference (cf. (9b))[7] but only under very specific circumstances, i.e. accompanied by the thematiser *to*. Otherwise they are coreferent with an object in the previous sentence, such as the policemen in (8) or the bottle in (9c). It is worth noticing that in (9b) *ta* can be accompanied by a noun (*ta dziewczyna* 'this girl'); when a noun is added in (9c) (*ta butelka* 'this bottle), *ta* changes its function from pronominal (anaphoric) to demonstrative (deictic)[8] and at the same time relative (with the meaning 'this exactly which. . .'). Diessel (2012: 2427) claims that "[t]hird person pronouns are used to continue a previously established discourse referent that is already in the interlocutors' focus of attention, whereas anaphoric demonstratives are used to

---

7 Of all the uses presented here, sentences of this kind correspond most to definite-article contexts, as discussed in Bacz (1991), Bartnik (2015) (cf. Himmelmann 1997).
8 In the case of this particular sentence, the addition of a noun makes the whole context odd. (9c) conveys a sequence of events, whereas repeating the noun *butelka* (obligatorily accented in this case, which points to a topic shift, cf. Nakajima and Allen (1993)) attracts attention to the object rather than the action. However, in a context where the second sentence can be transformed into a relative clause, like *Asia upuściła butelkę. Ta butelka* [or *która* 'which'] *należała do jej pradziadka i kosztowała fortunę.* 'Asia dropped a bottle. That bottle belonged to her great-grandfather and was worth a fortune.', is absolutely normal. Interestingly, *ta* can enter a postposition here, which is blocked for sentences of the type (9b).

indicate a topic shift, i.e., they direct the addressee's attention to a new discourse participant." Such a topic shift is also a foundation of prosententialization.[9]

(8) Ger. *Peter bemerkte einen Polizisten. Als er/der* ...
                                                  he / that one
      'Peter noticed a police officer. When he ...'
      (Diessel 2012: 2427)

(9) a. Pol. *Asia   upuściła   butelkę.   Ona   się*
              Asia   drop.PST.3SG   bottle.ACC.SG   she   REFL
              przestraszyła.
              get_scared.PST.3SG
              'Asia dropped a bottle. She got a fright.'
    b. Pol. *Asia   upuściła   butelkę.   Ta   to   jest*
              Asia   drop.PST.3SG   bottle.ACC.SG   this.F   this   be.PRS.3SG
              gapa.
              oaf.NOM.SG
              'Asia dropped a bottle. She is such an oaf.'
    c. Pol. *Asia   upuściła   butelkę.   Ta   się   stłukła.*
              Asia   drop.PST.3SG   bottle.ACC.SG   this.F   REFL   break.PST.3SG
              'Asia dropped a bottle. It broke.'
    d. Pol. *Asia   upuściła   butelkę.   To   było*
              Asia   drop.PST.3SG   bottle.ACC.SG   this   be.PST.3SG
              dziwne   [bo   zazwyczaj   jest   ostrożna]
              strange.N   because   usually   be.PRS.3SG   careful.F
              'Asia dropped a bottle. It was strange [because normally she is careful].'
    e. Pol. *Asia   upuściła   butelkę,   co   było   dziwne*
              Asia   drop.PST.3SG   bottle.ACC.SG   what   be.PST.3SG   strange.N

              [bo   zazwyczaj   jest   ostrożna].
              because   usually   be.PRS.3SG   careful.F
              'Asia dropped a bottle, which was strange [because normally she is careful].'
    f. Pol. *Karolina   powiedziała   mi,   że   Asia   upuściła*
              Karolina   tell.PST.3SG   I.DAT   that   drop.PST.3SG

---

9 Due to marking a topic shift these pronouns are often considered cohesive devices (cf. Halliday & Hasan 1976).

> butelkę, co było dziwne.
> bottle.ACC what be.PST.3SG strange.N
> 'Karolina told me that Asia dropped a bottle, which was strange.'

In modern Polish as well as in other Slavonic languages, all demonstrative pronouns can substitute for NPs (pronominalization) but only one of them can participate in prosententialization: *to* (cf. Cz. *to*, Russ. *ėto*), which morphologically is a neuter form of the pronoun *ten* (masculine), *ta* (feminine), *to* (neuter) 'this'. This makes Polish different from both Germanic languages, where *it / this* (and equivalents) can be coreferent with a previously mentioned object or a previous statement, and from languages having morphologically different forms for both types of anaphora at their disposal (such as Latin *hic* and *is* respectively). *To* covers all prosentential uses of English *it*, *this* and *that*. As pointed out by Diessel (2012: 2427; example (10) is taken from there), only *this* can participate in cataphoric arrangements, announcing a subsequent chunk of discourse. Apart from anaphoric contexts[10] (cf. (9d)), Polish *to* can participate in cataphoric ones, also based on the structure *it be* + adjective *that* + sentence (11).[11]

(10) Eng. *I forgot to tell you this (*that). Uhm Matt Street phoned while I was out.* (International Corpus of English)

(11) Pol. To było bardzo dziwne, że upuściła
      this be.PST.3SG very strange.N that drop.PST.3SG
      butelkę.
      bottle.ACC.SG
      'It was very strange that she dropped a bottle.'

There is also another prosententialiser in Slavonic: *tak* 'so'. As it is not found in the structures that are the central topic in this paper, we will not discuss it extensively. In general, the differentiation of prosentential *it* and *as* as presented in Cushing (1972) can be applied here: The verbs involved in taking a definite stance

---

10 We see prosententialization as one of the realizations of the anaphoric mechanism, in accordance with Piwek, Beun and Cremers (2008) and against e.g. Cornish (2011: 11–12), who claims that it "is not in fact (already) anaphora, since its function is essentially deictic (as its name suggests). It involves an act of cognitive pointing towards the result of processing a predication (or a part of a predication) in surrounding discourse, and creating a new discourse entity out of it."
11 Also frequent is the *to* + adjective + *ale* + sentence (*To dziwne, ale cię kocham.* 'lit. This (is) strange but I love you. = However strange it may be, I love you.').

with respect to the truth (or falsity) of a statement take *to* 'this/it' as a prosententialiser, while the ones involving "passive states of mind, with the subject acquiescing, or expressing a disposition, to the truth" of a statement prefer *tak* 'so' (Cushing 1972: 189), cf. (12) and (13) respectively. Following Cushing's differentiation of *it* as definite and *so* as indefinite, we propose the understanding of Polish *tak* as a prosentential marker not presupposing the truth-value of a statement it refers to, comp. (14a) and (14b). *To* presupposes that the antecedent is affirmed.

(12) Pol. *Nikt   nie   wierzy,   że   ona naprawdę*
         no-one not   believe.PRS.3SG that she   really
         upuściła   butelkę,   ale ja w   to   wierzę.
         drop.PST.3SG bottle.ACC but I   in   this.ACC believe.PRS.1SG
         'Nobody believes that she really dropped the bottle, but I believe it.'

(13) Pol. *Nie   wiem,   czy naprawdę   upuściła   butelkę,*
         not   know.PRS.1SG if   really   drop.PST.3SG bottle.ACC
         ale   tak sądzę.
         but   so   think.PRS.1SG
         'I don't know if she really dropped the bottle but I think so / I think that she did.'

(14) a. Pol. [*Asia upuściła butelkę.*] *Powiedziałam   im   o*
                                              say.PST.1SG   they.DAT about
                                              tym
                                              this.LOC
         '[Asia dropped a bottle.] I told them about it.'
     b. Pol. [*Asia upuściła butelkę.*] *Tak   im   powiedziałam.*
                                              so   they.DAT say.PST.1SG
         '[Asia dropped a bottle.] So I told them.'

Finally, it is important to distinguish prosentential *to* from the relative pronoun *co* 'which'[12] as in (9e), cf. also Table 2 below. Even though they both refer to the same object (in a wider sense) – the previously given statement (here, about Asia dropping a bottle), they do not have identical function. As a relative pronoun

---

[12] Polish *co* is not exactly equivalent to English *which*; it cannot refer to nominal antecedents, neither in restrictive uses (*Asia dropped a bottle which she got from her father*) nor in nonrestrictive ones (*Asia dropped a bottle, which rolled on a floor*). In both contexts *which* has a counterpart in Polish *który*.

introducing a supplementary clause,[13] *co* refers to a directly preceding object (a statement). In case of (9f), *co* can either refer to the same statement as in (9e) or, although less often, to the whole preceding statement (on Karolina saying this and that about Asia). *To*, on the other hand, resembles more pronominal personal pronouns and refers to the statement in a main clause of a previous sentence. Therefore, if (9f) were to be transformed into a *to*-sentence (. . . *To było dziwne.* 'This was strange.'), *to* would refer to Karolina saying something (cf. a possible continuation: . . . *To było dziwne, bo od dawna nie rozmawiałyśmy.* 'This was strange as we have not talked in ages.').

Table 2: Two types of Polish pronominalising and prosentecialising pronouns.

	pronominalisation	prosententialization
demonstrative	personal pronoun 3sg/pl *ten, ta, to* [+N]	*to, tak*
relative	*który, która, które*	*co*

"If discourse deictic expressions could speak", says Diessel (2012: 2426) quoting a graphic explanation from Karl Bühler, "they would speak as follows: look ahead or back along the band of the present utterance. There something will be found that actually belongs here, where I am, so that it can be connected with what now follows. Or the other way round: what comes after me belongs there, it was only displaced from that position for relief."[14] In this paper, we treat pronouns as having lexical meaning (Bolinger 1977). The core semantic component proposed for pronouns by Bogusławski (1991; 1994; 1996), and adapted here, refers to shared knowledge of the interlocutors: 'about what or whom I am saying you know what I am saying'. This is in line with Adger and Ramchand's description of pronouns as "always referentially dependent, whether on a discourse antecedent, a syntactic antecedent, or an assignment function required by connection to an operator" (Adger and Ramchand 2005: 173). In the case

---

13 It fulfills all criteria for nonrestrictives summed up in Denison and Hundt (2013); particularly interesting in this context is the quotation added by the authors on a distance between a relative pronoun and its antecedent: "There has been a continuing tendency since Middle English to reduce the degree of separation of a relative clause from its head noun, or to put it another way, an increasing tendency for nonrestrictive relative clauses to become more closely attached to their head nouns." (Montgomery 1989: 136–137).

14 "Jedenfalls aber sprächen alle anaphorischen Pfeile, wenn sie sprechen könnten, ungefähr so: schau vor oder zurück das Band der aktuellen Rede entlang! Dort steht etwas, das eigentlich hierher gehört, wo ich stehe, damit es mit dem Folgenden verbunden werden kann. Oder umgekehrt: dorthin gehört, was mir folgt, man hat es nur der Entlastung wegen versetzt." (Bühler 1934: 390).

of *to* 'this/it' having a discourse antecedent, the above component could be clarified as 'what has just been said, you know what I am talking about'.

The special value of *to* 'this/it' as a marker of prosententialization is also confirmed by historical material. In one passage of a Middle Polish text called *Prawdziwe wyobrażenie trojga dzieci barzo strasznych i dziwnych...* [A true image of three very terrible and strange children], a contemporary editor has altered the original pronoun *to* 'this/it' to *co* 'something' (cf. Kroczak 2007):

(15) Pol. Kiedy   ta   zasłona   na   twarzy   leżała,   tedy
         When   this.NOM   veil.NOM   on   face.LOC lie.PST.3SG then
         nosa,   oczu,   ust   nie   można   widzieć   i
         nose.GEN   eye.GEN.PL   mouth.GEN   not   can   see.INF   and
         nie   można   poznać,   jeśli   <c>o   pod   tą   zasłoną
         not   can   know.INF   if   anything   under   this.INS   veil.INS
         było.
         be.PST.3SG

'When this veil was on the face, one could not see and get to know the nose, eyes, mouth, and whether anything was under the veil.'

However, in our view this emendation fails to account for the prosentential usage of the pronoun *to* 'this/it' with its meaning 'what was mentioned above', i.e. 'the nose, eyes, mouth'. The singular neuter pronoun *to* does not refer here to three different objects (which would be an ungrammatical use) but rather to the enumerated objects treated as a whole. On this interpretation, we propose the following intended meaning of the sentence in question: "When this veil was on the face, one could not see and get to know the nose, eyes, mouth, and if any of this [what was mentioned] really was under the veil.' The change introduced by the editor removes this prosentential reading and introduces a new interrogative one.

In the second part of this article, we discuss historical Slavonic compositions of a preposition and a prosentential pronoun as in (4). It is therefore worth mentioning that also the prepositional element of the equation can, under certain circumstances, be meaningful. Even though it is a fact that in many cases a preposition is just one of the components of a larger language unit (most often verbal but also adjectival or nominal; cf. Kosek (1999)) or in special circumstances it may serve as a marker of case (cf. Kuryłowicz 1964: 176), it is not unlikely for a preposition to be an independent item with its own meaning and own requirements towards an adjoined noun. The prepositions forming composita discussed in this paper belong to the group of prepositions of place (such as 'at', 'beside(s)', 'next to', 'in', 'with', 'above', 'over', 'behind', 'beyond'). It is beyond the scope of this article to fully discuss their meaning, but their function can be generally described as follows: Typically, the prepositions localize the language context to which the pronoun refers (before, afterwards, above etc.), in other words, what is said can be understood linearly, mainly horizontally ('afterwards', 'next to', cf. Pol. *po, za*, Rus. *mimo*, Cz. *při*), and rarely vertically ('above', cf. *(po)nad*). Apart from prepositions operating in the two-dimensional space, there are also ones that place the utterance they introduce "outside" of what is being said (cf. Table 3). The statement that follows such a prepositional phrase is seen as supplementary (cf. Pol. *Jest zbyt leniwy do tej pracy, poza tym mamy już kandydata*. 'He is too lazy for the job, besides we already have a good candidate.'), while in case of vertical and horizontal prepositions the following statement is perceived (at least) as important as what has already been said (cf. Pol. *Jest zbyt leniwy do tej pracy, ponadto mamy już kandydata*. 'He is too lazy for the job, and most importantly we already have a good candidate.'). The spatio-temporal source of connectives has been observed in the literature for other languages (e.g. Giacalone Ramat and Mauri 2011).

Table 3: Main direction in a spatial domain given by prepositions in anaphoric composite.

	Russian	Polish	Czech
vertical	*sverx togo*	*nad+to, ponad+to*	*nad+to*
horizontal	*po+tomu, za+tem, pri+čem, po+čemu, za ėto*	*prze+to, za+tem, przy tym*	*po+tom* (cf. Bauer 1960: 31), *při+čem+ž, za+tím, za+to*
outside	*krome togo*	*poza tym, oprócz tego, mimo to*	*kromě toho*

It is also worth noticing that the constructions discussed here (cf. Table 3.) were by far less popular in Old Church Slavonic, which raises the question about what increased their popularity in later stages of the Slavonic languages' development. In OCS – as it is evidenced in *Slovník jazyka staroslověnského* (Kurz et al. 1966–1997) – only eight constructions corresponding to Polish, Czech or Russian connectors can be found: *po+tomь* (?) 'then, thereon, afterwards; moreover; no more', *počь+to* (?) 'why', *kъ tomu* 'then, afterwards' as well as *česo radi* 'why', *po+ně(že)* 'because', *za+ně(že)* 'because', cf. ex. (16):

(16) OCS *Pride   že   Ji⟨su⟩sъ   dvьremъ   zatvorenomъ. i*
         come.AOR.3SG so   Jesus   door.INS   closed.INS   and
         sta   po   srědě   jixъ   i   g⟨lago⟩la
         stand.AOR.3SG in   middle.LOC   they.GEN   and   say.AOR.3SG

> im   paky   mirъ   vamъ.   Po   tom   že
> they.DAT again   peace.NOM you.DAT.PL after this.LOC so
> g⟨lago⟩la   Thomě: prinesi   prъstъ   tvoj
> say.AOR.3SG   Thomas   bring.IMP.2SG   finger.ACC.SG your.ACC
> sěmo [...].
> there
>
> 'Jesus came to them in spite of the closed door and stood in among them and said: 'Peace be with you'. Then he said to Thomas: 'Put your finger there'.
> (*Assemani* 7b–7c, Jn. 20.26–27)

Here, the preposition *po* 'after' localizes the part of discourse to which the pronoun *tom* 'this.LOC' refers. At the same time the whole compound precedes and "announces" another direct utterance in the imperative mood addressed to Thomas: 'bring your finger'. This typical function of the compositions in question is observable in many examples in many languages, cf. Lith. *po to* 'thereafter', *be to* 'by the way' etc. Although most of such constructions evolve into connectors (cf. Bauer 1960; Łojasiewicz 1992; Wajszczuk 1997; Sannikov 2008; Apresjan and Pekelis 2011; Uryson 2011; Štícha et al. 2013, Grochowski, Kisiel and Żabowska 2014), only some of them specialize as linking particles (cf. Russ. *zatem* as a conjunction vs Pol. *zatem* as a linking particle). It is surprising that there is no linking particle based on prosentential pronouns in Russian. The data in Table 4 beg for an explanation why the discussed grammaticalization path is not present in East Slavonic languages. Several possible causes can be considered, e.g. the influence of non-Slavonic languages, a dialectal (in the wide sense) or even a geographical impact, and intra-language factors. To investigate them further, we will now turn to the analysis of three Slavonic examples of a preposition + pronoun construction.

Table 4: Modern North Slavonic de-anaphoric connectors.

	Russian	Polish	Czech
Conjunction	(*kak*) *budto, iz-za togo čto, krome togo čto, ottogo* (*čto*), *posle togo kak, potomu* (*čto*), *zatem* (*čto*(*by*)), *zato*	*dlatego, natomiast,* ?*przeto, toteż*	*proto*(*že*), *přestože, zatímco, zato* (cf. also: *anžto, jakožto, ježto, kdežto, kdyžto, přičemž*)
Linking Particle		*nadto, ponadto, poza tym, przeto, przy tym, zatem*	*beztoho, kromě toho, nadto, potom, přitom, totiž, zato*

3 The development of deprosentential linking particles in Slavonic

The historical data we have analyzed represents three levels (stages) of lexicalization of the constructions involving a preposition + pronoun. During the first stage, both elements of the construction represent separate lexical units. Both preposition and pronoun retain their original function: the former refers back to the previous sentence and links two utterances by moving the preposition to the level of the two-place connector, and the latter refers to the content of the previous sentence. Thus, such constructions as in (16) have a double-referential feature. The preposition is a marker of the quasi-conjunctive relation linking two syntactic units ("how we refer"), while the pronoun plays a referential function ("what we refer to"). While this composition gradually lexicalizes, its position in a sentence begins to stabilize. However, the direction of reference inherited from the early stage mechanism of prosententialization is preserved: the lexicalizing unit opens a leftward position for the rheme of a preceding utterance and joins the two originally direct clauses as syntactic units of a compound structure. However, the origins of the compound are still clear as the pronoun can be still "singled out" or "reconstructed". We can observe this in the conjunction *potomu* 'that's why' in (17), where the pronoun *t-omu* 'this-DAT' has more of an anaphoric than prosentential function and keeps the grammatical marking as required by *po* 'after' (namely the dative).

(17) ORuss. *Kak   my   sъ   toboju   šli   kъ   korolju,*
How   we.NOM   with   you.INS.SG go.PST.3SG to   king.DAT.SG
i   korolь   vъ   tu   poru   sъ
and   king.NOM.SG   in   this.ACC.SG time.ACC.SG with
pany   radilъ,   i   emu   ne   skazali,
lord.INS.PL   debate.PST.3SG and he.DAT.SG not   tell.PST.3PL
čto   ty   idešь,   i   potomu
that   you.NOM.SG come.PRS.2.SG and   that's_why
tobě   vstrěči   ne   bylo.
you.DAT.SG   meeting.GEN.SG not   be.PST.3SG
How you and I were going to the king, and the king at that time was consulting with the lords, and he was not told that you were coming, and that's why you did not have a meeting.
(*Slovar' russkogo jazyka XI – XVII vv.* [Dictionary of the Russian Language of the 11th–17th c.])

Finally, in the last stage the lexicalizing unit forms a grammaticalized expression with a function of connecting the elements of discourse (cf. Pol. *zatem, przy tym* etc.). It does not open up a leftward (or rightward) position for any syntactic component, although it does require a pretext, which is a trace of its origin. Unlike the original composition that operated on the sentence level, such a unit organizes the structure of the discourse, linking one theme-rheme structure with another, as is evident in the corresponding Czech and Polish examples from Table 4 above.

We assume that the second and the third level of "lexicalization" are in fact separate development paths. While compound conjunctions have derived from prepositions and anaphoric pronouns, compound linking particles in Slavonic languages have derived from prepositions and prosentential pronouns (cf. Section 2 and Sobotka 2019). The differences between the type of pronouns are the very reason for the possible delexicalization of the conjunctions, i.e. a possibility of reconstructing their original components, which is not possible in the case of particles (similarly to the example *dlatego* in (1b) and (1b')). The conjunctive compounds originally refer to an object, the particle compounds to the content of an utterance. This difference will be presented on a number of examples below.

Modern Czech *nadto* 'moreover' is usually classified as a particle that structures a text (cf. Štícha et al. 2013: 532). As a particle, it can co-occur with certain conjunctions, e.g. *a* 'and' as well as *ale* 'but'.

(18) Cz. takže   jest   i   z   jiných   zemí
        so   AUX.PRS.3SG   and from other.GEN.PL country.GEN.PL
        lidi   učené   nemalým   nákladem
        people.ACC.PL learned.ACC.PL considerable.INS.SG amount.INS.SG
        k   sobě   ale   vyvolával,   nad   to   i
        for himself.DAT.SG but call.LPTCP.SG.M over this and
        sám   také   mnohé   krajiny   shlédl.
        himself.NOM   also   many.ACC.PL   country.ACC.PL   see.LPTCP.SG.M
        'so, he has also invited scholars from other countries with a considerable amount of effort for himself, but moreover he himself has also travelled to many countries.'
        (CestPref 6; cf. Bauer 1960: 80)

The expression *ale nadto* is called by Bauer (1956) "a conjunction of gradation"[15] (cf. Karlík, Nekula and Pleskalová 2016: 1736–1737) and the word *nadto* 'moreover' is wrongly interpreted as an adverb. There can be no doubt that *nadto* in the above context and similar ones is more a discourse particle than an adverb.

---

15 I.e. "stupňovací spojka".

This is evidenced not only by its current functional characteristics but also by its historical development. Primarily, the structure with a preposition and a pronoun joined two direct utterances. As a direct utterance quotes somebody's saying, it always has a *de dicto* interpretation (cf. Coulmas 1986), so the connector between them should be also interpreted as a *de dicto* operator, i.e. it belongs to the domain of speech (for further discussion, cf. Frajzyngier 1991). It binds content of two utterances marked by a direct utterance.

(19) OCz. *Slyšeli   jste,   co   jest   řečeno*
         hear.LPTCP.PL AUX.2PL what   AUX.PRS.3SG say.PTCP.PASS
         dávno   starým: Oko   za   oko   a
         long_ago   old.INS.SG   eye.NOM.SG for   eye.ACC.SG and
         zub   za   zub.   Ale   já   vám
         tooth.NOM.SG for tooth.ACC.SG but   I.NOM   you.DAT.SG
         nadto   pravi: Neprotiviti   sě   zlému.
         over_that   tell.PRS.1SG not_resist.IMP.2PL REFL evil.DAT.SG
         'You have heard what was said once in the Old [Testament]: "Eye for eye and tooth for tooth". But I tell you over that: "Do not resist an evil [person].'
         (*Život Krista Pána*, Vokabulář webový)

The preposition *nad* 'over' vertically localizes non-linguistic phenomena (a moral norm in (19)) to which the pronoun refers. Therefore, since the particle does not so much join specific and isolated speech messages as it does the content associated with them, it is also possible to use it as a speaker comment on any two discursive contents. The speaker, by saying something, indicates at the same time that this is not everything that should be said, and that something more than what was said needs to be added so as to form a fuller picture of the situation.

(20) OCz. *jeho   Bóh   ze   všeho   toho*
         he.ACC.SG   god.NOM.SG   from   all.GEN.SG this.GEN.SG
         vysvobodil,   a   nadto   pánem   nade
         disentangle.LPTCP.SG.M   and   moreover   lord.INS.SG   over
         vším   královstvem   jej   ustavil
         whole.INS   kingdom.INS.SG   he.ACC.SG.M   establish.LPTCP.SG.M
         pro   jeho   vieru.
         for   he.GEN.SG   faith.ACC.SG
         'God released him from everything, and moreover he made him the Lord of his whole kingdom for his faith.'
         (*Štítný ze Štítného* 64r, Vokabulář webový)

Thus, as we see in (20), which is an echo of Ps 105, 20–21, the particle does not bind together two direct utterances as in (19), but it rather refers to an indirect utterance and functions as a discursive comment. Thus, the shift involves switching from the prosentential function of the pronoun to the comment function of the grammaticalized unit. This is exactly the function of the contemporary Czech particle *nadto* 'moreover'. Its development illustrates our hypothesis that the particle function of depronominal connectors has developed from a prosentential pronoun that refers to a discursive component, not to an object.

The same mechanism of grammaticalization is observed in Polish. However, an interesting shift can be noted in the 15th century Apocrypha called *The Przemyśl Meditation*. It turns out that discursive particles could join not only sentence arguments in a direct utterance but also arguments referring to someone's thinking. This shows that over time, an utterance did not necessarily have to be expressed on the surface of the text (cf. [content] *zatem* [content] → [unexpressed on the surface thought referring to an unknown content] *zatem* [content]). However, this does not change the fact that the connector connects the content.

(21) OPol. *Tako wtem wieliką myśl miała[...],*
So suddenly great.ACC.SG thought.ACC.SG have.PST.3SG
a zatem wziąwszy i poczęła czyść
and thus take.PST.PTCP and start.PST.3SG read.INF
ten psalm: „Błogosławiłeś, Gospodnie,
this.ACC.SG psalm.ACC.SG bless.PST.2SG Lord.VOC.SG
ziemię twoję".
land.ACC.SG your.ACC.SG
'So, she suddenly got a great idea, thus she has taken [it] and started to read this psalm: "Oh, Lord, you have blessed thy land".'
(*Rozmyślanie Przemyskie* [The Przemyśl Meditation] 48/21–25)

A slightly different development can be observed in the case of depronominal conjunctions. The preposition and pronoun compositions from which these conjunctions derived refer to a previously mentioned object. Everything seems to indicate that connectors of this kind were originally *de re* operators, i.e. they belong to the domain of real or mental objects. A *de re* connector allows the speaker to alter the form of the original utterance in accordance with what it means on the basis of this knowledge of the world in such a way that it may include inferences of which the original speaker is unaware. The pronoun as a part of the connector has an anaphoric character (in (22) it refers to Křizomysl as not a good name).

(22) OCz. *Po něm byl knězem Křizomysl,*
After he.LOC.SG be.LPTCP.SG.M prince.INS.SG Křizomysl
syn jeho. Ti všichni
son.NOM.SG he.GEN.SG this.NOM.PL all.NOM.PL
neostavili jsú jmene dobrého, nebo
not_leave.LPTCP.PL AUX.3PL name.GEN.SG good.GEN.SG because
biechu jich hlúpí nravi a
be.IMPERF.3PL they.GEN foolish.NOM.PL moral.NOM.PL and
pro to o nich
for this.ACC.SG about they.LOC.PL
písmo nic nepraví.
scripture.NOM.SG nothing not_speak.PRS.3SG
'Křizomysl, his son, became prince after him. They didn't give him a good name because of their moral foolishness and this is why the scripture doesn't tell about them.'
(*Dalimilova kronika* [Dalimil Chronicle], I-247 – folio 5r, Vokabulář webový)

Comparative analysis shows that while Western Slavonic languages prefer linking particles, Eastern Slavonic languages favor conjunctions appearing in similar contexts, or have no connectors at all. No conjunction can play a role of a linking particle or can be used in its function. In the contemporary Russian translation (cf. (4b)) of the example (4), here repeated as (23a)), the marker of the discursive relation is the particle *itak* 'so, now then'.

(23) a. OPol. *Pan* [...] *rzekł jemu:* [...]. *A zatym*
master.NOM.SG say.PST.3SG he.DAT.SG and then
rzekł swym sługam:
say.PST.3SG REFL.POSS.PRON.DAT.PL servant.DAT.PL
Weźmicie [...].
take.IMP.2PL
'The master said to him: [...]. And then he said to his servants: Take [...].'
b. RussCS. *Gospodinъ ego reče emu:* [...].
master.NOM.SG he.GEN.SG say.AOR.3SG he.DAT.SG
vъzъmete [...]
take.IMP.2PL
'His master said to him: [...]. Take [...].'
(*Ostromirovo evangelie* [Ostromir Gospel], l. 150 ob., The National Library of Russia)

The reason for the differences between the two groups of North Slavonic languages probably lies in different linguistic traditions. While in the East Slavonic languages the translations of the New Testament referred to Old Church Slavonic and Greek, in the West Slavonic languages the pattern for translations was Latin (cf. Greek (23c) and Latin (23d) fragments parallel with the Old Polish (23a) and Old Russian (23b)). In Greek, the particle of inference *oun*, an equivalent to Polish *zatem*, has been completely grammaticalized with no clear motivation (cf. Bakker 2009: 42–43). The Latin particle *ita-que*, on the other hand, had a clearly motivated structure, very close to Slavonic pronoun compounds. Latin (but not Greek) influence on West Slavonic pronominal and pronoun constructions therefore seems to be possible. Latin *ita-que* can be considered as a textual operator of inference, formed by combining the primary pronoun *ita*[16] and the particle *-que*. Thus, we can summarize that the Old Polish prosentential marker *zatym* is functionally similar to the Latin construction. In the analyzed contexts, looking at Latin helps to determine the depth of grammaticalization of the constructions in question.

(23) c. Gr. ὁ   κύριος   αὐτοῦ   εἶπεν   αὐτῷ [...]
            ho   *kurios*   *autou*   *eipen*   *autō:* [...].
            DET   master.NOM.SG   he.GEN.SG   say.AOR.3SG   he.DAT.SG
            ἔδει   σε   οὖν   βαλεῖν
            edei   *se*   *oun*   *balein* [...]
            behoove.IMPERF.3SG   you.ACC.SG   then   put.AOR.INF
            'his master said to him: [...]. it behooved you therefore to put [...].'
            (Mt 25, 26-27, Nestle et al. 1997: 73)
      d. Lat. *dominus*   *eius*   *dixit*   *ei:* [...].
            master.NOM.SG   he.GEN.SG   say.PERF.3SG   he.DAT.SG
            Tollite   *itaque*   *ab*   *eo* [...]
            take_up.IMP.2PL   thus   from   he.ABL.SG
            'his master said to him: [...]. Take up therefore from him [...].'
            (Mt 25, 26-28, Nestle et al. 1997: 73)

What is even more interesting for comparative analysis, when discourse deictic demonstratives are routinely used in particular constructions, they often develop into grammatical markers, e.g. the English definite article *the* and the third person pronouns *he* and *it* (cf. Diessel 1999). Slavonic demonstratives that are

---

[16] According to de Vaan (2018: 311) *ita* probably goes back to a "compound pronoun", namely a combination of PIE *$h_i i$ 'it' and *to- 'that'.

used with reference to content elements in discourse provide a common historical source for focus (discursive) markers. Moreover, the grammaticalization of demonstratives is cross-linguistically so common that central aspects of grammar such as definiteness marking and clause combining are crucially determined by this process (cf. Diessel 2012: 2428).

4 Conclusion

We have shown that Slavonic connectors composed of a preposition and a demonstrative pronoun can be divided into two basic types: *de dicto* and *de re* connectors. The former combines two discursive parts of an utterance, while the latter combines sentences or their parts. Originally, the pronoun of *de dicto* connectors functioned as a prosentential pronoun while the pronoun of *de re* connectors was an anaphorical pronoun. Thus, the former referred to some content, the latter to some object in a previous sentence. *De dicto* connectors evolved into linking particles, whereas conjunctions are derived from *de re* connectors. *De dicto – de re* distinction may be applied to explain both differences between the two sets of anaphora (referring to objects and referring to contents of sentences) and the different origins of the depronominal Slavonic compound conjunctions and linking particles. This explanation implies that *de dicto* pronouns and prepositions are encoded rather for discursive markers in Slavonic languages. However, due to the surface and formal identity of conjunctions and particles, the boundary between the two classes is difficult to delineate and nowadays it seems to be blurred. Linking particles, based on the analyzed pattern, developed much more productively in West Slavonic languages than in East Slavonic languages. We have conjectured that this may be due to the influence of Latin, in which such connectors had a clear structure. However, the grammaticalization of these connectors in question is primarily the result of intra-language factors and perhaps the influence of Czech on Polish. Polish is one of the languages with a particularly rich system of discursive lexis (like Greek or Gothic in the past). The etymological and historical evidence proves that the Polish language owes this status partly to the influence of the Czech language as nearly 30 Polish function words have been borrowed directly from Czech (cf. Sobotka 2018: 293–296).

References

Adger, David & Gillian Ramchand. 2005. Merge and Move: *Wh*-Dependencies Revisited. *Linguistic Inquiry* 36(2). 161–193.

Apresjan, Valentina Ju. & Ol'ga E. Pekelis. 2011. Sojuz [Conjunction]. In Vladimir A. Plungjan (ed.), *Russkaja korpusnaja grammatika* [A Russian corpus grammar]. Moskva: IRJa RAN. http://rusgram.ru (accessed 25 September 2018).

Bacz, Barbara. 1991. On some article-like uses of the demonstrative *ten* [this] in Polish. Could *ten* become an article? *Langues et Linguistique* 17. 1–16.

Bakker, Stéphanie J. 2009. On the curious combination of the particles γάρ and οὖν. In Stéphanie Bakker & Gerry Wakker (eds.), *Discourse cohesion in Ancient Greek*, 41–61. Leiden–Boston: Brill.

Bartnik, Artur. 2015. Demonstrative or article? The case of *ten* in Polish. *Roczniki Humanistyczne* 63(11). 7–20.

Bauer, Jaroslav. 1956. Vývoj stupňovacího souvětí v češtině [The development of the sentences of gradation in Czech]. *Sborník prací Filozofické fakulty brněnské univerzity* A4. 24–36.

Bauer, Jaroslav. 1960. *Vývoj českého souvětí* [The development of the Czech sentence]. Praha: Nakladatelství Československé akademie věd.

Blum-Kulka, Shoshana. 2004. Shifts of cohesion and coherence in translation. In Lawrence Venuti (ed.), *The translation studies reader*, 290–305. 2nd edn. New York & London: Routledge.

Bogusławski, Andrzej. 1991. THIS. In Maciej Grochowski (ed.), *Problemy opisu gramatycznego języków słowiańskich* [Problems of the grammatical description of the Slavonic languages], 23–29. Warszawa: Instytut Języka Polskiego PAN.

Bogusławski, Andrzej. 1994. Pronouns as proxies and pronouns as dummies. In Andrzej Bogusławski (ed.), *Sprawy słowa. Word Matters*, 377–403. Warszawa: Wydawnictwo Veda.

Bogusławski, Andrzej. 1996. Pronominalizacja w zdaniowych uzupełnieniach predykatów mentalnych [Pronomialization in clausal complements of mental predicates]. In Maciej Grochowski (ed.), *Anafora w strukturze tekstu*, 43–48. Warszawa: Wydawnictwo Energeia.

Bolinger, Dwight. 1977. *Pronouns and repeated nouns*. Bloomington: Indiana University Linguistics Club.

Bühler, Karl. 1934. *Sprachtheorie. Die Darstellungsfunktion der Sprache*. Jena: G. Fischer.

Cornish, Francis. 2009. Quel sens pour la linguistique? Texte d'une présentation (non publié) lors du Symposium organisé dans le cadre de l'octroi d'un doctorat honoris causa au Professeur Sir John Lyons par l'Université de Toulouse-Le Mirail, 23–24 avril 2009.

Cornish, Francis. 2011. 'Strict' anadeixis, discourse deixis and text structuring. *Language Sciences* 33(5). 753–767.

Coulmas, Florian. 1986. Reported speech. Some general issues. In Florian Coulmas (ed.), *Direct and indirect speech* 31. 1–28. Berlin, New York & Amsterdam: Mouton de Gruyter.

Crompton, Peter. 2017. Complex anaphora with *this*: variation between three written argumentative genres. *Corpora* 12(1). 115–148.

Cushing, Steven. 1972. The Semantics of sentence pronominalization. *Foundations of Language* 9(2). 186–208.

Davidse, Kristin. 2014. On specificational *there*-clefts. *Leuven Working Papers in Linguistics*. 1–34.

Declerck, Renaat. 1994. The taxonomy and interpretation of clefts and pseudo-clefts. *Lingua* 93(2). 183–220.

Denison, David & Marianne Hundt. 2013. Defining relatives. *Journal of English Linguistics* 41(2). 135–167.
Diessel, Holger. 1999. *Demonstratives: Form, function, and grammaticalization*. Amsterdam & Philadelphia: John Benjamins.
Diessel, Holger. 2012. Deixis and demonstratives. In Claudia Maienborn, Klaus von Heusinger & Paul Portner (eds.), *Semantics: An international handbook of natural language meaning*, Vol. 3, 2407–2432. Berlin & Boston: De Gruyter Mouton.
Dixon, R.M.W. 2003. Demonstratives: A cross-linguistic typology. Studies in Language 27(1). 61–112.
Dufter, Andreas. 2009. Clefting and discourse organization: Comparing Germanic and Romance. In Daniel Jacob & Andreas Dufter (eds.), *Focus and background in Romance lnguages*. 83–121. Amsterdam & Philadelphia: John Benjamins.
Fichtner, Edward G. 1993. Cleft sentences in English: A comprehensive view. *WORD* 44(1). 1–30.
Fillmore, Charles J. 1997. *Lectures on deixis* (CSLI lecture notes 65). Stanford, Calif.: CSLI Publications.
Frajzyngier, Zygmunt. 1991. The *de dicto* domain in language. In Elizabeth Closs Traugott & Bernd Heine (eds.), *Approaches to grammaticalization*, 219–252. Amsterdam & Philadelphia: John Benjamins.
Francis, Gill. 1994. Labelling discourse: an aspect of nominal-group lexical cohesion. In Malcolm Coulthard (ed.), *Advances in written text analysis*. London: Routledge.
Frei, Henri. 1944. Systèmes de déictiques. *Acta Linguistica* 4(1). 111–129.
Geluykens, Ronald. 1984. *Focus phenomena in English: An empirical investigation into cleft and pseudo-cleft sentences*. Wilrijk: Universitaire Instelling Antwerpen, Departement Germaanse, Afdeling Lingüistiek.
Giacalone Ramat, Anna & Caterina Mauri . 2011. The grammaticalization of coordinating interclausal connectives. In Heiko Narrog & Bernd Heine (eds.), *Oxford Handbook of Grammaticalization*, 656–667. Oxford: Oxford University Press.
Gray, Bethany. 2010. On the use of demonstrative pronouns and determiners as cohesive devices: A focus on sentence-initial *this/these* in academic prose. *Journal of English for Academic Purposes* 9(3). 167–183.
Grochowski, Maciej. 1996. O partykułach jako wykładnikach nawiązania. Analiza wyrażenia *wręcz* [On particles as markers of concatenation. An analysis of the expression *wręcz*]. In Maciej Grochowski (ed.), *Anafora w strukturze tekstu*, 97–104. Warszawa: Wydawnictwo Energeia.
Grochowski, Maciej, Anna Kisiel & Magdalena Żabowska. 2014. *Słownik gniazdowy partykuł polskich* [A dictionary of Polish particles]. Kraków: Polska Akademia Umiejętności.
Halliday, M. A. K. & Ruqaiya Hasan. 1976. *Cohesion in English*. London: Longman.
Hartmann, Katharina & Tonjes Veenstra (eds.). 2013. *Cleft structures* (Linguistik Aktuell/Linguistics Today (LA) 208). Amsterdam–Philadelphia: John Benjamins.
Hedberg, Nancy & Lorna Fadden. 2007. The information structure of it-clefts, wh-clefts and reverse wh-clefts in English. In Nancy Hedberg & Ron Zacharski (eds.), *The Grammar-pragmatics Interface: Essays in Honor of Jeanette K. Gundel*, 49–76. Amsterdam–Philadelphia: John Benjamins.
Higgins, Francis R. 1979. *The pseudo-cleft construction in English*. London: Routledge.
Himmelmann, Nikolaus P. 1997. *Deiktikon, Artikel, Nominalphrase zur Emergenz syntaktischer Struktur*. Tübingen: Niemeyer.

Kaiser, Elsi. 2011. Focusing on pronouns: Consequences of subjecthood, pronominalisation, and contrastive focus. *Language and Cognitive Processes* 26(10). 1625–1666.
Karlík, Petr, Marek Nekula & Jana Pleskalová (eds.). 2016. *Nový encyklopedický slovník češtiny* [New encyclopedic dictionary of the Czech Language], vol. 1–2. Praha: Nakladatelství Lidové noviny.
Kosek, Iwona. 1999. *Przyczasownikowe frazy przyimkowo-nominalne w zdaniach współczesnego języka polskiego* [Adverbal prepositional phrases in sentences of Modern Polish]. Olsztyn: Wydawnictwo Uniwersytetu Warmińsko-Mazurskiego.
Kroczak, Jerzy (ed.) 2007. *Staropolskie przepowiednie i mirabilia* [Old Polish prophecies and mirabilia] (Bibliotheca Curiosa 2). Wrocław: Oficyna Wydawnicza „Atut" – Wrocławskie Wydawnictwo Oświatowe – Wydział Filologiczny Uniwersytetu Wrocławskiego.
Kuryłowicz, Jerzy. 1964. *The inflectional categories of Indo-European*. Heidelberg: Winter.
Kurz, Josef, Antonín Dostál, Zoe Hauptová, František Václav Mareš & Markéta Štěrbová (eds.). 1966–1997. *Slovník jazyka staroslověnského – Lexicon linguae palaeoslovenicae*, vol. 1–4. Praha: Akademia – Nakladatelství Československé akademie věd.
Levinson, Stephen C. 2006. Deixis. In Laurence R. Horn & Gregory Ward (eds.), *The handbook of pragmatics*, 97–121. Oxford: Blackwell.
Lyons, John. 1979. Deixis and anaphora. In Terry Myers (ed.), *The development of conversation and discourse*, 88–103. Edinburgh: Edinburgh University Press.
Łojasiewicz, Anna. 1992. *Własności składniowe polskich spójników* [Syntactic properties of Polish conjunctions]. Warszawa: Wydawnictwa Uniwersytetu Warszawskiego.
Montgomery, Michael. 1989. The standardization of English relative clauses. In Joseph B. Trahern, Jr. (ed.), *Standardizing English: Essays in the history of language change, in Honor of John Hurt Fisher*, 111–138. Knoxville: University of Tennessee Press.
Nakajima, Shin'ya & James F. Allen. 1993. A study on prosody and discourse structure in cooperative dialogues. *Phonetica* 50(3). 197–210.
Nestle, Erwin, Barbara Aland, Kurt Aland, Johannes Karavidopoulos, Carlo M. Martini & Bruce M. Metzger (eds.). 1997. *Novum Testamentum Graece et Latine*. 27th edition, Stuttgart: Deutsche Bibelgesellschaft.
Panevová, Jarmila. 1996. Referenční platnost elidovaných aktantů (k některým otázkám koreference) [Referential validity of omitted actants (on some issues of coreference)]. In Maciej Grochowski (ed.), *Anafora w strukturze tekstu*, 23–34. Warszawa: Wydawnictwo Energeia.
Piwek, Paul, Robbert-Jan Beun & Anita Cremers. 2008. 'Proximal' and 'distal' in language and cognition: Evidence from deictic demonstratives in Dutch. *Journal of Pragmatics* 40(4). 694–718.
Polański, Kazimierz. 1967. *Składnia zdania złożonego w języku górnołużyckim* [The syntax of the compound sentence in Upper Sorbian]. Wrocław et al.: Ossolineum.
Saeboe, Kjell Johan. 1996. Anaphoric presuppositions and zero anaphora. *Linguistics and Philosophy* 19(2). 187–209.
Sannikov, Vladimir Z. 2008. *Russkij sintaksis v semantiko-pragmatičeskom prostranstve* [Russian syntax at the semantics-pragmatics interface]. Moskva: Jazyki slavjanskix kul'tur.
Sinclair, John M. 1993. Written discourse structure. In Michael Hoey Gwyneth Fox & John M. Sinclair (eds.), *Techniques of description. Spoken and written Discourse*, 6–31. London: Routledge.
Slovar' russkogo jazyka XI – XVII vv. [Dictionary of the Russian Language of the 11th–17th c.]. vol 18. 1992. Moskva: Nauka.

Sobotka, Petr [Piotr]. 2019. Ètimologija i smyslovoe razvitie severnoslavjanskix konnektorov, obrazovannyx ot mestoimenij [The etymology and the semantic development of North Slavonic depronominal connectives]. In Berezovič, Elena L'vovna (ed.), *Ètnolingvistika. Onomastika. Ètimologija. Materialy IV Meždunarodnoj naučnoj konferencii. Ekaterinburg, 9–13 sentjabrja 2019 g.*, 309–311. Ekaterinburg: Izdatel'stvo Ural'skogo universiteta.

Sobotka, Piotr. 2018. Polskie wyrażenia funkcyjne pochodzenia czeskiego [Polish function words of Czech provenance]. In Adam Dobaczewski, Andrzej Moroz & Piotr Sobotka (eds.), *Sens i konwencje w języku. Studia dedykowane Profesorowi Maciejowi Grochowskiemu*, 291–310. Toruń: Wydawnictwo Naukowe Uniwersytetu Mikołaja Kopernika.

Sobotka, Piotr & Magdalena Żabowska. 2017. Wyodrębnianie, dekodowanie i klasyfikacja historycznych jednostek języka [Differentiation, decoding and classification of historical linguistic units]. *LingVaria* 24(2). 113–133.

Štícha, František, et al. 2013. *Akademická gramatika spisovné češtiny* [Acadmic grammar of the Czech language]. Praha: Academia.

Uryson, Elena V. 2011. *Opyt opisanija semantiki sojuzov. Lingvističeskie dannye o dejatel'nosti soznanija* [On the semantic description of conjunctions. Linguistic data on the activity of the mind]. Moskva: Jazyki slavjanskix kul'tur.

de Vaan, Michiel. 2008. *Etymological dictionary of Latin and the other Italic languages*. Leiden: Brill.

Vanhove, Martine. 2010. Deixis, information structure and clause linkage in Yafi' Arabic (Yemen). In Isabelle Bril (ed.), *Clause linking and clause hierarchy. Syntax and pragmatics*, 333–354. Amsterdam & Philadelphia: John Benjamins.

Wajszczuk, Jadwiga. 1997. *System znaczeń w obszarze spójników polskich: wprowadzenie do opisu* [The system of meanings in the area of Polish conjunctions: an introduction to their description]. Warszawa: Katedra Lingwistyki Formalnej UW.

Wajszczuk, Jadwiga. 1999. Can a division of lexemes according to syntactic criteria be consistent? *Biuletyn Polskiego Towarzystwa Językoznawczego* 55. 19–38.

Wajszczuk, Jadwiga. 2005. *O metatekście* [On the metatext]. Warszawa: Katedra Lingwistyki Formalnej UW.

Wajszczuk, Jadwiga. 2010. Functional class (so called "part of speech") assignment as a kind of meaning-bound word syntactic information. *Cognitive Studies/Études cognitives* 10. 15–33.

Webber, Bonnie Lynn. 1991. Structure and ostension in the interpretation of discourse deixis. *Language and Cognitive Processes* 6(2). 107–135.

Agnieszka Słoboda
The influence of Latin on the syntax of Old Polish numerals

Abstract: Unlike parts of speech that are characterised by distinct morpho-syntactic features, the class of numerals emerged very late in the development of Slavonic languages. Proto-Slavonic numerals represented different morphological classes – nouns, pronouns, and adjectives. The formation of this class in the early stages of the emerging Slavonic languages was influenced by many external and internal factors. The processes that formed a new morpho-syntactic category of numerals in Polish reflected specific syntactic tendencies: the semantic and formal categorisation, structurisation and the tendency of language autonomisation. The most important external factors are literacy and the influence of syntactic and morphological patterns from various foreign languages, mainly Latin, German and Czech. This article focuses on the impact of Latin on the syntax of numeral phrases in medieval Polish. We put forward the hypothesis that the presence of numeral phrases in Latin texts, being the base of translation for Polish writers, and the use of Latin in bilingual texts, influenced the syntactic structure of numeral phrases in the Polish language. Latin phrases with adjectival numerals caused the most critical change involving syntactic agreement. This is the first stage of a longer line of subsequent changes in the morphology and syntax of numerals in Polish.

Keywords: numeral phrase, medieval syntax, Old Polish, Latin

1 Introduction

Both internal (analogy, competition, elimination, feedback[1]) and external factors belonging to different areas of cultural and social life (Krążyńska et al. 2012) cause languages to change. This paper is focused primarily on describing issues

---

[1] I assume that morphological change runs parallel to syntactic change: each step of the syntactic change is immediately scanned by morphology, and if that change has any consequence for the morphological system, the corresponding morphological operation is carried out. Feedback form morphology to syntax is also possible.

Agnieszka Słoboda, Adam Mickiewicz University in Poznań, e-mail: asloboda@amu.edu.pl

https://doi.org/10.1515/9783110651331-003

related to external factors, namely those of a cultural nature. In particular, this paper will seek to answer the question of how the language that was crucial – both culturally and socially – in the Middle Ages influenced the development of numerals in Old Polish.

Current research examining the influence of Latin on Old Polish focuses on syntactic borrowings found mainly in texts from the 16th and 17th centuries, when Latin became a written and spoken language of the intellectual and social elites (Safarewicz 1972; Siatkowska 1989; Siatkowska 1992; Dubisz 2007). However, the impact of Latin syntactic patterns on the syntactic constructions of Old Polish occurred in different ways before 1500, when Latin functioned primarily as an elite written language and a spoken subcode reproducing written texts. Here it was primarily used in theological communication (liturgy, Bible translations), in governance (diplomacy and law), and in literature, which at that time did not distinguish fiction (ars poetica) from rhetoric (ars rhetorica) (Dubisz 2007: 3).

The role of written communication grew in line with the development of the Polish state in the Middle Ages. Medieval Polish texts were shaped by spoken language, continuing the Proto-Slavonic legacy, and by the influence of foreign writing traditions (within the Indo-European language family). The Middle Ages were a period of transitions from an oral to a literary tradition in the history of Polish. This shift in communication has the effect of imposing a new interpretation of linguistic facts and initiated a number of language change processes that manifested themselves in different ways in the earliest state of the Polish language. Such changes include: the structurisation of statements based on spatial analysis, language elements becoming more abstract, structuring syntactic relations of sentence components, the development of correlated connectors in compound sentences (subordinate and superordinate), the formation of indirect speech, accumulating content within a simple sentence (nominalisation), and connecting a number of relatively short simple sentences into a compound sentence (Krążyńska et al. 2011: 35–38). Christian Vandendorpe perfectly captured the nature of this transition:

> By making it possible to record the traces of a mental configuration and reorganise them at will, writing introduced a new order in the history of humanity. Through writing, thoughts can be refined and reworked repeatedly, can undergo controlled modifications and unlimited expansion, without the repetition that characterises oral transmission. What was fluid and moving can become as precise and organised as crystal, and confusion can give way to system. In short, through writing, the productions of the mind enter the objective order of the visible. (Vandendorpe 2009: 9)

In most European languages (including Polish) the shift to written over oral communication occurred as a result of contact with foreign writing traditions and is closely related to bilingualism (Adams 2003). Written Polish was always learned after the acquisition of written Latin. Medieval writers educated in Latin used its grammar as a model for the written form of Polish, which was not always their native language. Consequently, medieval scribes perceived Polish through the prism of Latin which served as a meta-language and adapted Polish syntactic structures to Latin semantics and syntax (Masłej 2015). Latin grammar became both a model, which was imitated in written Polish by using the most appropriate semantic and structural equivalents from Polish, and a source of pattern borrowings.[2]

2 Cardinal numbers in early Polish

Cardinal numbers in early Polish represented different morphological classes – pronouns, adjectives and nouns – and reflected the division of numerals into a lower and a higher class occurring in most languages (Greenberg 1987: 285; Corbett 1983: 224–236; Hurford 2001;Rutkowski 2003; Słoboda 2011). Their morphological characteristics determined the syntax of numeral phrases. Therefore, the numerals 1–4 agree with the quantified noun in case and gender. Moreover, *dwa* is followed by a dual noun, while *trzy* and *cztyrzy* by a plural one:

(1) Pronouns (*jeden*, *dwa*):
    a. *jeden*   *człowiek*
        one.M.NOM.SG   man.M.NOM.SG
        'one man'
    b. *dwa*   *krol-a*
        two.M.NOM.DU   king-M.NOM.DU
        'two kings'

(2) Adjectives (*trzy*, *cztyrzy*):
    a. *trzy*   *grzywn-y*
        three F.NOM   mark-F.NOM.PL
        'three marks'
    b. *cztyrzy*   *koni-e*
        four.M.NOM   horse-M.NOM.PL
        'four horses'

---

[2] Old Polish sources include *sensu stricto* translations of religious texts (psalters, the Bible, some religious songs) and legal documents (ortyls, codes of law). Many texts are free translations based on Latin treatises and manuscripts popular in the Middle Ages. Furthermore, some of the manuscripts are bilingual (e.g., court oaths).

Numerals from *pięć* upwards, originally being abstract nouns (Moszyński 2006: 284), were followed by a noun in the genitive plural. The use of the genitive, in this case, is motivated by perceiving the number above '4' as a noun-like set separated from a larger whole of elements indicated by a noun in a plural form, and its function was therefore similar to a genitive of quantity (Kempf 1970; Klemensiewicz 1930: 86–96).

(3) Nouns (*pięć*, *sześć* etc.):
    a. *przed   ośmi-ą   lat*
       before eight-F.INS.SG   year.N.GEN.PL
       'before eight years will pass'
    b. *z   siedmi-ą   pan-ow*
       with   seven-F.INS.SG   noble-M.GEN.PL
       'with seven nobles'
    c. *na sześc-i   kon-i*
       on   six-F.LOC.SG horse-M.GEN.PL
       'on six horses'

Numerals from *pięć* upwards took a modifier agreeing with them in case, number, and gender:

(4) *nad   tę   pięć   grzywi-en*
    over this.F.ACC.SG five.F.ACC.SG mark-F.GEN.PL
    'more than these five marks' (Great Poland Oaths of Kościan. 15th c.)

(5) *wszytka   pięć   bracie*
    all.F.NOM.SG five.F.NOM.SG brotherhood.N.GEN.SG
    'all five brothers' (Great Poland Oaths of Kościan. 15th c.)

As a head of a noun phrase, cardinal numbers from *pięć* upwards also determine the verb form in a sentence. In Old Polish texts, two types of agreement in number occur: 'syntactic' agreement (verb in singular) and 'semantic' agreement (verb in plural):

(6) Syntax *ad formam*
    a. *sześć   niedziel   minęła*
       six.F.NOM.SG week.F.GEN.PL pass.PST.F.3SG
       'six weeks have passed' (Great Poland Oaths of Poznań. 15th c.)
    b. *ostała   pięć   grzywien*
       leave.PST.F.3SG five.F.NOM.SG mark.F.GEN.PL
       'five marks were left' (Great Poland Oaths of Poznań. 15th c.)

(7) Syntax *ad sensum*
   a. *pięć   jich   mowią*
      five.F.NOM.SG he.M.GEN.PL speak.PRS.3PL
      'five of them are speaking' (Great Poland Oaths of Kalisz, 15th c.)
   b. *Dziesięć   kmieci   jachali   na Jadamową*
      ten.F.NOM.SG peasant.M.GEN.PL invade.PST.M.3PL on Adam's
      dziedzinę
      estate.F.ACC.SG
      'ten peasants invaded Adam's estate' (Great Poland Oaths of Kościan. 15th c.)

3 The influence of Latin

Existing works concerning syntactic changes in NPs with cardinal numbers have ignored the impact of Latin on the numerals from *pięć* upwards and have explained this process of syntactic changes as a result of intralingual Slavonic tendencies (Suprun 1969: 141–193; Bogusławski 1966: 172; Siuciak 2008: 143–162; Krążyńska et al. 2015). The abstract meaning of numerals became more relevant to their syntactic features than their object-set reference. Consequently, the tendency to differentiate numeral determinants on a semantic, inflectional and syntactic level from other parts of speech involved compensatory and unifying processes as well as the reduction of the paradigm. Even though it is possible to describe the syntactic changes in view of intralingual tendencies, the fact that the syntactic structure of written vernacular languages was largely based on Latin cannot be omitted. This paper is concerned only with cardinal numbers of simple morphological form – from *dwa* 'two' to *dziesięć* 'ten'; neither compound forms (of the type *jedenaście* 'eleven', *dwadzieścia* 'twenty'), nor groups of cardinal numbers (of the type *pięćnaście a sto* 'fifteen and one hundred') will be analyzed (see Słoboda 2012).

3.1 Reduction of dual number in Polish

The lack of the dual number in Latin enhanced the reduction of this category also in Polish. It is likely that the first step in the process that lead to the eventual loss of the dual in Polish involved adding modifiers in the plural form in NPs with the cardinal number *dwa*, so that the dual endings of nouns were only formal exponents of their agreement with cardinal numbers (Walczak 1993: 351):

(8) *ty   dwa   konia*
    these.M.NOM.PL two.M.NOM   horse.M.NOM.DU
    'these two horses' (Great Poland Oaths of Poznań. 15th c.)

(9) *o   pośledn-ich   dwu   świadk-u*
    about next-M.LOC.PL two.M.LOC witness-M.LOC.DU
    'about next two witnesses' (Rozmyślanie przemyskie. 15th c.)

Although dual forms of a noun following the cardinal number *dwa* dominate in the oldest manuscripts, a process of replacing them with plural forms can be observed, especially in texts translated from Latin:

(10) *uczyniłeś   dwie   wielik-i   świc-e*
     make.PST.M.2SG two.F.ACC   big-F.ACC.DU   candle-F.ACC.PL
     'you made two big candles' (Rozmyślanie przemyskie. 15th c.)

(11) *z   tych   dwu   zwolenik-ow*
     of   these.M.GEN.PL   two.M.GEN follower-M.GEN.PL
     'of these two followers' (Rozmyślanie przemyskie. 15th c.)

We can observe that agreement in number remains stronger between subjects and verbs (12). However, according to a much more general pattern,[3] the plural form of a verb occurs when the verb and the counted noun are further away from each other (13):

(12) *naśladowa-ła   jego   dwa   ślep-a*
     follow-PST.M.3DU   him   two.M.NOM   blind-M.NOM.DU
     'two blind men followed him' (Rozmyślanie przemyskie. 15th c.)

(13) *przysz-ła   dwa   krzyw-a   i*
     come-PST.M.3DU   two.M.NOM   perjuring-M.NOM.DU   and
     fałszywa   świadk-i   i   rzek-li
     false.M.NOM.DU   witness-M.NOM.DU   and   say-PST.M.3PL
     'two perjurers and false witnesses came and said' (Rozmyślanie przemyskie. 15th c.)

---

[3] As Corbett writes: "When two forms of agreement may occur with a given item, 'strict' or 'syntactic' agreement (in this instance dual agreement) and 'loose' or 'semantic' agreement (here plural), then the nearer the agreeing item is to the controller in terms of syntactic distance [...] the more likely is strict agreement, and the further away [...] the more likely is loose agreement". (Corbett 1978: 9)

3.2 Roman notation of number and code-switching

The significance of using Roman numerals in Latin and Polish texts lies in the fact that different morphological classes are represented by a uniform system of symbols. The Roman notation, especially numbers higher than 10, corresponded structurally to the construction of Polish cardinal numbers. However, the strong influence of Latin syntax, in which the cardinal number was a formally dependent element of the NP obviously resulted in insecurities as to which form should be used after the numeral. Thus, instead of the proper syntax of agreement or government, incorrect constructions would appear,[4] e.g.:

(14) *Zawisza nie zapłacił za mię* **XXII grzywien**
 Zawisza NEG pay.PST.M.3SG for me XXII mark.F.GEN.PL
 'Zawisza didn't pay twenty two marks for me' (Great Poland Oaths of Pyzdry. 15th c.).

(15) *wzięła* **XXIIII grzywien**
 take.PST.F.3SG XXIIII mark.F.GEN.PL
 'she took twenty four marks' (Great Poland Oaths of Kościan. 15th c.).

(16) *Jako cso pachołek zajął* **konie XXVI**
 As what menial capture.PST.M.3SG horse.M.ACC.PL XXVI
 'that the menial captured twenty six horses' (Great Poland Oaths of Kościan. 15th c.).

These difficulties caused the Roman notation to be used reluctantly. In the Great Poland Court Oaths, which include bilingual records, it can be seen that the numerical notation was more prevalent, and therefore likely more convenient, when the whole NP was written in Latin, e.g.:

(17) *Godzwin dał Dzierżce* **X marcas**
 Godzwin give.PST.M.3SG Dzierżka X mark.F.ACC.PL
 et **V** *za Żydowego żywota*
 and V in Jew's life.M.GEN.SG
 'Godzwin gave Dzierżka ten marks and five during the Jew's life' (Great Poland Oaths of Kościan. 15th c.).

---

4 According to both the older and the contemporary state, constructions in (14), (15), (16) should have the following forms: XXII grzywnie$_{du}$ or grzywny$_{pl}$, XXIIII grzywny$_{pl}$, konie$_{gen\,pl}$ XXVI.

(18) pani   Margorzata pomagała   Dorocie prawa
     lady   Margaret   help.PST.F.3SG   Dorothy law.N.GEN.SG
     pro XVI marcis   scoltecie   in   Woczechowo
     for   XVI mark.F.ABL.PL   parish.F.GEN.SG   in   Wociechowo
     'lady Margaret helped Dorothy in trial on sixteen marks from the parish in Wociechowo' (Great Poland Oaths of Kościan. 15th c.).

(19) jako   Tomisław   Tutewski   **cum**   **duobus**   **tam**
     as   Tomislaw   Tutewski   with   two.M.ABL.PL   as
     bonis sicut est solus   et   XX   inferioribus
     good   as   is   himself and twenty   worse.M.ABL.PL
     'that Tomisław Tutewski with two men as good as himself and with twenty worse men' (Great Poland Oaths of Kościan. 15th c.).

Since Polish writers reluctantly used Roman notation, in most medieval texts cardinal numbers are expressed lexically, both in Latin and in Polish. However, medieval scribes were more comfortable using Latin as a written L1, especially when writing official documents. Polish orthography had not been established yet, and graphical representation of words or phrases varied from text to text. The Polish cardinal numbers with palatalised or fricative consonants and nasal vowels might have been difficult to write at a fast pace. It was easier to switch into a refined and practised code.[5] The code-switching in medieval Polish mixed-language texts includes single words as well as complex phrases:

(20) co   na   mię   żałował   Cześnik   o
     what   about   me   sue.PST.M.3SG   cupbearer.M.NOM.SG   for
     szeć   **marcas**
     six.F.ACC.SG   mark.F.ACC.PL
     'that the cupbearer sued me for six marks' (Great Poland Oaths of Pyzdry. 15th c.).

---

[5] Code-switching has been attested from Latin antiquity (see Adams 2003) and seems to have been widespread in medieval and early modern Europe (see Schendl 2000a; Schendl 200b; Schendl 2005; Schendl and Wright 2011).

(21) Cso   mi   Mikołaj   dał   **novem**   **scotos**
    what   me   Nicholas give.PST.M.3SG   nine.ACC   cattle.N.ACC.PL
    et   **sex**   **mensuras**   **avene**
    and   six.ACC measure.F.ACC.PL   oat.F.GEN.SG
    'that Nicholas gave me nine cattle and six measures of oat' (Great Poland Oaths of Kościan. 15th c.).

The following example is particularly worthy of mention because it is emblematic of how natural it was for court scribes to switch from one language to another:

(22) wziął   jest   szkody (...)   jako   **sexczdzisącz**
    take.LPTCP.SG.M   AUX.3SG   loss.F.GEN.SG   as   sixty
    grzywien
    mark.F.GEN.PL
    'he suffered a loss of sixty marks' (Great Poland Oaths of Pyzdry. 15th c.).

In the above example, the clerk started writing the number *sześćdziesiąt* in Latin, as he probably usually did in a draft,[6] or, intentionally used Latin *sex* to avoid difficulties with notation of Polish *sześć*.

3.3 The influence of Latin inflexion

According to Siuciak (2008: 145), the syntactic unification of cardinal numbers in Polish was strongly affected by the agreement pattern of NPs with the cardinal numbers 2 – 4. In Latin, however, the structure „indeclinable cardinal number + noun" with the noun being the head of the NP extended to all NPs with cardinal numerals.

By analogy with Latin syntax, the morphological category of number (singular for Polish cardinal numbers 5 – 10) lost its influence on other components of the NP. The following examples represent peculiar and rare constructions with a specific order, namely agreement followed by a genitive insertion, e.g.:

---

[6] The relationship between a draft and a clean copy of court oaths of Kościan show that very often Latin phrases from the draft were translated into Polish when written as a final version.

(23) mogę   sąd   w   moich
     can.PRS.1SG trial in   my.LOC.PL
     piąci   smysłow   sędzić
     five.LOC.SG sense.GEN.PL judge.INF
     'I can conduct a trial according to my five senses' (Maciejowski's Ortyls. 15th c.).

(24) napełnili   **ony**   **sześć**   **sędow**
     filled.PST.M.3PL these.ACC.PL six.ACC.SG   vessel.GEN.PL
     'they filled these six vessel' (Rozmyślanie przemyskie. 15th c.)

In the examples (23) and (24) the pronouns agree with cardinal numerals only in case, but their number is determined by the plural meaning of the whole expression. In contrast, the nouns remain in the genitive plural as subordinates to cardinal numbers. Such constructions seem to be a staging post for structuralisation processes leading to the reversed structure with the noun as the phrasal head. The consensus that is the backing for this assumption is that in the medieval texts at our hands there is only one example of pronoun agreement in number and gender with the cardinal numeral and only in case with the noun, e.g.:

(25) ja nie   wziął   **tej**
     I   NEG   take.LPTCP.SG.M   these.F.DAT.SG
     piąci   kmieciem   imienia
     five.F.DAT.SG peasant.DAT.PL   property.N.GEN.SG
     'I did not take from these five peasants their property' (Great Poland Oaths of Kościan. 15th c.).

The next stage of the unification process concerns NPs only in oblique cases. The syntactic independence of the nominative case and the syncretism of the nominative and accusative forms of nouns in the plural was the reason for why government as syntactic relation on numeral phrases is still present in Polish in these cases, except for NPs with masculine personal nouns (Siuciak 2008: 190–194).

According to Klemensiewicz (1930: 100), the change in syntax in phrases with cardinal numbers from *pięć* upwards first had an effect on NPs in the locative due to its semantic role. Basaj (1974: 232) in reference to Old Czech formulated a similar claim. Nevertheless, the evidence from different Old Polish texts shows that agreement in NPs occurs simultaneously in the locative, dative and instrumental cases,[7] e.g.:

(26) numerical phrases in the dative:
    a. *onym   siedmi   mężom*
        this.M.DAT.PL   seven.F.DAT.SG   man.M.DAT.PL
        'to these seven men' (Queen Sophia's Bible. 15th c.)
    b. *dziesiąci   dziewicam*
        ten.F.DAT.SG   virgin.F.DAT.PL
        'to ten virgins' (Rozmyślanie przemyskie. 15th c.)

(27) numerical phrases in the locative:
    a. *Młodzieniec **w ośmi**   **dnioch**   będzie*
        lad.M.NOM.SG in eight.F.LOC.SG day.M.LOC.PL AUX.FUT.3SG
        obrzazan
        circumcised.PTCP.PASS
        'A lad will be circumcised in eight days' (Queen Sophia's Bible. 15th c.)
    b. *Przykład **o**   **dziesiąci**   **dziewicach***
        example about ten.F.LOC.SG virgin.F.LOC.PL
        'the example about ten virgins' (Rozmyślanie przemyskie. 15th c.)

(28) numerical phrases in the instrumental:
    a. *Iże-śmy   zgrzeszyli **siedmią**   **śmiertnymi***
        that-AUX.1PL sin.LPTCP.PL seven.F.INS.SG mortal.M.INS.PL
        grzechy
        sin.M.INS.PL
        'that we have sinned by seven mortal sins' (from Słownik staropolski. 14th c.)
    b. *Jan przyjachał (...) **s**   **piącią**   **podlejszymi***
        John come.PST.3SG with five.F.INS.SG worse.M.INS.PL
        'John came with five worse men' (Great Polish Oaths of Pyzdry. 15th c.)

The occurrence of agreement in these cases might have resulted not only from the semantic role of cases but also from the impact of Latin morphological patterns. In most examples, the Polish structures are the equivalents of Latin phrases with the ablative or dative, which in plural were syncretic forms. Prepositional phrases

---

[7] The influence of the Czech language on the medieval syntax of numerals in Polish was described in Słoboda 2014.

with nouns in the locative or instrumental are, in most instances, translations of Latin prepositional phrases with the ablative. It can be assumed that the pattern of distinct ablative/dative (*-is, -ibus*) endings interfered with the syntactic structure of Polish phrases, especially in mixed-language texts, e.g.:

(29) ablative:
    a. *Jan   szedł   cum tribus   nobilibus   tam*
       John go.PST.M.3SG with three.ABL noble.M.ABL.PL as
       bonis   sicut est   solus, cum sex
       good.M.ABL.PL as   be.PRS.3SG himself with six
       kmethonibus
       peasant.M.ABL.PL
       'John went with three nobles as good as himself and with six peasants'
       (Great Poland Oaths of Kościan. 15ᵗʰ c.).
    b. *Jan   przyjachał (…) se   trzemi   s   tako*
       John come.PST.M.3SG with three.M.INS.PL with as
       dobrymi   jako sam   a   s   piącią
       good.M.INS.PL as   himself and with five.F.INS.SG
       podlejszymi
       worst.M.INS.PL
       'John came with three men as good as himself and with five worse men'
       (Great Poland
       Oaths of Pyzdry. 15ᵗʰ c.).

(30) dative:
    a. *Tunc simile erit regnum caelorum **decem** **virginibus*** (Mt 25.1)
    b. *Tedy będzie   przypodobano krolewstwo*
       Then be.FUT.3SG similar.N.SG kingdom.N.NOM.SG
       *niebieskie   **dziesiąci**   **dziewicam***
       of.heaven.N.NOM.SG ten.F.DAT.SG virgin.F.DAT.PL
       'At that time the kingdom of heaven will be like ten virgins' (Rozmyślanie przemyskie. 15ᵗʰ c.)

3.4 The effect of change

The change of the hierarchy of elements in NPs with the cardinal numbers from '5' upward, caused the noun, as a head of the phrase, to become independent of the cardinal number and dependent on the verb. However, this is only applicable in cases other than the nominative and accusative. Thus, the counted noun took the same case values as the cardinal number; this syntax consequently stabilised as an agreement between the cardinal numeral and the noun. During the ensuing centuries, cardinal numbers, under the influence of their new, attributive function, gradually fused their inflectional and syntactic characteristics (Siuciak 2008). The syntactic variability observed in Old Polish manuscripts is evidence of the initial stage of this process. It is worth pointing out that medieval scribes sometimes used both patterns (genitive and agreement) in the same text, e.g.:

(31) *podkomorzam* ***po*** *sześci* *grzywnach*,
chamberlain.M.DAT.PL in six.F.LOC.SG mark.F.LOC.PL
komornikom (...) ***po*** *sześci* *skot*
bailiff.M.DAT.PL in six.F.LOC.SG skojec.M.GEN.PL
'[to pay] chamberlains six marks each, bailiffs six skojecs each' (Działyński's Codex. 15th c.)

(32) *komornikom* *<**po**>* *sześci* *grzywien*, (...),
bailiff.M.DAT.PL in six.F.LOC.SG mark.F.GEN.PL
jinszym *kastellanom, (...),* ***po*** *sześci* *grzywnach*
other.DAT.PL castellan.M.DAT.PL in six.F.LOC.SG mark.F.LOC.PL
'[to pay] bailiffs six marks each, other castellans six marks each' (Suleda's Codex. 15th c.)

4 Conclusions

The contact of Old Polish and Latin in a medieval written context, of which Latin was acquired as a second language mainly in writing, and the first language was spoken, may lead to specific kinds of interference. Latin represented a standardised and structured system, whereas Old Polish syntax was still largely determined by semantic principles and the morphological rules were just being shaped. Factors influencing the degree of interference include, among other things, the way each of the two languages is taught and the functional style of each language depending on the subject and the communicative situation (Weinreich 2007: 46). The impact of Latin on the development of the grammatical category of cardinal numbers in Old Polish was systemic in nature and manifested itself as a gradual formal categorisation of cardinal numbers (Krążyńska at al. 2015: 98–102). The factors contributing to the formation of the new syntactic pattern in Old Polish are as follows: 1) The lack of a dual number in Latin caused a transition from a distinct hierarchy to a parity of meaning from the noun to the cardinal number *dwa/dwie*. Simultaneously, the distinction between 'one', 'two' and 'many' turned into the binary opposition of individuality and plurality. Consequently, the dual form of the noun, as well as its modifiers, became the syntactic variant of agreement with the cardinal number *dwa/dwie*. 2) Roman cardinal numbers, as written representations only of numerical value, did not inform about the morphological categories of cardinal numbers. This may have been the reason for why the noun form became the head of the phrase in dependent cases. 3) The bilingualism of medieval scribes and their preference for using Latin, which became manifest in mixed-language texts as code-switching, may have interfered in the syntax of Polish NPs of cardinal numbers from 5 and above. This is likely given that Latin cardinal numbers from *quattor* upwards were uninflected and the noun was the head of a nominal phrase. 4) Latin ablative noun forms, syncretic with the dative, had specific endings: *-is* or *-ibus*. Since most Polish dative, locative and instrumental structures were the translation of Latin ablative constructions, one can expect that the distinctiveness of these endings focused the scribe's attention and caused pattern borrowing, even though the ablative was translated in different ways. The examples from the *Great Polish Oaths* demonstrate that translations were not the only source of this influence, but that the bilingualism of medieval scribes and their custom to use Latin patterns in writing was also to blame.

The arguments raised in this article in favour of the impact of Latin on the syntax of cardinal numbers in Old Polish might also be valid for the analysis of other Slavonic languages. The influence of language contact, particularly with a written form of Latin, Greek, Old Church Slavonic or German, might shed new light on syntactic changes and explain differences and similarities in Slavonic numeral syntax.

References

Adams, James Noel. 2003. *Bilingualism and the Latin Language*. Cambridge: Cambridge University Press.
Basaj, Mieczysław. 1974. *Morfologia i składnia liczebnika w języku czeskim do końca XVI wieku* [Morphology and syntax of cardinal numbers in the Czech language until the 16th century]. Wrocław – Warszawa – Kraków – Gdańsk: Zakład Narodowy im. Ossolińskich.
Bogusławski, Andrzej. 1966. *Semantyczne pojęcie liczebnika i jego morfologia w języku rosyjskim* [A semantic concept of cardinal number and its morphology in Russian]. Wrocław – Warszawa – Kraków: Zakład Narodowy im. Ossolińskich.
Corbett, Greville G. 1978. Problems in the Syntax of Slavonic Numerals. *The Slavonic and East European Review* 56(1). 1–12.
Corbett, Greville G. 1983. *Hierarchies, Targets and Controllers: Agreement Patterns in Slavic*. London: Croom Helm.

Dubisz, Stanisław. 2007. Wpływ łaciny na język polski [Latin influence on the Polish language]. *Poradnik Językowy* 5. 3–13.
Greenberg, Joseph H. 1978. Generalizations about Numeral Systems. In Joseph H. Greenberg, Charles A. Ferguson & Edith A. Moravcsik (eds.), *Universals of Human Language, Volume 3: Word Structure*, 249–295. Stanford: Stanford University Press.
Hurford, James R. 2001. Languages treat 1–4 specially: Commentary on Stanislas Dehaene's précis of *The Number Sense*. *Mind and Language* 16(1) [Special issue]. 69–75.
Kempf, Zdzisław. 1970. Rozwój i zanik polskiego partitiwu [The development and decay of the Polish partitive]. *Język Polski* 50(3). 181–194.
Klemensiewicz, Zenon. 1930. *Liczebnik główny w polszczyźnie literackiej. Historia formy i składni* [The cardinal numbers in the literary Polish language. The history of form and syntax]. Warszawa: Skład główny w Księgarni E. Wendego.
Krążyńska, Zdzisława, Tomasz Mika & Agnieszka Słoboda. 2012. *Składnia średniowiecznej polszczyzny. Część I. Konteksty – metody – tendencje* [Old Polish syntax. Part I. Contexts – Methods – Tendencies]. Poznań: Rys.
Masłej, Dorota. 2015. O wyjątkowym średniowiecznym komentarzu do tłumaczenia modlitw [On one exceptional medieval commentary on translation of prayers], *LingVaria* 2(20). 221–234.
Moszyński, Leszek. 2006. *Wstęp do filologii słowiańskiej* [An introduction to Slavonic philology]. Warszawa: Wydawnictwo Naukowe PWN.
Rutkowski, Paweł. 2003. Neuropsychologiczne uwarunkowania składni liczebników głównych [Neuropsychological determinants of the syntax of cardinal numbers]. *Scripta Neophilologica Posnaniensia* 5. 209–233.
Safarewicz, Jan. 1972. Wpływ łaciński na system gramatyczny polszczyzny [The Latin influence on the grammatical system of Polish]. In Jan Zalewski (ed.), *Symbolae Polonicae in honorem Stanislai Jodłowski*, 145–150. Wrocław – Warszawa – Kraków: Zakład Narodowy im. Ossolińskich.
Schendl, Herbert & Laura Wright (eds.). 2011. *Code-Switching in Early English*. Berlin & New York: Mouton de Gruyter.
Schendl, Herbert. 2000a. Linguistic Aspects of Code-Switching in Medieval English Texts. In David A. Trotter (ed.), *Multilingualism in Later Medieval Britain*, 77–92. Cambridge: D.S. Brewer.
Schendl, Herbert. 2000b. Syntactic constraints on code-switching in medieval texts. In Irma Taavitsainen, Terttu Nevalainen, Päivi Pahta & Matti Rissanen (eds.), *Placing Middle English in Context*, 67–86. Berlin & New York: Mouton de Gruyter.
Schendl, Herbert. 2005. English historical code-switching in a European perspective. In Christine Dabelsteen & Jens Normann Jørgensen (eds.), *Languaging and language practices*, 194–208. Copenhagen: University of Copenhagen.
Siatkowska, Ewa. 1989. Historia wpływów łacińskich w językach zachodniosłowiańskich [The history of Latin influence in West Slavonic languages]. *Poradnik Językowy* 4. 229–239.
Siatkowska, Ewa. 1992. Rola wpływów obcych w rozwoju języka na przykładzie wpływu łaciny na język czeski i polski [The role of foreign influence on language change: the case of Latin influence on Czech and Polish]. In Krystyna Handke (ed.) *Słowiańskie pogranicze językowe. Zbiór studiów*, 141–145. Warszawa: Slawistyczny Ośrodek Wydawniczy.
Siuciak, Mirosława. 2008. *Kształtowanie się kategorii gramatycznej liczebnika w języku polskim* [The development of the grammatical category of number in Polish]. Katowice: Wydawnictwo Uniwersytetu Śląskiego.

Słoboda, Agnieszka. 2011. Pozajęzykowe uwarunkowania średniowiecznej morfologii i składni liczebników głównych [Extra-linguistic factors of medieval morphology and syntax of cardinal numbers], *LingVaria* 2. 91–102.

Słoboda, Agnieszka. 2012. *Liczebnik w grupie nominalnej średniowiecznej polszczyzny. Semantyka i składnia* [The numeral in the Old Polish noun phrase. Semantics and syntax]. Poznań: Rys.

Słoboda, Agnieszka. 2014. Oddziaływanie łaciny i czeszczyzny na składnię liczebników w średniowiecznej polszczyźnie [The impact of Latin and Czech an the syntax of numerals in the Medieval Polish language], *Prace Filologiczne* 65(1). 387–402.

Słownik staropolski [Dictionary of the Old Polish language]. 1953–2002. Wrocław: Zakład Narodowy im. Ossolińskich; Wydawnictwo PAN.

Suprun, Adam E., 1969, *Slavjanskie čislitel'nye. Stanovlenie čislitel'nych kak osoboj časti reči* [Slavonic numerals. The formation of numerals as a part of speech]. Minsk: Izdatel'stvo BGU im. V. I. Lenina.

Vandendorpe, Christian. 2009. *From papyrus to hypertext. Toward the Universal Digital Library.* Urbana and Chicago: Universtity of Illinois Press.

Walczak, Bogdan. 1993. Jeszcze o formach typu dwa braty, dwa świadki [More about forms like dwa braty, dwa świadki]. In Mieczysław Basaj & Zygmunt Zagórski (eds.), *Munera linguistica Ladoslao Kurzaszkiewicz dedicata*, 349–356. Wrocław: Zakład Narodowy im. Ossolińskich.

Weinreich, Uriel. 2007. Języki w kontakcie [Languages in contact]. In Ida Kurcz (eds.), *Psychologiczne aspekty dwujęzyczności* [Psychological aspects of bilingualism], 43–55. Gdańsk: Gdańskie Wydawnictwo Psychologiczne.

Pavel Kosek, Radek Čech and Olga Navrátilová

The influence of the Latin Vulgate on the word order of pronominal enclitics in the 1st edition of the Old Czech Bible

Abstract: This study is devoted to the word order of the short pronominal forms *mi*, *sě*, *tě* 'me.DAT, REFL. ACC, you.ACC' dependent on a finite verb in the 1st edition of the Old Czech Bible. The forms studied – permanent enclitics in modern Czech – are numerous enough so that their analysis is possible (unlike other pronominal enclitic forms, i.e., *si*, *ti*, *ho*, *mu* 'REFL.DAT, you.DAT, he.ACC, he.DAT'). In the introduction and Section 2, we summarize the results of the previous research dedicated: 1. to the degree to which the forms *sě* and *tě* were enclitics, 2. to the factors that influence the competition between the post-initial word order and a 'contact' word order of pronominal (and verbal) enclitics (the competition is documented well into the beginning of the 20th century in Czech). In the analytical part (Sections 3 and 4), we investigate the possible influence of the Latin word order of the Vulgate (Parisian Bible) on the word order of the forms examined.

Keywords: Old Czech, clitics, word order, Latin

1 Introduction

The present article analyzes the word order of pronominal enclitics in the oldest complete Old Czech translation of the Bible (i.e., the 1st edition of the Old Czech Bible). It is one of the results of a long-term research project on the development of the word order of Czech enclitics (Kosek 2011 and 2017a,b – see here also for relevant references).[1] At present, the research is focused on the word order of the Czech pronominal enclitics in selected older Czech Bible translations (from 14th to 21st century). In previous research, we concentrated on the methodology, the frequency of the pronominal forms *mi*, *sě*, *tě*, we analyzed their 'enclitic'

---

[1] The paper is part of the research supported by the grant project *Development of the Czech pronominal (en)clitics*, awarded by the Grant Agency of the Czech Republic (GA17-02545S).

Pavel Kosek, Masarykova univerzita, e-mail: kosek@phil.muni.cz
Radek Čech, Ostravská univerzita, e-mail: radek.cech@osu.cz
Olga Navrátilová, Masarykova univerzita, e-mail: olga@phil.muni.cz

https://doi.org/10.1515/9783110651331-004

status, their distribution within a clause, including the factors that influence this distribution – note, however, that we focused only on the cases of pronominal enclitics dependent on a finite verb (Kosek, Čech, Navrátilová and Mačutek 2018a; 2018b; Kosek, Čech and Navrátilová 2018a; 2018b). In these studies, we but briefly touched upon possible Latin influence on the word order of the studied forms. In previous papers, we did not concentrate on the possible influence of a Latin word order on the Czech one, and, thus, we dedicate this study to this angle. Moreover, of all the pronominal forms, only the forms *mi, sě, tě* are frequent enough in the 1st edition of the Old Czech Bible, and thus, we analyze the influence the original Latin word order might have had on the Czech translation only for these forms.

The paper is organized as follows: In Section 2, we summarize the results of the research on the word order properties of the pronominal forms *mi, sě, tě* (we pay special attention to the word order characteristics and frequency of the given forms in the analyzed biblical text). Here, we also introduce the results of our research concerning the development of the word-order positions of Czech pronominal enclitics, esp. the competition between the post-initial and the contact positions of the pronominal enclitics. At the end of this section, we discuss the factors that influence this competition. In Section 3 and 4, we focus on the main objective: the influence of the original Latin Bible on the word order of the Czech pronominal forms.

2 Summary of the current research

In our research,[2] we deal with enclitic forms, which – in modern Czech – are treated as so-called permanent enclitics:[3] *mi, si, ti, ho, mu, sě, tě* 'me.DAT, REFL. DAT, you.DAT, he.GEN/ACC, he.DAT, REFL.GEN/ACC, you.GEN/ACC'. These forms cannot – in neutral contexts in modern Czech – bear a word stress, thus, they use the preceding stressed word as their phonological host.[4] To all of these pronominal forms, there exist their long counterparts (that can bear stress) in modern Czech: *mi – mně, si – sobě, ti – tobě, ho – jeho, mu – jemu, se – sebe, tě – tebe*.

---

2 As already mentioned, in this part, we published our observations in Kosek, Čech, Navrátilová and Mačutek (2018b); Kosek, Čech & Navrátilová (2018a, 2018b).
3 For the terminology and classification of enclitics in modern Czech, see Uhlířová, Kosta and Veselovská (2017); Junghanns (2002) and Kosek (2011).
4 Under certain circumstances, these forms can be proclitics: if they are the first element after a pause, it is the following word that becomes their phonological host. Typical examples include *Se nezblázni* 'Don't get crazy' or *Petra, který byl opilý, se nedalo zbavit* 'Petr, who was drunk, could not be avoided'. Junghanns (2002), therefore, considers the Czech clitics as phonologically indifferent and claims that they are either proclitics or enclitics, depending on the phonological context.

From the point of their development, these studied forms appear to be rather heterogeneous: 1. only the forms *mi, si, ti* are original (Proto-Slavic) enclitics, the other forms could originally bear stress (and they became permanent enclitics only during the historical development of Czech), 2. the short dative and accusative forms of the reflexive, i.e., *si, sě*, are on the boundary between being a pronominal and a free morpheme (in particular, the accusative form participates in a number of grammatical operations such as deagentivization or intransitivization),[5] 3. the individual forms differ in their frequency.

For the development of Czech enclitics, we can posit a developmental competition between several clausal[6] positions: 1. the post-initial position, where the enclitic is in the second position in the clause (on the concept 'the second position' more below), 2. the non-post-initial contact position, where the enclitic is placed in a position other than the post-initial one, yet in the immediate vicinity of its governor, 3. the non-post-initial isolated position, where the enclitic is placed in the middle of a sentence without any contact with its governor. From the point of view of the development of Czech, we observe a tendency for the enclitics to be either in the post-initial position or in the non-post-initial contact position. In modern Czech, the post-initial position prevailed – though it is generally assumed that this process was completed only during the 20th century (Ertl 1924: 266–267; Avgustinova and Oliva 1997: 26; Toman 2004: 74).

However, these types of the enclitic positions within a clause have variants depending on the grammatical structure of the clause and its prosodic division. To illustrate these variants, we adopt the (modern Czech) sentences first used by Ertl (1924) in his canonical article on the word order of the Czech enclitics (here, we modified some of the positions). These examples are constructed and they are not meant to represent the enclitic word order positions of modern Czech, but to demonstrate the enclitic positions documented in the older developmental phases of Czech. The example sentence is made up of four phrases: 1. *starý strom* 'old tree', 2. *skácel se*[7] 'fell down', 3. *v zahradě* 'in the garden', 4. *rázem* 'all of a sudden'. The various arrangements of these phrases allow us to document the clausal positions of the enclitics dependent on a finite verb in older Czech (before 1775).

The post-initial position is common when the first phrase is just a single word, as shown in the example[8] (1a):

---

[5] See Pergler (2016: 104) for an analysis of *sě* in Old Czech.
[6] The term 'clause' means a sentence with a finite verb (verbum finitum), and also a matrix clause (the governing clause) with potential embeddings of other clauses (embedded / dependent clauses).
[7] This *se* is the enclitic dependent on the finite verb – the enclitic that assumes various positions in the clause, as described in the text.
[8] We use the square brackets to indicate syntactic units, i.e., clause and/or phrase. The enclitic is underlined, while its governor is marked by regular typeface.

(1) a. [Rázem]₁ se₂ [starý strom]₃ [v zahradě]₄ [skácel]₂

If the initial position in the sentence is a (passive) transgressive *byv podťat* 'being chopped' (1b) or a dependent clause *Když byl podťat* 'When [the tree] has been chopped,' (1c), the enclitic is placed after the first word/phrase in the matrix (governing) clause:

    b. [[Byv podťat,]₁ [rázem]₂ se₃ [starý strom]₄ [v zahradě]₅ [skácel]₃]
    c. [[Když byl podťat,]₁ [rázem]₂ se₃ [starý strom]₄ [v zahradě]₅ [skácel]₃][9]

Suppose that the first phrase is made up of two (or more words). In the earlier phases of Czech, the enclitic could appear: 1. after the first stressed word of the phrase (the so-called 2W-position – Halpern 1995), as in (1d);[10] 2. after the last word of the phrase (the so-called 2D-position – Halpern 1995), as illustrated in (1e).

    d. *[Starý]₁ se₂ [strom]₁ [rázem]₃ [skácel]₂ [v zahradě]₄
    e. [Starý strom]₁ se₂ [rázem]₃ [skácel]₂ [v zahradě]₄

In addition to the post-initial position, an enclitic may be in the contact position, i.e., in the immediate vicinity of its governor. This position is documented in other Slavonic languages (e.g., in modern Bulgarian and Macedonian – see Franks and King 2000) as well. There are two variants of the contact position recorded in the history of Czech: 1) the contact position after the governor (the so-called post-verbal position) shown in (2a) and (2b), 2) the contact position before the governing phrase, i.e., the pre-verbal position illustrated by examples (2c) and (2d).[11]

(2) a. [Starý strom]₁ [skácel se]₂ [v zahradě]₃ [rázem]₄
    b. [Starý strom]₁ [v zahradě]₂ [rázem]₃ [skácel se]₄

---

9 In contemporary Czech (and under certain grammatical circumstances), an (en)clitic can be placed after a pre-posed clause, as shown by this example: *Že se Petr nemyl, se Marii vůbec nelíbilo* 'That Petr didn't wash, didn't please Marie a bit.' For discussion, see Kosek (2011).
10 In various phases in the development of Czech, such word order positions of enclitics are well documented (Gebauer 1929: 91; Trávníček 1956: 147), however, their counterparts in contemporary Czech are ungrammatical. Among the Slavonic languages, only modern Croatian (Franks and King 2000) still seems to have this enclitic position.
11 If the finite verb has an analytical form (*bude kácet* 'will fall'), the enclitic is then found between the two stressed verbal forms – an auxiliary and an infinitive of the lexical verb, cf. *starý strom rázem k zemi bude se kácet* 'the old tree suddenly to the ground will [se] fall'. In these cases, it is not easy to determine whether we deal with a pre-verbal or post-verbal position, and – for purely technical reasons – we classify these cases as the so-called inter-verbal position.

c. [Starý strom]₁ [rázem]₂ [se skácel]₃ [v zahradě]₄
d. [Starý strom]₁ [v zahradě]₂ [rázem]₃ [se skácel]₄

From the examples cited it is clear that the contact position is to a large extent dependent on the word order position of the governing phrase (i.e., the finite verb) within the clause: 1. If the governing finite verb is in the middle of the clause, then the enclitic can be placed either in the post-verbal position, example (2a), or in the pre-verbal position (2c). 2. If the governing finite verb is at the end of the clause, the enclitic can be placed either in the (final) post-verbal position (example (2b)) or in the (pre-final) pre-verbal position, as in the example (2d).

The last clausal position, in which an enclitic can appear, is a non-post-initial (medial) isolated position – in this case, the enclitic is in the middle of a sentence without any direct contact with its governor; however, the enclitic always has to be to the left of its governor (Franks and King 2000: 112–114). This position, exemplified in (3), is rather infrequent in both Old and Modern Czech, and the position is usually linked to another (discursive, pragmatic) function (Franks and King 2000: 115–117; for further references, see Kosek 2011: 38).

(3) [Starý strom]₁ [rázem]₂ se₃ [v zahradě]₄ [skácel]₃

2.1 Annotation

Each instance of an enclitic obtained from the eight biblical books (or their parts; for details, see Section 1.2) has been provided with a manual annotation determining its word order position. It follows from the previous discussion that to fully classify a word order position of an enclitic, two perspectives must be combined:[12]

1. The position of the enclitic within a clause (initial – post-initial – medial – pre-final – final).[13]
2. The position of the enclitic with respect to its governor (contact position, i.e., pre-verbal – post-verbal – inter-verbal, vs. isolated).

---

[12] This annotation was used in earlier research on the word order of the Czech enclitics (Kosek 2011; 2017a; 2017b).

[13] The initial position = the position at the beginning of a clause; the post-initial position = the second position in the clause (examples (1a)–(1e); the medial position = in the middle of a clause (examples (2a), (2c), (3)); the pre-final position = the penultimate position right before the governing finite verb (the last element in the clause), example (2d); the final position = the position at the end of a clause, after the governing finite verb (example (2b).

At this point, we should emphasize that our classification is only instrumental and its primary goal is to sort the examples obtained from the Old Czech texts; these word-order positions also serve as a prerequisite for assessing the competition between the three word-order positions of older Czech enclitics mentioned above (see also Kosek 2011: 45–49). On methodological limitations on the research in the earlier stages of the development of Czech, see Kosek (2011: 44–45); Čech, Kosek, Navrátilová and Mačutek (2019b).

2.2 Language material

We have already stated that the word-order properties of the selected pronominal forms are analyzed in the younger copies of the first Old Czech Bible translation: *Bible of Olomouc* (BiblOl) and the *Bible of Litoměřice-Třeboň* (BiblLitTřeb). An analysis of older developmental phases of a language based exclusively on the analysis of the Bible translation is potentially dangerous: the findings may be distorted by the specific character of the Bible, especially given that the translators of a Bible tend to yield to a certain level of stylization. Furthermore, the Bible comprises texts of very different types and genres and, consequently, one must be cautious about this factor which can influence the results significantly (cf. Kosek, Čech, Navrátilová and Mačutek 2018b). To offset the risk, we chose different books both from the New and Old Testament of the oldest complete Czech biblical translation, so that our sample 1. contains different kinds of texts and 2. they are translated by different translators, according to Kyas (1997: 43). Therefore, we chose four books of each Testament: Gospel of Matthew, Gospel of Luke, the Acts of the Apostles, the Book of Revelation (of St. John), Genesis, Isaiah, Sirah, and the Book of Job.

Most of the analyzed books are from the *Bible of Olomouc*, only the Acts of the Apostles are from the *Bible of Litoměřice-Třeboň*. We have chosen these text variants, because they convey the original text of the 1st edition of the Old Czech Bible and they are relatively complete; moreover, they are the basis of the critical edition of the Old Czech Bible, as Kyas conceived it (Kyas 1981; 1985; Kyas, Kyasová and Pečírková 1996; Pečírková et al. 2009).[14]

---

[14] It is assumed that the oldest complete translation of the Bible into Old Czech was created in the 50s of the 14th century and that about ten anonymous translators were involved (Kyas 1997: 43; Vintr 2008: 1883a). We don't have the oldest autograph, the oldest text we have is the younger copies: the *Bible of Dresden* from the 60s of the 14th century, the *Bible of Litoměřice-Třeboň* from 1411–1414 and the *Bible of Olomouc* from 1417 (Kyas 1997: 57; Vintr 2008: 1883b). However, these texts are not completely identical with the original version, which is due to the following factors: 1. not all of these texts have been preserved, 2. the original text was slightly revised in the

We compare the Old Czech translation with the original Latin text. According to Kyas (1997: 51–52), the Old Czech translation is based on an old-fashioned version of the medieval Latin Vulgate such that it "contained a considerable amount of variants from the so-called Paris Bible" (Kyas 1997: 27, 52; translation PK, RČ & ON). Following Kyas (1981: 33), we use the critical editions of medieval Vulgates with a range of variants of the medieval biblical texts: 1. *Nouum testamentum domini nostri Iesu Christi Latine* (Wordsworth – White, eds. 1889–1898; 1954), 2. *Biblia sacra iuxta vulgatam versionem ad codicum fidem iussu Pii PP. XI.* 1926–1957 (quoted as BiblVul).

2.3 Summary of the results of the previous research

In total, we have collected more than three thousand occurrences of the pronominal forms in the selected books of the 1st edition of the Old Czech Bible; more than two and a half thousands of these occurrences are enclitics dependent on a finite verb (for a summary of the pronominal forms and their governor, see Kosek, Čech and Navrátilová 2018b). However, there are significant differences in the frequency of the forms analyzed, as shown in Table 1. It shows the distribution of the clausal positions of the enclitic pronominal forms dependent on a finite verb.

Table 1: Word order positions of the pronominal enclitics in the *BiblOl* a *BiblLitTřeb*.

	Initial	Post-initial	Medial	Pre-final	Final	∑
mi	0	240	11	0	13	264
	0%	90.9%	4.2%	0%	4.9%	
ť	0	29	1	0	0	30
	0%	96.7%	3.3%	0%	0%	
ho	0	6	0	0	0	6
	0%	100%	0%	0%	0%	

---

younger (=our) transcriptions, 3. some original parts were replaced by the younger translations; the *Litoměřice-Třeboň* and *Olomouc* versions, for instance, feature a new translation of Matthew's Gospel (known as Matthew's Gospel with Homilies); a part of the Epistles with the Acts of the Apostles in the *Bible of Olomouc* comes from the second edition of the Old Czech Bible translation (Kyas 1997: 42, 61–62; Vintr 2008: 1883b). The least complete, alas, is the oldest version – the *Bible of Dresden*, which was completely destroyed during the First World War. There is just a torso of (photo)copies of certain parts of the text: Kyas estimates it as a third of the original text of the *Bible of Dresden*, Kyas (1997: 37).

Table 1 (continued)

	Initial	Post-initial	Medial	Pre-final	Final	∑
mu	0	7	0	0	0	7
	0%	100%	0%	0%	0%	
sě	0	1680	262	63	63	2068
	0%	81.2%	12.6%	3.1%	3.1%	
tě	1	155	18	6	20	200
	0.5%	77.1%	9%	3%	10.4%	
∑	1	2117	292	69	96	2575
	~0.0%	82.2%	11.3%	2.7%	3.8%	

Table 1 documents a significant disproportion with respect to the frequency with which the forms are documented: there are thousands of occurrences (*sě*), to hundreds of occurrences (*mi*, *tě*) up to the forms found in dozens of tokens (*ho*, *mu*, *ť*) and to the unattested forms (*si*, *ti*). In line with our expectations – based on the development of Czech – the most frequent form is *sě*. Our expectation is – similarly – confirmed for the relatively high frequency of the forms *mi* and *tě*, and the absence of the dative form *si* and *ti*: the literature on the historical development of Czech details rather thoroughly that it is only the bi-syllabic pronoun *sobě* that is used commonly and the enclitic form *si* appears rarely and only from the 2nd half of the 15th century (Gebauer 1896: 527; Havránek 1928: 100; Vážný 1964: 121). What – on the other hand – strikes us as surprising, is the absence of the pronoun *ti*. Again, given what is known about the historical development of Czech – we might interpret it so that the non-syllabic form *ť* stands where the enclitic would have been expected, positing thus an apocope *ti* > *ť*. We discussed this form elsewhere (Kosek, Čech and Navrátilová 2018a), let us just add in passing that only a small number of the *ť* forms are interpretable as a clear dative form: in the vast majority of occurrences, the *ť* form must be interpreted as a discursive particle (as follows from the comparison of the Latin original text and the Old Czech translation).

The overview in Table 1 depicts clear differences in the frequency of the individual word-order positions: the post-initial position is the basic one, yet, the medial, pre-final and final positions (aka: 'non-post-initial' positions) compete with the post-initial position. Based on this overview, we can conclude that the frequency of each position mirrors the developmental competition between the post-initial and the contact position. We attempt to establish the effect that the contact word order has on the non-post-initial positions by examining the word-order position of the enclitic (in the non-post-initial position) and its governor. The results are summarized in Table 2.

Table 2: The position of an enclitic (in a non-post-initial positions) with respect to its finite verb.

	Contact WO			Isolated	∑
	Pre-verbal	Post-verbal	Inter-verbal		
mi	1	22	0	1	24
	4.2%	91.6%	0%	4.2%	
ť	0	1	0	0	1
	0%	100%	0%	0%	
sě	74	283	20	11	388
	19.1%	72.9%	5.4%	2.6%	
tě	9	33	0	3	45
	20%	73.3%	0%	6.7%	
∑	84	339	20	15	458
	18.3%	74%	4.4%	3.3%	

The results presented in Table 2 show that the overwhelming majority of all non-post-initial positions are cases where the enclitic is in a contact position with its governor. The medial isolated position is represented by only three percent of all the examples. Table 2 also shows that the post-verbal position is the most frequent among the contact positions. The enclitic's need to be 'in touch' with its governing finite verb (i.e., the post-verbal position) is so overpowering that it even violates Ertl's (1924) rhythmic rule, according to which the enclitics avoid the position at the end of a clause, e. g. the final position (see Table 1). In principle, style could be the motivating factor behind the extraordinary frequency of the post-verbal position; the following facts corroborate it: 1. In the previous research on Baroque Czech (Kosek 2011), we found a significantly higher number of enclitics in the post-verbal positions (including final positions in a clause) in the *Bible of St. Wenceslas* than in texts of other genres (such as historiography, entertainment literature, educational and religious literature, law and journalistic texts, etc.) 2. The frequency of the enclitic in a post-verbal position in the *BiblOl* and *BiblLitTřeb* depends on the style of the text: texts that incline to be poetic (such as Job, Sirah, Isaiah) are more likely to have enclitics in the post-verbal position with much a higher frequency than other texts (Kosek, Čech, Navrátilová and Mačutek 2018b).

However, there are also other factors that influence the distribution of the enclitics in the individual positions: 1. In the previous research, we analyzed the influence of prosodic factors (Kosek, Čech, Navrátilová and Mačutek 2018b; Kosek, Čech and Navrátilová 2018a; 2018b). We showed a strong correlation between the length of the first syntactic phrase[15] and the position of the enclitic – we found out that the longer the first phrase is, the higher the probability of the non-post-initial position of the enclitic.[16] 2. We also discussed the influence of the complexity of the clause on the distribution of the word-order position of the enclitic. We tested the hypothesis "the more dependent phrases (including subordinate clauses) a given finite verb has (i.e., the higher the number of nodes the finite verb immediately dominates in a syntactic dependency tree), the higher is the probability of the non-post-initial position" (Čech, Kosek, Navrátilová and Mačutek 2019a). The hypothesis was not falsified in this study. This can be understood as a tendency to place the enclitic in the immediate vicinity of its governor, and, thus – in a more complex clause – to prevent the possibility that the syntactic relationship between the enclitic and its governor is not easy to identify or interpret correctly.

2.4 What is the enclitic status of *sě*, *tě*?

As we have already mentioned at the beginning, the accusative forms *sě*, *tě* have changed into permanent enclitics gradually during the historical development of Czech. The biblical books analyzed reflect this process, and we found (rather infrequent) manifestations of their original orthotonic status (i.e., as stressed words), shown by the following facts: 1. These pronouns can be modified by

---

[15] We define the 'length of a phrase' in two ways: by the number of letters the phrase contains on the one hand and by the number of words in the phrase (Kosek, Čech, Navrátilová and Mačutek 2018b; Kosek, Čech and Navrátilová 2018a; 2018b). We chose the number of letters because the analyzed texts were transcribed by the new Czech spelling with a strong tendency to equate 1 grapheme with 1 phoneme (Uličný 2017).

[16] Undoubtedly, this behavior is determined prosodically: a long (complex and/or modified) first phrase means a closed prosodic unit from the perspective of intonation (Palková 2017); its boundaries are usually signaled by a pause. Since an actual enclitic avoids a post-pause position, it is placed after the first phrase following the first (complex) phrase. The effect of this rhythmic rule can be divided into the following points: i. If a phrase is long, it is usually followed by a pause, ii. An enclitic cannot follow a pause, iii. The enclitic needs another word order position, preferably close to its governor. In the previous research, this behavior was interpreted as an effort to avoid a position after a pause (Ertl 1924) or as the so-called *heavy constituent constraint* (Radanović-Kocić 1996: 435) or as a *clitic third* principle (Franks and King 2000: 229). However, the existence of pauses (assuming the text is divided into phonemic clauses) is hypothetical and empirically very difficult to verify (in fact unmeasurable) in the case of older development stages of a language. Therefore, we have chosen empirically traceable phenomena that correspond to the length of the phrase: 1. number of letters, 2. number of words (see the discussions in the articles cited above).

another pronoun, 2. They are used in comparison, 3. They follow the conjunction *a* 'and'. Furthermore, for *tě* there are these additional properties: a. We found (a single) occurrence of *tě* in an initial position, as shown in the Table 1. b. It can be coordinated.

However, in the overwhelming majority of cases, both pronominal forms behave as enclitics: 1. They mostly appear in the post-initial position (the typical position of enclitics); 2. Usually, they do not come after a pause; these forms are avoided in positions after a pre-posed transgressive, subordinate clause, after vocative, apposition, etc.; 3. Usually, they do not follow the conjunctions *a, ale, i* 'and, but, also' (see Kosek, Čech, Navrátilová and Mačutek 2018b; Kosek, Čech and Navrátilová 2018b).

3 The influence of the Latin Vulgate

The main goal of this article is to investigate a link between the distribution of the post-initial and non-post-initial positions of Old Czech pronominal enclitics and their Latin counterparts. Here, however, we must emphasize that our aim is not to investigate the motivation of the Latin word order of the original Latin pronominal form, but rather whether the word order of the Latin text influenced the word order of the pronominal forms in the 1st edition of the Old Czech Bible. Therefore, we start with the assumption that the linear organization of the Latin original version could become a model for the linear organization of the Old Czech translation. In this case, thus, we start with the possibility of an interference (word order interference, to be more precise) from the original Latin text in the Czech translation. The prerequisite for such a text-based interference is that the original source text had the status of a model. There are two reasons to believe that this, indeed, was the case: 1. We deal with a translation of the Holy Scripture (a text written in the sacred language) – the form of the original text is, therefore and by nature, a religious authority; 2. In the Middle Ages and the early modern times, Latin was a model of an advanced language, a model of written communication and an instrument of education (among other things, it is safe to assume that translators obtained their literary education in Latin). Given these circumstances, a linguistic influence of the Latin text on the Czech text is to be expected; moreover, it has already been documented for the word order in older Czech translations (Navrátilová 2016).[17]

---

[17] However, the degree with which the translations were influenced by the Vulgate varies in the individual biblical translations, e.g., Navrátilová (2016: 99–100) states that in the word order

Looking at this phenomenon, we assume that the Latin original could have influenced the Old Czech enclitic position, given the possibility of various positions for enclitics, as discussed above. This influence was possible because there were systematic prerequisites for it. But we do not look for these prerequisites in the rules of the Latin word order (as already mentioned), since the Latin (pronominal) forms were most likely not permanent enclitics (Spevak 2010: 94). We see the systematic conditions for Latin interference in the Czech translation in the fact that the position of the Old Czech enclitics varied between the two above described positions (and their variants) within a clause, i.e., between the post-initial position and the non-post-initial position (primarily contact position).[18] Thus, we assume that the influence of the Latin original text came into the picture with the translator: he could succumb to the tendency to use that of the two competing positions, which was contained in the Latin text.[19]

From the overview above, it follows that the non-post-initial position was less common among the positions the Old Czech enclitics could take. This position could have been motivated by various factors (style, length of the initial phrase, degree of complexity of the clause). Here, we want to explore whether the word order of the Latin original text could be one of the factors that influence the frequency of non-post-initial positions. Therefore, we juxtaposed all the examples of non-post-initial enclitic positions in the Old Czech texts with their parallel pronominal forms in the Vulgate. Given the number of the actual tokens of the enclitics in the text, we decided to compare only these three enclitics: *mi, sě, tě*.

Already at first glance, we see that it is necessary to separate the results: on the one hand, *mi, tě* match up (in most cases) with the corresponding Latin pronominal forms *mihi, me* (for *mi*) and *te, tibi* (for *tě*) and, on the other hand, there is the form *sě* which usually is not matched by any pronominal form. There-

---

of possessive pronouns, there is a distinct difference between the Old Czech Bible of the 1st and 2nd editions: even though there are some cases of the influence of the Latin word order in the 1st edition, it is only from the 2nd edition that the influence of the Latin Vulgate text becomes more dominant (similarly Kyas 1997: 100).

18 This competition between post-initial and the non-post-initial positions of both pronominal and auxiliary clitics is well documented since the oldest Czech texts into the first half of the 20th century (Kosek 2011; Kosek 2017a; 2017b; Kosek, Čech, Navrátilová and Mačutek 2018a). This competition was not primarily influenced by Latin – it was attested in original Czech texts.

19 A similar mechanism was observed in the case of the influence of Greek original texts on Old Church Slavonic translations – from competing syntactic equivalent forms, the translators preferred the Old Church Slavonic form that was closest to the form in the Greek original text (Večerka 1971: 142).

fore, the following analysis is divided into two parts: 1. the relationship of the non-post-initial positions of *mi*, *tě* and the Latin version, and 2. the relationship of the non-post-initial positions of *sě* and the Latin version.

3.1 The non-post-initial positions of *mi*, *tě* and the Latin original

For these forms, the situation is rather straightforward: in the overwhelming majority of cases, the non-post-initial position correspond to the position of the Latin pronominal form (*mihi, me, tibi, te*), as evidenced by the medial post-verbal positions shown in (4) and (6) and the final position (5), (7):

(4) a. [Na tom] chváliti bude <u>tě</u>
      on this.LOC.SG.N extol.INF be.AUX.FUT.SG you.ACC.SG
      dóm silný ...
      house.NOM.SG.M strong.NOM.SG.M
      'So a strong nation will extol you'[20]
   b. *super hoc* laudabit <u>te</u> *populus fortis*...
      (BiblOl Isa 25,3|BiblVul)

(5) a. nebť náhle přijde jeho hněv a |
      [v času své pomsty]
      in time.LOC.SG.M his.GEN.SG.F vengeance.GEN.SG.F
      zatratí <u>tě</u> |
      destroy.FUT.3SG you.ACC.SG
      'For his wrath shall come on a sudden, and in the time of vengeance he will destroy thee'
   b. *subito enim venit ira illius et in tempore vindictae* disperdet <u>te</u>
      (BiblOl Sir 5,9|BiblVul)

---

[20] A complete translation of the Old Czech examples would lengthen this paper to an unacceptable extent; for this reason, we generally cite one example of a particular phenomenon, with a simple gloss of just the relevant part of examples (the glossed parts of the examples are indicated by a vertical line |). – The English Bible-translations have been taken from the *New English Translation* (NET Bible) (http://www.bible.org/netbible/index.htm) or from the *Douay–Rheims Bible* (http://vulsearch.sourceforge.net).

(6) a. [Hospodin   bóh]   otevřěl   *mi*
       Lord.NOM.SG.M   God.NOM.SG.M   open.LPTCP.M.SG   me.DAT.SG
       jest   ucho. . .
       be.AUX.PRS.3SG   ear.ACC.SG.N
       'The Lord God hath opened my ear'
   b. *Dominus Deus* aperuit *mihi aurem*. . .
       (BiblOl Isa 50,5|BiblVul)

(7) a. *Učenie, jímžto mě treskceš, uslyším a* |
       [duch   mého   rozuma]   otpovie
       spirit.NOM.SG.M my.GEN.SG.M   sense.GEN.SG.M   answer.FUT.3SG
       mi |
       me.DAT.SG
       'When I hear a reproof that dishonors me, then my understanding prompts me to answer'
   b. . . . *et spiritus intelligentiae meae* respondebit *mihi*. . .
       (BiblOl Job 20,3|BiblVul)

The influence of Latin is clearly visible on a single occurrence of the initial position of the form *tě* in (8a). This is the only case of the initial position of more than 2,500 tokens of the pronominal forms:

(8) a. [Juda,]   [*tě*   budú   chváliti
       Judah.VOC.SG.M   you.ACC.SG   be.AUX.FUT.3SG   praise.INF
       bratřie   tvoji,] . . .
       brother.NOM.PL.M   your.NOM.PL.M
       'Judah, your brothers will praise you'
   b. *Iuda te* laudabunt *fratres tui*
       (BiblOl Gen 49,8|BiblVul)

However, there are several examples of non-post-initial positions where the clause positions in Latin and Czech do not match, as shown in (9), (10) and (11). Moreover, the mismatch is more frequent for the pronoun *tě*: the Czech form is in a different position from its Latin counterpart in 13 cases (out of 44); it is just a single case (out of 24) for the pronominal form *mi* (however, given the relatively low number of the documented examples, these differences are statistically negligible – see Tables 1 and 2):

(9) a. *A   v   prosbě   za   Izmahele   sem*
       and   in   prayer.LOC.SG.F for   Ishmael.ACC.SG.M   be.AUX.PRS.1SG
       tě   uslyšal
       you.ACC.SG   hear.LPTCP.M.SG
       'As for Ishmael, I have heard you'
   b. *super Ismahel quoque exaudivi te*
       (BiblOl Gen 17,20|BiblVul)

(10) a. *Ty budeš nad mým domem a tvých úst kázanie má veš lid poslušen býti, | než*
        [jedinú]₁   tě   [stolicí]₁   královú
        only.INS.SG.F   you.ACC.SG   throne.INS.SG.F   king.POSS.INS.SG.F
        převýším |
        exceed.FUT.1SG
        'You will oversee my household, and all my people will submit to your commands. Only I, the king, will be greater than you'
    b. *... uno tantum regni solio te praecedam*
        (BiblOl Gen 41,40|BiblVul)

(11) a. *Najprvé dary jeho okojím, ježto napřed ženú, |*
        [a   potom   pro   to   [když   sě
        and   then   for   that.ACC.N.SG   [when.COMP   REFL.ACC
        s   ním   uzřím,]   snad   mi   bude
        with   him.INS.SG.M   see.FUT.1SG   perhaps   me.DAT.SG   be.FUT.3SG
        pro   to   milostivějí]
        for   that.ACC.SG.N   merciful.NOM.SG.M
        'I will first appease him by sending a gift ahead of me. After that I will meet him. Perhaps he will accept me'
    b. *dixit enim placabo illum muneribus quae praecedunt et postea videbo forsitan propitiabitur mihi*
        (BiblOl Gen 32,20|BiblVul)

It is an exception, if there are no pronominal forms corresponding to the Old Czech forms *mi, tě* in the Latin original: for instance, there is no 'you' in the Latin counterpart to *zbaví tě* '(get) rid of you' (12) and no 'me' in the Latin counterpart to *nepodal-s mi* 'you didn't give (it) to me' in (13):[21]

---

[21] Since we did not find any examples of *mi* in the non-post-initial position that would not correspond to the Latin text, we give an example of a post-initial position instead.

(12) a. *Tři síta třie jsú ještě dnové,* |
[po   nichžto   farao   zbaví   tě
after they.REL.LOC.SG.M Pharaoh.NOM.SG.M rid.FUT.3SG you.ACC.SG
hlavy   tvé]
head.GEN.SG.F your.GEN.SG.F
| *a oběsí tě na kříži a zderúť ptáci maso tvé*
'The three baskets represent three days. In three more days Pharaoh will decapitate you and impale you on a pole. Then the birds will eat your flesh from you'
b. *tria canistra tres adhuc dies sunt post quos* auferet *Pharao caput tuum ac suspendet te in cruce et lacerabunt volucres carnes tuas*
(BiblOl Gen 40,18–19|BiblVul)

(13) a. *Všel sem v tvój dóm;* |
nepodal-s   *mi*   *vody*
NEG.give.LPTCT.M.SG-AUX.PRS.2SG me.DAT.SG water.GEN.SG.F
nohám, ... |
foot.DAT.DU.F
'I entered your house. You gave me no water for my feet'
b. *intraui in domum tuam aquam pedibus meis* non dedisti
(BiblOl Lk 7,44|BiblVul)

We summarize our findings in the following tables. In Table 3, we look at the pronominal forms *mi* and its Latin counterpart and indicate, in which contexts the pronouns appear in the same position in the clause (the second row in Table 3) and in different clausal positions (third row) in the Old Czech and Latin. Table 4 captures the parallel facts for the Old Czech pronominal form *tě*:

Table 3: The non-post-initial position of the pronominal form *mi* in the Old Czech translation related to the position of the corresponding pronoun in the Vulgate.

Vulgate	Old Czech mi	Gen	Job	Sir	Isa	Mt	Lk	Acts	Rev	∑	%
pronoun	The clausal position is identical	10	4	2	4	0	1	1	1	23	95.8
	The clausal position is different	1	0	0	0	0	0	0	0	1	4.2
	No pronominal form	0	0	0	0	0	0	0	0	0	
∑		11	4	2	4	0	1	1	1	24	

Table 4: The non-post-initial position of the pronominal form *tě* in the Old Czech translation related to the position of the corresponding pronoun in the Vulgate.

Vulgate	Old Czech tě	Gen	Job	Sir	Isa	Mt	Lk	Acts	Rev	∑	%
Pronoun	The clausal position is identical	0	7	2	14	2	3	1	0	29	65.9
	The clausal position is different	4	0	0	5	1	1	1	1	13	29.5
	No pronominal form	1	0	1	0	0	0	0	0	2	4.6
∑		5	7	3	19	3	4	2	1	44	

3.2 The relation of the non-post-initial positions of *sě* and the Latin original

There are few examples, in which the Latin and Old Czech texts have the pronoun *sě* (*se*, *te*, *me* in Latin) in the same (reflexive) context, as in *opáše sě – praecinget se* in the example (14), *poddaj sě – trade te* in (15) and *pomním sě – aestimo me* in (16). Even though the cases where Old Czech *sě* corresponds to the Latin reflexive are not numerous, the Latin influence on the position of the pronominal form is clear.

(14) a. … *věrně pravi vám,* |
    [*že   opáše   sě   káže   jim*
     that.COMP dress.FUT.3SG   REFL.ACC   order.PTCP.PRS.M.SG   them.DAT
     za   stuol   siesti…] |
     at   table.ACC.SG.F   sit.INF
     'I tell you the truth, he will dress himself to serve, have them take their place at the table'
  b. *quod* praecinget *se et faciet illos discumbere*
     (BiblOl Lk 12,37|BiblVul)

(15) a. *A   protož   poddaj   sě   hospodě*
     and   therefore   submit.IMP.2SG   REFL.ACC   master.DAT.SG.M
     mému,   králi   assyrskému, …
     my.DAT.SG.M   king.DAT.SG.M   Assyrian.DAT.SG.M
     'Now make a deal with my master the king of Assyria,…'
  b. *et nunc* trade *te domino meo regi Assyriorum*
     (BiblOl Isa 36,8|BiblVul)

(16) a. *Králi Agrippa,* |
  [[*ve všem   v tom,   [z něhožto   na*
  in all.LOC.SG.N in that.LOC.SG.N [of REL.GEN.SG.N on
  mě   Židé   žalují,]   pomním
  me.ACC.SG Jew.NOM.PL.M   accuse.PRS.3SG] remember.PRS.1SG
  sě, |
  REFL.ACC
  [*jež ot tebe za spravedlného jmien budu, kdež sě mám dnes obrániti*]]
  'Regarding all the things I have been accused of by the Jews, King Agrippa, I consider myself fortunate that I am about to make my defense before you today'
  b. *de omnibus quibus accusor a iudaeis rex agrippa* aestimo me *beatum apud te cum sim defensurus me hodie*
  (BiblLibTřeb Acts 26,2|BiblVul)

There are only two examples (in the non-post-initial position) – *sě domní – se putat* in (17) and *nestrachuj sě – non te terreat* in (18) in which the Old Czech pronoun is placed in a position different from its Latin counterpart.

(17) a. *Muž ješitný v pýchu sě výší a* |
  jako hřiebě   divokého   osla   svobodně
  like   colt.NOM.SG.N wild.GEN.SG.M   donkey.GEN.SG.M freely
  urozeného   sě   domní
  born.GEN.SG.M   REFL.ACC   think.PRS.3SG
  'But an empty man will become wise, when a wild donkey's colt is born a human being'
  b. *vir vanus in superbiam* erigitur *et tamquam pullum onagri* se *liberum natum* putat
  (BiblOl Job 11,12|BiblVul)

(18) a. | *Alevšak divu   mého   nestrachuj*
  but   miracle.GEN.SG. my.GEN.SG.M   NEG.worry.IMP.2SG
  sě |
  REFL.ACC
  a má výmluva nebuď tobě těžká,...
  'Therefore no fear of me should terrify you, nor should my pressure be heavy on you'
  b. *verumtamen miraculum meum* non te *terreat et eloquentia mea non sit tibi gravis*
  (BiblOl Job 33,7|BiblVul)

However, in the overwhelming majority of examples, there is no pronominal form corresponding to *sě* in the Latin text. In more than two-thirds of the original Latin clauses, there is a synthetic verbal form (corresponding to the Old Czech *sě* and a finite verb), so we cannot observe any (even if potential) effects on the word order of the Old Czech pronominal forms. This can be demonstrated by comparing the verb forms *sě výšší – erigitur* in (17), *zjevil sě – affuit* in (19), and *třasú sě – contremescunt* in (20).

(19) a. Pak   jednoho   dne,   [když   biechu
     then   one.GEN.SG.M   day.GEN.SG.M   [when.COMP   be.AUX.IMPERF.3PL
     přišli   synové   boží,
     come.LPTCP.PL   son.NOM.PL.M   god.ADJ.NOM.PL.M
     [aby
     [COMP.be.AUX.COND.3PL
     stáli   před   hospodinem,]]   zjěvil
     stay.LPTCP.PL   before   lord.INS.SG.M]]   arrive.LPTCP.M.SG
     sě   také   mezi   nimi   Sathan...
     REFL.ACC   also   among   they.INS.SG.M   satan.NOM.SG.M
     'Now the day came when the sons of God came to present themselves before the Lord – and Satan also arrived among them'
   b. *quadam autem die cum venissent filii Dei ut adsisterent coram domino adfuit inter eos etiam Satan*
     (BiblOl Job 1,6|BiblVul)

Besides these examples, there is a specific set of examples of non-post-initial position of *sě* corresponding to the Latin clause with the analytical perfect of the *iudicatus est* type. This periphrastic Latin form contains a form of the auxiliary verb *esse* and the past passive participle, as shown in (20) (*sě zbierají – congregata sunt*) and (21) (*sě otevřely – aperti sunt*).

(20) a. *Slúpové nebeští třasú sě a bojie sě jeho vóle,* |
     jeho   silú   náhle   sě   mořě
     his.GEN.SG.M   power.INS.SG.F   suddenly   REFL.ACC   sea.NOM.PL.N
     zbierají |
     gather.PRS.3PL
     a jeho múdrost ztratí pyšného
     'The pillars of the heavens tremble and are amazed at his rebuke. By his power he stills the sea; by his wisdom he cut Rahab the great sea monster to pieces'

b. *columnae caeli* contremescunt *et pavent ad nutum eius in fortitudine illius repente maria* congregata <u>sunt</u> *et prudentia eius percussit superbum*
(BiblOl Job 26,11–12|BiblVul)

(21) a. |*Tehdy nebesa sě otevřely,*|
then heaven.NOM.PL.N. REFL.ACC open.LPTCP.M.PL
i uzřě ducha božieho s nebes sstupujíce jako holúbka
'the heavens opened and he saw the Spirit of God descending like a dove'
b. *et ecce aperti* <u>sunt</u> *ei caeli*
(BiblOl Mt 3,16|BiblVul)

In the examples (20) and (21), the positions of the reflexive in Old Czech and the auxiliary in Latin are different. However, in the vast majority of the other examples, the positions are the same. This is demonstrated in the following cases of post-verbal positions: 1. The medial position shown in (22) *vzdviže sě – factus est*; 2. The final position in (23) *rozmohl sě – roboratus est* (clear medial pre-verbal and pre-final positions were not found, probably because both clause positions occur rather rarely in these Bible translations):[22]

(22) a. *Tehdy búřě veliká vzdviže*
then storm.NOM.SG.F great.NOM.SG.F developed.AOR.3SG
<u>*sě*</u> *na moři,*
REFL.ACC on sea.LOC.SG.N
'And a great storm developed on the sea so that the waves began to swamp the boat'
b. *et sire motus magnus* factus est *in mari, ita ut navicula operiretur fluctibus...*
(BiblOl Mt 8,24|BiblVul)

---

[22] The variants of non-post-initial positions of pronominal (and also auxiliary) enclitics in (22a) – (23b) are well documented from the oldest Czech texts till the second half of the 20th century (Kosek 2011; Kosek 2017a; 2017b; Kosek, Čech, Navrátilová and Mačutek 2018a). These variants were not primarily influenced by Latin – there were attested occurences in original (e.g. non-translated) Czech texts.

(23) a. ... neb jest ztáhl svú ruku proti bohu
[a   proti   všemohúciemu   rozmohl   sě]
and   against   almighty.DAT.SG.M   vaunt.LPTCP.M.SG   REFL.ACC
'for he stretches out his hand against God, and vaunts himself against the Almighty'
b. ... et contra Omnipotentem roboratus est
(BiblOl Job 15,25|BiblVul)

Such cases of the Latin auxiliary and the Czech reflexive *sě* having the same word-order position are common even when there is preterite used in the Old Czech translation. Therefore, the Old Czech reflexive and auxiliary usually form an enclitic cluster, and the position of the whole cluster corresponds to the Latin position; as illustrated in the following example *pokřtili sú sě – baptizati sunt* in (24):

(24) a. A   v   túž   hodinu,   [kteříž   sú
and   at   that.ACC.SG.F   hour.ACC.SG.F   [REL.NOM.PL.M   be.AUX.PRS.3PL
přijěli   řěč   jeho,]
accept.LPTCP.M.PL   speech.ACC.SG.F   his.GEN.SG.M
pokřtili   sú   sě
baptize.LPTCP.M.PL   be.AUX.PRS.3PL   REFL.ACC
'So those who accepted his message were baptized'
b. qui ergo receperunt sermonem eius baptizati sunt
(BiblLitTřeb Acts 2,41|BiblVul)

The frequency of various positions in the Latin original and the Old Czech translations are summarized in Table 5:

Table 5: The relation of non-post-initial positions of *sě* and the Latin original – *all occurrences*.

Vulgate	Old Czech sě	Gen	Job	Sir	Isa	Mt	Lk	Acts	Rev	∑	%
Pronoun	The clausal position is identical	1	0	8	2	0	5	1	5	22	5.7
	The clausal position is different	0	2	0	0	0	0	0	0	2	0.5
Periphrastic verbal form	The clausal position is identical	6	10	3	15	12	6	13	1	66	17
	The clausal position is different	0	1	3	2	5	2	2	3	18	4.6
Synthetic verbal form		18	52	66	25	42	27	30	13	273	70.4

Table 5 (continued)

Vulgate	Old Czech sě	Gen	Job	Sir	Isa	Mt	Lk	Acts	Rev	∑	%
No Latin form		0	1	1	0	1	0	4	0	7	1.8
∑		25	66	81	44	60	40	50	22	388	

Table 5 illustrates what has been explained above: 1. More than two-thirds of the word order positions of *sě* cannot be influenced by the Latin version, because they contain a synthetic verbal form (273 occurrences). 2. In the remainder of the occurrences (approximately one-third), which contain an element whose position the Old Czech reflexive *sě* can mimic, the Latin influence is still dominant: a. if the Vulgate contains a pronoun, then *sě* appears in the same position in the Old Czech translation as well (in 22 out of 24 cases); b. if the Vulgate contains a periphrastic passive (of the type *iudicatus est*), then (in 66 occurrences out of the total of 84 cases) the position of the Old Czech reflexive *sě* corresponds to the Latin auxiliary position (78% of the cases). Based on this data, we can conclude that the word order of the Latin Vulgate affects the non-post-initial positions of *sě*, if the Latin original text has an element (a pronoun or an auxiliary) whose position can be imitated in the Old Czech translation.

Descriptively, the situation is clear, but from a linguistic perspective it is surprising that the word order of the reflexive enclitic *sě* could be influenced by the word order of Latin auxiliaries. Hence, we appear to deal with a situation where the Czech reflexive imitates the word order position of the Latin model, although the grammatical function and meaning of a (Old Czech) reflexive and a (Latin) auxiliary are different: 1. In Latin, an analytical passive consists of a passive participle of a lexical verb (*roboratus*, *baptizati*) and a finite form of an auxiliary verb (*est*, *sunt*), whereas the Czech form consists of a lexical verb (*rozmohl*, *pokřtili*) and the reflexive pronoun *sě* (see examples (23) and (24)); 2. the Latin form is a resultative and the event is presented from the perspective of the affected object, in the Czech form, on the other hand, the form suggests that the object is co-referent with a subject, or signals that the agent position in the surface realization of the clause has been blocked (deagentivization). Nevertheless, there are certain grammatical features these two forms share: 1. Formally, both types can be interpreted as analytical and – at the level of the linear organization of the sentence – both forms have a discrete element, i.e., a free morpheme (especially when the Old Czech *sě* has a function of intransitivization or deagentivization or when *sě* is a part of a reflexive tantum verb), 2. From the perspective of meaning, both forms are means of deagentivization. These two grammatical features, then, created systemic (intra-language) conditions for a textual interference. However, the non-linguistic conditions (introduced at the beginning of this section, i.e., the authority of the translated biblical text) must have been met first.

4 The relation between the word order of the Latin Vulgate and the post-initial positions in the Old Czech translation

In the previous sections, we found that the word order of the Latin text affects the non-post-initial positions of pronominal forms. Such an observation suggests the influence of the Latin source text on the distribution of non-post-initial positions of *mi, sě, tě*, but it does not disclose the overall influence of the Latin source text on the word order of these pronominal forms. Therefore, we explore also the relationship of post-initial positions of the Old Czech enclitics and the Latin original. Based on the research of non-post-initial positions, we can formulate the following assumption: the word order of the enclitic forms *mi, sě, tě* is influenced by the word order of the Latin original, provided there is a Latin counterpart to the Old Czech enclitic. Since we now look at a much greater number of cases (which is practically impossible to analyze manually), we decided to analyze a random sample of the corpus. Specifically, from each Biblical book in the corpus, we randomly choose 25% of examples, which leads to creating a sample with 519 examples, see Tables 6–8. As for the procedure of generating the sample, we assigned a number to each example and, further, we generated random numbers from a given interval of examples for each particular book. For the generation of random numbers, we used the statistical software R (R Core Team 2019).

Table 6: The relation between the pronoun *mi* in the post-initial position and the Latin original version.

Vulgate	Old Czech mi	Gen	Job	Sir	Isa	Mt	Lk	Acts	Rev	∑	%
Pronoun	The clausal position is identical	8	2	0	2	4	4	4	2	26	43.3
	The clausal position is different	11	4	2	0	3	0	2	0	22	36.7
	No pronominal form in Latin	5	3	1	0	0	1	1	1	12	20
∑		24	9	3	2	7	5	7	3	60	

Table 7: The relation between the pronoun *tě* in the post-initial position and the Latin original version.

Vulgate	Old Czech tě	Gen	Job	Sir	Isa	Mt	Lk	Acts	Rev	∑	%
	The clausal position is identical	1	1	4	7	0	2	3	0	18	46.2
	The clausal position is different	5	2	1	4	3	1	1	0	17	43.6
	No pronominal form in Latin	1	0	1	0	1	1	0	0	4	10.2
∑		7	3	6	11	4	4	4	0	39	

Table 8: The relation between the post-initial position of *sě* and the Latin original version.

Vulgate	Old Czech sě	Gen	Job	Sir	Isa	Mt	Lk	Acts	Rev	∑	%
Pronoun	The clausal position is identical	2	1	0	0	0	2	3	1	9	2.1
	The clausal position is different	0	1	2	0	0	0	1	1	6	1.4
Periphrastic verbal form	The clausal position is identical	6	1	4	8	8	22	6	6	61	14.5
	The clausal position is different	3	2	2	2	6	8	14	4	41	9.7
Synthetic verbal form		33	47	40	28	37	53	49	9	296	70.4
No form in Latin		1	2	1	0	0	1	3	0	8	1.9
∑		45	54	49	38	51	86	76	21	420	

A Latin influence can be inferred from the tables above, namely from the frequency of matches between the word order of the Old Czech pronouns *mi*, *sě*, *tě* and their Latin counterparts. In the case of the post-initial positions of *mi* and *tě*, the Latin influence is still rather strong, but not as prevailing as in the case of the non-post-initial positions. The situation is similar also for the enclitic *sě*: 1. For most of the *sě* occurrences, there is no Latin counterpart. 2. If there is an element in the Vulgate for which there is an Old Czech equivalent, the Old Czech word order of *sě* copies the word order of the Latin counterpart in 60% of the occurrences (i.e., in 9 out of 15 cases) and in the case of a periphrastic passive, the word order position of *sě* corresponds to the word order position of the Latin counterpart in about 60% of the occurrences (i.e., in 61 out of 102 cases). We can observe that the distribution of the post-initial position of pronominal clitics in more than half of all examples copies the word-order positions of the Latin pronouns or Latin auxiliary verb forms.

5 Conclusion

In this work, we investigated the possibility that the (post-initial and non-post-initial) position of the pronominal forms *mi*, *sě*, *tě* in the Old Czech Bible of the 1st edition is affected by the original Latin word order. We have concluded that in the case of the forms *mi* and *tě*, this effect is rather striking, even though perhaps less so in the case of *mi* (recall, however, that the number of occurrences is low). In the case of the reflexive pronoun *sě*, two-thirds of the original Latin counterpart sentences do not contain any element whose clausal position could have been imitated by the Old Czech reflexive pronoun *sě*. Yet, in those cases where there was a Latin pronoun, the Old Czech translation mimics also its clausal position (in the vast majority of cases). We also established that (in more than two thirds of the cases) if the reflexive *sě* translates the Latin periphrastic passive (of the type *iudicatus est*), the clausal position of the *sě* in the Old Czech translation is the same as the verbal auxiliary in the Latin original. A similar situation emerges from the comparison between the Latin original and the Old Czech translation with respect to the post-initial positions of the pronominal forms. Our analysis shows that the competition between the post-initial and non-post-initial position for the pronominal forms in Old Czech, as it appears in the Old Czech translation of the Bible of the 1st edition, is to a large extent influenced by the word order of the Latin original.

Having compared the occurrences of Old Czech non-post-initial positions, it follows that the influence of the Latin original must be considered a relevant factor that affected the word order positions of pronominal enclitics. However, this influence has clear limits: the overwhelming majority of occurrences of the Old Czech reflexive enclitic *sě* do not have a Latin counterpart, and its word order position varies in the same way as the word order positions of the enclitics *mi* and *tě* that are the translations of/for their Latin counterparts. The Latin influence, then, can be understood as an external stimulus, and Old Czech selects the variant that is closer to Latin.

References

Avgustinova, Tania & Karel Oliva. 1997. On the nature of the Wackernagel position in Czech. In Uwe Junghanns & Gerhild Zybatow (eds.), *Formale Slavistik*, 25–47. Frankfurt am Main: Verlag Vervuert.

BiblVul = Wordsworth, John, Henry Julian White & Alexander Ramsbotham (eds.). 1889–1898, 1954. *Nouum testamentum domini nostri Iesu Christi Latine I–III*. Oxford: Typographeo Clarendoniano.
= 1926–1987. *Biblia sacra iuxta vulgatam versionem ad codicum fidem iussu Pii PP. X. I–XVII*. Rome: typis polyglottis Vaticanis.

Čech, Radek, Pavel Kosek, Olga Navrátilová & Mačutek Ján. 2019a. Full valency and the position of enclitics in the Old Czech. In Xinying Chen & Ramon Ferrer-i-Cancho (eds.), *Proceedings of the First Workshop on Quantitative Syntax (Quasy, SyntaxFest 2019)*, 83–88. Stroudsburg, PA (USA): Association for Computational Linguistics.

Čech, Radek, Pavel Kosek, Olga Navrátilová & Ján Mačutek. 2019b. Wackernagel's position and contact position of pronominal enclitics in historical Czech. Competition or cooperation? *Jazykovedný časopis* 70. 267–275.

Douay–Rheims Bible. Available at http://vulsearch.sourceforge.net

Ertl, Václav. 1924. Příspěvek k pravidlu o postavení příklonek [A contribution on the norm of the position of enclitics]. *Naše řeč* 8(9). 257–268; 8(10). 293–309.

Franks, Steven & Tracy H. King 2000. *A handbook of Slavic clitics*. Oxford: Oxford University Press.

Gebauer, Jan. 1929. *Historická mluvnice jazyka českého IV. Skladba* [A historical grammar of the Czech language IV. Syntax]. Ed. by František Trávníček. Praha: Česká akademie věd a umění.

Gebauer, Jan. 1896. *Historická mluvnice jazyka českého III/1. Tvarosloví – skloňování* [A historical grammar of the Czech language III/1. Morphology – inflection] Praha: F. Tempski.

Halpern, Aaron. 1995. *On the placement and morphology of clitics*. Stanford: CSLI Publications.

Havránek, Bohuslav. 1928. *Genera verbi v slovanských jazycích 1* [The category of voice in the Slavonic languages]. Praha: Královská česká společnost nauk.

Junghanns, Uwe. 2002. Klitische Elemente im Tschechischen: eine kritische Bestandsaufnahme. In Thomas Daiber (ed.), *Linguistische Beiträge zur Slavistik IX. München*, 117–150. München: O. Sagner.

Kosek, Pavel. 2011. *Enklitika v češtině barokní doby* [Enclitics in Czech in the baroque era]. Brno: Host.

Kosek, Pavel. 2017a. Wortstellung des Präteritum-Auxiliars in der alttschechischen Olmützer Bibel. *Die Welt der Slaven* 62(1). 22–41.

Kosek, Pavel. 2017b. Die Wortstellung des Präteritum-Auxiliars in den ältesten tschechischen Prosatexten. *Zeitschrift für Slawistik* 62(4). 621–646.

Kosek, Pavel, Radek Čech, Olga Navrátilová & Ján Mačutek. 2018a. On the development of Old Czech (en)clitics. *Glottometrics* 40(1). 51–62.

Kosek, Pavel, Radek Čech, Olga Navrátilová & Ján Mačutek. 2018b. Word order of reflexive *sě* in finite verb phrases in the first edition of the Old Czech Bible translation. *Studia Linguistica Universitatis Iagellonicae Cracoviensis* 133(3). 177–200.

Kosek, Pavel, Radek Čech & Olga Navrátilová. 2018a. Starobylá dativní enklitika *mi, si, ti* ve staročeské bibli 1. redakce [The old dative enclitics *mi, si, ti* in the 1st edition of the Old

Czech Bible]. In Malčík, Petr (ed.), *Vesper Slavicus. Sborník k nedožitým devadesátinám prof. Radoslava Večerky*, 137–151. Praha: Nakladatelství lidové noviny.

Kosek, Pavel, Radek Čech & Olga Navrátilová. 2018b. Slovosled staročeských pronominálních enklitik závislých na VF ve staročeské bibli 1. redakce [The word order of the Old Czech pronominal enclitics depending on VF in the 1st edition of the Old Czech Bible]. *Slavia* 87(1–3), 189–204.

Kyas, Vladimír. 1997. *Česká Bible v dějinách národního písemnictví* [The Czech Bible in the history of the national literature]. Praha: Vyšehrad.

Kyas, Vladimír (ed.). 1981. *Staročeská bible drážďanská a olomoucká: kritické vydání nejstaršího českého překladu bible ze 14. století. I. Evangelia* [The Old Czech Bible of Dresden and Olomouc: a critical edition of the oldest Czech bible translation from the 14th century. I. Gospels]. Praha: Academia.

Kyas, Vladimír (ed.). 1985. *Staročeská bible drážďanská a olomoucká: kritické vydání nejstaršího českého překladu bible ze 14. století s částmi Bible litoměřicko-třeboňské. II. Epištoly. Skutky apoštolů. Apokalypsa* [The Old Czech Bible of Dresden and Olomouc: a critical edition of the oldest Czech bible translation from the 14th century. II. Letters. Acts of the Apostles. Apocalypse]. Praha: Academia.

Kyas, Vladimír (ed.). 1988. *Staročeská bible drážďanská a olomoucká: kritické vydání nejstaršího českého překladu bible ze 14. století. III. Genesis–Esdráš* [The Old Czech Bible of Dresden and Olomouc: a critical edition of the oldest Czech bible translation from the 14th century. III. Genesis – Book of Ezra]. Praha: Academia.

Kyas, Vladimir; Věra Kyasová & Jaroslava Pečírková (eds.). 1996. *Staročeská bible drážďanská a olomoucká: kritické vydání nejstaršího českého překladu bible ze 14. století. IV. Tobiáš–Sirachovec* [The Old Czech Bible of Dresden and Olomouc: a critical edition of the oldest Czech bible translation from the 14th century. IV. Book of Tobit – Book of Sirach]. Padeborn: Schöningh.

New English Translation. Available at <www.bible.org/netbible/index.htm>

Navrátilová, Olga. 2016. *Slovosled posesivních zájmen ve staré češtině* [The word order of possessive pronouns in Old Czech]. PhD. disertace, FFMU, dostupné na <https://is.muni.cz/auth/th/sl156/?fakulta=1421;obdobi=7244>.

Palková, Zdena. 2017. Promluvový úsek [The phonemic clause]. In Petr Karlík, Marek Nekula & Jana Pleskalová (eds.), *Nový encyklopedický slovník češtin*, 1428–1433. Praha: Nakladatelství Lidové noviny.

Pečírková, Jaroslava et al. (eds.). 2009. *Staročeská Bible drážďanská a olomoucká s částmi Proroků rožmberských a Bible litoměřicko-třeboňské, V/1 Izaiáš–Daniel, V/2 Ozeáš–2. kniha Makabejská* [The Old Czech Bible of Dresden and Olomouc with parts of the Rožmberk prophets and the Bible of Litomořice-Třeboň]. Praha: Academia.

Pergler, Jiří. 2016. K otázce tzv. akuzativního *se* v češtině: pohled (nejen) diachronní [On the questeion of the so-called accustive *se* in Czech. A (not only) diachronic perspective]. *Slovo a slovesnost* 77(2). 102–122.

R Core Team 2019. R: *A language and environment for statistical computing*. R Foundation for Statistical Computing, Vienna, Austria. URL https://www.R-project.org/.

Radanović-Kocić, Vesna. 1996. The placement of Serbo-Croatian clitics: A prosodic approach. In Aaron Halpern & Arnold Zwicky (eds.), *Approaching second: second position clitics and related phenomena*, 429–445. Stanford, CA: CSLI.

Spevak, Olga. 2010. *Constituent order in Classical Latin prose*. Amsterdam & Philadelphia: John Benjamins.

Toman, Jindřich. 2004. Ertlova diskuse českých klitik [Ertl's discussion of the Czech clitics]. In Zdeňka Hladká & Petr Karlík. (eds.), *Čeština – univerzália a specifika* 5, 73–79. Brno: Nakladatelství Lidové noviny.

Trávníček, František. 1956. *Historická mluvnice česká 3. Skladba* [A historical Czech grammar 3. Syntax]. Praha: Státní pedagogické nakladatelství.

Uhlířová, Ludmila, Petr Kosta & Ludmila Veselovská. 2017. Klitikon [Clitic]. In Petr Karlík, Marek Nekula & Jana Pleskalová (eds.), *Nový encyklopedický slovník češtiny*, 808–818. Praha: Nakladatelství Lidové noviny.

Uličný, Oldřich. 2017. Český pravopis [Czech orthography]. In Petr Karlík, Marek Nekula & Jana Pleskalová (eds.), *Nový encyklopedický slovník češtiny*, 236–239. Praha: Nakladatelství Lidové noviny.

Večerka Radoslav. 1971. Vliv řečtiny na staroslověnštinu [The influence of Greek on Old Czech]. *Listy filologické* 94(2). 129–151.

Vážný, Václav. 1964. *Historická mluvnice česká II. Tvarosloví 1. Skloňování* [A historical Czech grammar II. Morphology 1. Inflection]. Praha: Státní pedagogické nakladatelství.

Vintr, Josef. 2008. Bible (staroslověnský překlad, české překlady) [The Bible (Old Slavonic translation, Czech translations]. In Luboš Merhaut et al. (eds.). *Lexikon české literatury. 4/II U–Ž, Dodatky A–Ř*. Praha: Academia.

Sanja Perić Gavrančić
The *accusativus cum infinitivo* in 16th–19th century Croatian texts. Contact-induced and internally motivated syntactic change

Abstract: The focus of this paper is on the occurrence and origin of the *accusativus cum infinitivo* (AcI) construction, which was used as a syntactic equivalent of the declarative clause in the pre-standard period of the Croatian language. After a short overview of the status of this construction in the Classical, Medieval and Neo-Latin periods, confirmations of the AcI syntactic pattern in Croatian writings have been observed in texts translated directly from Latin templates. A separate analysis has been conducted on the texts initially written in the vernacular, in which the occurrence of the AcI construction is not necessarily conditioned by the adherence to the Latin syntactic pattern. The analysis has revealed that the AcI construction has not only been reproduced in translated, but has also been adopted in original Croatian writings. It seems that these adoptions are predominantly governed by *verba sentiendi* and the verb *činiti* 'make' followed by a causative AcI complement. The rise of this construction in the texts originally written in Croatian appears to be the result of externally motivated language change induced by sociolinguistic circumstances. Conversely, the restructuring of the genuine Latin AcI construction and its limited usage, restricted to the above-mentioned matrix verb groups, can be interpreted as an internally motivated syntactic change.

Keywords: *accusativus cum infinitivo* construction, pre-standard Croatian writings, Latin language influence, syntactic pattern replication, contact-induced syntactic change

---

Sanja Perić Gavrančić, Department of the Croatian Language History and Historical Linguistics, Institute of the Croatian Language and Linguistics, Zagreb, e-mail: speric@ihjj.hr

https://doi.org/10.1515/9783110651331-005

1 Introduction

The question of Latin influence on the Croatian pre-standard written language[1] has been addressed in previous scholarly research dealing with language patterns that were influenced by, or modelled after, Latin syntax (Zima 1887; Vinja 1951; Pranjković 2001; Hudeček 2001; Vrtič 2009). The same question has been discussed in the case of some other Slavonic languages as presented in the paper of Jaroslav Bauer (1972: 55–65), who elaborates on the impact of Latin on Slavonic syntax, Czech and Polish in particular. He points out that Latin, as the second literary language in the history of the Czech and Polish written traditions, was considered not only a prestigious language but was also a model for improving and cultivating vernacular literacy. According to Bauer, these traditions and attitudes created the prerequisites for the deep influence on the formation of vernacular literary languages.

Latin played the same role in the history of the Croatian language. In their seminal paper on Croatian Latinity, Gortan and Vratović (1971) emphasize that the Latin language was continuously used in Croatian speaking regions from the 9th century onwards. Being the official language of administration, education, and public life in Croatian territories, Latin was used longer than in many other European regions. This applies particularly to political life where Latin was used in written as well as in spoken language (until 1847 it was in public use as the official language in the Croatian Parliament). Furthermore, the importance of the Latin language in the Croatian literary tradition is reflected in the fact that the literary production in Latin preceded the vernacular one and therefore heavily influenced vernacular Croatian in its literary use. According to Gortan and Vratović (1971: 37–38), this situation led to continuous bilingualism of the 15th to the 19th century Croatian literature and, consequently, the occurrence of Latin syntactic constructions in vernacular writings. The aim of this paper is to find out how far this presumption applies to the diffusion of the *accusativus cum infinitivo* (henceforth AcI) construction in 16th–19th century Croatian.

---

[1] Regarding the name of the language that is described in this paper, it should be noted that some authors from a sociolinguistic point of view deny the validity of the term "Croatian" in designating the pre-standard written language used in the Croatian lands in the period of the 16th to 19th century. These authors point out the nomenclature inconsistency in the early modern period and the fact that many writers used various names for their own languages (cf. e.g. J. Fine 2006; Kordić 2010: 263–276). For this reason, they dispute the standpoint that the notions "slovinski / slovênski", "ilirski", etc. correspond with "Croatian", which is commonly accepted in Croatian philology (cf. e.g. Bogišić 1985; Katičić 1992: 312–328; Matasović 2011: 472–473).

2 Language contact and syntactic change

Regarding bilingualism[2] as a phenomenon related to language contact in written language usage, we refer to Herbert Schendl (2012: 505), who dealt with Middle English language contact and change: "Contact-induced change in general presupposes some degree of bilingualism or, in the case of dialect or closely related languages, mutual intelligibility. In situations of no or limited literacy, language contact predominantly happens in oral communication [. . .]. Contact with Latin, on the other hand, primarily involved a written language of culture."

The research, which is entirely reliant upon written texts, inevitably raises questions associated with specific extra-linguistic circumstances for contact-induced change: the status of the source language (in our case Latin as a 'prestigious' language of the learned), the range of adherence to foreign language systems depending on the type of written discourse (translated or original vernacular texts), and the author's choice of language register which may differ in literary and non-literary texts.

When it comes to various linguistic levels of contact-induced changes, lexical borrowing in language contact situations is considered the most widespread and straightforward type of borrowing, while "foreign influence on structural changes is much more difficult to establish than lexical borrowing, and there has been a great deal of controversy in this area, especially with syntactic change" (Schendl 2012: 514). In their study on language contact and grammatical change, Heine and Kuteva (2005: 157) emphasize that "throughout the history of contact linguistics there has been a mainstream assumption to the effect that syntax is largely immune to replication". They are opposed to Winford's conclusion (2003: 97) "that syntactic structure very rarely, if ever, gets borrowed" (his term "borrowing" includes replication) and that "in stable bilingual situations, there are very strong constraints against such a change, even in languages subjected to intense pressure from a dominant external source". In the introduction to the chapter on new syntactic profiles, Heine and Kuteva argue that "a wide range of replications in some way or other resulted in syntactic change" even in situations of stable bilingualism (Heine and Kuteva 2005: 158).

Schendl (2012: 511) elaborates on another aspect of the problem: "In many cases of assumed structural borrowing, language-internal, native factors have also been proposed as possible causes of change, especially by mainstream linguistic, while contact linguistics has, like earlier philological approaches, emphasized the

---

[2] On Latin-vernacular biligualism in a broader European context cf. Bloemendal (2015), Winkler and Schaffenrath (2019).

importance of linguistic contact for linguistic change. Part of this ongoing controversy is linked to the question whether one looks for monocausal explanations of change or accepts that multiple causation, where foreign influence triggers or supports a native development, should also be considered as contact-induced change."

In this research, we follow Schendl's guidelines (2012: 518) in examining contact-induced syntactic change in pre-standard Croatian writings: "contact-induced change has to be approached in the sociohistorical context of the various languages in contact, and both extra-linguistic and linguistic factors must be taken into account". The first guideline is in accordance with our initial presumption that the occurrence of the AcI in 16th–19th century Croatian is the consequence of extended language contact with Latin language literacy, and that it was introduced into the pre-standard Croatian writings as a feature of a high register literary language due to the sociolinguistic circumstances while being reinforced by internal linguistic factors. Furthermore, since "contact-induced syntactic change is difficult to detect and even more difficult to prove", "certain criteria, such as type of contact, and their occurrence in translated texts may help in the decision" (Schendl 2012: 516). Therefore, evidence for this contact will firstly be drawn from the texts translated directly from Latin and afterwards from the texts originally written in Croatian in which the occurrence of the AcI construction is not directly conditioned by the adherence to the Latin template. Our research question is focused on the fact that the replication of the Latin AcI construction in Croatian vernacular texts is predominantly restricted to selected matrix verb groups, verbs of perception. Following this, we will examine the hypothesis that "foreign syntactic influence may trigger or reinforce the development of a construction that already exists in embryo in the receiving language" (Schendl 2012: 516), while constructions which are not native to a language have been abandoned (Sørensen 1957: 133). This would imply the rejection of certain Latin AcI types, which are not in accordance with the Croatian language system in their syntactic structure.

In this regard, the question of detecting genuine syntactic structures in written texts might be controversial when dealing with older periods of the Croatian language and literacy because of the bilingual (Latin and Old Croatian vernacular) and diglossic (Old Croatian vernacular and Croatian Church Slavonic – which may have triggered the influence of the Greek language) circumstances from the very beginnings of its development.[3] Essentially, it means that corresponding vernacular syntactic patterns of complementation cannot be traced before contact with Latin and, therefore, the language contact factor

---

3 On this subject cf. Kapetanović (2017).

cannot be excluded from our consideration. In his research of perception verb complements in Croatian Church Slavonic, Mihaljević (2011: 195) found out that the occurrence of the AcI construction governed by the mentioned matrix verbs is relatively rare and should be determined to be foreign language influence from Greek or Latin. Furthermore, according to Mihaljević (2009: 342), finite clauses introduced by the conjunction *da* were already attested in Old Church Slavonic in the same linguistic circumstances (cf. also Kurešević 2018: 266), while in Croatian Church Slavonic the declarative clause is attested as the most common type of complementation after the verbs of perception (Mihaljević 2009: 188).[4] As emphasized by Grković-Major (2018: 353) in her notice on the occurrence of the AcI as a perception verb complement in Slavonic, "Medieval Slavonic vernaculars used other strategies with perception verbs [. . .]. Accusative with infinitive could emerge as a secondary phenomenon, under foreign influence."

The question of the AcI construction in pre-standard Croatian writings has not been the subject of comprehensive research in the same way as it has been discussed in the case of some other Slavonic languages (in Czech cf. Gebauer 1929: 600–603; Bauer 1972: 55–65; Panevova 2008: 163; in Polish cf. Kropaczek 1928; Pisarkowa 1984: 152; Birzer 2018). However, there is a generally accepted assumption that the AcI construction in Croatian should be treated as the replication of the Latin syntactic pattern (Zima 1887: 309–310; Vinja 1951: 563; Pranjković 2001: 160). This paper presents a closer account on the occurrence of the AcI construction being used instead of a declarative clause in 16th to 19th century Croatian.

3 The AcI and *quod*-clause in Latin

In Classical Latin the AcI construction was usually required after the active forms of *verba dicendi, sentiendi, affectuum, voluntatis*, some impersonal verbs (e.g. *oportet*) and after particular verbs such as *iubeo, veto, sino, patior*. This general rule was applied in the case of both object and subject control structures: *Pater sperat filium venturum esse.* 'Father hopes the son will come.' *Pater sperat se*

---

[4] The broader Slavonic context on this subject is provided by Grković-Major (2018: 353) in her paper on the development of perception verb complements in Serbian: "Thanks to the *irrealis* semantics of the PS infinitive, dative(-locative) by origin, it could not be used as a perception verb complement in Slavonic (Grković-Major 2013: 78). The construction is not found in the vernacular texts from the 12th to the 15th century, except for several examples of its passive counterpart, as a result of language contact." A significant contribution to this subject matter is made by Kurešević (2018) who discussed the earliest period of the Slavonic language history in her paper on the status and origin of the AcI construction in Old Church Slavonic.

venturum esse. 'Father hopes he (himself) will come.' The exception to the rule (the absence of an accusative case) appears after *verba voluntatis* in the subject control situation: *Pater vult venire.* 'Father wants to come.' The usage of the AcI construction in Classical Latin prevails over the finite declarative clause with *quod*, the latter being rarely confirmed in texts before the 3rd century AD (cf. Bartoněk 2010: 20, 103).

From the 3rd century onwards, the Latin language system tends to abandon the AcI construction in favour of a finite clause, which was already confirmed in the syntax of Bible texts. Eventually, in Medieval Latin, the above-mentioned infinitive construction disappeared almost completely after *verba dicendi, affectuum* and *voluntatis*. However, it still remained a possibility after *verba sentiendi* (cf. Bartoněk 2010: 23, 104).[5] Then again, the AcI complement clause after the verb *facere* (Tekavčić 1970: 143; Biville 1995) was attested in Latin syntax from the 3rd century onwards (Kühner and Stegmann 1912: 694) as a starting point in the development of the causative constructions in Romance languages (cf. Chamberlain 1986).[6] Scholars point out several possible reasons for the replacement of the AcI construction with the *quod*-clause in Latin. The hypothesis that this change was due to the influence of Greek syntax (a replication of the subordinate clause introduced by ὅτι *hoti*) is abandoned by some authors who claim that "a construction like *dicere quod* would have developed independently within Latin itself" (Cuzzolin 2013: 29–31). According to Tekavčić (1970: 140–141), this phenomenon is connected with the fact that Classical Latin allows two types of sentential complementation after *verba affectuum*, both AcI and the subordinate clause (*gaudeo te valere – gaudeo quod vales*), without the same being possible after other verb classes such as *verba dicendi* (*dico te valere – ø*). Gradually, this syntactic variation, which was previously attested only after *verba affectuum*, has been introduced as a possibility after other verb groups, filling in the empty place within the language system (*dico te valere – dico quod vales*). Cuzzolin's research (1991) on sentential complementation after *verba affectuum* shows that the possibility of

---

5 Bartoněk (2010: 104): "Since the 3rd century AD, however, the constructions of Acc. + Inf. and Nom. + Inf. were gradually disappearing.[. . .] During the following centuries the above-mentioned infinitive constructions totally disappeared after the *verba dicendi* and *putandi*, remaining henceforth in a number of modern European languages only after the *verba sentiendi*."
6 Chamberlain (1986: 140) emphasizes: "The infinitive complement was the rule for causatives in Latin as early as the sixth century", while Vincent (2016: 297) adds that it was confirmed "a good deal earlier given the biblical uses and the third-, fourth-, and fifth century passages [. . .] plus occasional examples from writers such as Tertullian and Cyprian." However, Lehmann (2016: 939) claims: "In the written standard of the Latin language, there was no established grammaticalized causative construction. It was only in Proto-Romance that the complex sentence based on *facio* plus *a.c.i.* was grammaticalized as a dedicated causative construction."

replacing the AcI construction with a subordinate clause led towards an ongoing process of substitution "which affected and changed the whole system of subordination in Latin" (Cuzzolin 1991: 202). This process was verified by the research of Jozsef Herman (1989: 133) who confirmed that in Late Latin AcI clauses and *quod*-clauses were concurrently used after *verba sentiendi* and *dicendi*, sometimes even by the same authors and in the same texts, especially by Christian authors.

Calboli (1983: 52–53) provides another perspective on the topic, suggesting that it is the change from the SOV to the SVO word order that "provokes the fall of the cases (at least for subject-object opposition), and it also provokes the fall of the mechanism that sustains AcI." Several statistical studies of the ratio of AcI to *quod*-clauses in texts form different periods (Classical, Late, and Medieval Latin) reveal the progressive process of language change that led towards the prevalence of subordinate *quod*-clauses over AcI constructions in Medieval Latin (Wirth-Poelchau 1977; Bamman, Passarotti and Crane 2008) and influenced the early development of the subordination system in Romance languages (Herman 1963).

A reverse process took place in Renaissance Neo-Latin as a high register literary language based upon the canon texts of the Classical authors.[7] Neo-Latin was not the continuation of Medieval Latin, which followed an organic development and became farther removed from Classical Latin over time, but rather an artificially transplanted Latin of the classical period (Gortan and Vratović 1971: 56). It shows a decline of distinctive syntactic features with the traits of the spoken language which were incorporated in Medieval Latin syntax and a revival of Classical Latin syntactic patterns. The result is a newly established predominance of the AcI construction over subordinate *quod*-clauses (cf. Wirth-Poelchau 1977: 98–166).

While investigating the AcI construction occurrence in 16th–19th century Croatian, it is important to pay attention to the above-mentioned circumstances, especially when we try to determine whether a particular AcI construction is a result of a syntactic pattern replication conditioned by a Latin template. Our

---

7 "Neo-Latin, sometimes called New Latin, is the term typically applied to the use of Latin as a language for original composition, translation or occasionally general communication from the period of the Italian Renaissance up to the modern day. [. . .] Its most defining feature is that, since it never represented the living tongue of a given speech community, Neo-Latin lacked in many ways the traditional patterns and traits of development that are generally associated with spoken languages. [. . .] Lacking as it did any firm roots in the regular spoken exchanges of a unified society, the language had to formalize itself by reference to existing Latin texts. [. . .] Such written texts determined the grammatical and syntactical rules and patterns, vocabulary and, to a lesser extent, style within which such writers composed their own Neo-Latin" (Butterfield 2011: 303–304).

presumption is that the AcI construction, wherever found in Croatian texts, could be linked to both Classical Latin and Neo-Latin texts, but to a lesser extent to Medieval Latin literacy. Furthermore, we expect that the occurrence of AcI depends on the nature of the written documents, their literary register, and the range of their adherence to the Latin template translated or adapted into the vernacular.

4 The AcI and *da*-clause in Croatian

In our research, the AcI construction in Croatian writings is observed both in the texts translated directly from Latin templates and those written in the vernacular, in which the occurrence of the AcI construction is not necessarily conditioned by the adherence to the Latin syntactic pattern. Our presumption is that for the syntactic development in general non-literary writings such as liturgical texts are as important as literary ones, since they show some fixed and inherited syntactic patterns. Having in mind that those texts are predominantly the vernacular translations of the Latin templates and therefore particularly relevant in terms of contact-induced syntactic change, the first part of our research is based on a comparison with the corresponding Latin source text in order to trace the origin and formation of the AcI construction in 16th–19th century Croatian. In the second part, we will examine its maintenance and status in the vernacular literary language.

The corpus used in this research consists of literary and non-literary texts collected from various sources for the scholarly research within the research project *The textology of the Croatian written tradition* conducted from 2008 to 2013 at the Institute of the Croatian Language and Linguistics in Zagreb. Since the corpus has not yet been established as a unified digital version with annotations and query possibilities, it cannot offer a verified insight into the distribution and frequency of the two syntactic models in question (AcI and finite clause). For the same reason it cannot provide a comparative account of the AcI dissemination range in the three dialectal stylizations Kajkavian, Čakavian and Štokavian.[8] In addition, it has to be emphasized that the historical development of these three varieties, which is dependent on their geographical distribution, raises the question of different language contact situations. The occurrence of the AcI construction in

---

[8] On dialectal varieties within the Croatian literary language in the early modern period, cf. Katičić (2011: 570): "Different dialectal features are not different dialectal bases of different literary languages but merely dialectal stylizations of one language". Cf. also Tadić, Brozović-Rončević and Kapetanović (2012: 53–55) and Katičić (2017).

Kajkavian could possibly be ascribed to the influence of German (especially with verbs of perception, e.g. *sehen* 'see' and *hören* 'hear') while in Čakavian and Štokavian it is rather the influence of Italian (with verbs of perception and the causative clause governed by the verb *fare* 'make').[9] We argue that the possible impact of German or Italian on the occurrence of the AcI construction in Croatian took place predominantly in the domain of the spoken language and should be treated as a secondary phenomenon, which could have supported and reinforced the primary influence of Latin syntax on the Croatian pre-standard written language.

Accordingly, this research focuses both on identifying language-external circumstances which could have triggered, and language-internal factors which could have enabled the replication of a Latin syntactic pattern in the 16th–19th century Croatian.

4.1 AcI pattern replication in translated texts

In the first part of this research, we looked for instances of the AcI in texts translated directly from Latin templates, including both literary and non-literary writings, literal and non-literal translations, the latter ones being more open to syntactic modifications. We analyzed quotes from Bible translations compiled by different authors (Bernardin's *Lectionary*, Kašić's and Katančić's *Bible*), selected liturgical and devotional texts translated from Latin originals and a translation of a Classical Latin literary text. All instances of the AcI that we identified by crosschecking the Croatian texts were verified in Latin templates (listed in the reference below[10]).

---

[9] Cf. Grković-Major (2018: 353) on the AcI: „From the beginning of the 16th century, it is documented in the language of the writers from Dubrovnik and coastal Montenegro, as a calque of Romance pattern, directly or through Croatian Čakavian. As Zima (1887: 309) pointed out, this complement was a contact-induced feature of older Čakavian. In the literary works of writers from Vojvodina, it emerged under German influence."

[10] Examples from the following texts are included in this research: LATIN TEXTS: *Vulgata* (https://www.wilbourhall.org/pdfs/vulgate.pdf),; *De imitatione Christi* by Thomas à Kempis (Transcription: http://www.disc.ua.es/~gil/de-imitatione-christi.pdf); *De miraculis beatae Mariae virginis* by Johannes Herolt (https://reader.digitale-sammlungen.de/de/fs1/object/display/bsb10685871_00001.html); *Testimonium bilabium* by Filip Lastrić (Transcription by Ruggero Cattaneo: http://www.croatianhistory.net/etf/filip_lastric1755.pdf); *Fabulae Aesopiae* by Phaedrus (www.perseus.tufts.edu); CROATIAN TEXTS: 16th century texts: ŠTOKAVIAN – Marin Držić, *Dundo Maroje, Hekuba, Tirena*; Mavro Vetranović, *Suzana, Pjesni razlike*; ČAKAVIAN – *Bernardinov lekcionar* (1495); Marko Marulić, *Od naslidovanja Isukarstova*; Petar Zoranić *Planine*; Petar Hektorović, *Ribanje i ribarsko prigovaranje*; KAJKAVIAN – Antun Vramec, *Postilla*; 17th

As expected and according to the fact that the Classical Latin AcI construction is rarely attested in the text of the Vulgate (Plater and White 1926: 120–121), the possibility of the replication of the AcI pattern in Croatian Bible translations was restricted to a few examples following the Latin pattern with *iubeo*[11] as the matrix verb (1a, 1c, 1d, 2c, 3a, 3b).[12] These examples show that the AcI pattern (with the passive infinitive *adduci, reddi, duci*) governed by *iubeo* was not supported by vernacular syntactic structure and was consequently modified into an active infinitival complementation of the matrix verb, whereas the accusative *njega, ga, tilo* lost its function as the subject of the AcI construction which became an object complement of the infinitive (*privesti, dovesti, dati, odvesti, vodit*).

In addition, two examples should be distinguished due to the semantic modification of the matrix verb in the translation process: examples (1c) and (3b) represent a shift from the declarative to a causative infinitival complement introduced by the verb *činiti* 'make' (lat. *facere*) instead of *zapovijediti* 'order' (lat. *iubere*). Other instances of the causative construction governed by *činiti* can be classified as literal translations of the Latin template (examples 4, 5a and 5b).

Furthermore, the parallel analysis of Bible quotations translated into Croatian showed a general tendency towards the abandonment of the Latin syntactic model in favour of a declarative *da*-clause (1b, 2a, 2b, 2d, 6, and 7). Interestingly, this syntactic shift is confirmed also after *verba sentiendi* (6, 7), despite the fact that a replication of the Latin AcI construction was generally accepted in Slavonic languages if governed by the verb *audire* or *videre* (Bartoněk 2010: 23, 104). This means that a breakthrough of vernacular expression happens even when in contact with a text of the utmost authority such as Holy Scripture, where a strict adherence to the Latin template was highly expected or even required.

---

century texts: ŠTOKAVIAN – Bartol Kašić, the Bible translation and *Od nasledovanja Gospodina našega Jezusa*; Matija Divković, *Sto čudesa blažene divice Marije*; Ivan Gundulić, *Arijadna*; Junije Palmotić, *Kristijada*; Petar Kanavelić, *Sveti Ivan*; ČAKAVIAN/ŠTOKAVIAN – Jerolim Kavanjin, *Bogatstvo i uboštvo*; KAJKAVIAN – Krajačević (ed. Petretić), *Sveti Evangeliomi*; 18th century texts: ŠTOKAVIAN – Filip Lastrić, *Testimonium bilabium* (Croatian version); Nikola Lašvanin, *Ljetopis*; Andrija Kačić Miošić, *Razgovor ugodni naroda slovinskoga*; Ignjat Đurđević, *Uzdasi Mandalijene pokornice*; Josip Reljković, *Kućnik*; KAJKAVIAN – [anonym.] *Kalendarium horvacki / Evangeliumi nedeljni*; 19th century texts: ŠTOKAVIAN – Matija Petar Katančić, the Bible translation; Đuro Ferić, *Fedra pričice Esopove*; KAJKAVIAN – Ignac Kristijanović, *Danica zagrebečka ili Dnevnik za prosto leto*; Matija Valjavec, *Pripovjedke* (according to Zima 1889: 312).

11 On AcI with *verba imperandi* in Latin cf. Pinkster (1990: 128). On AcI occurrences governed by *iubeo* in Kašić's translation of the Bible cf. Vrtič (2009: 275) and on the same topic in Croatian Church Slavonic cf. Mihaljević (2009: 342).

12 Kropaczek (1028: 469) emphasizes that AcI is a rare phenomenon in the Polish translations of the Bible because this type of construction was not congruent with the Polish language system.

(1) a. *Isus   zapovidi   njega   k sebi   privesti.*
    Jesus.NOM order.AOR.3SG he.ACC   to himself   bring.INF
    'Jesus ordered to bring him over to him.'
    (Bernardinov lekcionar 63)
  b. *Jesus   zapovjedje   da   bi   ga   priveli*
    Jesus.NOM order.AOR.3SG that AUX.COND   he.ACC bring.LPTCP.PL
    k   sebi.
    to   himself
    'Jesus ordered that he should be brought over to him.'
    (Kašić, Biblija. Lk. 18:40)
  c. *Isus   učini   ga   dovesti   k   sebi.*
    Jesus.NOM make.AOR.3SG he.ACC bring.INF   to himself
    'Jesus made him be brought over to him.'
    (Katančić, Biblija. Lk 18:40)
  d. *Jesus   zapoveda   njega   k sebe* [sic!] *pripeljati.*
    Jesus.NOM order.PRS.3SG he.ACC to himself   bring.INF
    'Jesus orders to bring him over to him.'
    (Sveti Evangeliomi, Ev. S. Lukača vu 18. delu)
    Lat. *Jesus iussit illum adduci ad se.*
    (Vulg. Lk. 18:40)

(2) a. *Tada   Pilat   zapovidi   da   mu   se   da*
    Then   Pilate order.AOR.3SG that he.DAT REFL give.PRS.3SG
    tilo   Isusovo.
    body.NOM   of_Jesus
    'Then, Pilate ordered that the body of Jesus should be handed over to him'
    [e.g. to Joseph].
    (Bernardinov lekcionar 41a)
  b. *Tada Pilat   zapovjedje   da   se   poda   tijelo.*
    Then Pilate.NOM order.AOR.3SG that REFL give.PRS.3SG   body.NOM
    'Then, Pilate ordered that the body should be handed over.'
    (Kašić, Biblija. Mt. 27:59)
  c. *Tada Pilat   zapovidi   dati   tilo.*
    Then Pilate.NOM order.AOR.3SG give.INF   body.ACC
    'Then, Pilate ordered to give the body.'
    (Katančić, Biblija. Mt 27:59)

d. *Teda   Pilatus   zapoveda   da   mu*
   Then   Pilate.NOM   order.PRS.3SG that he.DAT
   se   da   telo.
   REFL   give.PRS.3SG   body.NOM
   'Then, Pilate orders to give the body to him.'
   (Vramec, Postilla 86)
   Lat. *Tunc Pilatus jussit reddi corpus.*
   (Vulg. Mt 27:59)

(3) a. *zapovijedi   ga   odvesti   meju   vojsku*
       order.AOR.3SG   he.ACC   take.INF   to   military (camp)
       'He ordered to take him into the military camp.'
       (Kašić, Biblija. Dj 21:34)
    b. *učini   ga   vodit   u   tabor*
       make.AOR.3SG   he.ACC   take.INF   to   military_camp
       'He made him be brought to the military camp.'
       (Katančić, Biblija. Dj 21:34)
       Lat. *iussit duci eum in castra*
       (Vulg. Acts 21:34)

(4) *činjaše   silaziti   oganj   s   neba   na zemlju*
    make.IMPERF.3SG   descend.INF   fire.ACC   from   sky.GEN   to earth.ACC
    'He made fire to descend down to the earth.'
    (Kašić, Biblija. Otk 13:13)
    Lat. *ignem fecerat de caelo descendere in terram*
    (Vulg. Apoc. 13:13)

(5) a. *i   njega   odisgara   sjediti   činiše*
       and   he.ACC   above   sit.INF   make.IMPERF.3PL
       'And they made him sit above.'
       (Kašić, Biblija. Mt 21:7)
    b. *i   njega   su   gore   učinili   sedeti*
       and   he.ACC   AUX.PRS.3PL   above   make.LPTCP.PL   sit.INF
       'And they have made him sit above.'
       (Evangeliumi nedeljni, Ev. S. Mat. vu 21. delu)
       Lat. *et eum desuper sedere fecerunt*
       (Vulg. Mt 21:7)

(6) ere   sam   ja   čuo   da   vi   govorite
    PTCL AUX.PRS.1SG I.NOM hear.LPTCP.M.SG that you.NOM talk.PRS.2PL
    'I heard that you were talking.'
    (Kašić, Biblija. Br 11:18)
    Lat. *ego enim audivi vos dicere*
    (Vulg. Nm 11:18)

(7) čuo   sam   da   ih   ti   primudro
    hear.LPTCP.M.SG AUX.PRS.1SG that they.ACC   you.NOM   wisely
    tumačiš
    interpret.PRS.2SG
    'I have heard that you interpret them very wisely.'
    (Kašić, Biblija. Post 41:15)
    Lat. *Quae audivi te sapientissime conicere.*
    (Vulg. Gn 41:51)

The examples (8) – (14) below have been selected from devotional and homiletic Late Medieval writings and their translations into Croatian. The AcI construction is only occasionally attested in the analyzed texts, written by Marulić, Divković and Lastrić, due to its low frequency in the Medieval Latin templates compiled by Kempis and Herolt (see fn. 10). However, even this limited sample reveals a certain regularity in the usage of the AcI complement clauses in the Croatian examples: AcI is used after *verba sentiendi* – *čuti* 'hear', *vidjeti* 'see' (8, 9, 10), and the verb *činiti* 'make' (14), while avoided after other verb groups such as *verba voluntatis*, e.g., *htjeti* 'want'. This finding indicates that the Croatian language system generally accepted only those AcI models where the subject of the AcI clause can at the same time be interpreted as the object of the matrix verb.

The abandonment of the AcI construction in favour of a declarative *da*-clause is clearly shown in the quotation from 16th century Marulić's translation (11), where the Latin AcI governed by the verb *volo* 'want' could have easily been replaced by introducing a prolative infinitive (*hoće nas sebi podložiti* 'he wants us to submit to him'). Instead, Marulić chooses a *da*-clause, which provides obviation. Another quotation of the same author (12) shows syntactic instability in alternating two syntactic patterns: the Latin AcI governed by the impersonal verb *oportet* is translated both with *da*-clauses (*da tarpi . . . da uskarsne* 'to suffer. . .to resurrect') and with an infinitive clause (*ulisti* 'enter').

Similar syntactic variation of two different clause structures deriving from the Latin AcI construction after the verb *video* is confirmed in a 17th century text written by Divković (10 and 13a). This situation raises the question of whether the occurrence of different syntactic patterns (AcI and the *da*-clause) could have some functional reason in terms of distinguishing perception and acquired knowledge, as has been detected in the research of the diachronic complementation of *widzieć* 'see' in Polish (Birzer 2018: 29–30). Since the examples drawn from our corpus do not reveal the same distinction even in the writings of the same author, this hypothesis cannot be confirmed in the case of Croatian without further research. On the other hand, although the difference between knowledge acquired and the object of perception is often encoded as finite vs. nonfinite clauses, according to Grković-Major, this difference was established in Serbian by using different complementizers after perception verbs: "*da*-clauses for knowledge acquired and *kako*-, *gde*- clauses for object of perception" (2018: 339). In this regard, the Croatian examples (13a) with the *da*-clause and (13b) with the *gdi*-clause could be relevant in determining this kind of semantic differentiation.

While examples (11), (12) and (13a), as discussed above, represent an inclination towards the use of the *da*-clauses, in example (14) we encounter the reverse process. The causative AcI model governed by the verb *činiti* (lat. *facio*, 'make') was applied in Croatian translations, although the Latin template did not motivate it. This could bring us to the conclusion that this particular construction inherited from Latin was accepted and adopted into the Croatian language of the period, which means that it structurally conformed to the Croatian syntactic system. However, for this conclusion it is necessary to examine the instances of the causative AcI construction in original Croatian texts where the syntactic change is not directly conditioned by the Latin template (see the next section). In this regard, it has to be emphasized that this kind of syntactic model could have been reinforced by the influence of the Italian causative construction with the matrix verb *fare* 'make' followed by an infinitive and accusative as complements.[13]

(8) *dok te čujem pivati kralju nebeskom*
 while you.ACC hear.PRS.1SG sing.INF king.DAT of_heaven.DAT
 'While I hear you singing to the king of heaven'
 Lat. *Dum ergo te sentio cantare Regi coelesti.*
 (Laštrić, Testimonium 27, 21)

---

[13] As previously emphasized, the construction *facere* + AcI was a productive pattern in Late and Medieval Latin, and consequently in Proto-Romance and Romance languages (cf. Vincent 2016). Therefore, the attestation of this construction in Croatian can possibly be a result of syntactic borrowing not only from Latin but also from Italian. However, this depends on extra-linguistic circumstances and the languages in contact.

(9) kadano   te   vidjeh   [...] u   grob   staviti.
    when   you.ACC   see.AOR.1SG   in grave.ACC put.INF
    'When I saw you being put in the grave.'
    (Divković, Sto čudesa 13)
    Lat. *cum te vidi poni in sepulchro*
    (Herolt, De miraculis 12)

(10) vidje   vele svijetlu   družbu   ul'jesti   u   ćelicu
     see.3SG.AOR   very bright.ACC   company.ACC.SG enter.INF   into cell.ACC
     'He saw a luminous crowd entering the cell.'
     (Divković, Sto čudesa, 60)
     Lat. *Turbam candidissimam introire vidit.*
     (Herolt, De miraculis 59)

(11) Jer   Bog   hoće   da   se   svaršeno   njemu
     because   God.NOM   want.PRS.3SG that REFL completely   he.DAT.SG
     podložimo.
     submit.PRS.1PL
     'Because God wants us to submit to him completely.'
     (Marulić, Od naslidovanja Isukarstova I, 14, 3)
     Lat. *Quia Deus vult nos sibi perfecte subjici.*
     (Kempis, De imitatione Christi I, 14, 3)

(12) od potribe   biše   da   Isukarst   tarpi   i   da
     of necessity.GEN be.IMPERF.3SG that Jesus.NOM   suffer.PRS.3SG and that
     uskarsne   od   martvih   i   tako ulisti
     resurrect.PRS.3SG from dead.GEN.PL and so   enter.INF
     u   slavu   svoju.
     into glory.ACC   his.ACC
     'It was necessary that Christ has suffered, resurrected from the dead and entered his glory.'
     (Marulić, Od naslidovanja Isukarstova II, 12, 6)
     Lat. *Oportebat autem Christum pati et resurgere a mortuis et ita intrare in gloriam suam.*
     (Kempis, De imitatione Christi II, 12, 6)

(13) a. *vidješe   da   izliječu   vele   lijepe*   [...]
    see.AOR.3PL that fly_out.INF very beautiful.NOM.PL
    golubice
    dove.NOM.PL.
    'They saw that beautiful doves are flying out.'
    (Divković, Sto čudesa 40)
    Lat. *columbas speciosas vidit emergere*
    (Herolt, De miraculis 40)
  b. *vidje   gdi   starci   ulažahu   u   crkvu*
    see.AOR.3SG where old_man.NOM PL enter.IMPERF.3PL into church.ACC
    'He saw oldmen entering the church.'
    (Divković, Sto čudesa 58)

(14) *blažena   Divica   Marija   [...] čini   me*
    blessed.NOM virgin.NOM Mary.NOM   make.PRS.3SG I.ACC
    progovoriti
    speak.INF
    'The Blessed Virgin Mary makes me speak.'
    (Divković, Sto čudesa 29.)
    Lat. *beata virgo dedisset ei loquellam*
    (Herolt, De miraculis 29)

As expected, the AcI occurrence in the translation of Phaedrus *Fables* is much more frequent then in the vernacular versions of the Medieval Latin writings because of its common usage in Classical Latin literary texts:

(15) *vidim   te   ja   jesti*
    see.PRS.1SG you.ACC I.NOM eat.INF
    'I see you eating.'
    (Ferić, *Pričice* IV, 20, 21-22)
    Lat. *te video pasci.*
    (Phaedrus, *Fabulae* IV, 20, 21)

(16) *prasicu viš   zemlju   rijati*
    pig.ACC see.PRS.2SG soil.ACC dig.INF
    'you see a pig digging the soil'
    (Ferić, *Pričice* II, 4, 11-12)
    Lat. *fodere terram vides aprum*
    (Phaedrus, *Fabulae* IV, 20, 21II, 4, 8-9)

(17) *mojemučju   visjeti   videći*
    monkey.ACC hang.INF see.PTCP
    'having seen a monkey hanging'
    (Ferić, *Pričice* III, 3, 1-2)
    Lat. *pendere vidit simium*
    (Phaedrus, *Fabulae* III, 3, 1-2)

The analysis of the fables corpus led us to the following conclusions:

1. The AcI is found only after the matrix verb *vidjeti* 'see', with no records of its replacement by a declarative *da*-clause.
2. The text lacks causative infinitival clauses governed by the verb *činiti*, which is presumably caused by the absence of the construction in Classical Latin (according to Chamberlain 1986: 140).

4.2 Occurrences of the AcI pattern in vernacular literary texts

The second part of this research was focused on texts originally written in Croatian in which the AcI occurrences are not conditioned by the Latin templates. Nevertheless, many examples show the existence of the AcI construction in 16th to 19th century Croatian literary texts. This phenomenon has already been explored by the 19th century scholar Luka Zima (1887: 309–310), who attested the occurrence of the AcI in Croatian literature from the 16th century onwards, but without discussing its provenance in detail. Along with some examples from Zima's citation catalogue, we analysed original texts from our corpus including selected authors that belong to the literary canon of the period. This research has shown that the AcI syntactic pattern was extensively used in the vernacular literary language as the syntactic equivalent of the *da*-clause.

The following instances of the AcI construction appear in the same linguistic circumstances as presented in the examples of texts translated directly from Latin (1) – (17): after the *verba sentiendi vidjeti, ugledati* 'see'; *čuti* 'hear' (18–33) and after *činiti* 'make' as a matrix verb followed by a causative infinitive clause (34, 35, 36):

(18) *vilu   na zlati   jabuci   priplivati ugledah*
    fairy.ACC.SG. on golden.LOC apple.LOC swim.INF see.AOR.1SG
    (Zoranić, *Planine* XXI)
    'I saw a fairy swimming on a golden apple.'

(19) i   pokle ga   dojti   ugleda
    and later he.ACC.SG.   come.INF   see.AOR.3SG
    'And later he saw him coming.'
    (Zoranić, *Planine* IX)

(20) vidjeh   u   prah   Troju   iti
    see.AOR.3SG   into dust.ACC   Troy.ACC.   go.INF
    'I saw the city of Troy turning into dust.'
    (Držić, *Hekuba* II, 439)

(21) kad   te   čuh   govorit
    when you.ACC   hear.AOR.1SG   speak.INF
    'When I heard you speaking.'
    (Držić, *Dundo Maroje* I, 1)

(22) perivoj   uljesti   ako   ju   vidimo
    park.ACC   enter.INF   if   she.ACC   see.PRS.1PL
    'If we see her entering the park.'
    (Vetranović, *Suzana* I, 2)

(23) kada   su   te   začuli   moje   ime   klikovati
    when AUX.PRS.3PL   you.ACC   hear.LPTCP.PL   my.ACC   name.ACC   acclaim.INF
    'When they heard you acclaiming my name'
    (Hektorović, *Ribanje i ribarsko prigovaranje* II)

(24) starce   vidim   šetat
    old_man.ACC.PL   see.PRS.1SG   stroll.INF
    'I see old men strolling.'
    (Držić, *Tirena,* Prolog 29)

(25) vidim   hodit   djevojčicu
    see.PRS.1SG   walk.INF   girl.ACC.SG
    'I see a girl walking.'
    (Gundulić, *Arijadna* IV, 1123)

(26) njega   mrijeti   zemlja   vidje
    he.ACC   die.INF   land.NOM   see.AOR.3SG
    'The land saw him dying.'
    (Palmotić, *Kristijada* I, 21-22)

(27) doći   ugleda   zrak   gorući
    come.INF see.AOR.3SG air.ACC   burning.ACC
    'He saw the burning air coming.'
    (Kanavelić, *Sveti Ivan* XX, 107-108)

(28) vidim   pâsti   stada
    see.PRS.1SG graze.INF   cattle.ACC.PL
    'I see cattle grazing.'
    (Kavanjin, *Bogatstvo i uboštvo* V, 99)

(29) ugleda   ležat   tuj   na putu   koprenicu raskinutu
    see.AOR.3SG lie.INF here on path.LOC veil.ACC   torn.ADJ.ACC
    'He saw a veil torn apart lying on the path.'
    (Đurđević, *Razlike zgode* V, 71-74)

(30) vidiše   sviće   gorit
    see.AOR.3PL candle.ACC.PL burn.INF
    'They saw candles burning.'
    (Lašvanin, *Ljetopis*; according to Pranjković 2001: 160)

(31) bil   videl   stradati   Gabela
    AUX.PST.3SG see.LPTCP.M.SG perish.INF Gabael.ACC
    'He had seen Gabael perishing.'
    (Kristijanović, *Danica zagrebečka*, 12)

(32) vidi   tri   devojke   sedeti
    see.PRS.3SG three girl.ACC.PL sit.INF
    'He sees three girls sitting.'
    (Valjavec, *Pripovjedke*, 153)

(33) ja   ga   naški   prozivati   ne   čuh
    I.NOM he.ACC in our language call.INF   NEG hear.AOR.1SG
    'I did not hear him calling in our language.'
    (Reljković, *Kućnik*, 134)

(34) vilo,   pisati   i   peti   čini   me
    fairy.VOC write.INF and sing.INF make.IMP.2SG I.ACC
    'Fairy, make me write and sing.'
    (Zoranić, *Planine* XX)

(35) činjaše   i   rijeke   stat
    make.IMPERF.3SG and river.ACC.PL stop.INF
    'He made rivers be stopped.'
    (Vetranović, *Pelegrin*, v. 3467)

(36) u   volujsku   kožu   čini   ga   sašiti
    into OX.ADJ.ACC skin.ACC make.PRS.3SG he.ACC sew.INF
    i   u   vodu   baciti
    and into water.ACC   throw.INF
    'He makes him be sewn into the ox skin and thrown into the water.'
    (Kačić Miošić, *Razgovor ugodni*, 16.)

Examples (37) and (38), in comparison with (18) and (20), reveal a certain variability between two syntactic patterns in the writings of the same authors. This syntactic instability has also been confirmed in texts that are dependent on Latin templates, as discussed in Section 4.1.

(37) čuju   da   mi   se   sardačce   razdira
    hear.PRS.3PL that I.DAT REFL heart.NOM tear_apart.PRS.3SG
    'They hear that my heart is being torn apart.'
    (Zoranić, *Planine* IX)

(38) s   sinovmi   činila   [je]   da   dođem   k
    with son.INS.PL make.LPTCP.F.SG AUX.PRS.3SG   that come.PRS.1SG to
    njojzi
    she.DAT
    'She made me come to her with (my) sons.'
    (Držić, *Hekuba* V, 1)

5 Conclusion

The analysis of the above listed examples from our corpus (Section 4.1. and 4.2.) has brought us to the following conclusions:
1. The AcI syntactic pattern was attested as a result of contact-induced syntactic change both in texts translated from Latin and in texts originally written in Croatian.

2. When attested, the AcI construction is predominantly governed by *verba sentiendi* (*vidjeti, ugledati* 'see'; *čuti, začuti* 'hear') and the verb *činiti* 'make', while rarely confirmed after other matrix verbs.
3. The parallel records of the AcI constructions and declarative clauses in the same text and under the same linguistic circumstances reveal syntactic variability between the two syntactic expressions in question, which cannot be ascribed to functional reasons (acquired knowledge vs. perception).

This research has brought us closer to answering the initial research question of how to interpret the occurrence of the AcI in 16th to 19th century Croatian. In this regard, it should be emphasized that the rise of this construction can have two origins, which lead to a terminological distinction between syntactic loan translation (syntactic calque) and learned borrowing (cf. Weinreich 1979: 51, 60)[14] or, in terms of recent theories on language contact and syntactic replication, between grammatical replication and grammatical borrowing (cf. Wiemer, Wälchli and Hansen 2012). From this point of view and according to observations and attestations from our corpus, the term syntactic calque or grammatical replication would refer to a non-native syntactic pattern modelled exactly after the Latin template (as discussed in Section 4.1.) According to Vinja (1951: 549), a syntactic calque can also be the result of the authors' unconscious imitation of the Latin syntactic model, due to the author's bilingual competence, as evident in the case of Marulić's vernacular writings, e.g. in the example of AcI after the verb *htjeti* 'want', where the particular syntactic pattern is not immanent in the Croatian language system due to the literal imitation of the Latin construction.

(39) *hoteć   nas   živiti   životom   vikovstva*
     want.PTCP.PRS.ACT we.ACC live.INF life.INSTR. eternity.GEN.SG
     'wanting us to live an eternal life'
     (Marulić, *Od muke Isukarstove*, 48; according to Vinja 1951: 563)

---

[14] Cf. Večerka (1989: 28; 1997: 373, 375) who applied the distinctive terms "syntaktische Nachahmungen" or "Calques" ('syntactic calques') and "schriftsprachliche Neologismen" ('bookish neologisms') when dealing with the Greek influence on OCS syntax. The same terminology distinction was applied by Kurešević (2018) in distinguishing two layers among syntactic Graecisms in OCS. Kurešević (2018: 279) came to a similar conclusion discussing the status and origin of the AcI construction in (O)CS: „Finally, if AcI with communicative and cognitive verbs in (O)CS is attested in many ancient Indo-European languages, had internal language motivation, as well as a special pragmatic function, we should consider it to be a bookish neologism rather than a syntactic calque."

Vinja's statement has been reaffirmed by Gortan and Vratović (1971: 38), who emphasized that the continuous bilingualism of the Croatian literature in the period from the 15th to the 19th century influenced the Croatian writers of the period "to invest their Croatian writings with the spirit of Latin syntax, believing it would enrich the expressiveness of their native language." This assumption refers to the increase of the Latin syntactic models in texts originally written in Croatian, where they emerge without the direct influence of the Latin templates (as discussed in Section 4.2.).

This leads us to the conclusion that the occurrences of AcI in those texts are the result of an externally motivated syntactic change induced by sociolinguistic circumstances. We identify them as grammatical borrowings in terms of "selective copying" where "only certain aspects of a unit from the model code are transferred" as pointed out by Wiemer and Wälchli (2012: 45). As a stylistic feature of the high register literary language, they were widely adopted due to the fact that their syntactic structure conformed to the Croatian language system within particular syntactic circumstances. Compliance with the vernacular syntactic system is the reason for the structural transformation of the genuine Latin AcI construction where the AcI counts as a separate constituent and can therefore, as a whole, function as a direct object. Because of the internally motivated language change, in pre-standard Croatian texts this construction was almost exclusively governed by the verb *činiti* 'make' and by perception verbs. The reason for its maintenance here, and a motivation for its loss elsewhere, is that the subject of the AcI clause can also be interpreted as the object of a perception verb or causative *činiti*, but not for other types of verb (except for the calques in the strict sense as in the example (37)).

Following this conclusion, we refer to Wiemer and Hansen (2012: 128–129), who discussed the same linguistic phenomenon in terms of contact-induced grammaticalization. They consider the rise of the AcI construction in Czech, in 16th to 19th century Polish and in some Croatian dialects "as an instance of grammaticalization, since it presents a condensation of two clauses which encompasses the merger of the subject position of the subordinate clause with the direct object position of the superordinate clause." Finally, as an instance of the AcI construction in Czech, the authors give the following example: *vidim Petra tančit*, which corresponds to similar AcI occurrences in 16th to 19th century Croatian covered in this paper.

The rise of the AcI construction as a syntactic pattern adopted from Latin into the Croatian pre-standard written language appears to be the result of an externally motivated language change induced by sociolinguistic circumstances. However, its development, which includes the restructuring of the genuine Latin AcI construction and its restricted usage, is influenced by internal language factors. The assumption that both language-external and language-internal factors are often simultaneously involved in the rise and development of a new syntactic expression corresponds with the concluding remarks of recent studies on similar research subjects in closely related languages.[15]

References

Bamman, David, Marco Passarotti & Gregory Crane. 2008. A case study in treebank collaboration and comparison: *Accusativus cum infinitivo* and subordination in Latin. *The Prague Bulletin of Mathematical Linguistics* 90. 109–122.

Bartoněk, Antonín. 2010. *A comparative Graeco-Latin sentence syntax within the European context*. München: Lincom Europa.

Bauer, Jaroslav. 1972. *Vliv řectiny a latiny na vývoj syntaktické stavby slovanských jazyků*. [The influence of Greek and Latin on the development of syntactic constructions in Slavonic languages.]. In *Syntactica Slavica. Vybrané práce ze slovanské skladby*, 47–67. Brno: Universiteta J. E. Purkyně.

Birzer, Sandra. 2018. On the diachronic complementation of *widzieć* 'see'. *Wiener Slawistischer Almanach* 81. 7–31.

Biville, Frédérique. 1995. Énoncés factitifs en latin: syntaxe et sémantique. In Dominique Longrée (ed.), *De usu. Études de syntaxe latine offertes en hommage à Marius Lavency*, 31–44. Louvain-La-Neuve: Peeters.

Bloemendal, Jan (ed.). 2015. *Bilingual Europe. Latin and vernacular cultures, examples of bilingualism and multilingualism c. 1300–1800*. Leiden & Boston: Brill.

Butterfield, David. 2011. Neo-Latin. In James Clackson (ed.), *A Companion to the Latin language*, 303–318. Chichester: Wiley-Blackwell.

Calboli, Gualtiero. 1983. The Development of Latin (Cases and Infinitive). In Harm Pinkster (ed.), *Latin linguistics and linguistic theory. Proceedings of the 1st International Colloquium on Latin Linguistics*, 41–58. Amsterdam & Philadephia: John Benjamins.

Chamberlain, Jeffrey T. 1986. *Latin antecedents of French causative* faire. New York: Peter Lang.

Cuzzolin, Pierluigi. 1991. On sentential complementation after *verba affectuum*. In József Herman (ed.), *Linguistic studies on Latin: Selected papers from the 6th International Colloquium on Latin Linguistics (Budapest, 23–27 March 1991)*, 201–210. Amsterdam & Philadelphia: John Benjamins.

Cuzzolin, Pierluigi. 2013. The Latin construction *dicere quod* revisited. *Graeco-Latina Brunensia* 18(1). 23–38.

Gebauer, Jan. 2007 [1929]. *Historická mluvnice jazyka českého. Díl 4. Skladba* [Historical grammar of the Czech language. Part 4. Syntax]. Praha: Academia.

Gortan, Veljko & Vladimir Vratović. 1971. The basic characteristics of Croatian Latinity. *Humanistica Lovaniensia: Journal of Neo-Latin Studies* 20. 37–68.

---

[15] Cf. studies on the AcI construction in Old Church Slavonic (cf. Kurešević 2018) and on perception verb complements in Serbian (cf. Grković-Major 2018).

Grković-Major, Jasmina. 2018. The development of perception verb complements in the Serbian language. In Björn Hansen, Jasmina Grković-Major & Barbara Sonnenhauser (eds.), *Diachronic Slavonic syntax: the interplay between internal development, language contact and metalinguistic factors*, 339–360. Berlin & Boston: Mouton de Gruyter.
Heine, Bernd & Tania Kuteva. 2005. *Language contact and grammatical change*. Cambridge: University Press.
Herman, Jozsef. 1963. *La formation du système Roman des conjonctions de subordination*. Berlin: Akademie Verlag.
Herman, Jozsef. 1989. Accusativus cum infinitivo et subordonnée à *quod, quia* en latin tardif – nouvelles remarques sur un vieux problème. In Gualtiero Calboli (ed.), *Subordination and other topics in Latin. Proceedings of the Third Colloquium on Latin Linguistics*, 133–152. Amsterdam & Philadephia: John Benjamins.
Hudeček, Lana. 2001. Glagoli govorenja i mišljenja u hrvatskome čakavskom književnom jeziku do 17. stoljeća – strani sintaktički utjecaji. [Verbs of speech and thought in the Croatian literary language until the end of the 16th century – foreign syntactic influences]. *Rasprave: Časopis Instituta za hrvatski jezik i jezikoslovlje* 27(1). 95–112.
Kapetanović, Amir. 2017. Languages and their registers in medieval Croatian culture. *Studia Ceranea* 7. 79–98.
Kropaczek, Stefan. 1928. Zwrot „Accusativus cum infinitivo" w języku polskim. [The phrase 'Accusativus cum infinitivo' in Polish]. *Prace Filologiczne* 13. 424–496.
Kühner, Raphael & Carl Stegmann. 1912 [1877]. *Ausführliche Grammatik der lateinischen Sprache. Zweiter Band: Satzlehre*. Hannover: Hahnsche Buchhandlung.
Kurešević, Marina. 2018. The status and origin of the *accusativus cum infinitivo* construction in Old Church Slavonic. In Björn Hansen, Jasmina Grković-Major & Barbara Sonnenhauser (eds.), *Diachronic Slavonic syntax: The interplay between internal development, language contact and metalinguistic factors*, 261–283. Berlin & Boston: De Gruyter Mouton.
Lehmann, Christian. 2016. Latin causativization in typological perspective. In Paolo Poccetti (ed.), *Latinitatis rationes: descriptive and historical accounts for the Latin language*, 917–941. Berlin & Boston: De Gruyter Mouton.
Mihaljević, Milan. 2009. *Hrvatski crkvenoslavenski jezik* [Croatian Church Slavonic]. *Povijest hrvatskoga jezika. 1. knjiga: srednji vijek*. 290–349. Zagreb: Hrvatska Sveucilisna Naklada.
Mihaljević, Milan. 2011. Dopune percepcijskih glagola u hrvatskome crkvenoslavenskom jeziku [Perception verbs complements in Croatian Church Slavonic]. *Suvremena linguvistika*. 37(72). 187–200.
Nigel, Vincent. 2016. Causatives in Latin and Romance. In James N. Adams & Nigel Vincent (eds.), *Early and late Latin. Continuity or change?*, 294–312. Cambridge: Cambridge University Press.
Panevová, Jarmila 2008. České konstrukce tzv. slovanského akuzativu s infinitivem. [So-called Slavonic *accusativus cum infinitivo* constructions in Czech.] *Slovo a Slovesnost* 69. 163–175.
Pinkster, Harm. 1990. *Latin syntax and semantics*. Translated by Hotze Mulder. London & New York: Routledge.
Pisarkowa, Krystyna. 1984. *Historia składni języka polskiego*. [Historical syntax of the Polish language]. Wrocław: Ossolineum.
Plater, William Edward & Henry Julian White. 1926. *A Grammar of the Vulgate*. Oxford: Clarendon Press.
Pranjković, Ivo. 2001. Hrvatski i klasični jezici. [Croatian and Classical languages]. *Zbornik Zagrebačke slavističke škole: Trideset godina rada (1972–2001)*. 156–163.

Schendl, Herbert. 2012. Middle English: Language contact. In Alexander Bergs & Laurel L. Brinton (eds.), *English historical linguistics. An international handbook. Vol 1*, 505–519. Berlin & Boston: De Gruyter Mouton.

Sørensen, Knud. 1957. Latin influence on English Syntax. *Travaux du cercle linguistique de Copenhague* 11. 131–155.

Tekavčić, Pavao. 1970. *Uvod u vulgarni latinitet*. [An introduction to Vulgar Latin]. University of Zagreb.

Večerka, Radoslav. 1997. The influence of Greek on Old Church Slavonic. *Byzantinoslavica* 58(2). 363–386.

Večerka, Radoslav. 1989. *Altkirchenslavische (Altbugarische) Syntax I. Die lineare Satzorganization*. Freiburg: Weiher.

Vinja, Vojimir. 1951. *'Calque linguistique' u hrvatskom jeziku Marka Marulića* ['Calque linguistique' in the Croatian language of Marko Marulić]. *Zbornik radova Filozofskoga fakulteta u Zagrebu*. 547–565.

Vrtič, Ivana. 2009. *Sintaksa Kašićeva prijevoda Svetoga pisma* [Syntax in Kašić's translation of the Holy Scripture]. Zagreb: University of Zagreb dissertation.

Weinreich, Uriel. 1979. *Languages in contact: findings and problems*. Preface by André Martinet. The Hague, Paris & New York: De Gruyter Mouton.

Wiemer, Björn & Björn Hansen. 2012. Assessing the range of contact-induced grammaticalization in Slavonic. In Björn Wiemer, Bernhard Wälchli & Björn Hansen (eds.), *Grammatical replication and borrowability in language contact*, 67–158. Berlin & Boston: De Gruyter Mouton.

Wiemer, Björn & Bernhard Wälchli. 2012. Contact-induced grammatical change: Diverse phenomena, diverse perspectives. In Björn Wiemer, Bernhard Wälchli & Björn Hansen (eds.), *Grammatical replication and borrowability in language contact*, 3–64. Berlin & Boston: De Gruyter Mouton.

Wiemer, Björn, Bernhard Wälchli & Björn Hansen (eds.). 2012. *Grammatical replication and borrowability in language contact*. Berlin & Boston: De Gruyter Mouton.

Winkler, Alexander & Florian Schaffenrath (eds.). 2019. *Neo-Latin and the vernaculars: bilingual interactions in the Early Modern Period*. Leiden & Boston: Brill.

Winford, Donald. 2003. *An Introduction to contact linguistics*. Malden: Blackwell Publishing.

Wirth-Poelchau, Lore. 1977. *AcI und quod-Satz im lateinischen Sprachgebrauch mittelalterlicher und humanistischer Autoren*. Erlangen-Nürnber: Friedrich-Alexander University dissertation.

Zima, Luka. 1887. *Njekoje, većinom sintaktičke razlike između čakavštine, kajkavštine i štokavštine*. [Some, mostly syntactic differences between Čakavian, Kajkavian and Štokavian]. Zagreb: L Hartman.

Barbara Sonnenhauser and Marisa Eberle
Relative coordination. *Kateri-/koteri*-relatives in 18th century Slovene and Kajkavian

Abstract: As compared to their contemporary varieties, 18th century Slovene and Kajkavian literary sources exhibit a larger range of relative clause constructions introduced by the interrogative-based pronouns *kateri/koteri* 'which'. Systematising this variation promises to add to the debate on the typology of relativisation strategies and relative clause structures, and to allow for a closer understanding of the emergence of the relativising function for *kateri/koteri* (and cognates).

Focusing in particular on the structures that are marginal or even obsolete in the contemporary varieties, the argument put forth in this paper is that in times of a developing literacy with specific needs in terms of content and elaboration, Latin might have served as a model for *kateri-/koteri*-constructions in 18th century Slovene and Kajkavian. More specifically, authors used language inherent means, i.e., interrogative pronouns of the type 'which of two', in new functions to adapt a structure available in Latin such as to meet particular genre-specific purposes. The fact that some of these structures went out of use with the diminishing role of the relevant genres illustrates how literary trends may coin functional and/or structural patterns that might appear marginal at first sight but are actually highly revealing for gaining insight into the processes that drive language contact and change.

Keywords: relative clause, Slovene, Kajkavian, language contact, Latin

1 Introduction

Remarkably, the origin of the relativising function for the originally interrogative pronoun of the type 'which of two' in North Slavonic, such as Russian *kotoryj*, Polish *który* and Czech *který*, is still unclear.[1] Even though contact with West Slavonic, in

---

[1] The research for this paper has been carried out through the project *Language description as filter and prism: the 'individuality' of Slovene*, funded by the Swiss National Science Foundation SNSF (grant number 10001B_162970/1). We would like to thank the two anonymous reviewers for their cricital remarks and valuable suggestions.

Barbara Sonnenhauser, Slavisches Seminar, Universität Zürich,
e-mail: barbara.sonnenhauser@uzh.ch
Marisa Eberle, Slavisches Seminar, Universität Zürich, e-mail: marisa.eberle@uzh.ch

https://doi.org/10.1515/9783110651331-006

particular with Polish, during the 17th century, seems as plausible trigger for Russian (and East Slavonic in general), the origin of the relativising function for these types of pronouns in West Slavonic remains unsettled (see Meyer 2017: 103, 110–111). Equally puzzling is the absence of this pronoun in a relativising function in the contemporary South Slavonic languages, with the exception of Slovene (cf. Gołąb and Friedman 1972 for an overview). The available data suggest the emergence of *kateri* as a relative pronoun in Slovene in the 16th century (e.g. Sonnenhauser 2013; 2018).[2] What has only been mentioned in passing so far is the availability of this pronoun in relativising function in yet another South Slavonic variety, i.e. Kajkavian, for which Gallis (1956: 111) notes the appearance of *koteri* in the literature of 1500–1800.

The present paper focuses on the usage of *kateri/koteri* as a relative pronoun in Slovene and Kajkavian literary sources of the 18th century. Documents dating to this time exhibit a variety of *kateri*-/*koteri*-structures that has been reduced again in more recent sources. Systematising the variation of *kateri*-/*koteri*-RC[3] constructions in 18th century Slovene and Kajkavian, the paper pursues a twofold aim: First, to place these constructions into the larger picture of RCs and mechanisms of clause linkage and thereby, second, to try to assess the factors driving the functional development of *kateri*-/*koteri*-structures. It will be argued that, given the context of gradually emerging literary norms against the backdrop of already established traditions of prestigious model languages and literatures, in particular Latin and German, these structures can be taken as evidence for the role of register in the consolidation of the relativisation function of *kateri* (and cognates). With a vernacular literary tradition beginning to emerge (Slovene) and striving to the peak of elaboration (Kajkavian), driven by well-educated people socialised in intellectual and clerical circles and familiar with the major cultural languages of that time, the processes observed for these two South Slavonic varieties might also provide one piece of evidence towards answering the more general question on the origin of the relativising function for this type of pronoun.

The paper is structured as follows: Section 2 provides an overview of the variety and development of *kateri*-RCs in Slovene, adducing also evidence from Kajkavian *koteri*-RCs. A structural and functional analysis of the RC types with *kateri/koteri* found in 18th century texts is provided in Section 3, with specific focus on structures with an overtly expressed head accompanying *kateri/koteri*. Section 4 discusses the role Latin might have played in the emergence (and loss) of these structures; Section 5 offers a short conclusion.

---

2 Mendoza (2018) makes a similar observation for Old Polish (late 14th–early 16th c.), where *który* appears later than the 'anaphoric' type *jenż(e)* and becomes the more frequent type towards the 16th c.
3 Abbreviations used: RC = relative clause, MC = main clause, Kjk = Kajkavian, Sln = Slovene.

2 Relativisation with *kateri* / *koteri*

Contemporary standard Slovene displays three main means of introducing RCs: the uninflected particle *ki*, (1), which is *accompanied* by a resumptive pronoun for non-subject relativisation (see *ki jih*), the adjectival pronoun *kateri*, (2), which is – unlike *ki* – also possible for the relativisation of prepositional objects (see *v kateri*), and the relative pronoun *kdor*, (3), for the introduction of free RCs.

(1) *kupci, ki tega [...] niso vedeli [...] kupovali izdelke, ki jih ni bilo* (Sln)

'the purchasers *who* did not know this bought products$_i$ *that* [they$_i$] did not exist' (Gigafida: *Delo Revije* 2003)

(2) *velikost datoteke, v kateri se slika nahaja* (Sln)

'the volume of the file *in which* the picture is stored' (Gigafida: neznani avtor, 2000)

(3) *Kdor jé meso, daje naročilo za ubijanje* (Sln)

'*Who* eats meat, gives the order to kill.' (Gigafida: *Dnevnik* 2004)

These three markers have specific restrictions and preferences in terms of the type of RC construction and the linearisation of RC and MC/external head, summarised in Table 1: for restrictive and appositive RCs, *ki* and *kateri* are both possible if they follow their external head. Differently from *ki*, *kateri* is also possible in pre-head position, i.e. in a correlative RC structure in which the main clause displays a correlative anaphoric element (rarely also without such anaphoric element). The second option for correlative RCs is *kdor*, which is otherwise used for free RCs, both in pre- and postponed position.

As this overview shows, *kateri* is the most versatile relativising element, overlapping in specific functions and structures with the other two options. In older stages of Slovene, it was possible in even more types of RC constructions. Until the 20th century, grammars of Slovene still regard *kateri* as an option for free RCs, as in (4), and RCs with an overtly expressed head accompanying the pronoun, see (5).

(4) *Kateri je volan iti peš, naj se oglasi.* (Sln)

Table 1: Main relativisation strategies in contemporary Slovene.

Element	RC marker	RC type	RC position
ki	uninflected particle	restrictive, appositive	post
kateri	adjectival pronoun	restrictive, appositive	post
		correlative (free)	pre
kdor	substantival pronoun	correlative, free	post / pre

(5) Kateri konj *sam teče, tega ni treba tirati*. (Sln)

'Which horse runs by itself, that one does not need to be rushed.'
(Breznik 1916: 212)

While *kateri* with free RCs still seems possible, albeit rare, in contemporary Slovene, constructions with overt internal heads as in (6) are marked as 'obsolete' in SSKJ 2016. Instead of establishing the link to the previous clause by means of *kateri* and the noun *mojster* 'master', which is co-referential to the previously introduced referent of *Michelangelo*, a paratactic construction is recommended. For (6), SSKJ suggests coordination with *in* 'and', and to establish the link to the previous clause by a demonstrative pronoun (*ta*), which accompanies a noun (*mojster*) to specify the referent.

(6) *ta stil vlada do Michelangela,* kateri mojster *pomeni začetek nove dobe* [= (*in*) *ta mojste*r] (Sln)

'This style prevailed until Michelangelo, *which master* meant the beginning of a new era [= (and) this master].'
(SSKJ)

Structures with *kateri* that are no longer possible in contemporary Slovene can also be found in earlier literary sources: (7) shows a free RC comparable to (4), (8) an RC with an overtly realised head, similar to (5).

(7) *Katire* sam na sebe gleda, [. . .] *je pokojn* (Sln)

'*Who(ever)* looks after himself only, is peaceful'
(IMP: *Marianske Kempensar*, Sailer, Sebastian, Pohlin, Marko; 1769)

(8) *Popolnema* pokorshena *pod eno duhovno Gosposko*, katira pokorshena [. . .]. (Sln)

'Complete *obedience* to one spiritual realm, *which obedience* . . .'
(IMP: *Mali katekizem*, Petrus Canisius et al.; 1768)

A further structure featuring *kateri* is illustrated in (9). As in (8), *kateri* accompanies a nominal (*besed*); however, the clause headed by *kateri* seems to be more autonomous than that in (8), since there is no identical co-referential NP in the previous clause. The *kateri*-structure resembles an interrogative clause, but at the same time establishes an (indirect) anaphoric link to the preceding one. In this kind of structures, *kateri* displays a twofold potential as an interrogative and relative pronoun.[4]

(9) *Poſluſheimo, kai nam S. Joannes cap. I. pokashe, inu povei: Ecce Agnus Dei,* [...]. *S'katirih beſed vidimo, de* [...] (Sln)

'Let us listen, what S. John, chapt. I shows and says: Ecce Agnus Dei [...]. From *which words* we see that'
(IMP: *Kristusovemu trpljenju posvečen post*, Gabriel Hevenesi, Gašpar Rupnik; 1773)

This structural and functional variance of *kateri* in the 18th century is remarkable not only because of the comparatively late appearance of this pronoun in a relativising function, but also because a considerable amount of variation has been reduced in contemporary standard Slovene by functional specialization, yielding the picture shown in Table 1.

The fact that *kateri* with overt RC-internal heads is unavailable in contemporary Slovene, and equally unattested in most contemporary varieties of Slavonic,[5] may be taken to suggest that the extension of *kateri* into these contexts and, potentially, into assuming a relativisation function at all, may have been

---

[4] This supports the assumption of such structures having constituted a bridging context between interrogative and relativising function. For older stages of Slavonic see Večerka (1983: 16; 2002: 179) sketches the starting point of this process for adjectival interrogatives/indefinites as in (ia)–(ib). As to the postposition of the *kotoryj-/kyj*-structure, (ic), he proposes an analogy to *iže*. The latter is possible only in postponed position, which can be accounted for by the anaphoric component figuring in the pronominal stem. Presuming that Slovene *ki* relates to *iže* (for a discussion see Sonnenhauser 2013 and references therein) would account for why *ki* is not possible for preponed RCs.

(i) a. **Kotoryi/Kyi mǫžъ pridetъ? / *Kotoryi/Kyi mǫžъ pridetъ. Viditъ.*
        'Which man comes? / Which(ever) man comes. He sees.'
    b. **Kotoryi/Kyi mǫžъ pridetъ, viditъ.*
        'Which man comes, sees.'
    c. **Mǫžъ, kotoryi/kyi pridetъ, viditъ*
        'The man, which comes, sees'

[5] Mendoza (2010) describes such structures for contemporary Polish; however, the relative pronoun *który* needs to be accompanied by the relativising element *to*. The early 20th century

accelerated by meta-linguistic influences such as prestigious model texts and the acquaintance of the authors with languages and literatures they classified as highly prestigious (see Section 4). This might have triggered a striving for imitation, in particular during the time of a consolidating literary norm concerning both language related and text/genre related aspects. The diminishing significance of these factors in the further development of Slovene literary language towards the end of the 19th century might provide an explanation for why these structures gradually vanished from written sources. This development would then be an instance of 'register-dependency', which Meyer (2017) observes for the development of relativising elements and complementisers in North Slavonic.

This assumption of the role of non-linguistic factors and, in addition, of individual authors' personal preferences concerning the usage of relativisation markers and specific kinds of RC structures is supported by observations on Kajkavian. In the 18th century Kajkavian literary language, *koji* and *koteri* are attested as relative pronouns, with *koji* appearing also in contracted forms, especially in the nominative masculine singular *ki*[6] (this contraction is sometimes marked as *kî*). Based on a sample of 570 randomly selected RCs from six texts by five authors, Eberle (2017: 103) shows that none of the typically cited factors such the animacy of the head noun, the position on the accessibility hierarchy or the type of RC (restrictive, appositive, free) seem to play a role in the choice of one or the other relativising element. Instead of strictly linguistic factors playing a role in choosing a particular relativising device, authors seem to use them at their own discretion. All authors employ the various types of RC structures discussed above and for all types, *koteri* may be used.

That is, in 18th century Kajkavian, *koteri* displays the same functional range as Slovene *kateri*; in addition to restrictive and appositive RCs, it is used for free RCs, (10), and RCs displaying overt internal heads. In (11), this overt head resumes an antecedent in the previous clause (*oblok* 'pedestal'), while in (12), it summarises a previous utterance (*Ferdinand ne ostavim te* 'Ferdinand I won't leave you') as *obečanje* 'promise'.

Štokavijan standard displays (rare) examples of overt internal heads with *koji*-RCs (Kordić 1995: 108–112).
6 Unlike Slovenian, Kajkavian *ki* is not accompanied by a resumptive pronoun. Most probably, this relates to its inflected status, by which it differs from Slovene *ki* as an uninflected particle. Whether Slovene *ki* originates from contracted *ki*, *ka*, *ko* is hard to tell by the available data (see Sonnenhauser 2013 and references cited therein for an overview of assumptions concerning the origin of Slovene *ki*).

(10) Ti o Bog moi nai bolye znas [. . .] kak lehko, koteri *terha nyegvoga poleg dufnofzti kerfchanfzke nepodnaffa Duffu fzvoju pogubiti more.* (Kjk)

'You, oh my God, know best how easily, *he who* doesn't fulfill his burden besides his Christian duty, can lose his soul.' (Berke 1775: 75–76)

(11) ov kip [. . .] *bil je* [. . .] *pofztavlen vu zid fztare Czirkve* na jeden oblok, koteri oblok *potlam y z-kipom fzkupa bil je za zidan* [. . .]. (Kjk)

'this statue was placed at the wall of an old church on a *pedestal, which pedestal* was later placed together with the statue at the wall' (Berke 1775: 4)

(12) Zveličitela s ovemi, kak se poveda, rečmi, Ferdinand ne ostavim te, *bi bil razveseljen*; kotero obečanje *takaj spunilo se je.* (Kjk)

'The saviour was encouraged with these words, as is told, *Ferdinand, I won't leave you; which promise* was fulfilled.' (Dijanić 1797: 51)

Towards identifying the factors that might have played a role in the diverse picture of RC strategies obtaining in the 18th century, the functional range of *kateri-/koteri*-structures, in particular those accompanied by an overt nominal head within the RC, and their distributional patterns will be elaborated on in Section 3.

3 Overt heads inside RCs: '*kateri /koteri* N'

In the following, the focus will be on those constructions that have become obsolete in more recent times, in particular in the course of standardisation (with Croatian finally being based on Štokavian, Kajkavian did not develop into a standard language[7]).[8] These structures share the presence of an overt lexical head (Mendoza 2010, 2018 speaks of 'internal nucleus') accompanying *kateri/koteri*, such that the RCs do not contain a gap.

---

7 A Kajkavian literary language developed from the 16th century onwards. However, it did not reach the status of an official standard language, for which the Štokavian dialect has been chosen as a basis. For more details on Kajkavian see Lončarić (2002), for a brief overview of the standardisation processes of Croatian see Lehfeldt (2014: 1455–1463).
8 In general, it needs to be noted that the structures with internal heads are not very frequent.

3.1 Structures

Since the structures under consideration here are characterised by an overt internal lexical head inside the RC, only markers of the adjectival type, i.e. those able to serve as determiners, may be used, such as the Slovene *kateri* or Kajkavian *koteri* and *koji*.[9] Pronominal elements such as *kdo(r)* and uninflected particles such as *ki* are not available for this kind of structure.

RCs with overt lexical heads appear in four basic types, schematically illustrated in (13), with X and Y representing overt nominal heads within the main clause (X) and the RC (Y).[10] The RCs may be pre- or postponed to their external heads, whereby this external head may be explicitly mentioned or left implicit. In the latter case, the RC relates to a structure larger than an NP referent, such as the proposition expressed by the clause or by the stretch of discourse this clause appears in.

(13) a. [...X_i...] [kateri Y_i ...]
 b. [...Ø...]$_i$ [kateri Y_i ...]
 c. [kateri Y_i...] [...X_i...]
 d. [kateri Y_i...]$_i$ [...Ø...]

Examples for type (13a) are given in (14) for Slovene and (15) for Kajkavian. In both cases, *kateri/koteri* accompanies a nominal with which it agrees in number and gender; this full NP agrees with the external head in both features. The nominal accompanied by *kateri/koteri* is the head of the RC it appears in. It is co-referential – in these examples even identical – with the external head (*kraj* and *oblok*, respectively).

(14) *in* [bo] *jih pahnil v' kraj$_i$ vezhne ſhtrafenge, kteri kraj$_i$ pekel imenujemo* (Sln)

'and he will throw them into a *place* of eternal punishment, *which place* we call hell'
(IMP: *Štiri poslednje reči*, Cigler, Janez; 1831)

(15) *ov kip* [...] *bil je* [...] *poſztavlen vu zid ſztare Czirkve na jeden oblok$_i$, koteri oblok$_i$ potlam y z-kipom ſzkupa bil je za zidan* [...]. (Kjk)

'this statue was placed at the wall of an old church on a *pedestal, which pedestal* was later placed together with the statue at the wall' (Berke 1775: 4)

---

9 Kajkavian displays a preference for *koji* in the structures under scrutiny here (Eberle 2017: 101).
10 The systematisation is based on Mendoza and Sonnenhauser (2017).

The structure of type (13b) is illustrated in (16) for Slovene and (17) for Kajkavian. In the Slovene example, the *kateri*-structure is not co-referential with some specific antecendent, but summarisingly relates to the main content expressed by the previous clause. In the Kajkavian example, the *koteri*-structure resumes in a summarising and paraphrasing way the description of the *duh* 'ghost' introduced in the previous stretch of discourse.

(16) [*Ali nikar koker jes ozhem, ampak koker ti ozheſh.*]$_i$ *Per katirih beſedah$_i$ le on zelo ſvojo volo v' to volo ſvoiga Nebeſhkiga Ozheta zhes dau.* (Sln)

'but not as I want, but as you want. *By which words he gave his will into the will of his Father in heaven.*'
(IMP: *Kristusovemu trpljenju posvečen post Hevenesi*, Rupnik, Gašpar; 1773)

(17) [. . .] *vu onom iſztom hipu pokazalmuſzeie* [*ieden peklenzki Duh, vu kruto ztrasne, u odurne ſzpodobe, koiega ov neſzrechniak piani zagledavſſi, preztraſſilzeie, y od velikoga ztraha napol pretresnil*]$_i$, *kotero ztraffilo peklenzko$_i$ opitalie pianecz, gdoie, kaije, odkudie, y kai onde ische?* (Kjk)

'in that very same moment a ghost from hell appeared to him, in cruel horrible, in disgusting guise, which this drunken unlucky fellow looked at, got frightened and trembled with great fear, *which hellish scarecrow the drunken fellow asked, who it was, what it was, and what it was looking for here?*' (Zagrebec 1727: 188)

With this type, the clause introduced by *kateri/koteri* may orthographically be separated by a full stop from the previous clause, as in (16). The same holds for (18). Here, *kateri Teſztament* anaphorically resumes the co-referent introduced by *Teſtamentuma Szoldachkoga*. It does so in a slightly Slavicised form (*Teſztament* instead of *Teſztamentum*), which is then additionally paraphrased by *iliti zadnye volye moje ochituvanye* 'or the proclamation of my last will'. Orthography thereby highlights the resemblance of those structures to independent clauses.

(18) [*Z*]*adnye vole moje ochituvanye, koje pod nachin navadnoga, y* [*od vſzeh ſztranih zverſſenoga Teſtamentuma Szoldachkoga*]$_i$ *imati hochu. Koteri Teſztament$_i$, iliti zadnye volye moje ochituvanye,* [. . .] *preporucham.* (Kjk)

'The proclamation of my last will, which I want to have in the mode of the testament of an ordinary soldier, carried out by all parties. *Which testament, or proclamation of my last will, I recommend.*'
(Berke 1775: 22)

For Kajkavian, Eberle (2017) observes that *koteri*-structures of type (13b) are often quite long, which can be taken as evidence that the RC internal head serves the purpose of facilitating the intelligibility of the overall construction. This fits the paraphrasing function identified above and supports the assumption that these structures differ from prototypical RCs as a means of modifying an NP by syntactically expanding it.

Instances of type (13c) are not very frequent; examples from Slovene are given in (19) and (20); see also (5) above.

(19) S' katiro miro$_i$ *boste vi mireli*, s' taisto$_i$ *se vam bode naſaj mirelu*. (Sln)

'*With which measure* you will measure, *with that one* you will be measured.
(IMP: *Mali katekizem*, Canisius, Petrus, Parhamer, Ignaz, Pohlin, Marko; 1768)

(20) Kateri$_i$ *zhes Simo* Zhebele$_i$ *nimajo perstaulene, perstavijo* taiste$_i$ *po skopnenim* (Sln)

'*Which bees* do not have supplement after winter, add *them* in the period of thaw'
(IMP: *Pogovor o čebeljih rojih*; 1776)

Displaying an anaphoric demonstrative in the main clause, these structures are correlative and resemble the 'archaic type' of RCs described by Zaliznjak and Padučeva (1997[1979]).[11] The availability of these inherited structures might have played a role as a catalyst in the emergence of structures of type (13a) and (13b). However, this question requires further empirical analyses.

Type (13d) is exemplified by (4) above. Very much alike free RCs, this RC structure constitutes an argument of the MC. It is hard to find in our data and will not be discussed in this paper.

3.2 Relative coordination

The structures of type (13a)–(13c) presented in Section 3.1 share one feature: the two clauses involved are rather loosely connected. The relation established by '*kateri/koteri* N' in these types of structures is coordinative, established by ana-

---

[11] See the Russian structure in (ii), which appears in Old Russian and is still attested in present-day non-standard and dialectal Russian (Zaliznjak and Padučeva 1997[1979]: 75):

(ii) *Kotoryj osel ubežal, togo my ljubili.*
    'Which donkey ran away, that one we loved.'

phoric or cataphoric reference.¹² In this regard they differ crucially from prototypical RCs, which have a modifying function. With the syntactic relation being one of coordination, speaking of 'matrix clause' and 'relative clause' does not seem very appropriate. Henceforth, both clauses will thus be referred to as '*kateri-/koteri*-structure' (i.e. the clause introduced by *kateri/koteri*) and 'structure of reference' (i.e. the structure containing the element the *kateri-/koteri*-structure relates to) respectively; the notion 'co-referent' will be used instead of 'matrix clause head / external head'.¹³

The structures in question are coordinative, but differ with respect to the level of coordination: coordination may take place at the level of the clause or of the discourse. For clause level coordination, illustrated in (21), the *kateri*-structure (here: *v' katirimu savupeinu*) may precede or follow the structure of reference; the structure of reference has to include an explicit nominal co-referent for the *kateri*-NP (here: *savupeine*).

(21) *Ozhe, v' nemu enu nar vezhi savupeine obudilu*, v' katirimu savupeinu *je on napreſtraſhenu* (Sln)
(IMP: *Kristusovemu trpljenju posvečen post* Hevenesi, Gabriel, Rupnik, Gašpar; 1773)

'Father, to whom most *trust* obtained, *in which trust* he is fearless'

The main function of clause level coordination can be described as ensuring reference tracking.

In cases of discourse level coordination, the *kateri*-structure does not establish a relation to a co-referent introduced by an NP, but to a situational referent

---

12 Modern Polish has a similar structure with the complex relative pronoun *który to*. With *który* being amended by the originally demonstrative element *to* (Mendoza 2010), the anaphoric relation is even more obvious. This also accounts for why, as Mendoza (2010) shows, this type of RCs cannot precede the external head.

13 The coordinative function for *kateri*-structures with internal heads can be observed also for Middle Russian 'pseudo-correlative constructions' (Mitrenina 2012). Here, the *kateri*-structure has to precede the structure of reference and both need to be connected by coordinative *a* or *i*, see (iii).

(iii) *A kotoraja gsdr' lošed poslanaja s nim* <...> *i ta lošed stala v Volodimere.*
 and which master horse sent with him <...> and that horse stayed in Vladimir
 'As for the horse that was sent with Stephan, that horse stayed in the city of Vladimir, master.'
 (Mitrenina 2012: 62; Gr 362)

These structures are different from the 'archaic type' by displaying an overt nominal head in the structure of reference.

described by the preceding clause or portion of discourse. In (22), this discourse consists in the enumeration of good deeds, which is referred to in a summarising way by *od katireh* 'from which'. This, again, establishes referential continuity.

(22) *Kolkajn sort je dobreh del? Tri. I. Molitva. II. Post. III. Wugejmedajanje. Od katireh se toku bére: dobra je molituv s' postam inu wugejme dajanjam.* (Sln)

'Of how many kinds are good deeds? Three: I. Prayer. II. Fast. III. Almsgiving. *From which* it reads as follows: good is a prayer with fasting and giving alms' (IMP: *Mali katekizem*, Petrus Canisius, Petrus, Ignza Parhamer, Marko Pohlin; 1768)

The plural form *katireh* in (22) indicates agreement with a preceding co-referent, which suggests it to be accompanied by an elliptical noun (such as, e.g., a very general *besed* 'words'[14]). Thereby, this structure differs from RCs with an indeclinable form of 'what', see (23), referring to the previous sentence without agreeing with a co-referent and without referentially continuing an antecedent.

(23) *Nepremičnine imajo pod hipotekami,* kar *pomeni, da* [. . .] (Sln)

'the real estate they have under mortgage, which means that [. . .]' (Gigafiada: Internet 2010)

In other cases, the lexical head accompanying the relative pronoun is explicitly spelled out, as in (24) and (25).

(24) *Poſluſheimo, kai nam S. Joannes cap. I.pokashe, inu povei: Ecce Agnus Dei,* [. . .]. S' katirih befed *vidimo, de* [. . .]. (Sln)

'Let us listen, what S. John, chapt. I shows and says: Ecce Agnus Dei [. . .]. *From which words* we see that [. . .]'
(IMP: *Kristusovemu trpljenju posvečen post*, Gabriel Hevenesi, Gašpar Rupnik; 1773)

---

14 Morphosyntactically, the 'three deeds' could also serve as this elliptical expression, as one reviewer suggested. The context, which reads like an explanation or paraphrase of the enumeration of deeds, seems to suggest the other option.

(25) *Nebojſe, sakaj gvishnu na tem ſvetu, ali na vnem bosh polonan, kakor te sag-vishata Modri rekozh: Beneſac juſto, & invenies retributionem magnam, & ſi non ab ipſo, certe à Domino.* Katero reſnizo *lahku morem poterdit s' exempelni.* (Sln)

'Don't be afraid [...]. *Which truth* I can confirm by means of examples.'
(IMP: *Sveti priročnik (vzorec)*, Janez Svetokriški; 1695)

Discourse relative coordination is possible only if the relation is anaphoric, i.e. only if the *kateri-/koteri*-structure follows the structure of reference. Differently from clausal relative coordination, the overt lexical head in the *kateri-/koteri*-structure does not need to be – and in fact cannot be – an identical copy of the antecedent, but, as a rule, constitutes a nominal expression providing a summarising keyword to introduce the subsequent paraphrase (see *besed* and *resnico* in (24) and (25)). This type of relative coordination serves one main function: it relates quotations, specific technical concepts, foreign terms, in particular from Latin, etc. to the main text, with '*kateri/koteri* N' introducing an explanatory paraphrase (see 18 above). To put it differently, '*kateri/koteri* N' relates some other's voice to that of the narrator and thereby establishes referential continuity of referents located at two levels of narration. In this sense, '*kateri/koteri* N' serves as indexical, intertextual marker.[15]

Both types of '*kateri/koteri* N'-structures, in particular those establishing discourse coordination, resemble structures known from Latin (especially from classical, less so from Early Latin, Pinkster 2012: 391) as 'relative connection'. These structures are characterised by relative expressions that serve as the connection for independent sentences (Pinkster 2012: 389) and the discourse continuation of a previously established referent (see also Bolkestein 1996; Pennell Ross 1996). This referent may be quite remote from the relative expression, as in (26). Here, the anaphoric link established by *quorum* referring back to *decuriones* 'members of the town council', while *oratione* in a summary way specifies the words by the town council thus serving as a lexical cue (Pennell Ross 1996: 517).

---

15 As to RCs with explicit internal heads in Polish, Mendoza (2010), too, proposes a discourse-based analysis in terms of thematic digression, with the internal head establishing co-reference to the external head.

(26) *Adventu Caesaris cognito, decuriones Auximi ad Attium Varum frequentes conveniunt; docent sui iudicii rem non esse; neque se neque reliquos municipes pati posse C. Caesarem imperatorem, bene de re publica meritum, tantis rebus gestis, oppido moenibusque prohiberi; proinde habeat rationem posteritatis et periculi sui.* quorum oratione *permotus Varus praesidum quod introduxerat ex oppido educit ac profugit.*

'Hearing of Caesar's arrival, the members of the town council of Auximum went in a body to see Attius Varus; they told him that [. . .]. Moved *by what they said*, Varus withdrew the garrison which he had put in, and fled.'
(Pennell Ross 1996: 517; Caes. Civ. 1.13.2)

In (27), *quo* refers to the sequence of events described in the previous discourse.

(27) *subito vi ventorum et aquae magnitudine pons est interruptus et reliqua multitudo equitum interclusa.* Quo cognito *a Petreio et Afranio* [. . .]

'the bridge was suddenly broken down by a storm of wind and a great rush of water, and a large force of cavalry that remained behind was cut off. *When* Petreius and Afranius *discovered* what had happened . . .'
(Pinkster 2012: 390; Caes. *Civ.* 1.40.3–4)

Since with relative connection, the relation between the two clauses involved is less hypotactic than paratactic, Pinkster (2012) speaks of autonomous – as opposed to adnominal – RCs; he illustrates the difference with (28) as adnominal vs. (29) as autonomous RC.

(28) *O Libane, uti miser est homo* qui amat.

'Oh Libanus! How miserable is a man *who's in love*.'
(Pinkster 2012: 379; Pl. As. 616)

(29) Qui homo *mature quaesivit pecuniam* / . . . *mature essurit.*

'The man that's [= *what man*] made money quickly . . . will quickly go hungry'
(Pinkster 2012: 380; Pl. Cur. 380–381)

Pinkster (2012) also regards (30) as instance of an autonomous RC, albeit one displaying a relative word instead of a relative phrase as in (29). A further difference to (29) consists in the absence of an internal head. However, in (30) the integration of the two clauses is tighter than in (29), i.e. the difference is not only one in terms of the relative expression and the missing internal head. The more important difference is that this structure constitutes an argument to the predicate in the main clause, i.e. is the subject of *adficitur*.

(30) *Qui amat... adficitur misera aerumna.*

'A man in love [= *Who loves*] ... is a sorry plight'
(Pinkster 2012: 380; Pl. Cur. 142)

Based on the structural and functional descriptions of '*kateri/koteri* N'-structures sketched in here, it is now possible to embedded them into the larger picture of RC types encountered in Slovene and Kajkavian.

3.3 Systematisation

The two types of '*kateri/koteri* N' coordination discussed in Section 3.2 differ from prototypical RCs in being referential instead of serving the modification of an external head NP. Restrictive RCs modify their external head by restricting its set of referents, appositive RCs modify the external head by providing additional information. By this additive modification they contribute to the overall reference of the head NP, but, differently from '*kateri/koteri* N'-structures, do not establish referential continuity. Autonomous RCs establish anaphoric co-reference by coordinating the external co-referent and their internal head.

As concerns the question of semantic reference, i.e. reference to the world, Grosu and Landman (1998) arrange the various types of relative constructions along a scale according to the relevance of the respective contributions of RC and external material. The scale ranges from 'only external material is relevant' (simplex phrase / XP) to 'no external material available' (simplex clause / CP), see (31). The relevance of external material decreases from appositives over restrictives towards free and correlative RCs[16] (Grosu and Landman 1998, 127). In other words, the structures towards the left of the scale are more autonomous than those towards the right.

(31) simplex XP – appositive – restrictive – free/correlative – simplex CP

---

[16] Grosu and Landman (1998) regard free and correlative RCs as 'maximalising' RCs. For the present purposes, this notion is not relevant.

Sonnenhauser (2019) maps RCs in contemporary Slovene onto that scale; adding the internally headed type yields the refinement as in (31'). Since autonomous RCs contribute to the reference on their own, they are positioned left of appositives.

(31') simplex   autonomous   appositive   restrictive   correlative   free   simplex CP
      XP   *kateri*   *ki, kateri*   *ki, kateri*   *kateri, kdor*   *kdor*

The various types of *kateri-/koteri*-structures are summarised in Table 2.

Table 2: Systematisation of *kateri-/koteri*-structures.

Head		*Kateri-/koteri-* structure	*Kateri-/koteri*-structure – structure of reference		
External	Internal	Position wrt external head / co-referent	Semantic reference	Textual relation	Syntactic relation
(i) Autonomous: clause					
+	+	pre-/post-head	RC, MC	ana-/cataphoric coreference	clausal coordination
(ii) Autonomous: discourse					
–	+	pre-head	RC, MC	anaphoric coreference	discourse coordination
(iii) Free					
(+)	–	pre-head	RC	N/A	argument
(iv) Restrictive					
+	–	post-head	MC	restrictive modification	NP extension
(v) Appositive					
+	–	post-head	RC, MC	additive modification	propositional extension

The question arises as to whether the availability of the relativsing function of *kateri* and its cognates as well as of the *kateri-/koteri*-structures in the 18th century Slovenian literary texts discussed here might be due to Latin influence. Evidence for this interpretation stems from the existence of autonomous RC-structures in Latin, in particular medieval Latin, and from the fact that Latin was among the languages of education and culture in the Habsburg Empire in general and in areas where Slovenian was spoken in particular (see Ahačič 2014 for a thorough description of the situation in the 16th century).

4 Latin as a role model?

There are various ways to interpret the fact that literary sources of the 18th century exhibit a richer variety of *kateri*-structures than contemporary Slovene does, in particular structures with overt lexical heads inside the RC. It could be interpreted as attesting to the then still ongoing functional extension of *kateri* from an originally interrogative pronoun to a pronoun assuming relativising functions (see the 'oscillating' nature of cases such as (9) above), or as a register and genre specific feature possibly resulting from an author's imitation of non-native patterns found in prestigious source texts (in particular Latin and German) by exploiting the maximum of this pronoun's functional potential. In fact, these processes might very well be interconnected. In the context of emerging literary languages, specific genres, in particular of the written register oriented at some model languages and their text traditions, may have fostered the usage of *kateri* in these particular functions, and, potentially, also the usage of *kateri* in a relativising function as such. The availability of a relativising function for interrogative pronouns of the type 'which (of two)' is not unique for the Slavonic languages; it is a more general phenomenon occurring in many languages of Europe (visible in, e.g., French *laquelle*, Italian *quale*, German *welche*, English *which*, Russian *kotoryj*, Albanian *i cili*, to mention but a view; see, e.g., Fiorentino 2007: 272). With the meaning 'which of two' presupposing a definite set of possible referents, these interrogatives may easily be interpreted as anaphorically or cataphorically referring to a co-referent established in a previous/subsequent clause or a previous stretch of discourse. This is facilitated also by their possibility of being used as attributive determiners, such that the co-reference relation may be specified by a nominal head accompanying the pronoun – even if there is no explicit single co-referent in the previous discourse. Based on Fleischer (2005: 176), who points out that the usage of such pronouns in relativising function originates in written and literary register, Meyer (2017: 111) interprets the spread of *który-/*který*-relatives in Polish and Czech as an "instance of register-dependency" (2017, 111; on the register dependency of the 'which'-series see also, e.g., Lehmann 1984: 392; Fiorentino 2007: 285).

Assuming a decisive role of register seems plausible for the Slovene and Kajkavian literary languages in the 18th century as well, in particular in the context of emerging literary norms within the linguistic context of the Habsburg Empire. In its Slavic parts, Latin and German were the main languages of higher education (*Kultursprachen* 'languages of culture', Haarmann 2003: 702; see Reindl 2008: 10–14 on Slovene–German bilingualism of the upper classes) and were used as meta-languages for grammatical descriptions and dictionaries until the 18th century.[17] Latin and German also served as main source languages for the translation of religious literature and as model languages for the intellectualisation of the vernacular. This socio-cultural and educational environment was shared by Kajkavian and Slovene authors in the 18th century. The fact that the extension of *kateri* and *koteri* as relativisation markers seems to have come into use not before the 16th century (see Section 1) and did not diffuse any further than to Kajkavian may give some clues as to how *kateri* and cognates in the other Slavonic languages developed this function: it presumably started within the German–Latin surroundings in the Habsburg lands and from there spread by transfer by translations from Polish into East Slavonic (via so-called 'interference-texts', see Meyer 2017: 107).

Nonetheless, whether the functional expansion of *kateri/koteri* towards a relativising function in general and the availability of the '*kateri/koteri* N'-structures in particular can be attributed to Latin influence is difficult to answer (for Polish *który*, Gallis 1956: 11 indeed assumes Latin influence). For one thing, the data basis – a restricted set of authors, texts and genres – is too small to allow for a thorough quantitative analysis providing insight into variation and change and into comparison with Latin (a further question would be: what kind of Latin). In addition, it is hard to clearly substantiate or rule out such influence by qualitative methods. Both approaches would necessitate a suitable way of differentiating between language contact and internal development – which is a problem far beyond the scope of the present paper. With the history of Europe being one of migrations of speakers and languages, it is hard to imagine any kind of linguistic development not to be contact-induced, and with Latin having played an important role throughout the history of ancient and medieval Central Europe, the question might better be asked the other way round, i.e.: how can we tell that specific structures were not influenced by Latin? Since contact influence on linguistic structures need not necessarily originate from face-to-face or text-to-text

---

17 For Slovene see, e.g., the grammars by Adam Bohorič (*Arcticae horulae succisivae*, 1584) or Hipolit Novomeški (*Grammatica Latino-Germanico-Slavonica*, 1715) translated into German in 1758 as *Grammatica oder Windisches Sprach-Buch* 'Grammar or Book of the Slovenian Language' (Toporišič and Reindl 2010: 912), and dictionaries such as *Dictionarium Latino-Carniolicum* 'Latin-Carniolan Dictionary' (1680–1710) by Matija Kastelec and Gregor Vorenc (Toporišič and Reindl 2010: 908). Junge (2020) provides an overview of the meta-languages used in Slovene grammar writing from the mid 16th to the mid 19th c. Concerning Kajkavian, see, e.g. the grammars by Ignacije Szentmártony (*Einleitung zur kroatischen Sprache*, 1783), Franjo Kornig (*Kroatische Sprachlehre oder Anweisung für Deutsche, die kroatische Sprache in kurzer Zeit gründlich zu erlernen, nebst beigefügten Gesprächen und verschiedenen Übungen*, 1795), Ignac Kristijanović (*Grammatik der kroatischen Mundart*, 1837). An overview of the Kajkavian tradition of grammar writing is provided in Štebih Golub (2018).

contact but might be very indirect, i.e. via adhering to particular literary fashions and trends, such questions are even harder to answer.

The observation that *kateri-/koteri*-RCs used in the coordinative structures discussed here have disappeared in more recent texts and that paratactic structures are preferred instead, i.e. structures that seem to be more typical of spoken registers, supports the assumption of register-based dependency.[18] Among the relevant genres, religious texts seem to be particularly prone to using discourse relative coordination, as a search in the corpus *Jezikovni viri starejše slovenščine* (IMP) for the second half of the 18th century has shown, whereas clausal relative coordination appears in texts for more practical purposes, such as in instructions on beekeeping.[19] This distribution fits the main functions of discourse vs. clausal relative coordination: the former are used to coordinate a paraphrase with a previous stretch of discourse as an antecedent, i.e. serve a mainly explanatory, instruction-related and didactic function, the latter resume a previously mentioned (or anticipate a subsequent) co-referent and hence enable reference tracking. Both kinds of structures thus can be said to facilitate written text comprehension.

Against this background, register-based dependency may indeed be the very place to look for (indirect) Latin influence,[20] in particular the usage of *kateri* and *koteri* in structures that are judged obsolete for the contemporary standard languages. It seems reasonable to assume that in the context of emerging literacy and the concomitant functional extension of Slovene (Kajkavian has not devel-

---

18 In the context of written registers, orthography needs to be considered as well. In particular for discourse-level relative coordination, punctuation adds to the particular oscillating status of *kateri-/koteri*-structures between being part of a biclausal unit or being independent main clauses. This yields specific effects that are not possible for oral language; such effects are still made use of in written language, as in the following recent example from German, where *die* 'that, which' introduces an RC-structure which is orthographically presented as main clause:

(iv) *Für die einen waren die Fundstücke am Strand eine Erinnerung an das Analogzeitalter, für andere ein Symbol für die Verschmutzung der Meere, und für alle war es eine kurios-rätselhafte Geschichte.* Die *sich nun weitgehend aufgeklärt hat*.

'For some it was [. . .], for others [. . .] and for all it was a mysterious story. *Which* has now found an explanation.'
(https://www.sueddeutsche.de/panorama, 29.03.2018)

19 The situation for Latin is similar: Bolkestein (1996: 588) shows genre preferences, Pinkster (2012: 381) identifies author-specific frequencies and thus speaks of "stylistic preferences" (2012: 391) in the usage of autonomous RCs.

20 See also Fiorentino (2007: 285) who regards relative pronouns of the 'which'-(**ille qualis*)-type "a Medieval (at least XII century) innovation which originated in a common written (literary) tradition, influenced by Latin language"; similarly, Lehmann (1984: 392).

oped into a standard language) towards a language serving diverse purposes, writers took the opportunity to exploit the functional potential of available structures under the influence of role models, such as Latin or German, to meet the specific needs of particular written genres.

5 Summing up: Relative clauses and kin

The variation of *kateri-/koteri*-RCs, notably the availability of structures with an overt internal head accompanying *kateri/koteri*, in 18th century Slovene and Kajkavian proves interesting in two respects: in a general perspective concerning the typology of RC structures and in a more specific perspective concerning the availability of *kateri* and cognates in relativising function in South Slavonic.

As to the former, '*kateri/koteri* N'-structures differ from canonical types of RCs in terms of being coordinative instead of modifying and establishing referential continuity. These features put into question the applicability of the notion of 'relative clause' for these structures, which in turn relates to the more general difficulty of linguistic categorisation, in particular when it comes to analysing non-standardised data (both in diachronic and diaphasic aspects). Among the most intricate issues is the problem of how to deal with 'oscillating' structures in the sense of Mendoza and Sonnenhauser (2017), i.e. structures that allow for a specific range of functions without being ambiguous between clearly identifiable options.

As to the latter, the emergence of a relativising function for *kateri/koteri* may have been facilitated by Latin influence in an indirect way. Latin played a crucial role in the sociocultural embedding of the emerging Slovene and Kajkavian literacy during the 18th century, with its specific needs in terms of content and language elaboration. Within these circumstances, authors may have used the linguistic means available in their varieties, employing them in new functions in order to adapt a structure that was available in Latin and that was considered to be necessary for particular register- and genre-specific purposes. In this way, the emergence of the relativising function for *kateri* and cognates can be seen as register-based, the usage of '*kateri/koteri* N'-structures as being supported by specific authors' preferences that at the same time fit the need of particular genres. In cases like this, individual preferences and general fashion trends may yield short-term functional and/or structural patterns that run danger of remaining unnoticed by diachronic research if it restricts the focus to the emergence and development of structures that persisted in the course of language history.

References

Ahačič, Kozma. 2014. *The history of linguistic thought and language use in 16th century Slovenia*. Frankfurt/Main: Institut d'études slaves et EUR'ORBEM.

Bolkestein, Machtelt. 1996. Is 'qui' 'et is'? On the so-called free relative connection in Latin. In Rosén, Hannah (ed.), *Aspects of Latin. Papers from the Seventh International Colloquium of Latin Linguistics. Jerusalem, April 1993*, 553–566. Innsbruck: Institut für Sprachwissenschaft.

Breznik, Anton. 1916. *Slovenska slovnica za srednje šole*. Celovec: Založila Družba sv. Mohorja.

Eberle, Marisa. 2017. Relativsätze im Kajkavischen. Die Distribution von *koji, koji* (kurz), *ki* und *koteri* in ausgewählten Texten des 18. Jahrhunderts. MA thesis. Universität Zürich.

Fiorentino, Giuliana. 2007. European relative clauses and the uniqueness of the relative pronoun type. *Italian Journal of Linguistics* 19(2). 263–291.

Fleischer, Jürg. 2005. Relativsätze in den Dialekten des Deutschen: Vergleich und Typologie. *Linguistik online* 24(3). 171–186.

Gallis, Arne. 1956. *The syntax of relative clauses in Serbo-Croatian. Viewed on a historical basis*. Oslo: Aschehoug.

Zbigniew, Gołąb & Victor A. Friedman. 1972. The relative clause in Slavic. In Paul Peranteau, Judith M. Levi & Gloria C. Phares (eds.), *The Chicago which hunt. Papers from the relative clause festival*, 30–46. Chicago: Chicago Linguistic Society.

Grosu, Alexander & Fred Landman. 1998. Strange relatives of the third kind. *Natural Language Semantics* 6. 125–170.

Haarmann, Harald. 2003. Slovenisch. In Thomas Roelcke (ed.), *Variationstypologie. Ein sprachtypologisches Handbuch der europäischen Sprachen in Geschichte und Gegenwart*, 684–703. Berlin & New York: Mouton de Gruyter.

Junge, Martin. 2020. Nicht nur Slovenisch, aber auch. Metasprachen und Beispielsprachen in den slovenischen Grammatiken. Patrizia Noel Aziz Hanna, Barbara Sonnenhauser & Caroline Trautmann (eds.), *Diskussionsforum Linguistik VII: Mehrsprachigkeit und Variation*. München: Open Access LMU, 41–46 (https://epub.ub.uni-muenchen.de/view/subjects/13282.html, accessed Sept. 15, 2020).

Lončarić, Mijo. 2002. Kajkawisch. In Okuka Miloš (ed.), *Lexikon der Sprachen des europäischen Ostens*, 257–264. Klagenfurt: Wieser.

Kordić, Snježana. 1995. *Relativna rečenica*. Zagreb: Hrvatsko Filologško Društvo.

Lehfeldt, Werner. 2014. Herausbildung der Standardsprache bei Serben und Kroaten. In Sebastian Kempgen, Peter Kosta, Tilman Berger & Karl Gutschmidt (eds.), *Die Slavischen Sprachen. Ein internationales Handbuch ihrer Struktur, ihrer Geschichte und ihrer Erforschung. Bd. 2*, 1446–1469. Berlin & New York: Mouton de Gruyter.

Lehmann, Christian. 1984. *Der Relativsatz*. Tübingen: Narr.

Mendoza, Imke & Barbara Sonnenhauser. 2017. Complexities in between. Oscillating clausal structures. *Paper presented at the 12th Annual Meeting of the Slavic Linguistics Society, Ljubljana Sept. 21–24, 2017*.

Mendoza, Imke. 2010. Relativsätze mit *który to*. *Wiener Slawistischer Almanach* 65. 105–118.

Mendoza, Imke. 2018. Zur Variation von Relativpronomina im Altpolnischen: Die Rolle der Relativisatoren. *Wiener Slawistischer Almanach* 79. 93–106.

Meyer, Roland. 2017. The C system of relative and complement clauses in the history of Slavic languages. *Language* 9(2). 97–113.

Mitrenina, Olga V. 2012. The syntax of pseudo-correlative constructions with the pronoun *kotoryj* ('which') in Middle Russian. *Slovene* 1(1). 61–73.
Pennell Ross, Deborah. 1996. Anaphors and antecedents in narrative text. In Hannah Rosén (ed.), *Aspects of Latin. Papers from the Seventh International Colloquium of Latin Linguistics. Jerusalem, April 1993*, 511–523. Innsbruck: Institut für Sprachwissenschaft.
Pinkster, Harm 2012. Relative clauses in Latin. Some problems of description. In Paula de Cunha Corrêa, Marcos Martinho, José Marcos Macedo & Alexandre Pineiro Hasegawa (eds.), *Hyperboreans. Essays in Greek and Latin poetry, philosophy, rhetoric and linguistics*, 377–393. São Paulo: Humanitas.
Reindl, Donald F. 2008. *Language contact: German and Slovenian*. Bochum: Brockmeyer.
SSKJ: *Slovar slovenskega knjižnega jezika* 2016. Ljubljana: ZRC SAZU.
Sonnenhauser, Barbara. 2019. Interrogative, indefinite, relative *kdo(r)*. Why Slovene is (not so) different. *Zeitschrift für Slavische Philologie* 75(1). 151–181.
Sonnenhauser, Barbara. 2018. Relativisation strategies in Slovene: diachrony between language use and language description. In Björn Hansen, Jasmina Grković-Major & Barbara Sonnenhauser (eds.), *Diachronic Slavonic syntax: The interplay between internal development, language contact and metalinguistic factors*, 387–406. Berlin: de Gruyter.
Sonnenhauser, Barbara. 2013. Relative clauses in Slovene: diachronic puzzles, synchronic patterns. *Wiener Slavistisches Jahrbuch. Neue Folge* 1. 150–187.
Štebih Golub, Barbara. 2018. Mali uvid u bogatu kajkavsku gramatikografiju. *Fluminensia* 30. 127–151.
Toporišič, Jože & Donald Reindl. 2010. Slovenian. *Revue Belge de philologie et d'Histoire*, 88(3). 897–920.
Večerka, Radoslav. 1983. Souvětí se závislými větami relativními v staroslověnštině. *Slovo* 32/33. 15–52.
Večerka, Radoslav. 2002. *Altkirchenslavische (altbulgarische) Syntax. Band 4: Die Satztypen. Der zusammengesetzte Satz*. Freiburg: Weiher.
Zaliznjak, Andrej A. & Elena V. Padučeva. 1997 [1975]. K tipologii otnositel'nogo predloženija. *Semiotika i informatika* 35 (Opera selecta). 59–107 (originally published in *Semiotika i informatika* 6. 51–101).

Sources

Berke, Petar. 1775 [1995]. *Kinch oszebuini szlavnoga orszaga horvatczkoga. To jefzt: Chudnovita pripechenya, y ofzebuine Milofche, kotere pri chudnovitom kipu Marie Bisztrichke viffe vre let fze fzkafuju*. Graecii. Za pretisak priredio i pogovor napisao Alojz Jembrih, Marija Bistrica.
Dijanić, Juraj. 1797 [1994]. *Hižna knižica. Horvatski dece prijatel*. Zagreb. Tekst transkribirao, za tisak priredio i popratnu studiju napisao Alojz Jembrih, Samobor.
Gigafida: http://www.gigafida.net/
Gr: Tarabasova, Nina I. & Sergej I. Kotkov (eds.). 1969. *Gramotki XVII–nač. XVIII veka*. Moskva: Nauka.
IMP: Erjavec, Tomaž. 2015. *Jezikovni viri starejše slovenščine*. url: http://nl.ijs.si/imp/
Mulih, Juraj. 1742 [2002]. *Regule roditelov i drugeh stareseh i Regule dvorjanstva*. Za tisak priredio tekst transkribirao, rječnik sastavio i pogovor napisao Alojz Jembrih, Zagreb.

Mulih, Juraj. 1744. *Skola kristusseva, kerschanszkoga navuka obilno puna.* Zagreb.
Oršić, J. 1772. *Betegujuche sivine vrachitel to jeszt szuprot vszakojachkomu sivinszkomu betegu jasznovita, vnogo puti probuvana,* ter isztinszka znaidena vrachtva iz vszakoiachkeh knig zvelikum marlivosztum zebrana, na horvaczki jezik obernyena, ter od jednoga Obchinſzke vſzega orſzaga, navlaſztito pako fziromahov haſzni Lyubitela na Szvetlo dana. Zagreb.
Zagrebec, S. 1727. *Hrana duhovna ovchicz kerschanzeh. Aliti zverhu Nedely od Perve Adventa, do Perve po Duhovom: z-prilosenemi nekoiemi zoſzebnemi za oſzebuineh vremen potreboche; Kakti Vu vremenu Jubileumzkoga Proschenia, Poſzvetil Czirkveneh, nad Novomesniki, y vu koiehgod obchinzkeh potrebochah oſzebuinum marlivoztium ukup ſzlosene, y na ſzvetlo dane.* Zagrebiae.

Part II: **The influence of Greek on Church Slavonic**

Anna Pichkhadze
Blocking of syntactic constructions without Greek counterparts in Church Slavonic

Abstract: The influence of Greek syntax on the syntax of Church Slavonic texts has been extensively studied in terms of the borrowing of Greek syntactic constructions in Church Slavonic. Restrictions and even prohibitions on the use of genuinely Slavonic syntactic constructions that had no support from Greek *analogues* have been examined to a lesser extent, although these constraints played an important role in the establishing of the syntactic norm of Church Slavonic. This paper analyses several syntactic phenomena that were not common in Church Slavonic because they were absent from Greek, namely a) participle and infinitive clauses, b) the reduction of usage frequency for light-verb constructions and c) the placement of enclitics according to Wackernagel's law.

Keywords: Greek, Church Slavonic, infinite constructions, light verbs, word order, clitics

1 Introduction

The influence of Greek syntax on the syntax of Church Slavonic texts has been extensively studied in the context of borrowing of Greek syntactic constructions in Church Slavonic. Restrictions on the use of certain Slavonic syntactic constructions that had no support from Greek analogues, have attracted far less attention. However, these constraints played an important role in the establishment of the syntactic norm of Church Slavonic. In this paper, I will discuss several syntactic phenomena that were not common in Church Slavonic because they were absent from Greek.

Anna Pichkhadze, Vinogradov Russian Language Institute of the Russian Academy of Sciences, Moscow, e-mail: rusyaz@yandex.ru

https://doi.org/10.1515/9783110651331-007

2 Infinite constructions introduced by conjunctions

2.1 Participle clauses

Such a significant feature of the Balto-Slavic syntax as the function of a participle as the predicate of a subordinate clause introduced by interrogative pronouns or by free choice pronouns/adverbs is only encountered sporadically in Church Slavonic. The necessary condition of its use was the referential identity of the subject of the matrix predicate and the subject of the participle construction. Participles as predicates of subordinate clauses occurred semi-regularly in certain kinds of syntactic constructions.

2.1.1 Indirect questions

A participle could be used instead of a finite verb in indirect questions. A few instances of participles being substituted for finite verbs in indirect questions are found in the Cyrillo-Methodian translation of the Gospel. For the most part, the participle construction is also attested in the Lithuanian translation in the same places where it appears in the Slavonic text, cf.:

(1) нє   вѣстаѩ   чєсо   просѩшта
    ne   věstasę   česo   prosęšta
    not know.PRS.2DU   what.GEN   ask.PTCP.ACT.PRS.DU.NOM
    'you do not know what you are asking' (Zogr., Mk. 10.38)
    = Lith. *ne žino ko prąszą* (Ambrazas 1990: 122)

(2) нє   вѣдѩтъ   что   творѩштє
    ne   vědętъ   čto   tvoręšte
    not know.PRS.3PL   what.ACC   do.PTCP.ACT.PRS.PL.NOM
    'they do not know what they are doing' (Sav., Ostr., Lk. 13.34)
    = Lith. *ne žino ką dárą*;

(3) самъ   бо   вѣдѣшє   что   хотѩ
    samъ   bo   věděše   čto   xotę
    himself.NOM   PTCL   know.IMPERF.3SG   what.ACC   want.PTCP.ACT.PRS.SG.NOM

сътворити
sъtvoriti
do.INF
'he himself knew what he would do' (Mar., Jn 6.6)
= Lith. *žinójo ką darysę̃s* (Růžička 1963: 195)

Participle clauses dependent on the verbs with the meaning 'to know' have been found in Old Czech and Old Polish (Potebnja 1958: 213). The participle construction can still be used in contemporary Lithuanian in indirect questions governed by verbs of perception and thought, although its use is considerably limited (Ambrazas 1990: 113–114, 135; Arkad'ev 2011: 48–49).

Already in the earliest manuscripts of the Slavonic Gospel, participles in indirect questions were replaced by finite verbs, but in Old Russian writings they are quite common:

(4) не знаетъ оу кого купивъ
    ne znajetъ u kogo kupivъ
    not know.PRS.3SG from who.GEN buy.PTCP.ACT.PST.SG.NOM
    'he does not know whom he bought it from' (Expanded version of the Russkaja Pravda, article 32; cited after Tixomirov 1953: 55, 94)

(5) вѣдѣ бо сѧ с ни(м) что молвивъ
    vědě bo sja s nimъ čto molvivъ
    know.PRS1SG PTCL REFL to him what.ACC talk.PTCP.ACT.PST.SG.NOM
    'I know what I talked to him about' (*Primary Chronicle*, PSRL I: 265)

Further examples can be found in Potebnja (1958: 211–214).

2.1.2 Relative clauses

Predications introduced by relative pronouns or adverbs constitute the largest group of subordinate clauses with participle predicate (cf. Pičxadze 2020: 258–270). A participle appears if the pronoun or adverb has a non-specific referent and/or expresses free choice, i. e., indicates an arbitrary chosen unspecified subject or accidental circumstance.

A large amount of examples is registered in Old Russian chronicles:

(6) ини   же   мъхъ   ꙗдаху · <...>   сосну,   кору
    ini   že   mъxъ   jadjaxu...   sosnu,   koru
    some.NOM.PL PTCL   moss.ACC   eat.IMPERF.3PL   pine.ACC   bark.ACC
    липову   и   листъ   ильмъ   кто   что
    lipovu   i   listъ   ilьmъ   kto   čto
    lime.ACC   and   leaves.ACC   elm_tree   who.NOM   what.ACC
    замысля
    zamyslja
    think.PTCP.ACT.PRS.SG.NOM

    'some ate moss <...>, pine, lime bark, and elm-tree leaves, whatever each could think of' (*Novgorod First Chronicle* 113b)

(7) а   прокъ   ихъ   разбежеся   куды   кто
    a   prokъ   ixъ   razbežesę   kudy   kto
    and   rest.NOM   of_them   flee.AOR.3SG   wherever   who.NOM
    видя,   нъ   тѣхъ   корѣла   кде
    vidja,   nъ   těxъ   korěla   kde
    see.PTCP.ACT.PRS.SG.NOM but   these.ACC.PL   Korel_people.NOM   wherever
    обидуче   въ   лѣсе   ли
    obiduče,   vъ   lěse   li
    surround.PTCP.ACT.PRS.PL.NOM   in   wood.LOC   PTCL
    выводаче   избиша
    vyvodjače   izbiša
    lead_out.PTCP.ACT.PRS.PL.NOM   kill.AOR.3PL

    'and the rest fled whatever way each saw, but these the Korel people killed, wherever they surrounded them – if in the woods, after having led them out' (*Novgorod First Chronicle* 103b)

(8) куда   же   ходяще   путемъ   по   своимъ
    kuda   že   xodjašče   putemъ   po   svoimъ
    wherever   PTCL   go.PTCP.ACT.PRS.PL.NOM   way.INS   in   your
    землямъ.   не   даите   пакости   дѣꙗти · ѡтрокомъ
    zemljamъ,   ne   daite   pakosti   dějati   otrokomъ
    land,   not   allow.IMP.2PL   damage   cause.INF warriors.DAT
    ни   своимъ ·   ни   чюжимъ
    ni   svoimъ   ni   čužimъ
    or   your_own_people   or   aliens

    'wherever you go in your land, do not allow your warriors to cause damage to your own people or aliens' (*Instruction of Vladimir Monomach*, PSRL I: 246)

There are numerous constructions of that kind in the Baltic languages, cf. Lettish: *vini salauzuši visu, ko nogrābuši* 'they broke everything [= whatever] they grabbed' etc. (Ambrazas 1990: 114).

Participle clauses with relative pronouns or adverbs are often connected with indefiniteness, indifference, and ignorance. This is illustrated by the following sentence from the Old Russian translation of the Life of St. Andrew the Fool:

(9) a. блж҃ныи   же   ан(д)рѣи   немощи   дѣмонѣ
       blaž<e>nyj   že   An(d)rěj   nemošči   děmoně
       blessed.NOM PTCL Andrew.NOM   powerlessness of_the_demon
       поругавсѧ.   пакы   вратисѧ   ѿкудѣ
       porugavsja,   paky   vratisja   otkudě
       having_derided   again return.AOR.3SG where
       пришедъ,
       prišedъ,
       come_from.PTCP.ACT.PST.SG.NOM
    b. ὅθεν   ἦλθεν
       hothen   ēlthen
       whence   come.AOR.3SG
       'and blessed Andrew having derided the powerlessness of the demon, returned again to where he had come from' (*Life of Andrew the Fool*, cited after Moldovan 2000: 218, 484)

The precise place from where Andrew came remains unknown because it is not important for understanding the situation, the author only notices that Andrew accidentally happened to be nearby.

The Life of St. Andrew the Fool narrates that one night Andrew's host heard Andrew crying and decided that the spirit that haunted the well had hit somebody he had encountered, and this person happened to be Andrew:

(10) a. розмысли   же   в   себе.   ӕко   дх҃ъ   кладѧжьныи
        rozmysli   že   v   sebe,   jako   duxъ   kladjažьnyj
        decided   PTCL in   himself   that   spirit.NOM.SG   of_the_well
        пришедъ.   надохнулъ   ѥсть.   ѥгоже
        prišedъ   nadoxnulъ   jestь,   jegože
        having_arrived   hit.LPTCP.SG.M   AUX.PRS.3SG   who.ACC.SG
        обрѣтъ   прѣдъ   собою.   да
        obrětъ   prědъ   soboju,   da
        encounter.PTCP.ACT.PST.SG.NOM before   self.INS and

	обрѣлъ	юсть	сєго,
	obrělъ	jestь	sego,
	encounter.LPTCP.SG.NOM	AUX.PRS.3SG	he.ACC.SG

b. παρακροῦσαι τὸν εὑρισκόμενον
parakrousai ton heuriskomenon
hit.INF the.ACC.SG.M encounter.PTCP.PASS.PST.ACC.SG.M

'decided that the spirit of the well, having arrived, hit the man that he [the spirit] encountered, and he encountered him (i. e., Andrew)' (*Life of Andrew the Fool*, cited after Moldovan 2000: 167, 456)

Here, the participle construction югожє обрѣтъ refers to an indefinite accidental subject, in contrast with the finite verb in the phrase обрѣлъ юсть сєго where a unique referent is involved.

In Slavonic languages, pronouns and adverbs that introduce participle clauses, may mostly be used as both interrogatives and relatives. Participle constructions with the pronoun иже, which is devoid of the meaning of indefiniteness and can only be used as a relative, are quite rare. They appear in generic contexts. A few instances are attested in Old Church Slavonic monuments, cf. in Euchologium Sinaiticum:

(11) а поѣсъ мрътвость тѣлоу ѡ нємьжє
a poěsъ mrъtvostь tělu o nemьže
and girdle.NOM mortification.ACC body.DAT around which

лєжѧ
ležę
lie.PTCP.ACT.PRS.SG.NOM

'the girdle [designates] mortification of a [=any] body which it lies around' (Euch. Sin. 67b10-11, cited after Vaillant 1977: 207)

(12) отъмываємъ же пакы грѣхы отъ сєбѣ. ꙗжє
otъmyvajemъ že paky grěxy otъ sebě, ježe
wash_away.PRS.1PL PTCL ADV sin.ACC.PL from ourselves which.ACC

по крьштєньи сътворьшє. покааниємь.
po krъštenьi sъtvorьše, pokaaniemь.
after baptism.LOC committ.PTCP.ACT.PST.PL.NOM contrition.INST

исповѣдаѭштесѧ боу
ispovědajǫstesę bogu
when we confess them to God
'we wash away [any] sins which we have committed after the baptism when we confess them to God with contrition' (Euch. Sin. 67b9-13, cf. also Vaillant 1977: 206)

Participle constructions with the participle of the verb хотѣти 'to want' are not unusual in Church Slavonic texts, since the meaning of this verb conforms perfectly to the meaning of free choice, as numerous examples show:

(13) a. ꙗкоже   влдка   стадоу :   ѥгда   хотѧ
       jakože   vladyka   stadu,   jegda   xotja
       as   owner.NOM   flock.DAT whenever   want.PTCP.ACT.PRS.SG.NOM
       посълетъ   и   приведетъ :   ꙗже   хоштетъ   овьца,
       posъletъ   i   privedetъ   jaže   xoštetъ   ovьcja,
       send.FUT.3SG and lead.FUT.3SG which want.PRS.3SG   sheep.ACC
    b. ὅτε   βουληθῇ
       hote   boulēthēi
       when   want.SBJV.3SG
       'as the flock owner will send whenever he wants and lead which sheep he wants' (Izbornik of 1076, 123b cited after Mušinskaya, Mišina 2009: 510)

(14) идѣте   ѥже   хотѧще   сътворите
     iděte   ježe   xotęšte   sъtvorite
     go.IMP.2PL   whatever.ACC want.PTCP.ACT.PRS.PL.NOM   do.IMP.2PL
     'go and do whatever you want' (Sinai Patericon of the 11th c., 59a cited after Golyšenko, Dubrovina 1967: 153)

(15) ѣсти.   ѥже   хотѧще   брашьно
     ěsti   ježe   xotjašče   brašьno
     eat.INF   whatever.ACC.SG want.PTCP.ACT.PRS.PL.NOM   food.ACC.SG
     'to eat whatever food you like' (Trinity Miscelany of the 12th–13th cc., 58b, f. 304.I, no. 12 in the Russian State Library in Moscow)

(16) a. тогда   неч(с̑)твыи   ѿметникъ   повелѣ
        togda   ne(č)<ъ>stivyj   otmetnikъ   povelě
        then   impious.NOM.SG   apostate.NOM.SG   order.AOR.3SG

антиохианемъ		бес	трепета	и	без
antioxianemъ		bes	trepeta	i	bez
inhabitants_of_Antiochia.DAT.PL		without	trembling	and	without
боꙗзни	принести [instead of прѣнести]	ѿтѹдѣ		и
bojazni	prinesti	ottudě		i
fear	remove.INF	from_there		and
положити	ꙗ	гдѣже	хотѧще,
položiti	ja	gděže	xotjašče,
put_down.INF	them.ACC.PL	wherever	wish.PTCP.ACT.PRS.PL.NOM

b. ὅπου δ' ἂν βούλοιντο,
hopou d' an boulointo
wherever PTCL wish.OPT.3PL

'The impious apostate then ordered the inhabitants of Antiochia to remove them [the remains] from there without trembling or fear and put them down wherever they wished' (*Life of Andrew the Fool*, cited after Moldovan 2000: 425–426, 613)

In Old Russian writings, participle clauses are even more frequent. Participles are always in the nominative masculine, singular or plural. Here are some examples from the *Questions of Kirik* from the 12th century[1]:

(17) а и роботою. или оубожьствомь. или како хотѧци
a i robotoju ili ubožьstvomь ili kako xotjaci
because of slavery or poverty, or how want.PTCP.ACT.PRS.PL.NOM
'because of slavery or poverty, or for whatever reason' (*Questions of Kirik*, 527a)

(18) а иже рѣзати в не(д)лю что хотѧче
a iže rězati v ne(d)<ě>l'u čto xotjače,
and that they slaughter on Sundays what.ACC want.PTCP.ACT.PRS.PL.NOM
нѣтоу бѣды
nětu bědy
there is nothing wrong
'and that they slaughter [cattle or poultry] on Sundays whatever they want, there is nothing wrong' (*Questions of Kirik*, 520b)

---

[1] Cited according to the Synodic Kormčaja of 1282 (Syn., no. 132 in the State Historical Museum in Moscow).

(19) в҃.ма свѣщами подобаѥть зажьныма быти или д҃.мъ
dvěma svěščami podobajetь zažьnyma byti ili četyrьmъ
2 candles must be lit, or 4,

или	колико	хотѧче		ладно
ili	koliko	xotjače		ladno
or	how_many.ACC	want.PTCP.ACT.PRS.PL.NOM		even_number.ADV

'2 candles must be lit, or 4, or whatever even number' (*Questions of Kirik*, 523a)

(20) а   коли   хотѧ   вдати.   вложи
     a   koli   xotja   vdati,   vloži
     and whenever   want.PTCP.ACT.PRS.SG.NOM   give.INF put.IMP.2SG

    часть   в   потирь   же   вина   влѣи.
    častь   v   potirь   že   vina   vlěi,
    part.ACC.SG into   the chalice, PTCL wine.GEN.SG pour.IMP2SG

    тако   даи
    tako   dai
    then   give.IMP2SG

'and whenever you want to give [the communion], put a part into the chalice, pour the wine and then give it' (*Questions of Kirik*, 520b–521a)

Similar examples can be found in more recent Russian business and legal texts:

(21) и   вол<ь>но   ѥму   Семену   онымъ   конем   як
     i   vol'no   jemu   Semenu   onym   konem   jak
     and   free.PRED   he.DAT   Semion.DAT this.INS.SG horse.INS.SG however

    хотячи   продат<ь>, дарова<ть>   и   заминят<ь>
    xotjači   prodat<ь>, darovat<ь>   i   zaminjat<ь>
    want.PTCP.ACT.PRS.SG.NOM   sell.INF   present.INF   or exchange.INF

    и   як   хотячи   влодет<ь>
    i   jak   xotjači   vlodet<ь>
    and   however   want.PTCP.ACT.PRS.SG.NOM   own.INF

'and he, Semion, is allowed to sell, present, or exchange this horse however he wants or to own it however he wants' (*Kaluga acts* № 19, 1671 cited after Markevič 1892: 49)

The meaning of free choice is realized properly in habitual / iterative contexts. The earliest instances of the use of participle constructions in habitual contexts describing a man's habits and behavior are attested in the Cyrillo-Methodian translation of the Gospels:

(22) вьземлеши   егоже   не   положь.
    vъzemleši   egože   ne   položь
    take_up.PRS.2SG what.GEN   not   lay_down.PTCP.ACT.PST.SG.NOM
    и   жьнеши   егоже   не   сѣвъ
    i   žьneši   egože   ne   sěvъ
    and   reap.PRS.2SG what.GEN   not   sow.PTCP.ACT.PST.SG.NOM
    'You take up what you did not lay down, and you reap what you did not sow'
    (Mar., Lk. 19.21)

(23) вьземлю   егоже   не   положь
    vъzemlju   egože   ne   položь
    take_up.PRS.1SG what.GEN   not   lay_down.PTCP.ACT.PST.SG.NOM
    'I take up what I did not lay down' (Ass., Lk. 19.22)

(24) събираѭ   идоуже   не   расточъ
    sъbirajǫ   joduže   ne   rastočъ
    gather.PTCP.ACT.PRS.SG.NOM   where   not   scatter.PTCP.ACT.PST.SG.NOM
    'gathering where I have not scattered seed' (Mar., Mt. 25.26)

(25) жьнѭ   идеже   не   сѣавъ
    žьnjǫ   ideže   ne   sěavъ
    harvest.PRS.1SG where   not   sow.PTCP.ACT.PST.SG.NOM
    'I harvest where I have not sown' (Ass., Mt. 25.26 cited after Růžička 1963: 197)

Notably, all the contexts are negative. In all the cited sentences, there are instances of finite verbs in the indicative mood in the Greek original. Slavonic manuscripts diverge in these passages: finite verbs are substituted for participles already in the earliest codices. Nevertheless, in the Lithuanian translation of the Gospel the same participle constructions are represented in the same places as in the most archaic Slavonic manuscripts: *piaughi ką nepasejes* (in the German original, there is a finite verb: *erndtest das du nicht gesset hast*) (Ambrazas 1990: 122). Participle constructions in habitual contexts are also found in Old Lettish: *cits. . . plitē ko dabuidams* 'he spends on drink whatever he earns', etc. (Ambrazas 1990: 115). A large number of participle clauses in habitual / iterative contexts occur in Old Russian writings, cf. in the *Questions of Kirik*:

(26) ци   приливати   воды   к   виноу,   коли   даюче
    ci   prilivati   vody   k   vinu,   koli   dajuči
    Q   add.INF   water.GEN   to   wine   whenever   give.PTCP.ACT.PRS.PL.NOM
    'should we add water to wine whenever we give it?' (*Questions of Kirik*, 276b)

Sometimes it is difficult to set clear-cut boundaries between free choice and habitual / iterative semantics, as in the following sentence from the Old Russian translation of the Jewish War[2]:

(27) a. исплънивса   ꙗрости.   идеже   ѡбрѣтъ
      isplъnivsja   jarosti, ideže   obrětъ
      full   rage.GEN wherever   meet.PTCP.ACT.PST.SG.NOM
      жидовина,   оубиваше,
      židovina,   ubivaše,
      Jew.ACC.SG   kill.IMPERF.3SG
   b. ὅσοις   ἐπετύγχανεν   Ἰουδαίοις
      hosois   epetugchanen   Ioudaiois
      who.DAT.PL   meet.AOR.3SG   Jew.DAT.PL
   'full of rage, wherever he met a Jew he killed him' (*Jewish War*, 358c15-16)

In a range of contexts, participle clauses with an unspecified object presumably express an additional meaning of condition, cause, or consequence. Most often, they are semantically close to conditional clauses, as is the sentences from *Codex Suprasliensis*[3] (28) and from the *Instruction of Vladimir Monomach* (29):

(28) a. а   єгоже   не   прѣимъ,   то   и
        a   jegože   ne   prěimъ,   to   i
        and   what.GEN not   perceive.PTCP.ACT.PST.SG.NOM this.ACC and
        глаголати   не   съмѣѭ,
        glagolati   ne   sъmějǫ,
        tell.INF   not   dare.PRS.1SG
   b. ὃ   δὴ   οὐ [variant reading: μὴ]   παρέλαβον
      ho   dē   u [variant reading: mē]   parelabon
      what.ACC PTCL not   perceive.AOR.1SG
   'and what I have not perceived (= if I have not perceived) I do not dare to tell' (Supr., 501.21)

(29) егоже   оумѣючи   того   не
     egože   umějuči   togo   ne
     whatever.GEN   know_how_to_do.PTCP.ACT.PRS.PL.NOM this.GEN not

---

[2] Cited according to Pičxadze et al. (2004).
[3] Codex Suprasliensis (henceforth Supr) is cited according to Kapaldo, Zaimov (1982–1983).

забываите	доброго,	а	ѥгоже	не
zabyvaite	dobrogo,	a	jegože	ne
forget.IMP.2PL	good.GEN	and	whatever.GEN	not

оумѣючи			а	тому	сѧ	оучите
umějuči,			a	tomu	sja	učite
know_how_to_do.PTCP.ACT.PRS.PL.NOM				this.DAT	REFL	learn.IMP.2PL

'whatever good thing you know how to do (= if you know how to do a good thing), do not forget it, and whatever (= if) you do not know how to do, learn it' (*Instruction of Vladimir Monomach*, PSRL I: 246)

In the following sentence from the Old Russian translation of the Pčela the participle clause seems to have the meaning of condition and cause simultaneously:

(30)
ни	конѧ	бо	скора	нар⟨ч⟩емъ	иже	ѿ
ni	konja	bo	skora	nar⟨i⟩(č)emъ	iže	ot
not	horse.ACC.SG	PTCL	quick.ACC.SG	call.PRS.1PL	which.NOM.SG	from

скора	родивсѧ.		оже	самъ	не
skora	rodivsja,		ože	samъ	ne
quick.GEN	bear.PTCP.REFL.PST.SG.NOM		if	itself.NOM	not

скоръ	є(с̂)
skorъ	e(s)⟨tь⟩
quick.NOM	is

'we do not call quick a horse which (= if it = because it) was born to a quick [parent], if it is not quick itself' (PSRL I: 246 cited after Pičxadze, Makeeva 2008: 832)

Presumably, the notion of a consequence is involved in the participle clause in the following example from the Volhynian chronicle:

(31)
Володимерь	же	иꙁ	Берестьꙗ.	посла	к	нимъ.
Volodimerъ	že	iz	Berestьja	posla	k	nimъ
Vladimir.NOM	PTCL	from	Berestiye.GEN	send.AOR.3SG	to	them

жито	в	лодьꙗхъ.	по	Боугоу	с	людми.	с
žito	v	lodьjaxъ	po	Bugu	s	ljud'mi	s
corn.ACC	in	boats.LOC	along	Bug.DAT	with	people.INS	with

добрꙑми.	комоу	вѣра
dobrymi,	komu	verja
honest.INS	who.DAT	trust.PTCP.ACT.PRS.SG.NOM

'Vladimir sent to them corn in boats from Berestiye along the Bug river, with honest people whom he trusted' (*Volhynian chronicle*, PSRL II: 879)

This sentence is reminiscent of Latin relative clauses with the meaning of consequence where the verb is in the subjunctive, like *sunt qui dicant* 'there are people who say (= there are such people that would say')' etc. In Latin, if a relative clause expresses the notion of condition, cause, or consequence, the verb is to be used in the subjunctive mood.

It has been stated in the literature that free choice items are incompatible with environments that describe a single action or event in the real world and typically occur in possibility modal contexts, in generic, habitual, hypothetical, and counterfactual sentences (Haimann 1974: 343–344; Giannakidou 2001; Tatevosov 2002: 146–150). Identical environments seem to favour participle constructions instead of finite ones in Slavonic and Baltic languages. Pronouns or adverbs, which introduced clauses of this kind, can be most often interpreted as free choice items. Some of these participle constructions have an additional adverbial flavour, especially that of condition.

2.1.3 Lack of evidence and incomplete knowledge

In Old Slavonic texts, participles in predicative positions occur occasionally in sentences which describe specified unique events and express ignorance or incomplete knowledge of a situation that has not been witnessed by the speaker. In the following passage from the Codex Suprasliensis, the narrator and his audience do not know and are unable to comprehend how after his resurrection Jesus could appear to his disciples though the door of the room where they were sitting together, was closed (Jn. 20.19). Only Jesus himself knew how he had passed through the closed door; for the others it was inconceivable:

(32) a. вьлезѣ   ꙗкоже   ѥдинъ   вѣды
      vьleze   jakože   jedinъ   vědy
      come_in.AOR.3SG how   alone.NOM know.PTCP.ACT.PRS.SG.NOM
      самъ,
      samъ,
      himself.NOM
   b. εἰσῆλθεν   ὡς   οἶδεν   αὐτὸς   μόνος
      eisēlthen   hōs   oiden   autos   monos
      come_in.AOR.3SG how know.AOR.3SG himself.NOM alone.NOM
      'he came in – only he himself knew in what way' (Supr., 501.8)

One may assume that participle clauses were used to render reported speech and thought. Consider the following examples:

(33) a. и   съповѣдавъше кмоу   вьса   ꙗже
     i   sъpovědavъše jemu   vьsa   jaže
     and   having_told   him   everything which.ACC
     слышавъше   отъ   с҃тааго   савина,
     slyšavъše   otъ   s<vę>taago   savina,
     hear.PTCP.ACT.PST.PL.NOM from   saint.GEN   Savin.GEN
  b. ἅπαντα   τὰ   δηλωθέντα   αὐτῷ
     hapanta   ta   dēlōthenta   autōi
     everything.ACC the.ACC.PL.N   tell.PTCP.PASS.PST.ACC.PL him.DAT
     'and having told him everything they had heard from saint Savin' (Supr., 152.10-11)

(34) да   на   ротоу   ходить.   по   своеи   вѣрѣ.   ꙗко
     da   na   rotu   xoditь   po   svoei   věrě,   jako
     PTCL to   oath.ACC go.PRS.3SG according_to   his   religion.DAT that
     не   имѣꙗ   ничтоже.   ти   тако
     ne   iměja   ničtože,   ti   tako
     not   have.PTCP.ACT.PRS.SG.NOM   nothing.ACC   and   then
     пущенъ   боудеть
     puščenъ   budetь
     absolve.PTCP.PASS.PST.SG.NOM   AUX.FUT.3SG
     'he must swear according to his religion that he has nothing, and then he will be absolved' (*Rus'–Byzantine Treaty* of 945, PSRL I: 52)

For further examples see (Pičxadze 2020: 271–272).

However, these examples are too few and for this reason do not seem quite reliable. Yet, bearing in mind the similarities of the participle syntax in the Slavonic and Baltic languages, it may be reasonable to consider the above Slavonic examples because in Baltic languages, participles are regularly used in evidential functions.

Thus, participle clauses functioning as sentential complements occur in Church Slavonic and Old Russian mostly in counterfactual environments: they express indefiniteness, indifference, uncertainty, and ignorance. A participle takes the place of a finite verb in the presence of indefinite constituents, in generic sentences, in indirect questions and, perhaps, in reported speech and thought. In Baltic languages, a participle functioning as a finite verb is used in similar contexts and much more regularly (Ambrazas 1990: 121–122). The use of a participle in the position of the predicate of a subordinate clause, which expresses various counterfactual meanings, is a Balto-Slavic innovation. The fact that the Baltic languages have retained the participle clauses functioning as finite clauses whereas the Slavonic languages have lost them completely can be explained by the strong influence of Greek and Latin texts on Slavonic writings.

It is symptomatic that the subjunctive mood was used in Latin in contexts similar to those where Slavonic and Baltic participle constructions appear – in iterative sentences with the conjunction *cum*, in relative subordinate clauses carrying an additional adverbial meaning, in indirect questions, and in reported speech and thought.

2.1.4 Immediate anteriority

In Old Russian, adverbial participle clauses were used to depict actions that immediately preceded the situation described in the main clause (Pičxadze 2020: 277–281). Consider the following sentences:

(35) се ѩко въꙁьрѣвъ видѣ
    se jako vъzьrěvъ vidě
    and as_soon_as glance.PTCP.ACT.PST.SG.NOM see.AOR.3SG
    прѣподобьнааго ѳеодосиѩ въ свѣтѣ томь. посрѣдѣ
    prěpodobьnaago theodosija vъ světě tomь, posrědě
    venerable.ACC Theodosius.ACC in light.LOC this.LOC in_the_middle_of
    манастырѧ прѣдъ црквию стоѩща
    manastyrja prědъ crkviju stojašča
    monastery.GEN in_front_of church.INS staying.ACC
    'and having glanced [at the mysterious light] he saw venerable Theodosius in this light, staying in the middle of the monastery in front of the church' (*The Life of St. Theodosius of the Caves*; Uspenskij Miscellany from the 12th–13th cc., 55d27–28)

(36) потече противоу Татариноу. како
    poteče protivu Tatarinu, kako
    run.AOR.3SG toward Tatar.dat as_soon_as
    стекасѧ
    stekasę
    run_into.PTCP.ACT.PST.SG.NOM
    [in the Pogodin and Xlebnikov codices: съшедсѧ]
    [in the Pogodin and Xlebnikov codices: sьšedsja]
    [run_into.PTCP.ACT.PST.SG.NOM]

```
        с     нимъ. тако оуби        Татарина
        s     nimъ, tako ubi         Tatarina
        with  he.INS then kill.AOR.3SG Tatar.ACC
```
'he ran toward the Tatar, and as soon as he ran into him he killed the Tatar'
(*Galician chronicle*, PSRL II: 853)

(37)
```
     Былъ          ми        е(с),        сноу,    ꙗ(к)       и      грець,
     Byl           mi        je(s)<i>,    synu,    ja(k)<o>   i      grec,
     be.LPTCP.SG.M I.DAT     AUX.PRS.2SG  son.VOC  like       and    dog.NOM
     в       теплъ    хра(м)       влѣ(з)    согрѣтсѧ.    и     ꙗ(к)
     v       teplъ    xra(m)       vlě(z)    sogrětsę,    i     ja(k)
     into    warm.ACC house.ACC    came      get_warm.SUP  and   as_soon_as
     согрѣвсѧ,                начне(т)          на     г̅адарь       свои
     sogrěvsę,                nаčne(t)          na     g<osp>adarь  svoi
     get_warm.PTCP.ACT.PST.SG.NOM  begin.FUT.3SG  at    host         its
     лаꙗти
     lajati
     bark.INF
```
'You were towards me, my son, like a dog that came into the house to get warm, and as soon as it gets warm it begins to bark at its host' (*The Tale of Akir the Wise*, cited after Grigor'ev 1913: 221).

Miklosich illustrates this construction by examples from Old Ukrainian writings (Miklosich 1868–1874: 835). Since analogues are absent in Greek, the construction had no chance to be accepted by Church Slavonic.

2.2 Infinitive clauses

Infinitive clauses registered in Church Slavonic are mainly calques of the Greek construction "ὥστε *hōste* + infinitive", which has the meaning of consequence. Likewise, infinitive clauses were exploited as corresponding to the Greek construction "article in the genitive + infinitive" indicating a goal:

(38) a.
```
     нынѣ    възвращѫсѧ.   ꙗко    въратитисѧ       кнѧземъ         прьсьскомъ,
     nyně    vъzvraštǫsę,  jako   vъratitisę       knęzemъ         prъsьskomъ,
     now     return.FUT.1SG COMP  make_war.INF     princes.DAT     of_Persia.DAT
```

b. τοῦ πολεμῆσαι
tou polemēsai
the.GEN.SG wage_war.INF
'now I will return to make war with the princes of Persia' (Dan. 10.20, cited after Sreznevskij 1903:1654–1655)

This model is a regular construction in modern Russian: *а сейчас я возвращусь, чтобы воевать а seičas ja vozvraščus', čtoby voevat'*. Both infinitive constructions are adverbial clauses; the predicates of the matrix clauses do not require any complement denoting consequence or goal.

At the same time, another infinitive construction was in use in Slavonic languages that functioned as sentential complement (for more details see Pičxadze 2019). It was governed by predicates of purpose. I have managed to find one single example in Church Slavonic writings, but it is not indicative of a larger trend because it is a calque from Greek:

(39) a. съвѣтъ сътворишѧ вьси архиереи старьци
   sъvětъ sъtvorišę vьsi arxierei starьci
   counsel.ACC took all.NOM chief_priests.NOM elders.NOM
   людьсции на и҃са. ѣко оубити и,
   ljudьscii na i<su>sa. ěko ubiti i,
   of_the_people.NOM against Jesus.ACC COMP put_to_death.INF he.ACC
b. συμβούλιον ἔλαβον (variant: ἐποίησαν)... ὥστε
   sumboulion elabon (variant: epoiēsan)... hōste
   counsel.ACC.SG take.AOR.3PL (take.AOR.3PL) COMP
   θανατῶσαι
   thanatōsai
   put_to_death.INF
   'all the chief priests and elders of the people took counsel against Jesus to put him to death' (Mt. 27.1)

Since in Greek such a construction with a purpose predicate is quite rare, it occurs only occasionally in Church Slavonic texts, which follow their Greek originals very closely.

On the contrary, in Old Russian chronicles and in other sources, infinitive clauses in the position of a sentential complement governed by a purpose predicate are frequent. They are being used with verbs expressing mental intention: мыслити *mysliti* 'to think of doing something, to plan', доумати *dumati* 'idem', съмотрити *sъmotriti* 'idem', печаловатисѧ *pečalovatisja* 'to be worried about doing something, to care, to be concerned', печаль имѣти *pečalь iměti* 'idem', льстити *lьstiti* 'to be cunning, to hatch', ловити *loviti* 'to watch for good time to do something':

(40) печалоуѧсѧ · абы коньцѧти и видети ц︵рковь
    pečalujasja, aby konьcjati i videti c<e>rkovь
    having_trouble COMP finish.INF and see.INF church.ACC
    съвѣршеноу · оукрашеноу
    sъvĕršenu ukrašenu
    complete.PTCP.PASS.PST.SG.ACC adorn.PTCP.PASS.PST.SG.ACC
    'having trouble to finish and see the church completed and adorned' (*Novgorod First Chronicle*, 57a)

(41) печаль имѣющю. како Днѣстръ перейти
    pečalь imějušču, kako Dnĕstrъ pereiti
    trouble.ACC having COMP Dniestr.ACC cross.INF
    'having trouble to cross the Dniestr river' (*Galician Chronicle*, PSRL II: 759)

(42) нача собѣ доумати. абы кде. за
    nača sobě dumati, aby kde. za
    begin.AOR.3SG REFL.DAT think.INF COMP somewhere beyond
    Берестьемь поставити городъ
    Berestjemь postaviti gorodъ
    Berestiye.INS build.INF town.ACC
    'he began to think where he might build the town beyond Berestiye' (*Volhynian chronicle*, PSRL II: 875)

(43) a. смотрѧше како оубити и
    smotrjaše kako ubiti i
    plan.IMPERF.3SG COMP kill.INF he.ACC
    b. σπεύδων ἀνελεῖν
    speudōn anelein
    seek.PTCP.ACT.PRS.SG.NOM kill.INF
    'he planned to kill him' (*Jewish War*, 355c14-15)

(44) a. дꙋмаста на мѧ, како мѧ оуморити,
    dumasta na mja, kako mja umoriti,
    conspire.IMPERF.3PL against me COMP I.ACC kill.INF

b. τὴν... ἐπιβουλὴν θανάτου
   tēn epibulēn thanatou
   the.ACC.SG.F conspiracy.ACC.SG.F death.GEN.SG.M
   'they conspired against me in order to kill me' (*Jewish War*, 373b12-13)

The predicate may be a noun, as in the sentence from the *Tale of the Holy Martyrs Boris and Gleb*:

(45) бѧше сънъ кго въ мънозѣ мысли и
    b'aše sъnъ jego vъ mъnozě <u>mysli</u> i
    was dream.NOM his in great contemplation and
    въ печали крѣпъцѣ и тѧжьцѣ и страшьнѣ.
    vъ <u>pečali</u> krěpъcě i tjažьcě i strašьně,
    in trouble great and deep and awful
    како предатисѧ на страсть, како пострадати
    kako <u>predatisja</u> na strastь, kako <u>postradati</u>
    COMP give.INF.REFL to suffering.ACC COMP suffer.INF
    и теченик съконьчати и вѣроу съблюсти
    i tečenije <u>sъkonьčati</u> i věru <u>sъbljusti</u>
    and path.ACC finish.INF and faith.ACC preserve.INF
    'his [Boris'] dream was full of contemplation and great, deep and awful trouble to give himself to suffering, to suffer and finish his path and preserve his faith' (*Uspenskij Miscellany*, 11a30-b6)

Notably, infinitive clauses appear with purpose predicates denoting mental intention but not with conative ones: the latter (тъснѫтисѧ *tъsnutisja* 'to try', тъщатисѧ *tъščatisja* 'idem') govern infinitives without conjunctions.

Another, more numerous group of predicates which function as heads of infinitive clauses are commissives, i. e. verbs constituting a statement that commits the speaker to some future action (for example: клѧтисѧ *klętisja* 'to swear'; cf. Vlasova 2014). Like infinitive clauses governed by purpose predicates, infinitive clauses governed by commissives are found exclusively in Old Russian sources, mainly in chronicles:

(46) a. и wбѣщасѧ   къ александру, ꙗко   битисѧ
        i <u>oběščasja</u> kъ aleksandru, jako <u>bitisja</u>
        and promise.AOR.3SG to Alexander.DAT COMP fight.INF
        самѣма,
        saměma,
        themselves.DAT

b. ὑπέσχετο... μονομαχῆσαι
hupescheto... monomachēsai
promise.AOR.3SG fight.INF
'And he promised Alexander that they would fight a duell' (*Alexandria*, cited after Istrin 1893: 83)

(47) цѣлоуи крⷭ҇тъ ꙗко имѣти братью въ любовъ
cělui kr<ьs>tъ jako iměti bratju vъ ljubovъ
kiss.IMP.2SG cross.ACC COMP have.INF brothers.ACC in peace
'kiss the cross to live in peace with your brothers' (*Kievan chronicle*, PSRL II: 318)

(48) извѣсти ми сѧ. ꙗко ти его. не
izvěsti mi sja jako ti ego ne
assure.IMP.2SG I.DAT REFL COMP you.DAT it.ACC not
ꙗвити никомуже
javiti nikomuže
tell.INF nobody.DAT
'assure me you would not tell anyone about it' (*Kievan chronicle*, PSRL II: 512)

(49) клѧласѧ бо бѣста. ꙗко wставшю
kljalasja bo běsta, jako ostavšu
swear.LPTCP.DU.M PTCL AUX.PST.3DU COMP having_stayed
в животѣ племени его. любовь имѣти
v životě plemeni ego l'ubovь iměti
in life kinfolk his peace have.INF
'they swore that the one who stays alive would live in peace with his kinfolk' (*Galician Chronicle*, PSRL II: 719)

A commissive predicate may involve a noun:

(50) и води и кр(с)тоу. како
i vodi i kr<ь>(s)tu, kako
and he_made_kiss him cross COMP
емоу не востати на рать
jemu ne vostati na ratь
him not make.INF in war.ACC
'and he made him kiss the cross not to make war' (*Kievan chronicle*, PSRL II: 689)

(51) а   поручникъ   бы(с̃)   Левъ.   ѩко
    a   poručnikъ   by(s)<tь>   Levъ,   jako
    and   guarantor.NOM be.COP.AOR.3SG   Lev.NOM   COMP
    вѣрноу   емоу   быти
    věrnu   emu   byti
    faithful.DAT he.DAT   be.INF
    'and Lev was the guarantor that he would be faithful' (*Galician Chronicle*, PSRL II: 829)

It seems reasonable to assume that purpose predicates and commissives govern the same construction because they are semantically very close: commissives serve to explicit purpose verbally through a speech act.

To summarize the above discussion, infinite constructions attached by conjunctions were more or less regularly used in medieval Slavonic languages in certain environments, whereas in Church Slavonic, a conjunction between a matrix clause and the participle or the infinitive in the constructions in question was forbidden. Eventually, infinite clauses fell into disuse. The extinction of these constructions in Slavonic languages is at least partly due to the fact that they were absent from Greek and, consequently, from authoritative Church Slavonic texts.

3 Collocations with light verbs

Permanent revisions of Church Slavonic translations according to their Greek originals reduced the use of productive collocations which included abstract nouns in the accusative and support verbs with the meaning 'to do', 'to make', 'to have', 'to give', 'to take' since these combinations were equivalents of a single Greek word.
According to SJS, the following collocations with the verbs имѣти *iměti* 'to have' and творити *tvoriti* 'to do', 'to make' are registered in Old Church Slavonic.

3.1 Collocations with имѣти, *iměti* 'to have'

завистъ *zavistъ* 'envy' > завистъ имѣти *zavistъ iměti* 'to envy' = φθονέομαι *phthoneomai*;
болѣзнь *bolězn'* 'disease' > болѣзни имѣти *bolězni iměti* 'to suffer pain' = ἀλγύνομαι *algunomai*;

мѫдрость mǫdrostь 'wisdom' > мѫдрость имѣти mǫdrostь iměti 'to be wise' = φρονέω phroneō;

стоудъ studъ 'shame' > стоудъ имѣти studъ iměti 'to be ashamed' = ἀναισχυντέω anaischunteō;

печаль pečalь 'sorrow' > печаль имѣти pečalь iměti 'to be sad' = περίλυπος εἶναι perilupos einai (SJS I 767–768).

3.2 Collocations with творити, tvoriti 'to do'

блѫдъ blǫdъ 'fornication' > блѫдъ творити blǫdъ tvoriti 'to fornicate' = πόρνος pornos, (ἐκ)πορνεύω ekporneuō, προσφθείρω prosphtheirō;

иzоуньшина izunьšina 'relief, release' > иzоуньшинѫ творити izunьšinǫ tvoriti 'to release (from difficulty)' (hapax of Supr) = λύω luō;

коуплıа kuplja 'purchase' > коуплıѫ творити kupljǫ tvoriti 'to trade' = πραγματεύομαι pragmateuomai;

любы ljuby 'love' > любы творити ljuby tvoriti 'to fornicate' = πορνεύω porneuō;

молитва molitva 'prayer' > молитвѫ творити molitvǫ tvoriti 'to pray' = ἐπεύχομαι epeuchomai, προσεύχομαι proseuchomai, συνεύχομαι suneuchomai;

нѫжда nǫžda 'coercion' > нѫждѫ творити nǫždǫ tvoriti 'to coerce' = βιάζομαι biazomai, καταναγκάζομαι katanagkazomai;

обида obida 'injustice' > обидѫ творити obidǫ tvoriti 'to do wrong, injure' = ἀδικέω adikeō, ἐπηρεάζω epēreazō;

огавие ogavije 'annoyance' > огавие творити ogavije tvoriti 'to cause one much annoyance' = παρενοχλέω parenochleō;

отъвѣтъ otъvětъ 'excuse' > отъвѣтъ творити otъvětъ tvoriti 'to speak in defence' = ἀπολογέομαι apologeomai;

пакость pakostь 'injury, harm' > пакость творити pakostь tvoriti 'to injury, harm' = βλάπτω blaptō, ἀδικέω adikeō, ἐπηρεάζω epēreazō, πολεμέω polemeō, ἐνοχλέω enochleō, κολαφίζω kolaphizō, ἐπιπλήττω epiplēttō, βιάζομαι biazomai;

прѣлюбы prěljuby 'fornication' > прѣлюбы творити prěljuby tvoriti 'to fornicate' = μοιχεύω moicheuō, πορνεύω porneuō;

съвѣтъ sъvětъ 'counsel' > съвѣтъ творити sъvětъ tvoriti 'to take counsel' = βουλεύομαι būleuomai;

трѣба trěba 'sacrifice' > трѣбѫ творити trěbǫ tvoriti 'to sacrifice' = θυσιάζω thysiazō, θύω thyō;

тъщета tъščeta 'damage' > тъщетѫ творити tъščetǫ tvoriti 'to do damage' = ἀδικέω adikeō, ζημιόω zēmioō (SJS IV: 437).

Russian chronicles feature collocations borrowed from Church Slavonic – for example, зъло / пакость (съ)творити *zъlo / pakostь (sъ)tvoriti* 'to harm' – as well as others, specific ones, e. g. възѩти / дати / сътворити миръ *vъzęti / dati / sъtvoriti mirъ* 'to make peace'. Novgorodian birchbark letters are especially abundant in such collocations: исправоу оучинити *ispravu učiniti* 'to arrange' (№ 361), зъло имѣти *zъlo iměti* 'to be angry' (№ 752), коуплю дѣѩти *kuplju dějati* 'to trade' (№ 877/572), миръ възѩти *mirъ vъzęti* 'to make peace' (№ 286), тѧжоу дѣѩти *tęžu dějati* 'to bring a case to court' (№ 831), оухо дати *uxo dati* 'to witness' (№ 25), въдати роукоу *vъdati ruku* 'to vouch' (Staraja Russa № 43), дати роукоу *dati ruku* 'idem' (№ 531), дати пороукоу *dati poruku* 'idem' (№ 389), даѩти дары *dajati dary* 'to present, to give gifts' (№ 831), (see Zaliznjak 2004).

The Slavonic Gospel text that has undergone multiple revisions demonstrates a persistent tendency to replace light-verb collocations by denominal verbs. The process of substitution began very early. According to the Greek-Slavonic Index, the Greek verb ἀπιστέω *apisteō* 'not to believe', which is translated in the Gospel both by the single-word equivalent невѣровати *nevěrovati* and the idiomatic utterance не ѩти / имѣти вѣры *ne jęti / iměti věry*, has the only counterpart невѣровати *nevěrovati* in the Apostle (ŘSl 6: 382). In the Didactic Gospel, compiled by Constantine of Preslav, the collocation вѣрѫ ѩти *věrǫ jęti* is used only once, the verb вѣровати *věrovati* 'believe' many times. Subsequently, denominal verbs substituted for light-verb collocations more and more intensively. As a result of revising the Bible texts in the 13th-14th centuries, the latter have been almost completely removed from Church Slavonic writings.

The expansion of denominal verbs may be illustrated by lexical substitutions made in various redactions of the Slavonic Gospel and Apostle (variant readings from Gospel manuscripts are cited according to Alekseev et al. 1998, Alekseev et al. 2005)[4]:

---

[4] Ar – f. 178, no. 1666 in the Russian State Library in Moscow, ComG – the Commentated Gospel, Čud – the Čudov New Testament, Db – Q.п.I.55 in the Russian National Library in St-Petersburg, Fl – F.п.I.14 in the Russian National Library in St. Petersburg, Gf – Gilf., no. 1 in the Russian National Library in St-Petersburg, Karp – Khlud., no. 132 in the State Historical Museum in Moscow, Mr – no. 1538 in the National Museum in Belgrade, Ostr – F.п.I.15 in the Russian National Library in St. Petersburg, Tp – f. 381, no.1 in the Russian State Archive of Ancient Documents in Moscow, Vl – f. 113, no.1 in the Russian State Library in Moscow.

Table 1: Lexical substitutions in various redactions of the Slavonic Gospel and Apostle.

		Cyrillo-Methodian translation	Subseqent redactions
ἀπολογέομαι *apologeomai* 'to apologize'	Rom. 2.15	отъвѣтъ даıати *otъvětъ dajati*	отъвѣщати *otъvěštati* – Christinopol Apostle (SJS II: 595)
ἐπηρεάζω *epēreazō* 'to injure, to trouble'	Mt. 5.44	творити напасти *tvoriti napasti*	напастьствовати *napastьstvovati* – Sav, зъломыслити *zъlomysliti* – Fl, искоушати *iskušati* – Čud
	Mt. 26.67	пакости дѣıати *pakosti dějati*	мѫчити *mǫčiti* – Čud
εὐχαριστέω *eucharisteō* 'to thank'	Mt. 15.36	хвалѫ въздати *xvalǫ vъzdati*	похвалити *poxvaliti* – Sav, Karp, благодарьствити *blagodarьstviti* – ComG, благодарити *blagodariti* – Čud
	Mt. 26.27	хвалѫ въздати *xvalǫ vъzdati*	благодарьствити *blagodarьstviti* – ComG, благодарити *blagodariti* – Fl, Čud
	Jn. 6.11, 23	хвалѫ въздати *xvalǫ vъzdati*	благодарити *blagodariti* – ComG, Čud
	Jn. 11.41	хвалѫ въздаıати *xvalǫ vъzdati*	благодарити *blagodariti* – Čud
κρίνομαι *krinomai* 'to judge'	Mt. 5.40	сѫдъ приıати *sǫdъ prijęti*	сѫдитисѧ *sǫditisę* – ComG, сѫдити *suditi* – Čud
μοιχάομαι *moichaomai* 'to fornicate'	Mt. 5.32	прѣлюбы дѣıати *prěljuby dějati*	любодѣıати *ljubodějati* – Preslav full Lectionary, любодѣиствовати *ljubodějstvovati* – ComG, Čud, прѣлюбодѣıати *prěljubodějati* – Fl, Vl

Table 1 (continued)

		Cyrillo-Methodian translation	Subseqent redactions
μοιχεύω *moicheuō* 'to fornicate'	Mt. 5.27	прѣлюбы сътворити *prěljuby sъtvoriti*	любодѣıати *ljubodějati* – Preslav full Lectionary, прѣлюбодѣиствовати *prěljubodějstvovati* – ComG, Fl, Čud
	Mt. 5.28	прѣлюбы сътворити *prěljuby sъtvoriti*	прѣлюбодѣиствовати *prěljubodějstvovati* – Fl, любодѣиствовати *ljubodějstvovati* – Čud
πιστεύω *pisteuō* 'to believe'	Mt. 21.25, Jn. 5.46 bis	вѣрѫ ıати *věrǫ jęti*	вѣровати *věrovati* – Preslav full Lectionary, ComG, Mr, Fl, Čud
	Mt. 21.32	вѣрѫ ıати *věrǫ jęti*	вѣровати *věrovati* – Preslav full Lectionary, ComG, Čud
	Mt. 24.23	вѣрѫ ıати *věrǫ jęti*	вѣровати *věrovati* – Preslav full Lectionary, ComG, Fl, Čud
	Mt. 24.26	вѣрѫ ıати *věrǫ jęti*	вѣровати *věrovati* – Čud
	Mt.27.42, Jn.19.35	вѣрѫ ıати *věrǫ jęti*	вѣровати *věrovati* – ComG, Fl, Čud
	Jn. 1.7	вѣрѫ ıати *věrǫ jęti*	вѣровати *věrovati* – ComG (commentaries), Čud
	Jn. 2.22	вѣрѫ ıати *věrǫ jęti*	вѣровати *věrovati* – ComG, Db, Čud
	Jn. 4.21, 48	вѣрѫ ıати *věrǫ jęti*	вѣровати *věrovati* – Čud
	Jn. 4.50	вѣрѫ ıати *věrǫ jęti*	вѣровати *věrovati* – ComG, Gf, Čud
	Jn. 5.24	вѣрѫ ıати *věrǫ jęti*	вѣровати *věrovati* – ComG, Tp, Čud
	Jn. 9.36	вѣрѫ ıати *věrǫ jęti*	вѣровати *věrovati* – ComG, Gf, Db, Fl, Čud
	Jn. 11.48, 13.19	вѣрѫ ıати *věrǫ jęti*	вѣровати *věrovati* – ComG, Db, Čud
	Jn.14.29	вѣрѫ ıати *věrǫ jęti*	вѣровати *věrovati* – Ostr, ComG, Db, Čud
	Jn. 17.21	вѣрѫ ıати *věrǫ jęti*	вѣровати *věrovati* – Ar, ComG, Čud

Table 1 (continued)

		Cyrillo-Methodian translation	Subseqent redactions
	Jn. 5.38, 5.47 bis, 6.30, 8.24, 45, 46, 9.18, 10.37, 38 bis, 11.15, 26, 42, 20.25	вѣрѫ ѩти *věrǫ jęti*	вѣровати *věrovati* – ComG, Čud
προσεύχομαι *proseuchomai* 'to pray'	Mt. 23.13	молитвѫ творити *molitvǫ tvoriti*	молитисѧ *molitisę* – Preslav full Lectionary, ComG, Mr, Fl, Čud
συμβουλεύω *symbouleuō* 'to take counsel'	Jn. 18.14	дати / сътворити съвѣтъ *dati / sъtvoriti sъvětъ*	съвѣщати *sъvěštati* – ComG, Čud

In the East Slavonic region, collocations including light verbs and abstract nouns continued to be used in business language and even became one of its characteristic features. They returned to Russian literary language in the 18th–19th centuries under the influence of European languages.

4 Word order

Church Slavonic translations from Greek imitated, among other things, the word order of their originals. In some cases, it resulted in the limitation and elimination of word orders fitting the Slavonic syntactic norm. This is exemplified, in particular, by the behavior of enclitics.

It is well known that the placement of enclitics in Old Church Slavonic texts followed the word order of their Greek originals and thus violated Wackernagel's law, which was obeyed by spoken Slavonic languages (Zaliznjak 2008). According to this law, for instance, the reflexive particle сѧ *sę* must occupy the second position following the first stressed word within its clause. But in Greek, the reflexive ending was inseparable from its verb, so in Slavonic translations the particle сѧ *sę* tends to follow its own verb but not the first stressed word of the clause. A. Zaliznjak (2008: 208–213) illustrates the frequency of the instances where the particle сѧ *sę* occupies its position according to Wackernagel's law by data summarized in Table 2 below. It shows that such instances occur mostly in original Slavonic writings and are very rare in translations (the Hexaemeron of Johann Exarch is an exception):

Table 2: Enclitic particle сѧ *sę* in Wackernagel position according to Zaliznjak 2008.

Life of St. Methodius	68%
Hexaemeron of Johann Exarch	70%
Novgorodian birchbark letters from 12th–13th centuries	77%
Kievan chronicle of 12th century (speech of personages)	65%
Sinai Psalter	2%
Codex Marianus	6%
Codex Suprasliensis	16%
Studite Typikon	0,6%
Jewish War	7%
Life of St. Theodosius of the Caves	3%
Tale of SSt. Boris and Gleb	5%

In spoken Russian, the particle сѧ *sę* gradually lost the ability to separate from the verb, but in Church Slavonic this process was much more intensive due to the influence of Greek patterns.

It seems that Greek influence supported free word order in Slavonic languages and weakened the tendency of its grammaticalization, which can be noticed in original Slavonic writings. Solid evidence has been recently provided by Ulitova (2016) in support of the claim that prenominal attributes already prevailed in the 17th century both in Russian business language and in Russian Church Slavonic writings – though in the latter to a lesser degree because the Greek influence through the medium of Church Slavonic inhibited the generalization of the preposition of attributes. In medieval Greek, there were no possessive adjectives and possessive pronouns were rare; possession was shown by a noun in the genitive case placed in postposition. In Slavonic translations, the latter were translated by possessive adjectives or pronouns that retained the postposition of Greek genitive attributes (Večerka 1989: 85–86; Minlos 2012: 22). This holds true also for medieval Croatian texts (Sudec 2013). The Greek model accounts for the postposition of the adjectives *божий božij* 'God's', *господень gospodenь* 'Lord's', *Давидовъ Davidovъ* 'David's', *человѣческий čelověčeskij* 'human', etc. as well as of possessive pronouns *мои moj* 'my', *твои tvoj* 'your', etc. in Church Slavonic writings. This pattern could have served as a model for non-possesive bookish adjectives like *велии velij* 'big' et al.

There is a range of other constructions not allowed in Church Slavonic because of their absence from Greek – for instance, repetition of prepositions before postpositive attributes, *nominativus absolutus*, certain models of prepositional government. In all likelihood, this list of constructions, which Slavonic languages have lost at least partly under the Greek influence, is not exhaustive and will be extended if medieval Slavonic texts are examined more thoroughly from this point of view.

References

Alekseev, Anatolij, Anna Pičxadze [Pichkhadze], Maja Babickaja [Babitskaja], Irina Azarova, Elena Alekseeva, Elena Vaneeva, Aleksej Pentkovskij, Varvara Romodanovskaja & Tat'jana Tkačenko [Tkachenko] (eds.). 1998. *Evangelie ot Ioanna v slavjanskoj tradicii* [The Gospel according to John in Slavonic tradition]. Sankt-Peterburg: Rossijskoe biblejskoe obščestvo.

Alekseev, Anatolij, Irina Azarova, Elena Alekseeva, Maja Babickaja [Babitskaja], Elena Vaneeva, Anna Pičxadze [Pichkhadze], Varvara Romodanovskaja & Tat'jana Tkačenko [Tkachenko] (eds.). 2005. *Evangelie ot Matfeja v slavjanskoj tradicii* [The Gospel according to Matthew in Slavonic tradition]. Sankt-Peterburg: Nestor-Istoria.

Ambrazas, Vytautas. 1990. *Sravnitel'nyj sintaksis pričastij baltijskix jazykov* [Comparative syntax of participles in the Baltic languages]. Vilnius: Mokslas.

Arkad'ev, Petr. 2011. Problemy sintaksisa konstrukcij «accusativus cum participio» v litovskom jazyke [On the syntax of «accusativus cum participio» constructions in Lithuanian]. *Voprosy jazykoznanija* 2011(5). 44–75.

Giannakidou, Anastasia. 2001. The Meaning of Free Choice. *Linguistics and Philosophy* 24. 659–735.

Golyšenko [Golyshenko], Vera & Vera Dubrovina (eds.). 1967. *Sinajskij paterik* [The Sinai Patericon]. Moskva: Nauka.

Grigor'ev, Aleksandr. 1913. *Povest' ob Akire Premudrom. Issledovanie i teksty* [The *Tale of Akir the Wise*. A study and the texts]. Moskva: Imperatorskoe obščestvo istorii i drevnostej rossijskix pri Moskovskom universitete.

Haimann, John. 1974. Concessives, conditionals, and verbs of volition. *Foundations of Language: International Journal of Language and Philosophy* 11(3). 341–359.

Istrin, Vasilij. 1893. *Aleksandria russkix xronografov: Issledovaniya i tekst* [The Alexandria of the Russian chronographs. A study and the text]. Moskva: Moskovskij universitet.

Knjazevskaja [Knyazevskaja], Ol'ga, Vladimir Dem'janov [Dem'yanov] & Maja Ljapon [Lyapon]. 1971. *Uspenskij sbornik XII-XIII vv.* [The Uspenskij Miscellany]. Moskva: Nauka.

Markevič A. I. 1892. *Kalužskie kupcy Dexterevy* [The merchants Dexterev from Kaluga]. Odessa: Tipografia V. Kirxnera.

Miklosich, Franz. 1868–1874. *Vergleichende Grammatik der slavischen Sprachen. Bd. IV. Syntax. 2. Theil.* Wien: Wilhelm Braumüller.

Minlos, Philip. 2012. Prenominal and postnominal position of adjective attributes in Old Russian. *Russian Linguistics* 36(1). 21–40.

Moldovan, Alexandr. 2000. *«Žitie Andreja Jurodivogo» v slavjanskoj pis'mennosti* [The *Life of St. Andrew the Fool* in Slavonic writings]. Moskva: Azbukovnik.

Mušinskaja, Marija [Mushinskaya, Maria], Ekaterina Mišina [Mishina] & Vera Golyšenko [Golyshenko] (eds.). 2009. *Izbornik 1076 g.* [The *Izbornik* of 1076]. T. I. Moskva: Rukopisnye pamjatniki Drevnej Rusi.

Pičxadze [Pichkhadze], Anna, Irina Makeeva, Galina Barankova & and Andrej Utkin (eds.). 2004. *«Istoria Iudejskoj vojny» Iosifa Flavija: Drevnerusskij perevod* [The *Jewish War* by Flavius Josephus. The Old Russian translation]. T. I. Moskva: Jazyki slavjanskoj kul'tury.

Pičxadze [Pichkhadze], Anna & Irina Makeeva (eds.). 2008. *«Pčela»: Drevnerusskij perevod* [The *Pčela*: The Old Russian translation]. T. I. Moskva: Rukopisnye pamjatniki Drevnej Rusi.

Pičxadze [Pichkhadze], Anna. 2019. Sojuznyj infinitiv v roli sentencial'nogo aktanta v drevnerusskom [Infinitive complement clauses in Old Russian]. *Voprosy jazykoznanija* 2019(4). 72–84.

Pičxadze [Pichkhadze], Anna. 2020. Slavjanskoe pričastie-skazuemoe v zavisimyx predikacijax [The Slavonic participle predicate in subordinate clauses]. In Anna Pičxadze [Pichkhadze] (ed.), *Očerki drevnerusskogo i starorusskogo sintaksisa*, 256–285. Sankt-Peterburg, Moskva: Nestor-Istoria.

Potebnja, Afanasij A. 1958. *Iz zapisok po russkoj grammatike* [From the notes on Russian grammar]. T. I-II. Moskva: Ministerstvo prosveščenija.

PSRL I – *Polnoe sobranie russkix letopisej. T. I. Lavrent'evskaja letopis'* [Complete collection of Russian chronicles. Vol. 1. The Laurentian chronicle]. Moskva: Jazyki russkoj kul'tury. 1997 [1926–1928].

PSRL II – *Polnoe sobranie russkix letopisej. T. II. Ipat'evskaja letopis'* [Complete collection of Russian chronicles. Vol. 2. The Hypatian chronicle]. Moskva: Jazyki russkoj kul'tury. 1998 [1908].

Růžička, Rudolf. 1963. *Das syntaktische System der altslavischen Partizipien und sein Verhältnis zum Griechischen*. Berlin: Akademie-Verlag.

ŘSI 2012 – *Řecko-staroslověnský index. T. I, fasc. 6.* [Greek – Old Slavonic index. Vol. I. issue 6.] Praha: Slovanský ústav AV ČR.

SJS I-IV – *Slovník jazyka staroslověnského*. T. I-IV. [Dictionary of Old Church Slavonic]. 1966–1997. Praha: Nakladatelství Československé Akademie věd.

Sreznevskij, Izmail I. 1903. *Materialy dlja slovarja drevnerusskogo jazyka* [Materials for an Old Russian Dictionary]. T. III. Sankt-Peterburg: Otdelenie russkogo jazyka i slovesnosti Imperatorskoj Akademii nauk.

Sudec, Sandra. 2013. Položaj pridjeva u imenskoj skupini u hrvatskom crkvenoslavenskom jeziku [Adjective position in noun phrases in the Croatian Church Slavonic Redaction]. *Rasprave Instituta za hrvatski jezik i jezikoslovlje* 39(2). 631–644.

Tatevosov, Sergej. 2002. *Semantika sostavljajuščix imennoj gruppy: kvantornye slova* [The semantics of noun phrase constituents: quantifiers]. Moskva: Nasledie.

Tixomirov, Mixail [Tikhomirov, Mikhail]. 1953. *Posobie dlja izučenia Russkoj pravdy* [A textbook for studying the *Russkaja Pravda*]. Moskva: Izdatel'stvo Moskovskogo universiteta.

Ulitova, Anastasija [Anastasiya]. 2016. *Porjadok slov v atributivnyx slovosočetanijax v pamjatnikax russkoj delovoj i knižnoj pis'mennosti XVII veka* [Word order in attributive phrases in the Russian business and literary writings of the 17th century]. Moskva: Moscow State university thesis.

Vaillant, André. 1977. *Grammaire comparée des langues slaves. T. 5. La syntaxe*. Paris: Éditions Klincksieck.

Večerka, Radoslav. 1989. *Altkirchenslavische (altbulgarische) Syntax I. Die lineare Satzorganisation*. Freiburg i. Br.: U. W. Weiher.

Vlasova, Ekaterina. 2014. Infinitiv i soslagatel'noe naklonenie v kosvennoj reči v russkix letopisjax XI–XVI vv. [The use of infinitive and subjunctive in indirect speech in Russian chronicles of the 11th–16th centuries] *Russkij jazyk v naučnom osveščenii* 1(27). 185–205.

Zaimov, Jordan & Kapaldo, Mario. 1982–1983. Suprasalski ili Retkov sbornik = Supraslskaja rukopis' [*Suprasl' Miscellany*]: V 2 t. / Uvod i koment. na starobălg. tekst Jordan Zaimov; Podbor i koment. na gr. tekst Mario Kapaldo. Sofia: Bălgarska Akademija na naukite.

Zaliznjak [Zaliznyak], Andrej A. 2004. *Drevnenovgorodskij dialekt* [The Old Novgorod dialect]. Moskva: Jazyki slavjanskoj kul'tury.

Zaliznjak [Zaliznyak], Andrej A. 2008. *Drevnerusskie ėnklitiki* [Old Russian enclitics]. Moskva: Jazyki slavjanskix kul'tur.

Jürgen Fuchsbauer
The article-like usage of the relative pronoun *iže* as an indicator of early Slavonic grammatical thinking

Abstract: The Greek definite article can be used for nominalizing non-nominal parts of speech and phrases. From the very beginning of Slavonic literacy, the authors of Old Church Slavonic texts have calqued many such nominalized phrases when translating from Greek, with the relative pronoun *iže* serving as equivalent of the Greek article. The present paper examines how these structural calques came to be used in Church Slavonic. Of course, the cause was Constantine's Greek understanding of language. It will be argued that the somewhat surprising choice of the relative pronoun has its reason in the terminology he was accustomed to: in traditional Greek grammar, the relative pronoun is termed "postposed article". When calquing these constructions, Constantine utilized the relative pronoun because he took it as an article.

Keywords: Old Church Slavonic, relative pronoun, definite article, Greek influence

1 Introduction

As is well known, the Greek definite article ὁ *ho*, ἡ *hē*, τό *to* usually has no lexical correspondent in Church Slavonic. Thus, John 1.4 (example 1a) is rendered in the codex Assemanianus as (1b):

(1) a. ἐν αὐτῷ ζωὴ ἦν, καὶ ἡ
       en aut-ōi zō-ē ē-n, kai hē
       in he-DAT.SG.M life-NOM.SG. be.AOR-3SG and the.NOM.SG.F
       ζωὴ
       zō-ē
       life-NOM.SG
    b. vъ t-omъ život-ъ bě· i život-ъ
       in this-LOC.SG.N life-NOM.SG be.AOR.3SG and life-NOM.SG

Jürgen Fuchsbauer, University of Innsbruck, e-mail: juergen.fuchsbauer@uibk.ac.at

https://doi.org/10.1515/9783110651331-008

a.	ἦν	τὸ	φῶς	τῶν	ἀνθρώπων
	ē-n	to	fō-s	tōn	anthrōp-ōn
	be.AOR-3SG	the.NOM.SG.N	light-NOM.SG	the.GEN.PL	man-GEN.PL
b.	bě		svět-ъ		člk-mъ.¹
	be.AOR.3SG		light-NOM.SG		man-DAT.PL

'In him [in the Logos, J.F.] was life; and the life was the light of men'² (Jn. 1.4)

Slavonic could, as is demonstrated by this example, generally not express the difference between ζωή *zōē* and ἡ ζωή *hē zōē*, 'life' and '*the* life'. The marking of definiteness was limited to noun phrases containing at least one adjective or participle, such as in John 1.9, where Greek (2a) corresponds to Old Church Slavonic (2b) in the codex Zographensis³ (the ending of the adjective is not readable in Assemanianus):

(2)	a.	ἦν	τὸ	φῶς	τὸ	ἀληθινόν
		ē-n	to	fō-s	to	alēthin-on
		be.AOR-3SG	the.NOM.SG.N	light-NOM.SG	the.NOM.SG.N	true-NOM.SG.N
	b.	bě		svět-ъ		ιstinъn-ъι
		be.AOR.3SG		light-NOM.SG		true-NOM.SG.LF

'That was the true Light' (Jn. 1.9)

As is usual in Slavonic, definiteness is expressed here morphologically, namely by the long ending of the adjective tracing back to the anaphoric pronoun **i*, and not, as in Greek, by a lexeme, the article.

Yet, apart from its main function, the expression of definiteness, the Greek definitive article could also be used for "nominalizing" non-nominal parts of speech and phrases, that is, for making non-substantives and non-adjectives function as substantives and adjectives within a sentence.⁴ In such constructions, the Greek article could be rendered in Church Slavonic with the help of the

---

1 My citations of Assemanianus rely on the edition of Vajs and Kurz (Evangeliarum Assemani 1955); the facsimile edition of Ivanova-Mavrodinova and Džurova of 1981 is considered as well.
2 The Greek New Testament is quoted according to the Nestle-Aland edition (1993), the English translations according to the King James Version (https://kingjamesbibleonline.org).
3 Cf. Jagić (1954: 136).
4 E.g. ἄνευ τοῦ ἔχειν λόγον δοῦναι *aneu tou*[GEN.SG.N] *echein*[INF.PRS.ACT] *logon*[ACC.SG] *dounai*[INF.AOR.ACT] 'without having a reason to give' (Plato, Symposium 202a). The article τοῦ *tou* has no other function as to make the infinitive ἔχειν *echein* combinable with the preposition ἄνευ *aneu*, which otherwise governs only substantives, adjectives, numerals, pronouns, and participles. Without the article, the expression would be ungrammatical.

relative pronoun *iže*.⁵ We encounter *iže* as the equivalent of nominalizing Greek articles already in the canonical documents of Old Church Slavonic (OCS). For instance, in Mt 6.23 the Greek text (3a) is rendered as (3b):

(3) a. τὸ   φῶς   τὸ   ἐν   σοὶ
       to   fō-s   to   en   soi
       the.NOM.SG.N light-NOM.SG the.NOM.SG.N in   you.DAT.SG
    b. svět-ъ   iže   vъ   tebě.
       light-NOM.SG. REL.NOM.SG.M in   you.LOC.SG
       'the light that is in thee' (Mt. 6.23)

This is the reading of both the OCS Tetra- (codices Zographensis and Marianus) and Aprakos Gospels (codex Assemanianus and Savina kniga). As we find a considerable number of further instances in the oldest translations from Greek, it is clear that Constantine the Philosopher and his collaborators already introduced this usage of *iže* into the literary language they founded in Constantinople before their departure to the so-called Great Moravian Empire.

In Middle Bulgarian translations from Greek, which surpass earlier translations in terms of the exactness of the rendering of the original, article-like *iže* is even more frequent. In the *Dioptra* we find numerous instances of substantivizing *iže*. For example, (4a) is translated into Slavonic as (4b).

(4) a. καὶ τοῖς   ἐν τῷ   νόμῳ
       kai tois   en tōi   nomō-i
       and the.DAT.PL   in the.DAT.SG.M law-DAT.SG
    b. i   iže   vъ   zakón-ě
       and REL.NOM.SG|PL.M in   law-LOC.SG

    a. καὶ τοῖς   ἐν τῇ   χάριτι
       kai tois   en tēi   charit-i
       and the.DAT.PL.M   in the.DAT.SG.F grace-DAT.SG
    b. i   iže   vъ   bl(a)g(o)/d/(a)t-i
       and REL.NOM.SG|PL.M in   grace-LOC.SG

---

5 Cf., for instance, Minčeva and Džurova (1968: 149–160); Večerka (1996: 176). A fairly inconsistent overview of the usage of *iže* as equivalent of the Greek article was given already by Dobrovský (1822: 608–611).

a. εἴθισται
   eithi-stai
   PRF.accustom-3SG.MED
b. *ωbyčn-o*   *estъ*.
   common-NOM.SG.N   be.PRS.3SG
   'it is common for those under the law and those in the grace'
   Dioptra P.a.6 (Miklas and Fuchsbauer 2013: 334–335)

However, the article-like usage of *iže* was not restricted to translations. We encounter it also in original works such as Euthymius of Tărnovo's *Life of Parasceva of Epibatai*; e.g.:

(5) *blagodějanï-a*   *že*   ... *jaže*   *vъ*   *epïvat-ochъ*,
    good_deed-ACC.PL   PTCL   REL.NOM|ACC.PL.N   in   Epibatai-LOC.PL
    jaže   *vъ*   *trakï-i*
    REL.NOM|ACC.PL.N   in   Thrace-LOC.SG
    'the good deeds ... which (she performed) in Epibatai, in Thrace'
    (Werke des Patriarchen... 1901: 60)

Instances of article-like *iže* occur also in Old Russian Church Slavonic, but far less frequently than in Middle Bulgarian. For example, in the *Tale of Dracula* we find the sentence

(6) *i*   *kako*   *t-i*   *sut'*,   *iže*   *na*
    and   how   this-NOM.PL.M   be.PRS.3PL   REL.NOM.SG|PL.M   on
    kolï-i
    stake-LOC.SG
    'And how are these that are on the stake?'
    (Povest' o Drakule 1964: 119)

Iže na kolïi again patterns the Greek construction without having a Greek model. Alternatively, this sentence might be understood as an elliptic relative clause, in which the copula is missing. Yet, the language of the main part of this text, which was written during the time of the second South Slavonic influence on Russian, is an archaic Church Slavonic (cf. Fuchsbauer 2021: 245–250). It is not unlikely that its author imitated a construction which he had become familiar with through the South Slavonic manuscripts then abundant in the *Rus'*.

Thus, the article-like usage of *iže* was firmly established in the Church Slavonic literary language. To the best of my knowledge, the question of how and why the relative pronoun came to be used as an – obviously – artificial correspondent to the

Greek article has not been solved yet. The following is another attempt at answering this hereto unanswered question.

2 The first occurrrences of *iže* as equivalent of the Greek article

According to the testimony of chapter XIV of his *Life*, Constantine the Philosopher started translating from *iskoni bě slovo*, that is from John 1.1 – ἐν ἀρχῇ ἦν ὁ λόγος *en archēi ēn ho logos*. As this is the beginning of the Aprakos, and not the Tetra-Gospel, it is generally assumed that the respective text, the first one translated to Slavonic, was indeed a short Aprakos Gospel like the one contained in the codex Assemanianus (cf., for instance, Koch 2000: 11–12). Therefore, this manuscript (MS) shall be the basis of argumentation for the remainder of this paper. In Assemanianus we encounter the first occurrence of *iže* as equivalent of the Greek article in line 16 of the first column of folio 4 verso.

(7) a. ὃν   ἔγραψεν   Μωϋσῆς   ἐν   τῷ
       hon   e-grap-s-en   Mōusē-s   en   tōi
       who.ACC.SG.M PST-write-AOR-3SG Moses-N.SG in the.DAT.SG.M
       νόμῳ
       nom-ōi
       law-DAT.SG
    b. *ego-že*   *pisa*   *mosi*   *vъ* *zakon-ě*
       REL.GEN/ACC.SG write.AOR.3SG Moses.N.SG in   law-LOC.SG

    a. καὶ οἱ   προφῆται   εὑρήκαμεν,
       kai hoi   prophēt-ai   heurē-ka-men,
       and the.NOM.PL.M   prophet-NOM.PL   find-PRF-1PL
    b. *i*   *pr/r/c-i:*   *obrět-omъ·*
       and   prophet-NOM.PL   find-AOR.1PL

    a. Ἰησοῦν   υἱὸν   τοῦ   Ἰωσὴφ
       Iēsou-n   huio-n   tou   Iōsēph
       Jesus-ACC.SG   son-ACC.SG   the.GEN.SG Joseph
    b. *iś-a·*   *sn̄-a*   *iosif-ov-a·*
       Jesus-GEN/ACC.SG son-GEN/ACC.SG   Joseph-POSS-GEN/ACC.SG

a. τὸν   ἀπὸ   Ναζαρέτ.
   ton   apo   Nazaret.
   the.ACC.SG.M of   Nazareth
b. iže   o/t/ nazaret-a.
   REL.NOM.SG.M of   Nazareth

'We have found him, of whom Moses in the law, and the prophets, did write, Jesus of Nazareth, the son of Joseph.' (Jn. 1.45[6])

Presuming that the short Aprakos Gospel was indeed the first text translated into Slavonic, this quote would mark the beginning of the article-like usage of *iže*. When Constantine and his helpers (*sъpospešnici*) translated the original phrase, they decided to render the Greek article τὸν *ton* as the Slavonic relative pronoun.[7]

In the codex Assemanianus we encounter before folio 4 verso containing John 1.45 some instances in which Constantine and his helpers did not use *iže* as the equivalent of the Greek substantivizing and attributizing articles.[8] Cf. Luke 24.16 in the Greek original (8a) and its OCS translation in lines 9–11 of the first column of folio 3 recto of Assemanianus (8b):

(8) a. οἱ   δὲ   ὀφθαλμοὶ   αὐτῶν
       hoi   de   ophthalm-oi   aut-ōn
       the.NOM.PL.M   PTCL   eye-NOM.PL   he-GEN.PL
       ἐκρατοῦντο
       e-krat-ounto
       PST-hold-IMPERF.3PL.MED

---

[6] Vajs and Kurz (Evangeliarium Assemani 1955: 8) give the verse number 46 (verse 38 is split here in two).

[7] In a recent paper Ol'ga Strachova (2015) adopted and discussed Pentkovskij's idea that in preparation of the mission to Rastislav's principality in 862/63 a liturgical Tetra-Gospel, and not a short Aprakos Gospel, was translated. If this was indeed the case, the first occurrence of article-like *iže* would be Mt. 6.23, which I quoted above (τὸ φῶς τὸ ἐν σοὶ – *světъ iže vъ tebě*, cf. example 3). As this corresponds structurally to Ἰησοῦν . . . τὸν ἀπὸ Ναζαρέτ – *iśa . . . iže o/t/ nazareta*, the conclusions to be drawn would be just the same.

[8] There are two further instances except for the two quoted in the text above (i.e. Lk. 24.16 and 24.33 – cf. example 10), Ὁ ὀπίσω μου ἐρχόμενος *Ho*$_\text{NOM.SG.M}$ *opisō mou*$_\text{GEN.SG}$ *erchomenos*$_\text{PTCP.PRS.MED.NOM.SG.M}$ – *grędy*$_\text{PTCP.PRS.ACT.NOM.SG.M.DET}$ *po mně*$_\text{LOC.SG}$ 'He that cometh after me' (John 1.15 and John 1.27; Slavonic: Assem. fol. 2r a11s. and fol. 2v c24) and τὰ ἐν τῇ ὁδῷ *ta*$_\text{NOM|ACC.PL.N}$ *en těi*$_\text{DAT.SG.FEM}$ *odōi*$_\text{DAT.SG}$ – *eže* $_\text{REL.NOM.SG.N}$ *byšę*$_\text{AOR.3PL.}$ *na pǫti*$_\text{LOC.SG}$ 'what things were done in the way' (Lk. 24.35; Slavonic: Assem. fol. 4r a1s.). In the latter instance the substantivized prepositional phrase was transformed into a relative clause by adding the copula.

b.	oč-ı	že	drъža-ste	sę
	eye-NOM.DU	PTCL	hold-AOR.3DU	REFL

a.	τοῦ	μὴ	ἐπιγνῶναι	αὐτόν
	tou	mē	epignō-nai	aut-on
	the.GEN.SG.N	not	recognize-AOR.INF.ACT	he-ACC.SG
b.	da	(e)go	ne	pozna-ete
	so_that	he.GEN/ACC.SG	not	recognize-AOR.3DU

'But their eyes were holden that they should not know him' (Lk. 24.16)

Here, a subordinate clause introduced by *da* corresponds to the Greek substantivized infinitive.[9] Yet, Greek substantivized infinitives were already calqued in the first Slavonic translations. The first instance in Assemanianus, presumably reflecting its first appearance in Slavonic literature on the whole, occurs in line 15 of the second column of fol. 115v; here the Greek original of Mark 12.33 (9a) is rendered in OCS as (9b):

(9) a. καὶ τὸ ἀγαπᾶν αὐτόν κτλ. (cf. example 14)
        kai to agapa-n aut-on
        and the.NOM.SG.N love-PRS.INF.ACT he-ACC.SG
    b. i eže ljubi-ti i etc.[10]
        and REL.NOM|ACC.SG.N love-INF he-ACC.SG.M
        'And to love him ...' (Mk. 12.33)

In John 1.45 (cf. example 7), Constantine might have decided to add a finite verb so as to transform the construction with *iže* into a complete relative clause, as he did in Luke 24.33, where the Greek text (10a) is translated as (10b), which we find in lines 21–25 of the second column of fol. 3v of Assemanianus.

(10) a. καὶ εὗρον ἠθροισμένους τοὺς ἕνδεκα
         kai eur-on ēthrois-men-ous tous hendeka
         and find-AOR.3PL PRF.gather-PTCP.MED-ACC.PL.M the.ACC.PL eleven

---

9 The folio is mutilated here. Parts of the clause were complemented in Cyrillic; however, Glagolitic *d. . . . poznaet.* is clearly legible in Ivanova-Mavrodinova and Džurova's facsimile edition of 1981. There can be no doubt that the initial Glagolitic text had a *da*-construction, and not an infinitive.
10 We find this reading also in the codices Zographensis and Marianus.

b. *i obrěto-ste   sovъ/kou/p-ъš-ę   sę*
   find-AOR.3DU gather-PTCP.PST.ACT-ACC.PL.M REFL
   edinogo na desęte:
   eleven

a. καὶ   τοὺς   σὺν   αὐτοῖς
   kai   tous   sun   aut-ois
   and   the.ACC.PL.M   with he-DAT.PL.M
b. *i   iže   bě-ach-ǫ   sъ   nimi*[11]
   and   REL.NOM.SG|PL.M be-IMPERF-3PL with he.INS.PL
   '[They] found the eleven gathered together, and them that were with them' (Lk. 24.33)

In John 1.45 (cf. example 7), however, he did not insert a finite verb form; *isa· sna iosifova· iže *estъ o/t/ nazareta* would have been perfectly fine – for me, at least. In constructions like this the article-like *iže* is not, as was stated by Večerka (1996: 176), used "als tatsächlicher Artikel zur Hervorhebung der anschließenden Satzglieder bzw. Sätze" [as actual article for the emphasis of subsequent clause constituents and clauses respectively – translation J.F.]. There is no special emphasis here. Its Greek equivalent has a specific syntactic function – it indicates that ἀπὸ Ναζαρέτ *apo Nazaret* is an incongruent attribute to Ἰησοῦν *Iesoun* (in the same way, the article is used obligatorily with a congruent attribute, e.g. Ἰησοῦς ὁ Ναζαρηνός *Iesous ho Nazarēnos* 'Jesus the Nazarene', Mk. 10.47).[12]

In John 1.45 the first translators into Slavonic could have simply left out *iže*, as it is omitted in the modern Russian version of the Gospels (*Iisusa, syna Iosifova, iz Nazareta*); the Vulgate expectably has no equivalent to the article either (*Iesum filium Ioseph a Nazareth*). However, as a Greek, Constantine would have felt the need to express formally that *of Nazareth* represents an attribute to Jesus. According to the model of Greek, he wanted to demonstrate that the prepositional phrase *o/t/ nazareta* is syntactically dependent on the noun *isa*.

---

[11] As is usual, the Vulgate has a relative clause here: *et invenerunt congregatos undecim et eos qui cum ipsis erant*.

[12] A missing article may change the meaning of a clause. For instance, Mk. 15.43 has the two variant readings ἐλθὼν Ἰωσὴφ ὁ ἀπὸ Ἀριμαθαίας *elthōn Iōsēph ho apo Arimathaias* and ἐλθὼν Ἰωσὴφ ἀπὸ Ἀριμαθαίας *elthōn Iōsēph apo Arimathaias*. The first variant, using the article, means 'Joseph of Arimathaea came', the second 'Joseph came from Arimathaea' ('... and went in boldly unto Pilate').

Thus, *iže* came to be used with prepositional phrases functioning as incongruent attributes (5 instances in Assemanianus[13]). In one case, the attribute is formed by a prepositional phrase only in Slavonic, while the original has a genitive.[14] In a further instance, a Slavonic prepositional phrase (which might have been already grammaticalized as an adverb) corresponds to a Greek adverb.[15] In a similar way, *iže* was used for rendering Greek substantivized prepositional phrases, such as in Lk 8.12, where Greek (11a) is translated as (11b) in Assemanianus (fol. 54r a1s.). There are 5 further instances in this MS.[16]

(11) a. οἱ   δὲ   παρὰ τὴν   ὁδόν
       hoi   de   para tēn   hodo-n
       the.NOM.PL.M PTCL by   the.ACC.SG.F way-ACC.SG
    b. eže   pri   pǫt-i
       REL.NOM.SG.N[17] by   way-LOC.SG
       'those by the way side' (Lk. 8.12)

3 The reason for the article-like usage of *iže*

Constantine's wish to render a specific syntactic pattern of his native tongue in Slavonic was presumably unconscious. However, since the Greek article ὁ *ho* has no immediate correspondent in Slavonic, he also had to make a deliberate decision, namely which word to use as its equivalent. Why did he decide for *iže* and not, say, for one of the demonstrative pronouns, which are semantically and

---

13 Mt 6.23 – (cf. example 3), Jn. 1.45 (cf. example 7) and Ἰωσὴφ ὁ ἀπὸ Ἀριμαθαίας *Iōseph*$_{NOM.SG.M}$ *ho apo Arimathaias*$_{GEN.SG}$ – *iosifъ*$_{NOM.SG}$ *iže*$_{REL.NOM.SG.M}$ *w/t/ arimaθeję*$_{GEN.SG}$ 'Joseph of Arimathaea' (Mk. 15.43; Jn. 19.38; Slavonic: Assem. 11v c17–19 and 106r b23s. (bis!); 106v c5–7).
14 ἡ δὲ τοῦ πνεύματος βλασφημία *hē*$_{NOM.SG.F}$ *de tou*$_{GEN.SG.N}$ *pneumatos*$_{GEN.SG}$ *blasphēmia*$_{NOM.SG}$ – *eže*$_{REL.NOM|ACC.SG.N}$ *na d(ou)chъ*$_{ACC.SG}$ *choula*$_{NOM.SG}$ 'the blasphemy against the [Holy] Ghost' (Mt. 12.31; Slavonic: Assem. 40c11s.).
15 οἱ ἐκεῖθεν *hoi*$_{NOM.PL.M}$ *ekeithen* – *iže*$_{REL.NOM.SG|PL.M}$ *otъ tǫdě* 'that would come from thence' (Lk. 16.26; Slavonic: Assem. 55v c9s.).
16 Lk. 8.12 (cf. example 11); ὁ ἐπὶ τοῦ δώματος *ho*$_{NOM.SG.M}$ *epi tou*$_{GEN.SG.N}$ *dōmatos*$_{GEN.SG}$ – *iže*$_{NOM.SG|PL.M.REL}$ *na krověchъ*$_{LOC.PL}$ 'him which is on the housetop' (Mt. 24.17; Slavonic: Assem. 83v c9s.); ὁ ἐν τῷ ἀγρῷ *ho*$_{NOM.SG.M}$ *en tōi*$_{DAT.SG.M}$ *agrōi*$_{DAT.SG}$ – *iže*$_{REL.NOM.SG|PL.M}$ *na selě*$_{LOC.SG}$ 'him which is in the field' (Mt. 24.18; Slavonic: Assem. 83v c13s.); οἱ δὲ ἐπὶ τὴν πέτραν *hoi*$_{NOM.PL.M}$ *de epi tēn*$_{ACC.SG.F}$ *petran*$_{ACC.SG}$ – *eže*$_{REL.NOM|ACC.SG.N}$ *na kameni*$_{LOC.SG}$ 'they on the rock' (Lk. 8.13; Slavonic: Assem. 54r13); τὸ δὲ ἐν τῇ καλῇ γῇ *to*$_{NOM|ACC.SG.N}$ *de en tēi*$_{DAT.SG.F}$ *kalēi*$_{DAT.SG.F}$ *gēi*$_{DAT.SG}$ – *iže*$_{REL.NOM.SG|PL.M}$ *na dobrě*$_{LOC.SG.F}$ *zem/l/i*$_{LOC.SG}$ 'that on the good ground' (Lk. 8.15; Slavonic: Assem. 54r b6s.).
17 Pro *iže* sicut in codice Mariano.

functionally closer to articles than relative pronouns? Since the relative pronoun in constructions with article-like *iže* always stands in the nominative case, they represent, as has already been noticed by Večerka (1996: 174), elliptic relative clauses lacking a finite verb form. Why did the translators not transform the phrase into a full relative clause by adding a finite verb? Indeed, sometimes they inserted a form of *byti* in order to turn phrases containing a substantivizing or attributizing article into complete relative clauses, as in Mt. 24.17:

(12) a. ἆραι   τὰ   ἐκ   τῆς
       ar-ai   ta   ek   tēs
       take-AOR.INF.ACT the.ACC.PL.N from   the.GEN.SG
       οἰκίας   αὐτοῦ
       oikia-s   aut-ou
       house-GEN.SG.   he-GEN.SG.M
    b. vъzę-tъ   iže[18]   estъ   vъ   dom-ou
       take-SUP REL.NOM.SG|PL.M   be.PRS.3SG   in   house-LOC.SG
       ego
       he.GEN.SG.M
       'to take anything out of his house' (Mt. 24.17; Slavonic: Assem. 83c11–13)

In my mind, there is yet another reason why Constantine used the relative pronoun *iže* as equivalent of the Greek article. He was, like any literate Byzantine, acquainted with traditional Greek grammatical thinking. In the *Art of Grammar* commonly ascribed to Dionysius Thrax, a succinct, but enormously influential handbook,[19] the article is defined as follows:

(13) Ἄρθρον ἐστὶ μέρος λόγου πτωτικόν, προτασσόμενον καὶ ὑποτασσόμενον τῆς κλίσεως τῶν ὀνομάτων. καὶ ἔστι προτακτικὸν μὲν ὁ, ὑποτακτικὸν δὲ ὅς (Uhlig 1883, 61).
Arthron esti meros logou ptōtikon, protassomenon kai hupotassomenon tēs kliseōs tōn onomatōn. kai esti protaktikon men ho, hupotaktikon de hos.

'The article is a declinable part of speech, preposed and postposed [or subordinated, J.F.] to the declension of nouns; and the prepositive is ὁ *ho* 'the', the postpositive ὅς *hos* 'who'.'

---

[18] Pro *eže* sicut in codice Mariano.
[19] For a brief overview of this work cf. Dickey (2007: 77–80).

Hence, there is a distinction between two types of articles (ἄρθρα *arthra*), namely the prepositive (προτακτικόν *protaktikon*) and the postpositive or subordinated one (ὑποτακτικόν *hupotaktikon*); the former represents ὁ *ho*, the article proper, the latter ὅς *hos*, the relative pronoun. Thus, when the founders of the Slavonic literary tradition decided to use the relative pronoun *iže* as an equivalent of the Greek article ὁ *ho*, in their conception they used one article, namely the postpositive, instead of the other, the prepositive. For a Greek there is no necessity to add a finite verb to a phrase introduced by an ἄρθρον *arthron*. This is presumably the reason why phrases with article-like *iže* could be left without a finite verb.

Once introduced into Slavonic, article-like *iže* could also be used for calquing another Greek construction which has no immediate equivalent in Slavonic, namely the substantivized infinitive. I already quoted the first instance that occurs in Assemanianus (cf. example 9): on fol. 115v Mark 12.33 Greek (14a) is rendered as (14b):

(14) a. καὶ   τὸ   ἀγαπᾶν   αὐτόν   ...
       kai   to   agapa-n   aut-on   ...
       and   the.NOM.SG.N   love-PRS.INF.ACT   he-ACC.SG.M   ...
   b. i   eže   ljubı-tı   i   ...
       and   REL.NOM.SG.N   love-INF   he.ACC.SG.M

   a. περισσότερόν   ἐστιν
       perisso-ter-on   estin
       great-COMPV-NOM.SG.N   be.PRS.3SG
   b. bole   estъ
       more   be.PRS.3SG

   a. πάντων   τῶν   ὁλοκαυτωμάτων   καὶ
       pant-ōn   tōn   holokautōmat-ōn   kai
       all-GEN.PL.N   the.GEN.PL.N   burnt_offering-GEN.PL   and
       θυσιῶν
       thusi-ōn
       sacrifice-GEN.PL
   b. vъsesъžagae-m-yich   žrъtvъ
       burn_whole-PTCP.PRS.PASS-GEN.PL sacrifice.GEN.PL

   'And to love Him [. . .] is more than all whole burnt offerings and sacrifices.' (Mk. 12.33; Slavonic: Assemanianus fol. 115v d17–116r a3)

Here *eže* is used to convert the infinitive construction into a functional substantive forming the subject of the sentence. In this case we are by no means dealing with an elliptic relative clause – *eže ljubiti i* cannot be complemented by a finite verb form.

Normally, a substantivized Greek infinitive is not rendered by the combination of article and infinitive in the oldest layer of Slavonic translations. In the codex Assemanianus there occur several correspondents of infinitives preceded by τοῦ *tou*, which usually express final meaning, namely final clauses introduced by *da*,[20] supines (after verbs of motion),[21] and, rarely, bare infinitives.[22] A Greek substantivized infinitive forming a part of a prepositional phrase may be translated as a *dativus absolutus*,[23] as a deverbal noun,[24] or as a subordinate clause introduced by *da*,[25] *egda*,[26] *zane*,[27] *prěžde daže ne*,[28] rarely, is an infinitive used

---

20 E.g. ζητεῖν τὸ παιδίον τοῦ ἀπολέσαι αὐτό *zētein*$_{INF.PRS.ACT}$ *to*$_{ACC.SG.N}$ *paidion*$_{ACC.SG}$ *tou*$_{GEN.SG.N}$ *apolesai*$_{INF.AOR.ACT}$ *auto*$_{ACC.SG.N}$ – *iskati*$_{INF}$ *otročjęte*$_{GEN.SG}$· *da pogoubitъ*$_{3SG.PRS}$ *e*$_{ACC.SG.N}$ 'seek the young child to destroy him' (Mt. 2.13; Slavonic: Assem. 134v21s.).

21 E.g. μετέβη ἐκεῖθεν τοῦ διδάσκειν *metebē*$_{PST.3SG.AOR}$ *ekeithen* *tou*$_{GEN.SG.N}$ *didaskein*$_{INF.PRS.ACT}$ – *prěide*$_{3SG.AOR}$ *o/t/ tǫdou oučitъ*$_{SUP}$ 'he departed thence to teach' (Mt. 11.1; Slavonic: Assem. 40r a8s.).

22 E.g. τοῦ δοῦναι θυσίαν κατὰ τὸ εἰρημένον *tou*$_{GEN.SG.N}$ *dounai*$_{INF.AOR.ACT}$ *thusian*$_{ACC.SG}$ *kata to*$_{ACC.SG.N}$ *eirēmenon*$_{PRF.PTCP.PASS.ACC.SG.N}$ – *dati*$_{INF}$ *žrъtvǫ*$_{ACC.SG}$ *po rečenoumou*$_{PTCP.PST.PASS.DAT.SG.N.DET}$ 'to offer a sacrifice according to that which is said' (Lk. 2.24; Slavonic: Assem. 141v21).

23 E.g. ἐν τῷ ὑποστρέφειν αὐτούς *en tōi*$_{DAT.SG.N}$ *hupostrephein*$_{INF.PRS.ACT}$ *autous*$_{ACC.PL.M}$ – *vъzvraštajǫštemъ sę*$_{PTCP.PRS.ACT.DAT.PL.M.MED}$ *imъ*$_{DAT.PL.M}$ 'as they returned' (Lk. 2.43; Slavonic: Assem. 136r14s.).

24 E.g. παραδίδοται εἰς τὸ σταυρωθῆναι *paradidotai*$_{PRS.3SG.PASS}$ *eis to*$_{ACC.SG.N}$ *staurōthēnai*$_{AOR.PASS.INF}$ – *prědanъ*$_{PTCP.PST.PASS.NOM.SG.M}$ *bǫdetъ*$_{FUT.3SG}$ *na raspjętie*$_{ACC.SG}$ 'is betrayed to be crucified' (Mt. 26.2; Slavonic: Assem. 87r b17–19).

25 E.g. πρὸς τὸ θεαθῆναι αὐτοῖς *pros to*$_{ACC.SG.N}$ *theathēnai*$_{AOR.PASS.INF}$ *autois*$_{DAT.PL.M}$ – *da vidimi*$_{PTCP.PRS.PASS.NOM.PL.M}$ *bǫdete*$_{FUT.2.PL}$ *imi*$_{INS.PL.M}$ 'to be seen of them' (Mt. 6.1; Slavonic: Assem. 73r a9–11).

26 E.g. ἐν τῷ κατηγορεῖσθαι αὐτὸν *en tōi*$_{DAT.SG.N}$ *katēgoreisthai*$_{INF.PRS.PASS}$ *auton*$_{ACC.SG.M}$ – *egda na nъ*$_{ACC.SG.M}$ *g(lago)laachǫ*$_{IMPERF.3PL}$ 'when he was accused' (Mt. 27.12; Slavonic: Assem. 107v c5s.).

27 E.g. διὰ τὸ εἶναι αὐτὸν ἐξ οἴκου καὶ πατριᾶς Δαυίδ *dia to*$_{ACC.SG.N}$ *einai*$_{INF.PRS.ACT}$ *auton*$_{ACC.SG.M}$ *ex oikou*$_{GEN.SG}$ *kai patrias*$_{GEN.SG}$ *Dauid* – *zane běaše*$_{IMPERF.3SG}$ *o/t/ domou*$_{GEN.SG}$ *I otč(ь)stviě d(avi)dova*$_{POSS.GEN.SG}$ 'because he was of the house and lineage of David' (Lk. 2.4; Slavonic: Assem. 132v18–20).

28 E.g. πρὸ τοῦ συλλημφθῆναι αὐτὸν ἐν τῇ κοιλίᾳ *pro tou*$_{GEN.SG.N}$ *sullēmphthēnai*$_{AOR.PASS.INF}$ *auton*$_{ACC.SG}$ *en tēi*$_{DAT.SG.F}$ *koiliai*$_{DAT.SG}$ – *prěžde daže ne začętъ sę*$_{3SG.AOR.MED}$ *vъ črěvě*$_{LOC.SG}$ 'before he was conceived in the womb' (Lk. 2.21; Slavonic: Assem. 136r3s.). Sentences starting with ἐγένετο ἐν τῷ *egeneto en tōi* + inf., which are typical of Luke, are often shortened in Assem. in comparison to the other OCS gospel MSS, e.g., Καὶ ἐγένετο ἐν τῷ ἐλθεῖν αὐτὸν εἰς οἶκον *Kai egeneto*$_{PST.AOR.3SG.MED}$ *en tōi*$_{DAT.SG.N}$ *elthein*$_{INF.PRS.ACT}$ *auton*$_{ACC.SG.M}$ *eis oikon*$_{ACC.SG}$ – *vъnide*$_{AOR.3SG}$ *i(isou)sъ*$_{NOM.SG}$ *vъ domъ*$_{ACC.SG}$ 'And it came to pass, as he went into the house' (Lk. 14.1; Slavonic: Assem. 63v c13–15); cf. Marianus: *i bystъ*$_{AOR.3SG}$ *egda vъnide*$_{AOR.3SG}$ *i(isou)sъ*$_{NOM.SG}$ *vъ domъ*$_{ACC.SG}$.

(the preposition is left out,[29] in its place *jako* may appear[30]). As an adnominal attribute a substantivized infinitive is usually rendered by an infinitive without an article.[31] Yet, Greek substantivized infinitives representing the subject of a sentence were unexceptionally transferred to Slavonic as *eže* + infinitive.[32] *Accusativi cum infinitivo* seem to be treated in the same way as bare infinitives.

I would be inclined to conclude that at the time of Constantine-Cyril the Slavonic infinitive, the old locative of an ĭ-stem deverbal noun (cf., for instance, Olander 2015: 172), still had a sufficiently nominal character so that it could fulfil two main nominal functions within a predication. Namely, it represented the subject and the direct object. It was, however, not declinable and, therefore, syntactically less flexible than Greek substantivized infinitives. As a locative it was apparently not particularly suitable for the expression of finality (as opposed to the supine, a petrified accusative of a ŭ-stem deverbal noun), nor could it be combined with prepositions requiring a certain case. *Eže* does not indicate that an appendant infinitive is used as a noun – it is not necessary to mark the nominal character of an infinitive – but that it represents the subject of a sentence.

The identification of *iže* with the Greek article is also reflected in the most important and most wide-spread Slavonic work on grammar before the grammars of L. Zyzanij and M. Smotryc'kyj were published, namely in the treatise *On the Eight Parts of Speech*. This text relies on several Greek sources, among them the *Art of Grammar*. It represents, however, not a translation but an adaptation of Greek grammatical thinking to Slavonic. The Slavonic treatise was presumably composed not in the 10th century by John the Exarch, to whom it is attributed in

---

29 E.g. καὶ δύναμις κυρίου ἦν εἰς τὸ ἰᾶσθαι αὐτόν (pro: αὐτοὺς) *kai dunamis*$_{NOM.SG}$ *kuriou*$_{GEN.SG}$ *ēn*$_{AOR.3SG}$ *eis to*$_{ACC.SG.N}$ *iasthai*$_{INF.PRS.MED}$ *auton*$_{ACC.SG.M}$ – *i sila*$_{NOM.SG}$ *g(ospod)ně*$_{POSS.NOM.SG.F}$ *bě*$_{AOR.3SG}$ *cěliti*$_{INF}$ *j̨ę*$_{ACC.PL.M}$ 'and the power of the Lord was present to heal them' (Lk. 5.17; Slavonic: Assem. 51r a18–20).

30 E.g. πρὸς τὸ κατακαῦσαι αὐτά *pros to*$_{ACC.SG.N}$ *katakausai*$_{AOR.INF.ACT}$ *auta*$_{ACC.PL.N}$ – *eko sъžešti*$_{INF}$ *j̨ę*$_{ACC.PL.M|F}$ 'to burn them' (Mt. 13.30; Slavonic: Assem. 126v7).

31 Eg. Τῇ δὲ Ἐλισάβετ ἐπλήσθη χρόνος τοῦ τεκεῖν αὐτὴν *Tēi*$_{DAT.SG.F}$ *de Elisabet eplēsthē*$_{PST.3SG.AOR.MED}$ *chronos*$_{NOM.SG}$ *tou*$_{GEN.SG.N}$ *tekein*$_{INF.PRS.ACT}$ *autēn*$_{ACC.SG.F}$ – *Elisabeti*$_{DAT.SG}$ *že isplъnišę sę*$_{AOR.3PL.MED}$ *denie*$_{COLL}$.Nom$_{SG}$ *roditi*$_{INF}$ *ei*$_{DAT.SG.F}$ 'Now Elisabeth's full time came that she should be delivered' (Lk. 1.57; Slavonic: Assem. 149r18s.).

32 Cf. example 14 above. There are only two further instances in Assemanianus, namely τὸ δὲ καθίσαι ἐκ δεξιῶν μου *to*$_{NOM|ACC.SG.N}$ *de kathisai*$_{AOR.INF.ACT}$ *ek dexiōn*$_{GEN.PL}$ *mou*$_{GEN}$ – A *eže*$_{REL.NOM|ACC.SG.N}$ *sěsti*$_{INF}$ *o desnǫjǫ*$_{ACC.SG.F.LF}$ *mene*$_{GEN.SG}$ 'But to sit on my right hand' (Mk. 10.40; Slavonic: Assem. 79r a24s.) and καὶ τὸ ἀγαπᾶν τὸν πλησίον ὡς ἑαυτὸν *kai to*$_{NOM|ACC.SG.N}$ *agapan*$_{INF.PRS.ACT}$ *ton*$_{ACC.SG.M}$ *plēsion*$_{ACC.SG.M}$ *hōs heauton*$_{ACC.SG.M}$ – *i eže*$_{REL.NOM|ACC.SG.N}$ *ljubiti*$_{INF}$ *iskrъněago*$_{GEN.SG.M.LF}$ *aky sebe*$_{GEN.SG}$ 'and to love his neighbour as himself' (Mk. 12.33 bis!; Slavonic: Assem. 115v d23–26).

some witnesses, but in early 14th century Serbia, Macedonia, or on Mount Athos (cf. Weiher 1977: 367). Referring to articles, it is stated towards the end of the text:

(15) "*Različie /ž/ je/s/ čestъ jedina ѡsmъ čestiĭ slova. skazatelno padežemъ samo ѡ sebě. i je/g/da glj̃emъ. iže, razli[č]je javichѡ/m/ pravou jedinъstvъnou mouž'skago imene.* (fol. 8r1–4)

[The article (literally: the discrimination) is one of the eight parts of speech, indicating cases by itself, and if we say *iže* we show the discrimination of the casus rectus singular of the masculine noun. – translation J.F.]"[33]

Then the Slavonic grammarian comments:

(16) "*padenija že imenъ različija ne trěboujutъ vъ slověn'skomъ jezycě. niže imoutъ prě/d/čin'ni/ch/* (fol. 8r11–13)

[The cases of nouns do not require an article in the Slavonic language, and they do not have prepositive ones – translation J.F.]"

However, they have, as he adds, "postpositive ones". Also, in connection with the infinitive the Slavonic grammarian points out that it may take an article:

(17) "*těm'že i različije imenou prijemletъ. jakože se. ježe čisti polъzno* (fol. 5v10–12)
[Thus the infinitive takes the article of the noun, as in *ježe čisti polъzno* – translation J.F.]"

Like Constantine, the compiler of this work considers *iže* to be an article, namely, the postpositive one, which can also be used for substantivizing infinitives.[34]

---

[33] This is a quotation according to the oldest MS, codex No 84 of Hilferding's collection in the National Library of Russia, which was edited by Weiher in 1977.
[34] In the preface to his translation of homilies of Isaac Syrus Paisij Veličkovskij (1722–1794) states that Greek has prepositive and postpositive articles (*prediduščyję i posledujuščyję arθry*), which are lacking in Slavonic; pronouns like *iže, onъ, sej, toj* are used instead (cf. Linţa 1983: 25–26 and Trunte 2006: 253–254). He seems not to be realizing that the traditional term *postpositive article* refers to relative pronouns.

4 Conclusion

The artificial introduction of a construction foreign to Slavonic, its further usage, as well as reflections on it, like the ones quoted, give us insight into the way Constantine the Philosopher, his helpers, and their successors reasoned on the language they created and used. For Constantine, as a Greek, nominalizing prepositional phrases and infinitives with the help of the ἄρθρον *arthron* available in Slavonic, *iže*, was only natural, and it was adopted by his Slavonic followers. On the whole, the article-like usage of *iže* is proof of a sometimes fairly methodical, but partly inadequate treatment of language, which does not necessarily correspond to modern conceptions. It relies on Constantine's Greek sense of language and on traditional Greek grammatical thinking, and we will need to bear this in mind when analysing older stages of Slavonic.

References

CCMH – *Corpus Cyrillo-Methodianum Helsingiense*. http://www.helsinki.fi/slaavilaiset/ccmh/ (accessed 27 February 2019).

Dickey, Eleanor. 2007. *Ancient Greek scholarship. A guide to finding, reading, and understanding scholia, commentaries, lexica, and grammatical treatises, from their beginnings to the Byzantine period*. Oxford: Oxford University Press.

Dobrovský, Josef. 1822. *Institutiones linguae slavicae dialecti veteris*. Wien: Typographie Anton Schmid.

Evangeliarium Assemani. 1955. *Evangeliarium Assemani. Codex Vaticanus 3. slavicus glagoliticus. Editio phototypica cum prolegomenis, textu litteris cyrillicis transcripto, analysi, annotationibus palaeographicis, variis lectionibus, glossario. Ediderunt Josef Vajs, Josef Kurz. Tomus II*. Prague: Academia Scientiarum Bohemoslovenicae.

Fuchsbauer, Jürgen. 2021. Zu Textüberlieferung und Autorschaft der altrussischen Draculaerzählung. In Jürgen Fuchsbauer & Emanuel Klotz (eds.), *Studien zum frühen Slavischen und zu älteren slavischen Texten. Unter Mitarbeit von Hanna Niederkofler*, 241–270. Berlin: Peter Lang.

Ivanova-Mavrodinova, Vera & Aksinija Džurova. 1981. *Asemanievoto evangelie. Starobălgarski glagoličeski pametnik ot X vek* [The Assemanianus Gospel: an Old Bulgarian Glagolitic Monument from the 10th century]. Sofia: Nauka i izkustvo.

Jagić, Vatroslav. 1954 [1879]. *Quattuor evangeliorum codex glagoliticus olim Zographensis nunc Petropolitanus*. Graz: Akademische Druck- und Verlagsanstalt.

King James Bible. http://www.kingjamesbibleonline.org (accessed 27 February 2019).

Koch, Christoph. 2000. *Kommentiertes Wort- und Formenverzeichnis des altkirchenslavischen Codex Assemanianus*. Freiburg i. Br.: Weiher.

Linţa, Elena. 1983. Paisij Veličkovski – edin između poslednite golemi cărkovnoslavjanski knižovnici [Paisij Veličkovski – one of the last great persons of Church Slavonic literacy]. *Palaeobulgarica* 7(3). 14–42.

Miklas, Heinz & Jürgen Fuchsbauer. 2013. *Die kirchenslavische Übersetzung der Dioptra des Philippos Monotropos. Band 1. Überlieferung. Text der Programmata und des ersten Buches.* Wien: Holzhausen.

Minčeva, Andželina & Aksinija Džurova. 1968. Anaforičeskoe upotreblenie drevnebolgarskogo mestoimenija *iže* v konstrukcijach s suščestvitel'nymi (K voprosu o grečeskom vlijanii na drevnebolgarskij sintaksis) [The anaphoric usage of the Old Bulgarian pronoun *iže* in constructions with nouns (On the question of Greek influence on Old Bulgarian syntax)]. In *Actes du premier congres international des études balkaniques et sud-est européennes. Tom VI. Linguistique,* 149–160. Sofia: BAN.

Nestle, Eberhard, Erwin Nestle & Kurt Aland. 1993. *Novum Testamentum Graece*, 27th edition, Stuttgart: Deutsche Bibelgesellschaft.

Olander, Thomas 2015. *Proto-Slavic inflectional morphology. A comparative handbook.* Leiden & Boston: Brill.

Povest' o Drakule. Issledovanie i podgotovka tekstov Ja. S. Lur'e [The Dracula story. Investigation and edition of texts by Ja. S. Lur'e]. 1964. Moscow & Leningrad: Izdatel'stvo Nauka.

Strachova, Ol'ga B. 2015. Četveroevangelie vs. Aprakos: kakie teksty pereveli Kirill i Mefodij? [Four Gospels vs. Aprakos: which texts did Cyril and Method translate?] *Palaeoslavica* 23(1). 199–284.

TITUS – *Thesaurus Indogermanischer Text- und Sprachmaterialien*. titus.uni-frankfurt.de (accessed 27 February 2019).

TOROT – *Tromsø OCS and Old Russian Treebank* https://nestor.uit.no/ (accessed 27 February 2019).

Trunte, Nikolaos. 2006. я҃сенъ сотворáти рáзумъ. Theorie und Praxis der Übersetzung des Paisij Veličkovskij. In Daniel Bunčić & Nikolaos Trunte (eds.), *Iter philologicum. Festschrift für Helmut Keipert zum 65. Geburtstag*, 251–262. München: Otto Sagner.

Uhlig, Gustav. 1883. *Dionysii Thracis ars grammatica*. Leipzig: Teubner.

Večerka, Radoslav. 1996. *Altkirchenslavische (altbulgarische) Syntax. Band III – Die Satztypen: Der einfache Satz.* Freiburg i. Br.: Weiher.

Weiher, Eckhard. 1977. Die älteste Handschrift des grammatischen Traktats. Über die acht Redeteile. *Anzeiger für slavische Philologie* 9(2). 367–427.

Werke des Patriarchen von Bulgarien Euthymius (1375–1393). Nach den besten Handschriften herausgegeben von Emil Kałužniacki. 1901. Vienna: bei Carl Gerold's Sohn.

Simeon Dekker
Past tense usage in Old Russian performative formulae. A case study into the development of a written language of distance

Abstract: Thanks to the corpus of Novgorod birchbark letters, which occupy an intermediate position on a continuum between orality and literacy, we can trace the development of a formal written language over a period of more than four centuries. Its emergence can partly be traced to (1) the adaptation of Church Slavonic norms to secular text types, and partly to (2) an adaptation of vernacular oral habits to the written medium.

The twofold origin of this development is presented by means of a case study, viz. the use of verbal tenses, especially the perfect and aorist, in performative formulae. In early texts, the use of the perfect in performative formulae is due to persisting patterns of oral formulation. In later texts, on the contrary, the aorist emerges, due to Church Slavonic influence and the development of a "language of distance". A comparison is made between the birchbark letters and the parchment letters from Novgorod and Pskov. The use of the aorist in performative formulae is also attested in Ancient Greek and in Old Church Slavonic translations from Greek. Thus, the use of verbal tenses enlightens the path of development of the Russian written "language of distance", through the lens of Greek and Church Slavonic (foreign) elements in interaction with oral (native) patterns of speech.

Keywords: performatives, birchbark letters, verbal tenses, literacy

1 Introduction

The Novgorod birchbark letters are about the closest we can get to face-to-face interaction in Old Russian (OR). It has been demonstrated in Dekker (2018a) that these letters occupy an intermediate position on a continuum between orality and literacy. Thanks to this corpus, we can trace the development of a formal written language over a period of more than four centuries. Its emergence can partly be

---

Simeon Dekker, Bern University – Institut für Slavische Sprachen und Literaturen, e-mail: simeon.dekker@issl.unibe.ch

traced to (1) the adaptation of Church Slavonic (CS) norms to secular text types, and partly to (2) an adaptation of vernacular oral habits to the written medium.

The twofold origin of this development is presented by means of a case study, viz. the use of verbal tenses, especially the perfect and aorist, in performative formulae. The increasing use of the aorist at a time when it was no longer part of the living OR language is due to external CS influence in the development of a Russian "language of distance" (cf. Koch and Oesterreicher 1985) in interaction with patterns of oral influence (internally motivated change). A comparison is made between the birchbark letters and the parchment letters from Novgorod and Pskov (GVNP). The use of the aorist in performative formulae is also attested in Ancient Greek and in Old Church Slavonic (OCS) translations from Greek. Thus, a comparison can be made both within and beyond the Slavonic realm.

A direct influence of CS and possibly Greek elements on the OR birchbark and parchment letters was postulated in Dekker (2020); the burden of the present contribution is to underpin this claim against the background of its pragmatic preliminaries. At various occasions, questions have been raised as to the topic's relation to genres and text types. This additional consideration leads to the question of how *direct* the pattern of influence might actually have been. The insertion of pragmatic and sociolinguistic factors will turn out to be indispensable in this respect. The methodology of the present investigation is one of philological close reading (a qualitative approach) combined with as large a corpus-linguistic (quantitative) component as is viable for the corpora in question.

The corpora will be briefly introduced in Section 2. The theoretical category of assertive declarations will be introduced in Section 3; the data from the birchbark corpus will be recapitulated there, too, and their performative interpretation substantiated by means of examples. The question will then be raised why past tenses (perfect and aorist) are used in these performative phrases and what the role of Greek (Section 4) and CS influence (Section 5) might have been in the development of the formulae in question. Two issues are vital here, viz. genres or text types (Section 6), and the relationship between OR and CS in the Middle Ages (Section 7).

2 The corpora

The birchbark letters[1] originate from Velikij Novgorod and its wide surroundings. They date from the early 11th to the late 15th century, which leaves us with over

---

1 The most commonly used Russian designation "berestjanye *gramoty*" 'birchbark documents' conveys the thought of official chancery documents, which is far from adequate. An important

450 years of attestations. This alone makes the corpus exceptionally valid for diachronic investigations. Linguistic developments can be traced over a reasonably long period. Thanks to the marshy clay soil conditions, the birchbark letters have been preserved. Virtually every summer, archeological excavations are conducted in Novgorod, which leads to the birchbark corpus growing over time. At the end of the 2019 archeological season, the corpus counted over 1200 individual letters (or fragments thereof), more than 1100 of which originated from the city of Novgorod. The letters' contents vary enormously, but with few exceptions they concern matters of everyday life (trade, taxation, law and order, estate management, family and church affairs). The term "pragmatic literacy" has sometimes been used to describe the social setting in which the birchbark letters functioned (Gippius 2012: 237; Schaeken 2012: 203). This term implies that the functions of the birchbark letters were of a mundane character, as opposed to literary or religious texts, whose value resided in the language of the texts themselves; and indeed, most of the birchbark letters pertain to matters of a practical kind. Does this allow us to view them as a separate genre? And what consequences might this terminological issue have for the receptivity of foreign (Greek and CS) syntactic elements and constructions? Were the birchbark letters receptive to such influences, or are the text types too different to postulate a direct influence? We shall come back to these questions below.

The relationship between the Novgorod birchbark letters and the much larger number of texts on parchment, which originate from the same period and geographical area (GVNP) can, frankly, be called problematic. It is only in a very limited sense that the commodity of one writing material versus another can be used as a satisfactory criterion to classify the texts they carry. Therefore, if made at all, a division between the two corpora must be based on the contents and must, out of necessity, be a scalar one. Many parchment letters are also of a 'pragmatic' nature, but less obviously so than most birchbark letters. Therefore, the data for this study has been selected from part of the GVNP corpus, viz. the sub-corpus of "*častnye gramoty*", i.e. such letters as deal with personal as opposed to governmental matters, e.g. wills, depositions, grants and deeds.

---

consideration for our topic is that the birchbark letters did not emerge as a consequence of a chancery that necessitated the production of legal documents, but rather as a spontaneous innovation that emerged in the context of everyday life, especially in business and trade. The present contribution follows common practice elsewhere (cf. Dekker 2018a: 7) by adhering to the traditional term 'birchbark letters', without claiming to make a statement about the actual textual genre to which they belong. This latter issue will be addressed in more detail in Section 6.

3 Assertive declarations

One case study to flesh out the linguistic behaviour of the birchbark and parchment letters on a pragmatic level has to do with the use of verbal tenses in performative or performative-like expressions. Performatives as such do not need any introduction here; I adhere to the well-known concept of performativity as defined by Austin (1962), which is further specified by Searle's (1975; 1979) more precise categories of illocutionary expressions. Of these well-known five classes of illocutionary expressions, only two are relevant for the purposes of the present contribution, viz. assertives and declarations. Especially relevant for present purposes is, however, the mixed class of "assertive declarations", which has received far less attention than the concept of performativity as such. Where assertives *describe* a situation in the world (e.g. *John is a Fascist*), and declarations *bring about* a change in the world (e.g. *I hereby pronounce you husband and wife*), both these elements are *combined* in the mixed class of assertive declarations. Searle coined this mixed class to classify instances where a statement is made about a situation in the world, but at the same time this situation is established and ratified authoritatively. For example, in the legal context of a courtroom, a judge may pronounce a defendant guilty in the following way:

(1) I (hereby) declare you guilty.

The defendant does not become guilty because of the judge's utterance; the judge finds him to be guilty on the basis of evidence (this is the assertive component), and by pronouncing the verdict, the judge only ratifies this conclusion institutionally (this is the declarational component). These are the two sides of an assertive declaration. In the context of the birchbark letters, as has been shown in Dekker (2018a), the use of assertive declarations can be connected to the concepts of orality and literacy.[2]

The 'epistolary past tense' is a well-known phenomenon from various ancient and classical languages, and has traditionally been explained as a switch to the reader's temporal perspective, i.e. the author looking *forward* to the moment of the letter's reception, when the act of sending will lie in the past. An alternative interpretation as to the OR data on birchbark has recently been put forward (Schaeken, Fortuin and Dekker 2014; Dekker 2018a: 115–136) in connection with the centrifugal verbal prefix *po-*. Consequently, the use of a past tense is to be

---

[2] An 'orality factor' in the birchbark letters had been noted before, mostly in connection with the role of the letter-bearer or messenger (Mendoza 2002; Gippius 2004; Schaeken 2011a; 2014).

traced to the author looking *back* on (a) his decision to send, (b) the preparations that have been made, so that now, finally, (c) the letter ratifies the act of sending and confirms it definitively. It is here that a connection with performative utterances comes to the fore. Two instances of the epistolary past tense (underlined) can be seen in the following letter, addressed to archbishop Semen (Simeon) of Novgorod (who occupied this position from 1416 until 1421, which is why this particular letter can be dated more precisely than usual):

(2) ѡсспо́дину · архи·ιєпискупу новъгоцкому · вл̄дкѣ семену ст̄ѣ · бц̄и · оуιєздъ · сиротѣ твои ѡшевьски погостъ ржевици · тебѣ ломъ · бьютъ вси · ѿ мала и до велика · ѡсподарю · послали ιєсме ѡспо́динє · дьака · ѡлекъсадра за[нежѣ и ѿєць] и дѣдъ · ιєго · пѣлъ · оу ст̄ѣ · бц̄и · в ошевѣ · и цто бъ ιєси ѡспо́динє · к ст̄ѣ бц̄и · того · дьака поставилъ попомъ · а с нимъ · ιєсме послали труфана ѿ погоста · занежѣ цѣрк̄въ · стоить бес пѣтьа [. . .]

Ospodinu arxijepiskupu novъgockomu vl̄dkě Semenu st̄ě B̄ci oujezdъ, sirotě tvoi oševъski pogostъ, rževici, tebě lomъ bьjutъ vsi, ot mala i do velika, ospodarju. <u>Poslali jesme</u>, ospodine, dьjaka Olekъsadra zaneže i otěcь i dědъ jego pělъ ou st̄ě B̄ci v Oševě. I cto by jesi, ospodine, k st̄ě B̄ci togo dьjaka postavilъ popomъ; a s nimъ <u>jesme poslali</u> Trufana ot pogosta. Zaneže cěrk̄vъ stoitь bes pětьja. [. . .]

'To the lord archbishop of Novgorod, holy archbishop Semen, your peasants from the Holy Mother of God district, the Oševo settlement, the people of Ržev, all bow to you, from young to old, lord. <u>We have sent</u>, lord, Deacon Oleksadr, because (his) father and his grandfather sang at the Holy Mother of God (Church) in Oševo. May you, lord, ordain that deacon as priest of the Holy Mother of God. And with him <u>we have sent</u> Trufan from the settlement, because the church is without services. [. . .]'
(N963 / 1416–1421 / NGB XII: 73–74 / DBG / translation Schaeken 2019: 125)[3]

By the use of the epistolary past tense, the letter is connected to its letter-bearers (in this case Oleksadr and Trufan) and, therefore, tied to the immediate context in which it was meant to function. The use of the perfect tense, therefore, emerged from a vernacular communicative pattern based on the context-dependent and orally-oriented function of a letter-bearer.

---

[3] The original Old Russian text is provided in a slightly simplified Latin transliteration system, adapted from Collins (2001: xix), and modern punctuation has been added for the sake of legibility.

The birchbark letters function in a period of *Verschriftlichung*.[4] I use this term as informed by the theory of Koch and Oesterreicher (1985), who distinguish between the medium and the conception of an utterance; thus, a text can be positioned on a scale from 'proximity' to 'distance'. This scale mainly refers to the degree to which a text is embedded in the context. In the case of the birchbark letters, this context is often personified by the abovementioned messenger or letter-bearer, who played an important role in conveying and elaborating on the written message orally. Consequently, the birchbark letters were formulated with this in mind; that is to say, the authors had an 'oral mindset', and made formulation choices that would seem unusual in our time. On the other hand, the Middle Ages were a period in which a 'language of distance' developed, i.e. the written texts become more and more independent from the physical context in which they are meant to function. This double orientation can clearly be seen in the assertive declarations. For clarity's sake, a number of examples will be recapitulated here (cf. Dekker 2018a: 137–176; 2020).

(3) ивαNαа молов́ила ѳимь любо коунь
восоли па^к ли дорго продаю

Ivanjaja <u>molovila</u> Fimъ: ljubo kounъ vosoli, pak li dorgo prodaju.

'Ivan's wife <u>has said</u> to Fima: You either send the money, or I will demand that a large fine be imposed on you.'
(St.R. 11 / 1160–1180 / DND: 446 / DBG)

(4) [ѿо пе]тра ко коузм[е] ıазо тобе братоу свокмоу приказалє про сєбє [так]о оурадил[о] ли сѧ со тобою ци ли не оурадил[о]сѧ ти ты со дроцилою по сомоло⹁
ве прави а ıазо сѧ кланєю

Oto Petra ko Kouzme. Jazo tobe, bratou svojemu, <u>prikazale</u> pro sebe tako: ourjadilo li sja so toboju ci li ne ourjadilosja, ti ty so Drociloju po somolove pravi. A jazo sja klaneju.

---

4 For lack of an English equivalent, the German term is retained here. It refers to a development towards literacy, in which not only the written medium is used for an increasing number of purposes, but also the formulation habits are increasingly accommodated towards the exigencies of the written medium, e.g. increasing context-independence. The result of this process is what Koch and Oesterreicher (1985) call a "Sprache der Distanz" 'language of distance'.

'From Petr to Kuz'ma. I <u>have instructed</u> [i.e. hereby instruct] you, my brother, concerning ourselves as follows: whether he has made an arrangement with you or has not made an arrangement, you execute [it] with Dročila according to the agreement. And I bow down.'
(N344 / 1300–1320 / DND: 526 / DBG)

Both these examples contain a *verbum dicendi* that is phrased in the perfect tense. In example (3), this is due to the procedure of dictation. Ivan's wife had given oral instructions to the scribe, who reproduces the message in its written form, using the past tense as looking back on its oral utterance. In this way, Ivan's wife's previous oral utterance is ratified in writing, which lends additional authority to her message. A similar analysis can be made of (4).

(5) се купило михало у кн҃за вели=
кого бороце у василиа ѡдреана
кузнеца и токову и ѡстровну
и ротковици кодраца и ведрово
да в҃ рубла и г҃ грины дасте
ꙗковъ атно се замѣшете миха=
лу брату ѥг дасте сере=
бро двоѥ

Se <u>kupilo</u> Mixalo u knzja velikogo boroce u Vasilija Odrejana kuzneca i Tokovu i Ostrovnu i Rotkovici Kodracja i Vedrovo. <u>Da</u> 2 rublja, i 3 griny daste Jakovъ. Atno se zaměšete Mixalu bratu jeg daste serebro dvoje.

'Hereby Mixal <u>has bought</u> from Vasilij, the great prince's tax collector, Odrejan the blacksmith and [the villages] Tokova, Ostrovna, Kodrač's Rokoviči and Vedrovo. [Mixal] <u>has given</u> 2 roubles, and Jakov has to give 3 grivnas. If any damage will occur, [the one who is guilty] shall pay the double amount to Mixal and his brother.'
(N318 / 1340–1360 / DND: 611 / DBG)

Here we have a slightly different situation. It is now not a speech act which is recorded and ratified, but a financial transaction. The transaction has been agreed on and carried out orally, the financial side has been settled, and now the document is drawn up retrospectively in order to ratify the transaction formally and definitively in the written medium. Thus, the oral transaction remains primary, whereas its written reflection is secondary.[5] Nevertheless, the fact that a written record was deemed a useful addition to the oral transaction also shows an increasing awareness of the status of the written word and its performative potential. This awareness testifies to a growing sense of 'trust in writing'.

Initially, therefore, the use of the perfect tense is an indicator of what I have called "speech-based orality" (Dekker 2018a: 44, 179), i.e. an element reflecting a document's oral origin and its context-dependent *Sitz im Leben*. Over time, however, the increasing use of the aorist in this specific function (see Tables 1 and 2)[6] has to be traced to CS influence, as the aorist had already disappeared from the spoken vernacular (cf. Uspenskij 2002: 215).[7] Thus, the speech-based origin of past-tense performatives was driven to the background and replaced by a feature of the language of distance. This is one element that shows how a document can become dislocated from its oral origins. We shall come back to the means by which this CS influence asserted itself below.

Table 1: Perfect and aorist forms in assertive declarations in the birchbark corpus.

No	Date	Perfect	Aorist
N525	1100–1120	√	
N384	1160–1180	√	
N211 (2x)	1240–1260	√	√
N198	1260–1280	√	
N197	1280–1300		√
N45	1320–1340		√

---

5 Cf. Seemann's (1983: 556) observation (concerning Old Russian legal texts) that "die schriftliche Fixierung der von Sprechakten begleiteten Rechtsgeschäfte ist [...] etwas sekundäres."
6 For practical reasons, the data presented in Dekker (2020) is reproduced in Tables 1 and 2. Table 1 covers the 879 letters from the birchbark corpus that contain a sufficient amount of text to be included into the electronic database of the Russian National Corpus (http://ruscorpora.ru/new/search-birchbark.html, accessed 13 December 2019). It should be borne in mind that each instance of the perfect and aorist had to be checked manually to make sure that only assertive declarations are included. These constitute but a tiny minority of all perfect and aorist tense forms (viz. 6 out of 514 perfects and 8 out of 42 aorists). This consideration shows that a quantitative method always needs to be supplemented by a qualitative (philological) component. Table 2 covers the Novgorodian "častnye gramoty" section of GVNP, consisting of 21 letters.
7 According to Živov (2017: 618), the aorist slowly disappeared from the spoken language of the Eastern Slavs by the beginning of the 13th century. This point of view has repeatedly been contested by Bjørnflaten (e.g. 2015), who posits a much later decline of the aorist, in fact postponing it to the early modern period. His examples are, however, not very convincing; see also Section 5.

Table 1 (continued)

No	Date	Perfect	Aorist
N318 (2x)	1340–1360	√	√
N136	1360–1380		√
N366 (3x)	1360–1380		√√√
N309	1410–1420	√	

Table 2: Perfect and aorist forms in assertive declarations in GVNP.

No	Date	Perfect	Aorist
GVNP 102	< 1147	√√	
GVNP 103	< 1147	√√	
GVNP 104	± 1192	√√√√	
GVNP 105	< 1270	√√	
GVNP 106	> 1359	√√	√√
GVNP 107	1389–1415		√√√
GVNP 108	1389–1415		√√
GVNP 109	1389–1415		√√√
GVNP 110	1393	√	√
GVNP 111	1435	√√√√	√
GVNP 112	1436–1456		√√(√)
GVNP 113	1456–1471		√
GVNP 114	1456–1471	√	
GVNP 115	± 1460		√
GVNP 116	mid-15th cent.		√√
GVNP 117	mid-15th cent.	√	√√
GVNP 118	mid-15th cent.		√√
GVNP 119	1466–1467	√√√	
GVNP 120	< 1471	√	√
GVNP 122	15th cent.	√√	√√√√

Zaliznjak (DND: 174) already noticed that the aorist ousted the perfect tense in performative formulae due to its stylistically more elevated character.[8] We shall come back to this issue below.

---

[8] Živov (2017: 614), who disagrees with Zaliznjak's assessment, allows for stylistic considerations in the case of state charters (*dogovornye gramoty*) with their high social status, but he sees no rea-

4 Greek

As I have argued elsewhere (Dekker 2020), the use of the aorist in assertive declarations can partly be traced to (O)CS. We can, however, take one more step back and refer to Greek sources from various stages of that language's history.

The first phenomenon to be investigated in connection with our topic is the 'epistolary past tense'. We can take an example from Biblical Greek:

(6) <u>ἀπεστάλκαμεν</u> οὖν Ἰούδαν καὶ Σιλᾶν καὶ αὐτοὺς διὰ λόγου ἀπαγγέλλοντας τὰ αὐτά. (UBS)

apestalkamen oun Ioudan kai Silan kai autous dia logou apaggellontas ta auta.

'We <u>have sent</u> therefore Judas and Silas, who shall also tell you the same things by mouth.' (KJV / Acts of the Apostles 15:27)

Clearly, Judas and Silas were sent simultaneously with the letter (i.e. as letter-bearers), as they were to elaborate orally on the letter's contents. The same analysis of the centrifugal prefix in OR (Schaeken, Fortuin and Dekker 2014; Dekker 2018a: 115–136; cf. Section 3) can be applied to the Greek data.

Interestingly, in Greek, a chronological development can be detected which is similar to the increasing use of the aorist at the expense of the perfect tense in performative OR utterances. As Koskenniemi (1956: 78–79, 189–200) already notes, in the Ptolemaic era, the perfect tense was still used predominantly for the epistolary past tense; in the Christian era, however, the aorist took over, along with an increasing use of the present tense.[9]

Tense variation can also be detected when we turn from the epistolary past tense to the closely related category of performative utterances. Perfect tense performatives can be identified in Biblical Greek; consider the following example:

---

son to suppose why the writer of an 'ordinary' purchase deed should strive after the use of a higher style. Consequently, he refuses to consider the aorist as a late derivative of the perfect tense.

9 In older research sometimes untenable claims can be found as to the reasons for the increasing use of the present tense. Koskenniemi (1956: 193), for instance, goes so far as to state that "das Präsens ist, wenn es gebraucht wird, lediglich sprachlicher Ungeschicklichkeit zuzuschreiben" 'if the present tense is used, it is to be attributed solely to linguistic clumsiness.' Needless to say, such clumsy statements need no longer be taken for granted. They do not concern us directly in the present study.

(7) κἀγὼ ἑώρακα, καὶ <u>μεμαρτύρηκα</u> ὅτι οὗτός ἐστιν ὁ υἱὸς τοῦ θεοῦ.

kagō heōraka, kai <u>memartureka</u> hoti houtos estin o huios tou theou

'And I saw, and <u>bare record</u> that this is the Son of God' (KJV / John 1:34).
'And I have seen and <u>bear witness</u> that this is the Son of God' (Andrason and Locatell 2016: 56).

Note that the perfect is not recognized as a performative in KJV and other older translations, whereas present-day translators realize that the present tense is the appropriate English rendition of performatives. The quotation of this one example does not mean that the perfect is the only tense used for performatives. The possibility of variation is witnessed by various manuscript traditions of the same text, where the perfect and present tense can be used in the same context:

(8) ἰδού, <u>δέδωκα</u> ὑμῖν τὴν ἐξουσίαν τοῦ πατεῖν ἐπάνω ὄφεων καὶ σκορπίων [...]. (UBS)

idou, <u>dedōka</u> humin tēn exousian tou patein epanō ofeōn kai skorpiōn [...]

ἰδού, <u>δίδωμι</u> ὑμῖν τὴν ἐξουσίαν τοῦ πατεῖν ἐπάνω ὄφεων καὶ σκορπίων [...]. (Byz.)

idou, <u>didōmi</u> humin tēn exousian tou patein epanō ofeōn kai skorpiōn

'Behold, <u>I give</u> unto you power to tread on serpents and scorpions' (KJV / Luke 10:19).[10]

The variation in tense usage may point to an instability of the status of performatives in the written language and thus to a typological similarity with OR, where the status of a written performative utterance is wrestled with in a transitional period of *Verschriftlichung*.

5 Church Slavonic

However interesting a comparison with Greek parallels may be, they can hardly have influenced OR without the intermediary of (O)CS. The first point that needs to be underlined is that the aorist was no longer in use as an alternative past tense in OR in the period in which the aorist started ousting the perfect in performative

---

10 A similar variation is reflected in various OCS manuscripts, where we find both "*Se <u>daxъ</u> vamъ vlastь*" (aorist) and "*Se <u>dajǫ</u> vamъ vlastь*" (present tense).

utterances (cf. Tables 1 and 2). Secondly, the specific use of the aorist in OR performative contexts can hardly be traced to the original meaning of the aorist in OCS, which would be an anachronism. What is more, it has often been noted (e.g. MacRobert 2013: 387–388) that the distribution of aorist and perfect was already problematic and far from transparent in OCS.

Bjørnflaten (2015) traces the use of the aorist in OR to its original grammatical meaning as late as the 13th century. However, interestingly enough, the only aorist examples which he cites are actually instances of performative formulae in a *dogovornaja gramota* (2015: 262). This significant deviation in aorist usage precludes a direct influence from OCS to OR along the lines of the grammatical properties of the aorist. In addition, one should be aware that here we have a completely different text type that shows speech acts which were not directly founded on OCS examples. Birchbark literacy was a "spontaneous by-product" of ecclesiastical writing (Gippius 2012: 237) and should, therefore, be credited with originality, although it was influenced by ecclesiastical writing habits, as we shall see below. A grammatically deviant use of the aorist in non-traditional linguistic contexts can be seen as an instance of hypercorrection.

The question thus arises to what extent the CS interference in the use of the aorist was intentional. Daiber (2018b: 111–112), when discussing Greek influence in OCS, distinguishes between "Gräzismen" 'graecisms' as unintentional interference due to incomplete second language competence and "Gräzisierung" 'graecization' as the intentional adoption of elements from a culturally authoritative language. When transferring these terms to our topic, the first option, i.e. unintentional interference, seems excluded: after all, the use of the aorist is restricted to very specific types of speech acts. However, when going for the second option, i.e. intentional adoption, this does not necessarily mean that users were aware of the aorist's original grammatical properties; all they were aware of was the higher status of CS elements (of which they had passive knowledge; cf. Section 6). They adopted some of these elements as a reflection of their growing awareness of the written word's performative potential, as distinct from its oral context.

As is proposed by Uspenskij (2002), and recently reaffirmed by Bounatirou (2018: 610) for CS sources of a slightly later period, perfect and aorist are to be viewed as verb forms of one and the same grammeme, which users would not even have distinguished as different tenses. I would not go so far for OR in the Middle Ages, but this observation reflects a further stage of the development, although it solely describes the problem in grammatical terms and leaves out matters of pragmatics and stylistics. Nevertheless, we can say something about the grammatical side of the issue. The original resultative meaning of the perfect tense would have been most useful to denote a performative formula.[11] The fact that the aorist starts taking over, i.e. a tense whose original meaning does not carry resultative connotations, provides an additional indication that the specific resultative meaning of the perfect tense had also been lost (otherwise it would still have been preferred over the aorist). Ivanov (1982: 94) observes the beginning of this tendency already from the 11th century onwards (although he does not claim its completion until after the 12th century; this is in accordance with the chronological distribution of the data presented in Tables 1 and 2).

It does not mean, however, that we should view the aorist as taking over a resultative meaning. Rather, the perfect had acquired a generalized past tense meaning; the aorist was subsequently reinterpreted as a stylistically higher variant of this general past tense. Thus, as the aorist, when it was still in active use, was not typically used in performative utterances, its use in assertive declarations can be called an innovative adaptation of a conservative element. Thus, the adoption and reinterpretation of the aorist is part of the process of *Verschriftlichung*. Mendoza (2016: 123) notes that the use of CS elements makes a text more "written", i.e. more "distant" in Koch and Oesterreicher's (1985) terms.[12] The adoption of perceived higher style variants is a well-known phenomenon from other languages and periods, too; for instance, Oesterreicher and Koch (2016: 36) mention a present-day example of a postcard in which a prestigious administrative idiom is imitated.[13] The relative proximity of the two Slavonic varieties (CS and OR) allows *Ausbau* of the informal register by means of the adoption and adaptation of elements from the high variety. These topics (literacy and diglossia) will be elaborated on in the following sections.

6 Text types and the development of literacy

Too often, the OR birchbark letters have tacitly been assumed to be a genre of its own, whereas the only element that links them together as a corpus is the material on which they are written. In Dekker (2020), I lamented the lack of in-depth

---

[11] Cf. Hewson's (2012: 515–519) observation that performatives and perfectives typically overlap because both represent a complete event in all its phases.
[12] "Wir können lediglich sagen, dass die Verwendung von Elementen aus dem Kirchenslawischen einen Text in der Regel ‚schriftlicher' macht" (Mendoza 2016: 123).
[13] "Andererseits finden sich in Beispielen einer Form der sogenannten *formalisation discursive* diskurstraditionell und varietätenbezogen von Sprechern/Schreibern fälschlich als stilistisch hoch eingeschätzte Sprachformen; dies kam zu Formulierungen wie „Das Wetter ist schön und ich hoffe dasselbige auch von Euch" (Postkarte aus dem Italienurlaub) [. . .], in denen [. . .] ein prestigebesetzter administrativer Sprachgebrauch ‚imitiert' werden soll" (Oesterreicher und Koch 2016: 36).

research on the issue of the genres to which the birchbark letters belong. A rather general description of each text's contents has been made in the edition (NGB, DND), but a more detailed sub-classification into genres is sorely lacking.[14] The aorist can be encountered in some written genres, but hardly or not at all in others (cf. Dekker 2018a: 169).

The most important consideration with respect to the different text types is whether there are differences in the degree of 'trust in writing' among the various genres. Lazar (2014: 27–28) makes a functional distinction between "Akte" and "Urkunden"; she considers the former to have a documenting function and the latter to be socially binding. It is important to observe that that goes only for a society in which 'trust in writing' has been firmly rooted. Assertive declarations are the documentation of an oral ceremony *plus* its socially binding written fixation. They show that in medieval Russian society, the two could not always be neatly divided into two separate genres, as the concept of literacy still functioned in a transitional period of *Verschriftlichung*.

Even the general term 'pragmatic literacy', though adequate to refer to the functional characteristics of the birchbark corpus, is problematic "because it does not discriminate enough between the spheres of birchbark and parchment writing; in the period and language area under discussion, quite a number of 'practical' texts were written on parchment, mostly legal documents (treaties, deeds)" (Schaeken 2012: 203). A similar term, "Gebrauchsschrifttum" 'functional writing', is used by Lazar (2014: 13) against clerical (ecclesiastical) writing.

These problems lead to the question to what extent the birchbark and parchment letters can actually be compared and brought under one common denominator. Is it not rather timely to no longer distinguish between the two corpora just on the basis of the writing material? This would in no way undermine the importance of the birchbark letters as a unique and separate source of linguistic information about the actual Novgorodian vernacular. That some birchbark letters function as draft versions, to be copied onto parchment, has repeatedly been emphasized (DND: 304; Dekker 2018a: 12). This function allows for the most tangible relation between the birchbark and parchment letters. It can, however, be postulated for only a minority of birchbark letters. An explicit clue for this procedure can be found in the following example (the closing sentence of a long birchbark letter dealing with a rather fuzzy legal issue, the precise nature of which remains unclear due to large lacunae in the letter's state of preservation):

---

[14] As Lazar (2014: 16) also notes, the only rough classification of the birchbark letters into genres can be found on the website http://gramoty.ru (accessed 12 November 2019). After a decade of apparent inactivity, this website has recently been updated to include the archaeological finds up to and including the 2017 season.

(9) а ты спе҂
пане пьрьпесаво на хароти҂
тию посъли жь (...)

[...] A ty, Spepane [sic], pьrьpesavo na xarotitiju, posъli žь.

'[...] And you, Stepan, having copied [this] onto parchment, send [it] away.' (N831 / 1140–1160 / DND: 303 / DBG)

Zaliznjak draws the conclusion that the more important letters were not written on birchbark, but on parchment, so that parchment letters were obviously perceived as more official or more respectable (DND: 304).[15] Consequently, indeed, in that sense there is a clear dichotomy between the two corpora. Nevertheless, upon closer inspection, the dichotomy turns out to be less simple than it may seem.[16] The main text types represented in this investigation are contracts, deeds, wills and depositions. All of these text types occur in both corpora.

So do these corpora have enough in common to categorize them as belonging to the same class? For our present purposes, this comes down to the following question: was there a difference in the amount of 'trust in writing' between birchbark and parchment?[17] Or was the notion of 'trust' connected to writing as such, quite apart from the material on which this writing was fixated? I contend for the latter option. The division into birchbark and parchment letters is a modern one and does not necessarily reflect the users' contemporary understanding. In spite of the difference in writing material, a significant number of basic text types are the same. In both corpora, 'low' texts aspired to 'high' status (which was traditionally assigned to ecclesiastical writing) because of an increased perception of the importance of trust in writing and the enhanced role of the written word. This allowed texts of pragmatic literacy to be receptive to 'high' elements from Greek via the intermediary of CS.

This view is supported by Uspenskij (1987: 49, 64, 71–72; cf. 2002: 78, 98–99, 110–111), as paraphrased by Collins (1992: 81): "Given the methods of education, the very act of writing became associated with the high language to a large extent.

---

15 "[. . .] наиболее ответственные письма писались не на бересте, а на пергамене. Очевидно, письмо на пергамене воспринималось как более официальное и/или более почтительное."
16 A substantial methodological problem might be that the parchment letters as collected and published by Valk (1949) are by far not as closed a corpus as the birchbark letters are. The latter corpus is small enough to comprise *all* tokens of birchbark letters found hitherto. The parchment documents are far more extensive in number and no claims are made as to the degree of completion of the now published collections.
17 For a more extensive treatment of the topic of 'trust in writing' in the birchbark letters, see Dekker (2018a: 45–46, 184–186).

This explains why Slavonic elements, especially formulae, could appear in business documents." Such an "epiphenomenon of the act of writing" (Collins 1992: 85) is only possible if writing as such has acquired a certain status.[18] This status is possibly due to the "sacred" origin of writing in the realm of CS texts (cf. Bulanin 1997), whereas pragmatic literacy was originally but a "spontaneous by-product" of such ecclesiastical writing (Gippius 2012: 237). Thus, both in its incipience and in its further development, the status and performative potential of medieval Russian pragmatic literacy depended on that of ecclesiastical literacy. Practically speaking, this development can be traced to the educational habits and their close interaction with a passive reading acquisition of CS.[19] This leads us to the second aspect of this analysis.

7 Diglossia

The second dimension in our discussion of the phenomenon in question has to do with the relative functions and status of OR and CS in the medieval East Slavonic lands. The interaction of the two has often been analyzed as a situation of extensive diglossia: CS as the 'high' variety and OR as the 'low' variety each figured in specific functional domains. CS influence can, therefore, not necessarily be described as a *foreign* element in OR texts. CS had taken root in local society, but was used actively only in the higher domains (predominantly religion and associated areas). In addition, it should be realized that the CS that was used in medieval Rus' was a hybrid form, containing many local East Slavonic elements (cf. Živov 2014: 1276, 1284). Thus, the correlation between the dimensions 'local vs. foreign' and 'high vs. low' becomes blurred.

An alternative take on the issue is thus to "call the use of Church Slavonic in the East Slavonic manuscripts not so much the use of another language, but

---

18 Collins's term "epiphenomenon" might suggest an inadvertent insertion of CS elements. However, we have ample indications for medieval Novgorodian writers' strong sociolinguistic awareness. Schaeken (2011b) shows this by drawing attention to the use of the local Novgorodian dialect vs. the supra-regional variety of Old Russian in certain birchbark letters. It should be borne in mind that the birchbark letters and, by extension, the parchment letters, too, operated on a continuum between CS, supra-regional Old Russian and the local Novgorodian variety (cf. Dekker 2018b).
19 Another area in which the influence of an education geared towards acquiring passive CS reading skills is reflected, is the co-existence of two orthographical systems in the birchbark letters and other Old Russian sources. According to Uspenskij (2002: 136–149), the emergence of the *"bytovaja orfografija"* was due to the ecclesiastical pronunciation of the semi-vowels ь and ъ. For more on the competing orthographies, see DND (21–28); Bunčić (2016); Dekker (2018b).

the use of emblematic 'high' elements" (Daiber 2018a: 138). This approach would diminish the barrier between OR and CS and allow for a more pronounced propensity towards adopting the CS elements in question, as they are not taken over from a *foreign* language but rather from a 'high' variety of the same *native* language. Collins (1992: 80) notes as to CS that "most pupils acquired it passively," whereas its "active use [. . .] required special training." This passive knowledge would have facilitated the implementation of CS elements in OR texts even by those writers who would not have been able to compose CS texts independently.

A strict division between CS and OR as completely separate languages is problematic for yet another reason, viz. users' awareness of both idioms' compatibility, as evidenced by the widespread existence of 'hybrid' texts. As Bounatirou (forthc.) comments, "there existed no completely clear-cut division between linguistic means belonging to ChS [CS] and those belonging to Slavonic vernacular languages. Instead, it seems that the border between ChS and vernaculars was in many respects rather fuzzy." This border being "rather fuzzy" facilitated the transfer of linguistic elements along pragmatic lines, as both idioms were not perceived as mutually exclusive.

A strict division between the two languages was facilitated artificially from the time of the '*knižnaja sprava*' onwards. Although Daiber (2018a) posits the beginning of this 'revision of books' in the 16th century, the phenomenon as such is usually restricted to (and was certainly at its height during) the reforms of patriarch Nikon in the 17th century (cf. Uspenskij 2002: 433). It was then that a more critical attitude towards mixing CS and vernacular elements emerged (cf. Daiber 2018a); this does not mean, however, that we should generalize such an approach to the preceding centuries, too. The emergence of the Second South Slavonic influence may have contributed to an awareness of OR and CS as being two separate languages, too, but the final outcome of that process lies beyond the timeframe of the present study.

8 Concluding remarks

A purely grammatical approach to the issue treated in this contribution would have missed out on some important reflections on the nature of syntactic variation and change. It has been demonstrated how pragmatic considerations can turn out to be exceedingly relevant to the manifestation of external influences (be it from other languages or from a 'high' or 'distant' variety of the same language).

The early history of the birchbark letters shows us that one important element of *Verschriftlichung*, viz. 'trust in writing', can develop without the adoption of 'high' elements. Vernacular OR writing started off as a by-product of CS religious writing, which in itself carried over a residue of 'trust' to the vernacular texts.

We started from the past tense in performatives as a reflection of an oral component in communication, which over time developed into a feature of the language of distance. This was possible thanks to the development of various text types towards 'trust in writing' and facilitated by the situation of diglossia in medieval Russia. Over the course of its development, OR could not but be influenced by CS. Thus, the category of assertive declarations has contributed towards elucidating the path of development of the Russian written "language of distance" through the lens of Greek and CS (foreign or 'high') elements in interaction with oral (native or 'low') patterns of speech.

Abbreviations

Byz.	Byzantine text of the New Testament
DGB	Drevnerusskie berestjanye gramoty gramoty.ru (accessed March 2021)
DND	*Drevnenovgorodskij dialekt* (Zaliznjak 2004)
GVNP	*Gramoty Velikogo Novgoroda i Pskova* (Valk 1949)
KJV	King James Version
N	Novgorod
NGB	*Novgorodskie gramoty na bereste*, vols. I–XII
NGB XII	Janin, Zaliznjak and Gippius (2015)
St.R.	Staraja Russa
UBS	United Bible Societies

References

Andrason, Alexander & Christian Locatell. 2016. The perfect wave: A cognitive approach to the Greek verbal system. *Biblical and Ancient Greek Linguistics* 5. 7–121.

Austin, John L. 1962. *How to do things with words*. Oxford: Clarendon Press.

Bjørnflaten, Jan Ivar. 2015. The perfect from a cross-linguistic perspective in Old East Slavic texts. *Slavia* 84(3). 259–267.

Bounatirou, Elias. 2018. *Eine Syntax des „Novyj Margarit" des A.M. Kurbskij: Philologisch-dependenzgrammatische Analysen zu einem kirchenslavischen Übersetzungskorpus*. 2 vols. Wiesbaden: Harrassowitz.

Bounatirou, Elias M. forthc. Church Slavic, Recensions of. In Marc L. Greenberg & Lenore A. Grenoble (eds.), *Encyclopedia of Slavic languages and linguistics*. Leiden & Boston: Brill.

Bulanin, Dmitrij. 1997. Der literarische Status der Novgoroder Birkenrinden-Urkunden. *Zeitschrift für Slawistik* 42(2). 146–167.

Bunčić, Daniel. 2016. Thirteenth-century Novgorod: Medial diorthographia. In Daniel Bunčić, Sandra L. Lippert & Achim Rabus (eds.), *Biscriptality: A sociolinguistic typology*, 129–139. Heidelberg: Universitätsverlag Winter.

Collins, Daniel E. 1992. On diglossia and the linguistic norms of medieval Russian writing. In A.A Barentsen, B.M. Groen & R. Sprenger (eds.), *Studies in Russian linguistics*, 79–94. Amsterdam & Atlanta: Rodopi.

Collins, Daniel E. 2001. *Reanimated voices: Speech reporting in a historical-pragmatic perspective*. Amsterdam & Philadelphia: John Benjamins.

Daiber, Thomas. 2018a. In contact with the medium: 'knižnaja sprava' in 16th-century Russia. *Russian Linguistics* 42(2). 137–158.

Daiber, Thomas. 2018b. Gräzismen in der Vita des hl. Kyrill. In Sebastian Kempgen, Monika Wingender & Ludger Udolph (eds.), *Deutsche Beiträge zum 16. Internationalen Slavistenkongress Belgrad 2018*, 111–116. Wiesbaden: Harrassowitz.

Dekker, Simeon. 2018a. *Old Russian birchbark letters: A pragmatic approach*. Leiden & Boston: Brill/Rodopi.

Dekker, Simeon. 2018b. Three dimensions of proximity and distance in the Old Russian birchbark letters. In Amir Kapetanović (ed.), *The Oldest Linguistic Attestations and Texts in the Slavic Languages*, 176–190. Vienna: Holzhausen.

Dekker, Simeon. 2020. Upotreblenie glagol'nyx vremën v drevnerusskix performativnyx vyskazyvanijax: pragmatičeskij podxod [The use of verbal tenses in Old Russian performatives: A pragmatic approach]. In Egbert Fortuin, Peter Houtzagers & Janneke Kalsbeek (eds.), *Dutch contributions to the sixteenth International Congress of Slavists*, 54–75. Leiden & Boston: Brill/Rodopi.

Gippius, Aleksej Alekseevic. 2004. K pragmatike i kommunikativnoj organizacii berestjanyx gramot [On the pragmatics and communicative organization of the birchbark letters.]. In Valentin Lavrent'evič Janin, Andrej Antol'evič Zaliznjak & Aleksej Alekseevič Gippius (eds.), *Novgorodskie gramoty na bereste XI (Iz raskopok 1997–2000 godov)*, 183–232. Moskva: Russkie slovari.

Gippius, Aleksej Alekseevič. 2012. Birchbark literacy and the rise of written communication in Early Rus'. In Kristel Zilmer & Judith Jesch (eds.), *Epigraphic literacy and Christian identity: Modes of written discourse in the newly Christian European North*, 225–250. Turnhout: Brepols.

Hewson, John. 2012. Tense. In Robert I. Binnick (ed.), *The Oxford handbook of tense and aspect*, 507–535. Oxford & New York: Oxford University Press.

Ivanov, Valerij Vasil'evič. 1982. Istorija vremennyx form glagola [The history of verbal tense forms]. In Ruben Ivanovič Avanesov & Valerij Vasil'evič Ivanov (eds.), *Istoričeskaja grammatika russkogo jazyka: Morfologija, glagol*, 25–131. Moskva: Nauka.

Janin, Valentin Lavrent'evič, Andrej Antol'evič Zaliznjak & Aleksej Alekseevič Gippius. 2015. *Novgorodskie gramoty na bereste (Iz raskopok 2001–2014 gg.). Tom XII* [Novgorodian letters on birchbark: From the excavations 2001–2014. Vol. XII]. Moskva: Jazyki slavjanskoj kul'tury.

Koch, Peter & Wulf Oesterreicher. 1985. Sprache der Nähe – Sprache der Distanz: Mündlichkeit und Schriftlichkeit im Spannungsfeld von Sprachtheorie und Sprachgeschichte. *Romanistisches Jahrbuch* 36. 15–43.

Koskenniemi, Heikki. 1956. *Studien zur Idee und Phraseologie des griechischen Briefes bis 400 n. Chr*. Helsinki: Finnish Academy.

Lazar, Marija. 2014. *Von Geld und guten Worten: Entwicklung des russischen Geschäftsbriefes als Textsorte*. München: Verlag Otto Sagner.

MacRobert, C. M. 2013. The competing use of perfect and aorist tenses in Old Church Slavonic. *Slavia* 82(4). 387–407.

Mendoza, Imke. 2002. Zur Nominaldetermination im Altostslavischen (Pronomina in den Birkenrindentexten). *Zeitschrift für slavische Philologie* 61(2). 291–311.

Mendoza, Imke. 2016. Alltagssprache, Alltagswelt: Die russischen Birkenrindentexte zwischen Mündlichkeit und Schriftlichkeit. In Anna Kathrin Bleuler (ed.), *Welterfahrung und Welterschließung in Mittelalter und Früher Neuzeit*, 117–133. Heidelberg: Universitätsverlag Winter.

Oesterreicher, Wulf & Peter Koch. 2016. 30 Jahre ‚Sprache der Nähe – Sprache der Distanz': Zu Anfängen und Entwicklung von Konzepten im Feld von Mündlichkeit und Schriftlichkeit. In Helmuth Feilke & Mathilde Hennig (eds.), *Zur Karriere von ›Nähe und Distanz‹: Rezeption und Diskussion des Koch-Oesterreicher-Modells*, 11–72. Berlin & Boston: De Gruyter.

Schaeken, Jos. 2011a. Don't shoot the messenger: A pragmaphilological approach to birchbark letter no. 497 from Novgorod. *Russian Linguistics* 35(1). 1–11.

Schaeken, Jos. 2011b. Sociolinguistic variation in Novgorod birchbark documents: The case of no. 907 and other letters. *Russian Linguistics* 35(3). 351–359.

Schaeken, Jos. 2012. The birchbark documents in time and space – revisited. In K. Zilmer & J. Jesch (eds.), *Epigraphic literacy and Christian identity: Modes of written discourse in the newly Christian European North*, 201–224. Turnhout: Brepols.

Schaeken, Jos. 2014. Don't shoot the messenger: Part two. Pragmaphilological notes on birchbark letters nos. 497 and 771 from Novgorod and no. 2 from Zvenyhorod. In Egbert Fortuin, Peter Houtzagers, Janneke Kalsbeek & Simeon Dekker (eds.), *Dutch contributions to the fifteenth International Congress of Slavists: Minsk, August 20–27, 2013. Linguistics*, 155–166. Amsterdam & New York: Rodopi.

Schaeken, Jos. 2019. *Voices on birchbark. Messages from medieval Russia: Daily life and communication*. Leiden & Boston: Brill/Rodopi.

Schaeken, Jos, Egbert Fortuin & Simeon Dekker [J. Sxaken, Ė. Fortejn & S. Dekker]. 2014. Ėpistoljarnyj dejksis v novgorodskix berestjanyx gramotax [Epistolary deixis in the Novgorod birchbark letters]. *Voprosy jazykoznanija* 2014(1). 21–38.

Searle, John R. 1975. A taxonomy of illocutionary acts. In Keith Gunderson (ed.), *Language, mind, and knowledge*, 344–369. Minneapolis: University of Minnesota Press.

Searle, John Rogers. 1979. *Expression and meaning: Studies in the theory of speech acts*. Cambridge: Cambridge University Press.

Seemann, Klaus-Dieter. 1983. Die „Diglossie" und die Systeme der sprachlichen Kommunikation im alten Rußland. In Reinhold Olesch et al. (eds.), *Slavistische Studien: Zum IX. Internationalen Slavistenkongress in Kiev*, 553–561. Köln & Wien: Böhlau.

Uspenskij, Boris Andreevič. 1987. *Istorija russkogo literaturnogo jazyka (XI – XVII vv.)* [History of the Russian literary language (11th–17th c.)]. München: Verlag Otto Sagner.

Uspenskij, Boris Andreevič. 2002. *Istorija russkogo literaturnogo jazyka (XI – XVII vv.)* [History of the Russian literary language (11th–17th c.)]. 3rd edn. Moskva: Aspekt Press.

Valk, Sigizmund Natanovič. (ed.). 1949. *Gramoty Velikogo Novgoroda i Pskova* [Documents from Great Novgorod and Pskov]. Moskva & Leningrad: Izdatel'stvo Akademii Nauk SSSR.

Zaliznjak, Andrej Antol'evič. 2004. *Drevnenovgorodskij dialekt* [The Old Novgorodian Dialect]. 2nd edn. Moskva: Jazyki slavjanskoj kul'tury.

Živov, Viktor M. 2014. Das Kirchenslavische bei den Ostslaven. In Karl Gutschmidt, Sebastian Kempgen, Tilman Berger & Peter Kosta (eds.), *Die slavischen Sprachen: Ein internationales Handbuch zu ihrer Struktur, ihrer Geschichte und ihrer Erforschung*, vol. 2, 1276–1294. Berlin & Boston: De Gruyter Mouton.

Part III: **The influence of Latin on Church Slavonic**

Vittorio S. Tomelleri
When Church Slavonic meets Latin. Tradition vs. innovation

Abstract: This paper deals with the Church Slavonic translation of a medieval Latin compilation, Bruno's commented Psalter (11th century), which was done in Novgorod, around the middle of the 16th century, by the well-known translator Dmitrij Gerasimov.

Some infinitive and participial constructions of the Slavonic text are here discussed and briefly compared with previous and later Church Slavonic translations from Latin. The aim is to put forward some syntactic features of the Slavonic text, which sometimes oscillates between the preservation of constructions inherited from the Church Slavonic tradition and the need of rendering in an appropriate way some peculiarities of Latin morpho-syntax. In the translation of the commentary on the Psalms one observes an increasing use of Accusativus-cum-infinitivo and participial constructions, due to the influence of the Latin model. This redistribution, or extension, of old patterns shows the particular nature of Church Slavonic syntax: at the outset departing from the local dialects, it became more flexible and permeable to syntactic calques (at the same time translation technique significantly moved toward literalism). Thus, although it was characterized by petrified forms and grammatical rules (or rather, textual fixed patters), Church Slavonic syntax still continued to experience changes and improvements due to the contact with external factors and or local dialects.

The collected material is intended as a first contribution to a broader typological investigation of syntactic constructions in Church Slavonic translations from Latin.

Keywords: (Old) Church Slavonic, Latin, syntax, accusative with infinitive, participial constructions

1 Introductory remarks

The present paper represents a first attempt at presenting some syntactic features found in a late Russian Church Slavonic translation from Latin and putting them in a broader "typological" context. The investigation is based on a preliminary

---

Vittorio S. Tomelleri, Università di Torino; St. Petersburg University, Department of General Linguistics, e-mail: vittoriospringfield.tomelleri@unito.it

https://doi.org/10.1515/9783110651331-010

analysis of Bruno's commented Psalter (*Tolkovaja Psaltir' Brunona*), a catena commentary compiled by Bruno, Bishop of Würzburg, in the middle of the 11th century (*Expositio psalmorum Brunonis, episcopi Herbipolensis*). The Latin text of the *Expositio psalmorum* was translated into Church Slavonic by Dmitrij Gerasimov in Novgorod in the second quarter of the 16th century on behalf of the then archbishop of Novgorod Macarius (1482–1563), who some years later would become Metropolitan of Russia.[1] Since no critical edition of Bruno's commented Psalter exists,[2] the material will necessarily be presented in a rather fragmentary and random way.[3] We shall not present corpus-based data or statistically relevant results; our more modest aim is to point out the importance, and at the same time difficulty, of combining a linguistic analysis with a philological-textual approach in order to properly analyze and understand the (Old) Church Slavonic tradition.

For the analysis, we have selected some Church Slavonic infinitive and participle constructions and their Latin (and sometimes also Greek) counterparts. The main issue will be first to establish certain syntactic patterns, peculiar to Bruno's commented Psalter, and to possibly explain whether they can be attributed to linguistic constraints or simply mirror the translator's attitude towards or dependence on the Church Slavonic tradition. At the same time, through a comparison with other Church Slavonic texts translated from Latin in different times and places, we shall try to provide an account of the diachronic evolution of the examined constructions.

Before starting, it is useful to remind of the artificial character, in the good sense of the word, of (Old) Church Slavonic, which was "shaped according to the syntactic patterns and stylistic norms of Greek" (Drinka 2011: 63). In the well-known fourth thesis of the Prague Linguistic Circle (*The immediate problems of Church Slavonic*), its author, identified with the Russian linguist Nikolaj Nikolaevič Durnovo (Keipert 1999: 124), rightly stressed that

> Dans une langue qui, dès ses débuts, n'était pas destinée à un besoin local, qui s'appuyait sur la tradition grecque littéraire, et qui a pris par la suite le rôle de *koinè* slave, on doit supposer à priori l'existence d'éléments artificiels, amalgamés et conventionnels. *Il y a donc lieu d'interpréter l'évolution du vieux-slave en fonction des principes qui président à l'histoire des langues littéraires.* (Mélanges 1929: 21–22)

---

1 In the colophon written by the translator himself we read that the work was accomplished on the 15th of October 1535 (Tomelleri 2004: 61).
2 The editor's preface, the translator's afterword and the tenth Psalm have been published in Tomelleri (2004: 274–337).
3 All quotations here are from the codex Nr. 16.12.7 (Osn. 1287) of the Library of the Russian Academy of Sciences, end of the 17th century, collated with the manuscript 1039 (1148) of the Soloveckij collection, mid-16th century, kept in the National Library of Saint-Petersburg.

[[i]n a language which from the beginning was not destined for a local need, which was based on the Greek literary tradition, and which later acquired the role of a Slavic "koinē," one must presuppose *a priori*, artificial, amalgamated, and conventional elements. *Therefore one must interpret the development of Old Church Slavonic on the basis of the principles which govern the history of standard literary languages.* (Steiner 1982: 18–19)]

His statement pertains primarily to the lexical (abstract, religious and, to a lesser extent, scientific concepts) and the syntactic domains of the translated texts. With respect to syntax, the basic principle, or rather practice, of translating religious texts requested that the word order of the Greek (or Latin) models be strictly reproduced in the Old Church Slavonic translation. This approach was based on the mystical conception that in the case of Holy Scriptures, according to Jerome's pregnant formulation in the Epistle 57 Ad Pammachium, even the word order is a mystery, *verborum ordo mysterium est* (Barr 1979: 313). Therefore, it is sometimes very difficult to properly understand and interpret Slavonic translations without considering the source text.

The fact that most Slavonic translations follow the word order of the original, has relevant consequences both at the clause and phrase levels for their interpretation and "considerably embarrasses the study of their syntax" (MacRobert 1986: 142). For example, in Latin, unlike Slavonic, the adnominal genitive can be placed before its head; let us now consider what happens when each single element of the genitive noun construction is mechanically reproduced in the order in which it occurs in the Latin original. In the Glagolitic Kiev Leaflets (presumably 10th century)[4] we encounter a prepositional phrase, with the preposition отъ (*otъ*) followed by two nouns in the genitive case: симь нъи отъ гръхъ сквръностии нашихъ оуисти – *simь ny otъ grěxъ skvrьnostiï našixъ očisti* (this.INS.SG we.ACC from sin.GEN.PL stain.GEN.PL our.GEN.PL clean.IMP.2SG; Nimčuk 1983: 104). Reading this passage, one would probably assume that the wordform гръхъ (*grěxъ*) 'sins' is directly governed by the immediately preceding preposition отъ (*otъ*) 'from', and that the second genitive сквръностии нашихъ (*skvrьnostiï našixъ*) depends on the preceding noun гръхъ (*grěxъ*) 'sins' as a modifier. The whole sentence can be accordingly rendered in English approximately as "By means of this clean us from the sins of our stains". Looking at the Latin text, however, we get a significantly different picture: *per haec nos a peccatorum nostrorum maculis emunda* (Nimčuk 1983: 105), i.e. "By means of these clean us from the stains of our sins". As the preposition *a/ab* 'from' requires the ablative case, in the Latin text, unlike in the Slavonic, there is no ambiguity: the preposition *a* does not govern the noun next

---

4 It should be noted, however, that the Kiev Missal, written more in the style of the Greek liturgy, reveals a relatively weak influence from the Latin source (Konzal 1994: 194).

to it, expressed in the genitive case, but the noun *maculis*, which follows the genitive phrase. Note, in addition, that in the source text the adjective *nostrorum* 'our' is syntactically related to the noun *peccatorum* 'sins'.

Should we complain about the Slavonic text because of its ambiguity? Should we consider it to be obscure or even wrong, if compared with its source? Is such a translation really tricky? It is impossible to properly answer these questions, as we do not know where and when this mass was celebrated and, in any case, how the text was understood by the preacher and/or his audience. To complicate the picture further, the possessive adjective нашихъ (*našixъ*) 'our' does not occur in the same position as in the Latin original. This deviation raises the question of whether we must suppose that the Slavonic translation follows here a Latin text different from that what is known to us or whether this incongruence is the result of some problems in the transmission of the Slavonic text. Thus, even a short request by a sinner contains a lot of philological and linguistic details which we should not underestimate. In the present paper we shall focus not so much on linear syntax than on patterns at the interclausal level, namely on some infinitive and participle clauses.

2 Syntactic overlapping

As was pointed out by Boris Andreevič Uspenskij, many Old Church Slavonic syntactic constructions and structures, patterned after the Greek model, were later preserved and further developed, being used in "original" texts too, and so becoming integral elements of the language:

> Многие синтаксические конструкции, будучи по происхождению синтаксическими кальками из греческого, употребляются затем и в оригинальных церковнославянских текстах; тем самым они оказываются не явлениями переводных текстов, но явлениями церковнославянского языка (Uspenskij 2002: 254)

> [Many syntactic constructions, being by origin syntactic calques from Greek, are then used also in the original Church Slavonic texts; thus, they are not phenomena of translated texts, but phenomena of the Church Slavonic language.]

Among them we find several participial and infinitive constructions, connected with the formal hierarchization of predicative units (Živov 2017: 328), which represent core features of the high bookish (*knižnyj*) register. These syntactic patterns, which were learned and transmitted by reading and copying extant texts, mainly former translations that contained them, did not conform, qualitatively and, above all, quantitatively to any spoken variety.[5] Therefore, the Neogrammarian approach, aiming at establishing the autochthonous or foreign nature of a given phenomenon, cannot be usefully employed for the oldest period and makes even less sense in later times of the development of the written language. Much more interesting, however, is the functional meaning and use of such constructions in quite specific situations related to a particular period in the history of Church Slavonic. As we shall demonstrate, the reduction or extension of the constructions examined here was tightly connected to linguistic contact at the textual (translatory) level.

The quite precise chronological, geographical, and cultural localization of Bruno's commented Psalter (Novgorod, first half of the 16th century) relieves us of the burden of tackling problems of dating, which can be very tricky in the case of Church Slavonic translations. However, the identification of the chronological and spatial environment refers only to the commentary (*Tolkovanija*) by the Latin Church Fathers (Cassiodorus, Augustine, Ps-Jerome and Beda). The verses of Psalms still show their direct or indirect dependence upon the Church Slavonic traditional text, which goes back to the literary activity of Saints Cyril and Methodius. However, there are some interesting cases of interplay between what I propose to call *the Greek-Slavonic heritage text* and *Latin-induced innovations*. The impact of Latin syntax upon an already existent text, originally translated from Greek, or, if you prefer, the interference of the old tradition, clearly emerges in the following example of syntactic mixing:[6]

(1) Ps. 149.8 (Tomelleri 2013: 199)

Exp ad alligand-os reg-es eorum in
to bind.GRDV-M.ACC.PL king-ACC.PL they.GEN in
comped-ibus et nobil-es eorum in manic-is
chain-ABL.PL and noble-ACC.PL they.GEN in manacle-ABL.PL
ferre-is
made_of_iron-ABL.PL

Br къ свазанїю ц҃рей ихъ пꙋты
kъ svęzanïj-u c̄r-ei ixъ put-y
to binding-DAT king-GEN.PL they.GEN chain-INS.PL

---

[5] In any case, the intellectual content of Church Slavonic texts, as well as their syntactic devices, were "far removed from the daily concerns of the Slavs" (Lunt 1987: 156).
[6] Abbreviations – **Exp**: Latin text of the *Expositio psalmorum*; **Br**: Church Slavonic translation of Bruno's Psalter; **GB**: Gennadius Bible (1499); **S**: Greek text of the Septuaginta.

	и	славныѧ	ихъ	рꙋчными	ѡковы
	i	slavny-ę	ixъ	ručn-ymi	ōkov-y
	and	renowned-ACC.PL	they.GEN	manual-INS.PL	chain-INS.PL

желѣзными
želězn-ymi
made_of_iron-INS.PL

GB свѧзати цр҃ѧ ихъ пꙋты и
svęza-ti cr̄-ę ixъ put-y i
bind-INF king-ACC.PL they.GEN chain-INS.PL and

славныѧ ихъ рꙋчными оковы
slavny-a ixъ ručn-ymi okov-y
renowned-ACC.PL they.GEN manual-INS.PL chain-INS.PL

желѣзными
želězn-ymi
made_of_iron-INS.PL

S τοῦ δῆσαι τοὺς βασιλεῖς
tou dēs-ai tous basil-eis
the.GEN.SG bind.AOR-INF the.ACC.PL.M king-ACC.PL

αὐτῶν ἐν πέδαις καὶ τοὺς
aut-ōn en ped-ais kai tous
they-GEN in chain-DAT.PL and the.ACC.PL.M

ἐνδόξους αὐτῶν ἐν χειροπέδαις
endox-ous aut-ōn en kheiroped-ais
renowned-ACC.PL they-GEN in manacle-DAT.PL

σιδηραῖς
sidēr-ais
made_of_iron-DAT.PL

'to bind their kings with chains and their nobles with fetters of iron'

One cannot overlook the syntactic incongruence in the Slavonic version of Bruno's text, namely the use of the accusative славныѧ (*slavnyę*), as in **GB**, instead of the genitive, as in the preceding noun phrase цр҃ей ихъ (*crei ixъ*). We have to do with a failed attempt to strike a balance between tradition and translation: on the one hand, one observes the stability of the traditional text – where the accusative is syntactically required by the infinitive form свѧзати (*svęzati*), like in the Greek model – and, on the other hand, the later influence of the Latin text. Indeed, Dmitrij Gerasimov used to render the gerundive purpose construction (in combination with the preposition *ad*) by means of a deverbal abstract action noun governing the genitive of the object, as in (2a):[7]

(2) a. Bruno's commentary
ad effundendum sanguinem – 'to shed blood' (13.6)
къ   пролитїю   крови
kъ   prolitij-u   krov-i
to   shedding-DAT.SG   blood-GEN.SG

ad inimicos dissipandos – 'to dissolve the enemies' (17.3)
ко   враговъ   разоренїю
ko   vrag-ovъ   razorenij-u
to   enemy-GEN.PL   dissolving-DAT.SG

ad faciendam vindictam in nationibus – 'to take revenge among the nation' (149.7)
къ   сотворенїю   ѡ(т)мщенїа   въ   ıазыцѣхъ
kъ   sotvorenij-u   ō(t)mŝenï-ę   vъ   jazyc-ěxъ
to   making-DAT.SG   revenge-GEN.SG   in   people-LOC.PL

Such a regular correspondence (Latin gerundive and Slavonic verbal noun) can be also observed in other (older and later) texts, e. g. in the "Forty Gospel homilies" by Gregory the Great (2b), in the Croatian tradition (2c) and in Kurbskij's translation of the "Exact exposition of the orthodox faith" by John of Damascus (2d):

b. Gregor the Great, Homilia 39, 187ba, 9–12 (Konzal 2006: 806)
Ad   insinuand-am   quoque   veritat-em
to   creep_in.GRDV-ACC.SG.F   even   truth-ACC.SG
dominic-ae   resurrection-is   notand-um
of_the_Lord-GEN.SG.F   resurrection-GEN.SG.F   notice.GRDV-NOM.SG.N
nobis   est
we.DAT   be.PRS.3SG

---

[7] An interesting case, very similar to the example above from the Kiev Leaflets, is the following: *converte*IMP.2SG, *Domine*VOC.SG, *oculos*ACC.PL *cordis*GEN.SG *NOSTRI*GEN.SG *ad cernendam*GRDV.ACC.SG.F *tui*GEN.SG *iudicii*GEN.SG *veritatem*ACC.SG – ѡбрати гн ѻчи срца нашего ко оуzрѣнїю твоего суда истинꙋ / *ōbrati*IMP.2SG *gi*VOC.SG *oči*ACC.DU *sr(d)ca*GEN.SG *našego*GEN.SG *ko uzrěniju*DAT.SG *tvoego*GEN.SG *suda istinu*ACC.SG 'Turn, Lord, the eyes of our heart, so that we see the truth of your sentence' (16, oratio). As the genitive *tui iudicii* precede the head noun *veritatem*, which in the Slavonic translation should stay also in the genitive, a quite different syntactic structure is obtained with the "accusativus pendens" истинꙋ (*istinu*), while твоего суда (*tvoego suda*) is directly governed by ко оуzрѣнїю (*ko uzrěniju*).

на разоумѣние   же   истинꙑ   гн҃ѧ
na razuměnij-e   že   istin-y   gń-ę
to understanding-ACC.SG and truth-GEN.SG of_the_Lord-GEN.SG
въскр҄ьниꙗ   повѣдати   намъ   ѥсть
vъskr(s)nij-a   pověda-ti   namъ   jestь
resurrection-GEN.SG announce-INF   we.DAT   be.PRS.3SG
'in order to understand the truth of the Lord's resurrection we have to notice'

c. Vatican Missal Illirico (Mihaljević 2018: 230)
Excit-a,   Domin-e,   [cord-a]   nostr-a   ad
stir_up-IMP.2SG lord-VOC.SG   heart-ACC.PL   our-ACC.PL.N   to
praeparand-as   Unigenit-i   [fili-i]
prepare.GRDV-ACC.PL.F   only_begotten-GEN.SG   son-GEN.SG
tu-i   vi-as
your-GEN.SG   way-ACC-PL
zbud-i   pros-im'   g(ospod)-i   sr(ьd)c-a
stir_up-IMP.2SG   beseech.PRS-1PL lord-VOC.SG   heart-ACC.PL
n(a)š-a   kъ   ugotovani-û   edinočed-ago
our-ACC.PL.N   to   preparing-DAT.SG   only_begotten-GEN.SG
s(i)n-a   tvo-ego   put-i
son-GEN.SG   your-GEN.SG   way-GEN.PL
'stir up our hearts, Lord, to prepare the way for your only son'

d. John of Damascus, Exposition of the orthodox faith (Besters-Dilger 1995: 414 and 415)
ad   ea   custodiend-a   quae
to   they.ACC.N   protect.GRDV-ACC.PL.N   REL.NOM.PL
sunt   secundum   natur-am
be.PRS.3SG   according_to   nature-ACC.SG
ко   сохранению   тѣ(х)   ꙗже
ko   soxranenij-u   tě(x)   jaže   sutь
to   saving-DAT.SG   they.GEN   REL.NOM.PL.N   be.PRS.3PL
по   естьствоу
po   estestv-u
according_to   nature-DAT.SG
'in order to protect those which are natural'

The contamination of the Greek and Latin syntactic patterns can involve participle forms too, or even the dative absolute construction. In example (3), the present participle of the verb бꙑти (*byti*) 'to be' is introduced by the subordinate conjunction єгда (*egda*) 'when' because the Latin verse of the Psalm has a temporal clause: *cum esset*. We could reverse the perspective, saying that the conjunction is followed by the participle сы (*sy*) because the traditional Slavonic verse, depending on the Greek text, had a participial form ὤν (*ōn*):

(3) Ps. 58.13 and 21 – verse (Tomelleri 2013: 200)

Exp	et	homo	<u>cum</u>	in	honor-e	<u>esse-t</u>
	and	man.NOM.SG	when	in	honour-ABL.SG	be.SBJV.IMPERF-3SG
Br	и	ч͞лкъ	<u>егда</u>	въ	ч͡(с)т-и	<u>сы</u>
	i	člk-ъ	egda	vъ	č(s)t-i	sy
	and	man-NOM.SG.	when	in	honour-LOC.SG	be.PTCP.PRS.NOM.SG.M
GB	и	ч͞лкъ		въ	чести	сы
	i	člk-ъ		vъ	čest-i	sy
	and	man-NOM.SG		in	honour-LOC.SG	be.PTCP.PRS.NOM.SG.M
S	καὶ	ἄνθρωπος		ἐν	τιμῇ	ὤν
	kai	anthrōp-os		en	tim-ēi	ōn
	and	man-NOM.SG		in	honour-DAT.SG	be.PTCP.PRS.NOM.SG.M

'and man being in honour'

Although the use of subordinate conjunctions with the dative absolute can be encountered in other texts from different periods and regions (Bulaxovskij 1958: 438–439),[8] the combination we find in example (4) has probably to be seen as another case of interference at the textual rather than the linguistic level:

(4) Ps. 31.3 (verse)

Exp	<u>dum</u>	<u>clamare-m</u>	tot-a	die
	when	cry.SBJV.IMPERF-1SG	all-ABL.SG.F	day.ABL.SG

---

[8] Bulaxovskij quotes an example form the Life of Saint Sergius of Radonezh (first quarter of the 15th century): и егда сему бываему, тогда оба абие пребываста алчуща / *i egda semu*_DAT.SG_ *byvaemu*_PTCP.PRS.DAT.SG_, *togda oba*_NOM.DU_ *abie prebyvasta*_AOR.3DU_ *alčuŝa*_PTCP.NOM.DU_ 'and when this was happening, then both of them immediately remained hungry' (439; see also Živov 2017: 344, n. 159). A similar case occurs in the second book Paralipomenon (30, 10) of the Ostrog Bible (1580/1581): *illis*_ABL_ *irridentibus*_PTCP.PRS.ABL.PL_ *et subsannantibus*_PTCP.PRS.ABL.PL_ *eos*_ACC_ – егда посмѣющимся и поругающимся имъ / *egda posmějušimsę*_PTCP.PRS.DAT.PL_ *i porugajušimsę*_PTCP.PRS.DAT.PL_ *imъ*_DAT_ 'whilst they laughed at them and mocked them' (Freidhof 1972: 138). Interestingly, this seems to be the product of a correction made on the previous version of the Gennadius Bible, where a genitive form is attested: тѣ(х) посмѣющихся и поругающихся и / *tě(x) posmějušixsę i porugajušixsę i(m)*. A further example from the Serbian medieval literature is provided by Kurešević (2006: 51).

Br	єгда	зовѫщѫ		ми	весь	днь
	egda	zovuŝ-u		mi	ves-ь	dn̄-ь
	when	cry.PTCP.PRS-DAT.SG		I.DAT	all-ACC.SG.M	day-ACC.SG
GB		зовѫщю		ми	весь	днь
		zovuŝj-u		mi	ves-ь	dn̄-ь
		cry.PTCP.PRS-DAT.SG		I.DAT	all-ACC.SG.M	day-ACC.SG
S	ἀπὸ	τοῦ	κράζειν	με	ὅλην	τὴν
	apo	tou	kraz-ein	me	hol-ēn	tēn
	from	the.GEN.SG	cry.PRS-INF	I.ACC	all-ACC.SG.F	the.ACC.SG.F
	ἡμέραν					
	hēmer-an					
	day-ACC.SG					

'from my crying all the day'

In fact, the translation of the commentary shows several counterexamples in which a Latin *ablativus absolutus*, preceded by a subordinate conjunction, is rendered with a finite verb form:

(5) 28.5 (commentary)[9]

    quos   Domin-us   confring-et   quando
    REL.ACC.PL.M lord-NOM.SG break-FUT.3SG when
    abiect-is   superb-is   humil-es
    depress.PTCP.PST.PASS-ABL.PL proud-ABL.PL humble-ACC.PL
    elig-at
    choose-FUT.3SG

ихже	гь	сокрѫшитъ	єгда	ѿверже
ixže	g̅-ь	sokruš-itъ	egda	ō(t)verž-e
REL.ACC.PL	lord-NOM.SG	break-PRS.3SG	when	depress-AOR.3SG
гордьі	а	смиреныхъ		изберетъ
gord-y(x)	a	smiren-yxъ		izber-etъ
proud-GEN/ACC.PL	but	humble-GEN/ACC.PL		choose.PRS-3SG

'whom the Lord shall break when he shall throw down the prouds and choose the humbles'

As the conjunction in the Latin original does not relate syntactically to the absolute construction, this odd solution suggests that the combination of conjunction and

---

[9] For some more examples see the commentary to 17.47, 31.10, 60.6, 88.23, 105.22.

dativus absolutus was felt by Dmitrij Gerasimov as odd or just misinterpreted. In favor of the second interpretation speaks the "correct" (or literal) translation in (6):

(6) 5.3 (commentary)
    cum   discuss-is   tenebr-is
    when dissipate.PTCP.PST.PASS-ABL.PL darkness-ABL.PL
    clar-i   lumin-is   advent-us   infuls-it
    bright-GEN.SG.N light-GEN.SG arrival-NOM.SG shine.PRF-3SG
    егда ѿшедшимъ   темнотамъ   ч͡стаго
    egda ō(t)šedš-imъ   temnot-amъ   č(s)t-ago
    when withdraw.PTCP.PST.ACT-DAT.PL darkness-DAT.PL pure-GEN.SG
    свѣта   пришествїе   ѿсїае͡т
    svět-a   prišestvï-e   ō(t)sïa-e(t)
    light-GEN.SG arrival-NOM.SG shine-PRS.3SG
    'when, after the dissipation of darkness, the arrival of bright light shines'

In the following, we shall concentrate on the commentary to the Psalms, which was for the first time translated from Latin in the middle of the 16th century. From a textual and linguistic perspective, it is less subjected to contamination phenomena and, moreover, contains qualitatively and quantitatively more interesting linguistic data. Some infinitive and participle constructions will be the main object of the analysis. The central question is about the role played by Latin in (re)modeling some syntactic patterns which were already attested in Church Slavonic, however with a different distribution. Along with the identification of regular patterns and correspondences between the Slavonic translation of the commentary and its Latin model, we have to determine whether some deviations from the "expected" translation are due to textual interference, as we have just seen, or to some other linguistic factors.

3 Linguistic constraints: active vs. passive

The preference given to the active voice in infinitive clauses, when in the Greek (or Latin) original a passive form occurs, is probably due to syntactic constraints. (Old) Church Slavonic often uses active constructions instead of the passive of their source originals, independently of the presence (7a) or absence (7b) of subordination:

(7) a. Mt. 18.25 (Kul'bakin 1921: 230)
    ἐκέλευσεν   αὐτὸν   ὁ   κύριος   αὐτοῦ
    ekeleus-en   aut-on   ho   kuri-os   aut-ou
    order.AOR-3SG   he-ACC   the.NOM.SG.M   lord-NOM.SG   he-GEN
    πραθῆναι
    prathē-nai
    sell.AOR.PASS-INF

    повелѣ   господь   его   да   продадѧтъ   и
    povelě   gospod-ь   ego   da   prodad-ętъ   i
    order.AOR.3SG   lord-NOM.SG   he.GEN   that   sell.PRS-3PL   he.ACC
    iuss-it   eum   domin-us   eius   venund-ari
    order.PRF-3SG   he.ACC   lord-NOM.SG   he.GEN   sell.PRS-INF.PASS
    'his lord commanded that he should be sold'

b. Mt. 19.12, Codex Marianus (Xodova 1980: 282)
    εἰσὶν   εὐνοῦχοι   οἵτινες   εὐνουχίσθησαν
    eisin   eunoukh-oi   hoitines   eunoukhisthē-san
    be.PRS.3PL   eunuch-NOM.PL   REL.NOM.PL   emasculate.AOR.PASS-3PL
    ὑπὸ   τῶν   ἀνθρώπων
    hypo   tōn   anthrōp-ōn
    by   the.GEN.PL   man-GEN.PL

    и   сѫтъ   каженици   ѩже
    i   sǫtъ   kaženic-i   ję̌e
    and   be.PRS.3PL   eunuch-NOM.PL   REL.ACC.PL
    исказишѧ   члов҇ци
    iskazi-šę   člověc-i
    emasculate.AOR-3PL   man-NOM.PL

    but cf. Savina kniga:
    и   сѫтъ   каженици   иже
    i   sǫtъ   kaženic-i   iže
    and   be.PRS.3PL   eunuch-NOM.PL   REL.NOM.PL
    сѧ   казишѧ   отъ   члов҇къ
    sę   kazi-šę   otъ   člověk-ъ
    REFL   emasculate.AOR-3PL   from   man-GEN.PL
    'there are eunuchs, who were made so by men'

This syntactic conversion is quite regular with *verba iubendi*; probably because of its modal value the Slavonic *dativus cum infinitivo* construction would not have been suitable for a proper rendering of the model (Večerka 1996: 223).[10] While in the Greek and Latin originals the jussive verb of the matrix clause governs a dependent clause, consisting of accusative with infinitive, in the Church Slavonic translations the nominal phrase in the accusative usually fulfills the syntactic role of direct object of the infinitive, with the active (!) infinitive directly depending on the verb of the matrix clause:

(8) a. Lectio in festo s. Feliciani pape et mart. (Mihaljević 2018: 230)
Hic   constitu-it   supra memori-as
he.NOM.SG   establish.PRF-3SG   over memory-ACC.PL
martyr-um   miss-as   celebr-ari
martyr-GEN.PL   mass-ACC.PL   celebrate.PRS-INF.PASS
si   post(a)vi   vr'hu pamet-i
he.NOM   establish.AOR.3SG   over memory-GEN.SG
m(u)č(e)n(i)k-i mis-e   služi-ti
martyr-GEN.PL   mass-ACC.PL   celebrate-INF
'he established that a mass should be celebrated in memory of the martyrs'

b. Martyrdom of Saint Vitus (Kappel 1974: 76; Mareš 1979: 136)
hoc   audiens   pater   eius   iuss-it
that.ACC   hear.PTCP.PRS.NOM.SG   father.NOM   he.GEN   order.PRF-3SG
infant-em   cathom-is   caed-i
child-ACC.SG   rod-ABL.PL   beat.PRS-INF.PASS
слышавъ   же   си   оцъ
slyša-v-ъ   že   si   oc-ь
hear-PTCP.PRF.ACT-NOM.SG.M   and   these.ACC father-NOM.SG
його   повелѣ   отрока   прутіѥмь   бити
jego   povelě   otrok-a   prutij-emь   bi-ti
he.GEN   order.AOR.3SG   child-GEN/ACC.SG   rod-INS.SG   beat-INF
'having heard that, his father commanded that the child should be beaten with rods'

c. Gennadius Bible, Mac. 2.13, 4 (Freidhof 1972: 31)
iuss-it,   ut   eis   est   consuetudo,
order.PRF-3SG   that   they.DAT   be.PRS.3SG   habit.NOM.SG

---

10 "Diese aksl. Konstruktion stellt eine syntaktische Umstellung der griech. Fügung dar, denn ihr mögliches Übersetzungsäquivalent mit passivem Infinitiv, die Konstruktion des *dativus cum infinitivo*, entspräche wahrscheinlich in semantischer Hinsicht nicht genau der Vorlage. Er hat nämlich eine zusätzliche modale Schattierung."

```
           apprehens-um                 in   eodem      loc-o           nec-ari
           arrest.PTCP.PASS-ACC.SG      in   same.ABL   place-ABL.SG    kill.PRS-INF.PASS
           повелѣ         ꙗко     имъ       єсть                  ѡбычаи
           povelě         jako    imъ       estь                  ōbyčai
           order.AOR.3SG  like    they.DAT  be.PRS.3SG            habit.NOM.SG
           ꙗта                          в     тӧ               мѣстѣ            оубити
           jat-a                        v     to(m)            měst-ě           ubi-ti
           arrest.PTCP.PASS-GEN/ACC.SG  in    that.LOC.SG      place-LOC.SG     kill-INF
           'he commanded, as the custom is with them, that he should be appre-
           hended and put to death in the same place'
```

d. John of Damascus, Exposition of the orthodox faith (Besters-Dilger 1995: 262 and 263)

```
           Oporte-ba-t              enim   et       solid-ari                et
           be_proper-IMPERF-3SG     for    and      strengthen.PRS-INF.PASS  and
           innov-ari               natur-am
           renew.PRS-INF.PASS      nature-ACC.SG
           подобало          оубо    оукрепїти         ї      ѡбновіти
           podoba-l-o        ubo     ukrepï-tï         ï       obnovï-tï
           be_proper-PST-N   for     strengthen-INF    and     renew-INF
           єстество
           estestv-o
           nature-ACC.SG
           'it was necessary to strengthen and renew the nature'
```

Bruno's Psalter behaves in the same way:

(9) a. 11, Argumentum
```
           pet-it         itaque      prophet-a           iniquitat-em
           ask.PRS-3SG    therefore   prophet-NOM.SG      iniquity-ACC.SG
           mund-i         destru-i
           world-GEN.SG   destroy.PRS-INF.PASS
           просит҃ъ        же      оубо      про̂рокъ
           pros-itъ        že      ubo       pr(o)rok-ъ
           ask.PRS-3SG     and     therefore prophet-NOM.SG
           неправду         мира            разорити
           nepravd-u        mir-a           razori-ti
           iniquity-ACC.SG  world-GEN.SG    destroy-inf
           'so, the prophet demands that the iniquity of the world be destroyed'
```

b. 16.6
    pet-it   ergo   Christ-us   pass-us   su-os
    ask.PRS-3SG therefore   Christ-NOM   step-ACC.PL his-ACC.PL.M
    custod-iri
    keep.PRS-INF.PASS

    проситъ   оубо   х͡с   стопы
    pros-itъ   ubo   x͡s   stop-y
    ask.PRS-3SG therefore   Christ.NOM   step-ACC.PL

    своѧ[11]   соблюсти
    svo-ę   sobljus-ti
    his-ACC.PL   keep-INF
    'therefore, Christus demands that his steps be kept'

Sometimes, however, we are faced with more interesting, and more complicated situations, where the reflexive "pronoun" (or, to say it better, the postfix) сѧ (sę) occurs in a syntactically unclear or ambiguous position:

(10) 21.21
    liber-ari   se   postula-t
    free.PRS-INF.PASS REFL.ACC   ask.PRS-3SG

    избавитисѧ   проситъ
    izbavi-ti-sę   pros-itъ
    free-INF-PASS   ask.PRS-3SG
    'he demands to be freed'

From a quantitative point of view, according to the principle of the one-to-one correspondence between translation and translated text, one could affirm that the passive infinitive *liberari* of the Latin text was "substituted" by the translator, as usually, with the active form избавити (*izbaviti*); this being the case, the element сѧ (*sę*) would render the accusative form *se* in the syntactic role of the subject of the infinitive construction. Such an explanation, however, is morphologically problematic and syntactically highly improbable. It is much more plausible to assume that in the Slavonic text the verb проситъ (*prositъ*) 'demands' governs a simple passive infinitive (избавитисѧ – *izbavitisę*) 'to be freed', and not an accusative with infinitive as in the Latin original. This is without any doubt the case in the next example, where the position of сѧ (*sę*) leaves no room for doubt:

---

[11] With the active infinitive we would expect the form его (*ego*) instead of the reflexive adjective своѧ (*svoe*).

(11) 138.23
    pet-it   se   deduc-i   in aetern-a   vi-a
    ask.PRS-3SG REFL.ACC conduct.PRS-INF.PASS in eternal-ABL.SG.F way-ABL.SG
    проситъ наставитисѧ на вѣчномъ пѹти
    pros-itъ nastavi-ti-sę na věčn-omъ put-i
    ask.PRS-3SG conduct-INF-PASS on eternal-LOC.SG way-LOC.SG
    'he demands to be conducted on the eternal way'

On the other hand, the occurrence of the full pronominal form себе (*sebe*) in example (12) produces a quite strange construction, as the reflexive meaning does not convey the sense of the Latin original, which is actually passive:

(12) 25.2
    prob-ari   se   rog-at   ecclesi-a
    examine.PRS-INF.PASS REFL.ACC ask.PRS-3SG church-NOM.SG
    искѹсити себе просить црквь
    iskusi-ti sebe pros-itъ crkv-ь
    examine-INF REFL.ACC ask.PRS-3SG church-NOM.SG
    'the church demands to be tempted'

The pronominal form себе (*sebe*) corresponds here to the Latin accusative *se*, denoting the subject of the infinitive clause, as in the following example:

(13) 29.7
    iur-e   dice-ba-t   se   mov-eri
    right-ABL say-IMPERF-3SG REFL.ACC move.PRS-INF.PASS
    non posse in aetern-um
    NEG can.PRS.INF in eternal-ACC.SG
    в правдѹ глаше себе подвижатисѧ
    v pravd-u gla-še sebe podviža-ti-sę
    in truth-ACC.SG say-IMPERF.3SG REFL.ACC move-INF-PASS
    не мощи въ вѣкъ
    ne mošî vъ věk-ъ
    NEG can.INF in century-ACC.SG
    'he rightly said that he could not be moved forever'

Therefore, passive infinitive forms seem to occur quite regularly with verbs that do not express request, command and so on. Consequently, it is tempting to suppose behind this alternation of voice a functional distribution, due to semantic (and syntactic) constraints, between passive voice in an infinitive clause, like in the Latin model, and active forms with jussive verbs, where the *accusativus cum infinitivo* construction is generally avoided.

The same holds true when the infinitive construction is replaced by means of a non-finite subordinate clause introduced by the conjunction *da*, see here example (14a) and (7a) above, here reproduced as (14b):

(14) a. Chronicle of George the Monk (Kopylenko 1957: 234)
    ἐπεζήτησεν   ἀποσταλῆναι   αὐτ-ῷ   τὸν
    epezētē-s-en   apostalē-nai   aut-ōi   ton
    request-AOR-3SG   send.AOR.PASS-INF   he-DAT   the.ACC.SG.M
    πατριάρχην   Νικόλαον   καί   τινας   τῶν
    patriarch-ēn   Nikola-on   kai   tin-as   tōn
    Patriarch-ACC.SG   Nicholas-ACC.SG   and   some-ACC.PL   the.GEN.PL
    μεγιστάνων
    megistan-ōn
    magnate-GEN.PL

    проси   же,   да   послеть   емоу   Николоу
    prosi   že,   da   posl-etъ   emu   Nikol-u
    request.AOR.3SG   and   that   send.PRS-3SG   he.DAT   Nicholas-ACC.SG
    патриарха   и   нѣкоих   вельможь
    patriarx-a   i   někoix   velьmož-ь
    patriarch-GEN/ACC.SG   and   some.GEN/ACC.PL   magnate-GEN/ACC.PL
    'he requested that the patriarch Nicholas and some of the magnates be sent to him'

b. Mt. 18.25 (Kul'bakin 1921: 230)
    ἐκέλευσεν   αὐτὸν   ὁ   κύριος   αὐτοῦ   πραθῆ-ναι
    ekeleu-s-en   aut-on   ho   kuri-os   aut-ou   prathē-nai
    order-AOR-3SG   he-ACC   the.NOM.SG.M   lord-NOM.SG   he-GEN   sell.AOR.PASS-INF
    повелѣ   господь   его   да   продадатъ   и
    povelě   gospod-ь   ego   da   prodad-ętъ   i
    order.AOR.3SG   lord-NOM.SG   he.GEN/ACC   that   sell.PRS-3PL   he.ACC
    iuss-it   eum   domin-us   eius   venund-ari
    order.PRF-3SG   he.ACC   lord-NOM.SG   he.GEN   sell.PRS-INF.PASS
    'his lord commanded that he should be sold'

There are, however, some exceptions, where a passive periphrastic form is used:

(15) 54.1
pet-it   prophet-a   exaud-iri   oration-em   su-am
ask.PRS-3SG prophet-NOM.SG   heed.PRS-INF.PASS   prayer-ACC.SG   his-ACC.SG.F
проси   пр҃рокъ   оуслышанѣ   быти
pros-i(t)   pr(o)rok-ъ   uslyšan-ě   by-ti
ask.PRS-3SG prophet-NOM.SG   heed.PTCP.PST.PASS-DAT.SG   be-INF
мл҃твѣ   его
mltv-ě   ego
prayer-DAT.SG he.GEN
'the prophet asks that his prayer be heard'

We may suppose here that the use of the dative, instead of the accusative case, has made the choice of the passive voice of the dependent predicate possible, like in the following example:

(16) 33.7
haud   dubi-um   est   timent-es
NEG   doubtful-NOM.SG.N   be.PRS.3SG   fear.PTCP.PRS-NOM.PL
Domin-um   ab   angel-is   custod-iri
lord-ACC.SG by   angel-ABL.PL   protect.PRS-INF.PASS
нѣсть   съмнѣнию   боѧщимсѧ
něstь   sumněnij-u   boęŝ-imsę
NEG.be.PRS.3SG doubt-DAT.SG fear.PTCP.PRS.DAT.PL
г҃а   ѿ   агглъ   хранимомъ   быти
ǧ-a   ō(t)   aǧgl-ъ   xranim-omъ   by-ti
lord-GEN/ACC.SG by angel-GEN.PL protect.PTCP.PRS.PASS-DAT.PL be-INF
'there is no doubt that who fears the Lord is protected by angels'

Unlike Greek and Latin, Slavonic does not possess genuinely passive infinitive forms, apart from the periphrastic forms with passive participle and the copula быти (*byti*) 'to be', as in examples (15) and (16). We can thus conclude that there exists a native tendency, or preference, to use active infinitive or finite forms rather than their corresponding passive contained in the Greek or Latin models. The observed voice-case correlation in subordinate clauses leads us to the next point.

4 Infinitive constructions

In the literature, Slavonic infinitive constructions where the subject of the subordinate clause is put in the accusative case while the predicate is expressed in the infinitive form (*accusativus cum infinitivo*) are usually considered ungrammatical or semi-grammatical (Večerka 1971: 140), an external Grecism pertaining to the surface (Pacnerová 1958: 269; Birnbaum 1971: 42).[12] They rarely occur in Old Church Slavonic texts, thus occupying a marginal and unstable position:

(17) Mt. 16.15 (Večerka 2002: 446)
    ὑμεῖς   δὲ   τίνα   με   λέγετε   εἶναι;
    hymeis   de   tina   me   leg-ete   einai?
    you.NOM.PL   and   who.ACC   I.ACC   say.PRS-2PL   be.INF
    вы   же   кого   мѧ   глаголете   бъіти
    vy   že   kogo   mę   glagol-ete   by-ti
    you.NOM.PL   and   who.ACC   I.ACC   say.PRS-2PL   be-INF
    Vos   autem   quem   me   esse   dic-itis?
    you.NOM.PL   but   who.ACC   I.ACC   be.INF   say.PRS-2PL
    'but whom do you say that I am?'

On the contrary, the accusative with participle or the *dativus cum infinitivo* constructions have been generally deemed to be the proper equivalent of the Greek construction (MacRobert 1986: 143).[13] The *dativus cum infinitivo* construction was more spread out, with the infinitive preserving its modal meaning, whereas the accusative was mostly, but not exclusively used with the participle with verbs denoting physical or intellectual perception (Večerka 1996: 195–196).

The question on the origin of the *accusativus cum infinitivo* construction does not matter here.[14] More relevant to our investigation is the presence, in Bruno's Psalter, of a great quantity of infinitive constructions, calqued on the Latin model; the subject occurs in the accusative or in the genitive also with inanimate refer-

---

12 For an interesting attempt at analyzing example (17) in the framework of the generative-transformational grammar see Růžička (1966: 84–85). It can be stated that "the infinitive is not a native means of expressing indirect statements in Old Church Slavonic (MacRobert 1986: 158).
13 By *dativus cum infinitivo* we mean here such cases, clearly based on the Greek model, where the dative-infinitive construction forms a dependent clause, with the dative being its subject, while the verb of the matrix clause does not govern the dative case: мнѣахѫ ѥмоу разболѣти сѧ / *mněaxǫ*$_{\text{IMPERF.3PL}}$ *jemu*$_{\text{DAT}}$ *razbolěti*$_{\text{INF}}$ *sę*$_{\text{REFL}}$ 'they thought that he would fall ill' (*Codex Suprasliensis* 551,1, quoted from Mrazek 1963: 121). Notwithstanding their use as an artificial stylistic device (искусственный стилизационный приём), they did not violate the Slavonic syntactic structure of the time, since purely Slavonic infinitive sentences were potentially polysemantic (Mrazek 1963: 114). For other infinitive constructions, looking similar on the surface and usually conveying some modal values, see the classification by Mrazek (1963) and the material collected in Pacnerová (1958) and Rothe (1960).
14 For further discussion and references see Kurešević (2018: 262) and Danylenko (2019).

ents, as in examples (18a) and (18b),[15] perhaps an overextension of the Russian constructional counterpart, or with the dative case, both with active (19a) and with passive voice (19b):

(18) a. 9.31

cum   dic-it   ocul-os   eius   in
when   say.PRS-3SG   eye-ACC.PL   he.GEN   in
pauper-em   scilicet   spirit-u   respic-ere
poor-ACC.SG   namely   spirit-ABL   look.PRS-INF
єгда   гл͠етъ   ѡчєсъ   єго   на
egda   gl-etъ   ōčes-ъ   ego   na
when   say.PRS-3SG   eye-GEN/ACC.PL he.GEN   at
нищаго   сирѣчь   д͠хомъ   зрѣти
niŝ-ago   sirěčь   dx̄-omъ   zrě-ti
poor-GEN/ACC.SG   namely   spirit-INS.SG   look-INF
'when he says that his eyes look at the poor namely in spirit'

b. 27, Argumentum

notand-um   igitur   hunc   psalm-um
notice.GRDV-NOM.SG.N   therefore   this.ACC.SG.M psalm-ACC.SG
terti-um   esse
third-ACC.SG   be.INF
вѣдомо   ж   оубо бꙋди   сєго
vědom-o   ž   ubo   bud-i   sego
known-NOM.SG.N   and   for   be.IMP-3SG   this.GEN/ACC
ѱалма   трєтїаго   быти
psalm-a   treti̇-ego   by-ti
psalm-GEN/ACC.SG   third-GEN/ACC.SG   be-INF
'notice also that this Psalm is the third'

(19) a. 9.19

dic-it   enim   non   per-ire   patienti-am
say.PRS-3SG   for   NEG   die.PRS-INF   patience-ACC.SG

---

15 The use of the genitive as the case of the direct object is codified in the Russian translation of the Latin *Donatus*-grammar and frequently attested in the works of Maksim the Greek (Keipert 1988: 108–109). This clearly demonstrates the influence of the "spoken" morphology upon Church Slavonic.

гл҃етъ   же   паки   не   погибнѫти   терпѣнїю
gl-etъ   že   paki   ne   pogibnu-ti   terpěnij-u
say.PRS-3SG and again   NEG   die-INF   patience-DAT.SG
'because he says that patience does not die'

b. 79.6
quia De-us   supra vir-es   nostr-as   tent-ari
for God-NOM.SG   over force-ACC.PL   our-ACC.PL.F   try.PRS-INF.PASS
nos   et vex-ari   non permitt-it
we.ACC and trouble.PRS-INF.PASS   NEG allow.PRS-3SG
еже   бг҃ъ   выше   силъ   нашихъ   искѹситисѧ
eže   bğ-ъ   vyše   sil-ъ   naš-ixъ   iskusi-ti-sę
that God-NOM.SG   over   force-GEN.PL   our-GEN.PL   try-INF-PASS
намъ   і   ѡзлоблѧтисѧ   не   попѹститъ
namъ   ï   ōzloblę-ti-sę   ne   popust-itъ
we.DAT and trouble-INF-PASS   NEG   allow.PRS-3SG
'because God does not allow us to be tried and harassed beyond our strength'

This conspicuous number of infinitive constructions clearly corresponds to the situation in the Latin original; thus, Latin influence has to be assumed. An analogous situation is to be observed in Kurbskij's translation of the "Exact exposition of the orthodox faith" by John of Damascus, where the vast majority of Latin *accusativus cum infinitivo* constructions have been calqued (Besters-Dilger 1982: 5).

However, even when Latin syntax seems to act as an element of considerable strength, we can still detect native morpho-syntactic categories, as the presence of the genitive-accusative, in a form which has been curiously extended to nouns with inanimate referents, independently of number (examples 18a and 18b). Beside this, the absence in Slavonic of a morphological category, namely the past active infinitive, has caused an increase of participial constructions in subordinate clauses, as will be shown in the next section.

5 Extension of participial constructions

A no less interesting categorical expansion is represented by the frequent occurrence of *accusativus cum participio* constructions, considered to be "autochthonous" and not imported (Birnbaum 1968: 57), which in Old Church Slavonic, as was already mentioned, tend to be used mainly with verbs denoting sense perception (Večerka 2002: 447–448):[16]

(20) Mk. 1.16 (Grković-Mejdžor 2010: 189)

εἶδεν	Σίμωνα	καὶ	Ἀνδρέαν	τὸν
eid-en	Símōn-a	kai	Andre-an	ton
see.AOR-3SG	Simon-ACC.SG	and	Andrew-ACC.SG	the.ACC.SG.M

ἀδελφὸν	Σίμωνος	ἀμφιβάλλοντας
adelf-on	Simōn-os	amphiballont-as
brother-ACC.SG	Simon-GEN	cast_a_net.PTCP.PRS.ACT-ACC.PL.M

ἐν	τῇ	θαλάσσῃ
en	tēi	thalass-ēi
in	the.DAT.SG.F	sea-DAT.SG

видѣ	симона	и	аньдрѣѭ
vidě	simon-a	ï	anьdrěj-ǫ
see.AOR-3SG	Simon-GEN/ACC.SG	and	Andrew-ACC.SG

братра	того	симона.
bratra	togo	simon-a.
brother-GEN/ACC.SG	that.GEN	Simon-GEN.SG

въметаѭща	мрѣжѧ	въ	море
vъmetajǫ̂-a	mrěž-ę	vъ	mor-e
throw.PTCP.PRS.ACT-ACC.DU	net-ACC.PL	in	sea-ACC.SG

'he saw Simon and Andrew his brother, casting nets into the sea'

In Bruno's Psalter, however, the participial construction is not related semantically to the presence of a *verbum sentiendi* nor does it necessarily mark the processual meaning expressed by the participle. Instead, it has the function of filling a morphological gap of Slavonic verbs, being employed as a useful syntactic tool for rendering Latin past infinite forms. Such an "augmented" use of subordinate participial constructions for expressing past time reference (or anteriority) can be easily found in other translations from Latin:

---

[16] Růžička (1963: 240) mentions four *verba sentiendi*, namely видѣти (*viděti*), оуꙃьрѣти (*uzъrěti*) both 'to see', слышати (*slyšati*) 'to hear' and обрѣсти (*obrěsti*) 'to find', which can have an activity as a complement.

(21) a. Sermons of Gregory the Great (Bes 10, 42bβ 18 – Haderka 1964: 523)
   omn-ia   quippe   element-a   auctor-em   su-um
   all-NOM.PL.N   in_fact   element-NOM.PL.N   creator-ACC.SG their-ACC.SG
   venisse   testatae sunt
   come.PRF.INF   attest.PRF.3PL

   вса   же   твари   творца
   vs-ę   že   tvar-i   tvorc-a
   all-NOM.PL   and   creature-NOM.PL   creator-GEN/ACC.SG

   своюго   пришедъша
   svoj-ego   prišedъš-a
   their-GEN/ACC.SG.M   come.PTCP.PST.ACT-GEN/ACC.SG

   съвѣдѣтелъствовали   соутъ
   sъvědětelъstvoval-i   sutъ
   attest.LPTCP-PL   AUX.PRS.3PL

   'since all the elements have attested that their creator has come'

b. Esther 7, 8 (Mihaljević 2018: 232)
   reper-it   Aman   super   lectum   corruisse
   find.PRF-3SG   Aman.ACC   on   bed-ACC.SG   fall.PRF.INF
   in   quo   iace-ba-t   Esther
   in   REL.ABL.SG   lie-IMPERF-3SG   Esther.NOM.SG

   v'z'obret-e   aman-a   na   postel-û
   find.AOR-3SG   Aman-GEN/ACC.SG   on   bed-ACC.SG
   spad'š-a   v   neiže   leža-še
   fall.PTCP.PST-GEN/ACC.SG   in   REL.LOC.SG.M   lie-IMPERF.3SG
   estor-ь
   Esther-NOM

   'he found Aman was fallen upon the bed on which Esther lay'

c. Guido delle Colonne's Trojan history (Ščepkin 1899: 1368)
   Quod   postquam   not-um   Parid-i
   REL.NOM.SG.N   after   known-NOM.SG.N   Paris-DAT
   factum   est   regin-am   vicem
   make.PTCP.PRF.PASS.N   AUX.PRS.3SG   queen-ACC.SG   instead
   Helen-am   Menela-i   reg-is   uxor-em
   Helen-ACC.SG   Menelaus-GEN.SG   king-GEN.SG   wife-ACC.SG
   ad   templ-um   ips-um   Vener-is   accessisse
   to   temple-ACC.SG   itself-ACC.SG   Venus-GEN.SG   arrive.PRF.INF

   єгда   же   вѣдомо   бысть   паридоу
   egda   že   vědom-o   bystь   Parid-u
   When   and   known-NOM.SG.N   be.AOR.3SG   Paris-DAT.SG

црцоу   еленоу   менелаа   цр҃а
cr̄c-u   Elen-u   Menela-ę   cr̄-ę
queen-ACC.SG Helen-ACC.SG   Menelaos-GEN.SG   king-GEN.SG

женоу   во   храмъ   афродита
žen-u   vo   xram-ъ   Afrodit-a
wife-ACC.SG in   temple-ACC.SG Aphrodite-GEN.SG

пришѣ̑дшоу
priše(d)š-u
arrive.PTCP.PST-ACC.SG.F

'and when Paris became aware of the fact that the queen Helen, wife of Menelaus, had arrived at the temple of Aphrodite'

d. John of Damascus (Besters-Dilger 1982: 6 = 1995: 298)

Dic-imus   autem   natur-am   nostr-am   surrexisse
say.PRS-1PL   and   nature-ACC.SG   our-ACC.SG.F   rise.PRF.INF

a   mortu-is,   assumptam esse,   et
from   dead-ABL.PL   take_up.PRF.INF.PASS and

sed-ere   ad   dexter-am   patr-is
sit.PRS-INF   at   right_side-ACC.SG   father-GEN.SG

ї   послѣдую̑е(м)   оубо   естество   нш҃е
ï   poslědu-e(m)   ubo   estestv-o   nš-e
and   follow.PRS-1PL   therefore   nature-ACC.SG   our-ACC.SG.N

воскр҃ше   от   мр҃твы̑(х)
voskr(s)š-e   ot   mr̄tv-y(x)
rise.PTCP.PST-ACC.SG.N   from   dead-GEN.PL

вознесен'но   быти,   ї   седѣти   о
voznesen'n-o   by-tï,   ï   sedě-ti   o
take_up.PTCP.PST.PASS-ACC.SG.N be-INF   and sit-INF   at

дес'ную   ot҃ца
des'n-uju   o(t)c̄-a
right_side-ACC.SG   father-GEN.SG

'but we say that our nature has risen from the dead,[17] has been taken up and sits at the Father's right hand'

---

[17] I do not totally agree with the German translation provided by Besters-Dilger (1982: 6), which assigns a temporal meaning to the first participle form воскр҃ше (voskr(s)še): "wir sagen aber, dass unsere Natur, nachdem sie von den Toten auferstanden ist, aufgenommen wird und zur Rechten des Vaters sitzt".

In Bruno's commented Psalter there are many participial constructions, with the accusative (22a) as well as with the dative case (22b):

(22) a. 101.18
  dic-it etiam respexisse Domin-um oration-em
  say.PRS-3SG even regard.PRF.INF lord-ACC.SG prayer-ACC.SG
  pauper-um
  poor-GEN.PL
  гл҃етъ   паки призрѣвша
  gl-etъ   paki prizrěvš-a
  say.PRS-3SG again regard.PTCP.PST-GEN/ACC.SG
  г҃а   на моленїе   нищихъ
  ğ-a   na molenï-e niŝ-ixъ
  lord-GEN/ACC.SG toward prayer-ACC.SG poor-GEN.PL
  'he says further that the Lord has regarded the prayer of poor men'

 b. 21.34
  apte   vero dict-um   est
  properly but say.PTCP.PST.PASS-SG.N be.PRS.3SG
  Christian-um popul-um Domin-um fecisse
  Christian-ACC.SG people-ACC.SG lord-ACC.SG make.PRF.INF
  ѿчасти[18] оубо речено   есть
  ō(t)časti ubo recen-o   estь
  partly but say.PTCP.PST.PASS-SG.N be.PRS.3SG
  хр҃тоименитыи   людеи   г҃у
  xr(s)toimenit-y(x) ljud-ei   ğ-u
  Christian-GEN/ACC.PL people-GEN/ACC.PL lord-DAT.SG
  сотворшу
  sotvorš-u
  PTCP.PST-DAT.SG
  'it is indeed correctly said that the Lord has made the Christian people'

Passive verb forms are rendered with the past passive participle plus the infinite of the auxiliary verb быти (*byti*) 'to be', almost exclusively with the accusative case:

---

18 This translation is probably the result of a wrong interpretation of the Latin abbreviation, read as *a parte* instead of *apte*.

(23) 85.12
su-am que anim-am dic-it esse
his-ACC.SG.F and soul-ACC.SG say.PRS-3SG be.INF
liberat-am ab infern-o inferior-i
free.PTCP.PST.PASS-ACC.SG.F from hell-ABL.SG lower-ABL.SG
свою же д͠шу г͠летъ быти
svoj-u že dš-u gl̃-etъ by-ti
his-ACC.SG.F and soul-ACC.SG say.PRS-3SG be-INF
изба́влен꙯ ѿ ада преисподнаго
izbavlen-u ō(t) ad-a preispodn-ęgo
free.PTCP.PST.PASS-ACC.SG.F from hell-GEN.SG lower-GEN.SG
'and he says that his soul has been freed from the lower hell'

A possible explanation for this restriction could be the modal meaning conveyed by the *dativus cum infinitivo* construction. There are, however, some rare examples of a mismatch between the accusative marking on the noun and the predicate in the dative (24a and 24b), which are attested also elsewhere in the Church Slavonic tradition (24c):

(24) a. 21.5
qu-os const-at venisse ad praemi-um
REL-ACC.PL.M be_known.PRS-3SG come.PRF.INF to reward-ACC.SG
ихже состоитса пришедшимъ къ
ixže sostoitsę prišedš-imъ kъ
REL.ACC.PL be_known.PRS.3SG come.PTCP.PST.DAT.PL to
возданїю
vozdanïj-u
reward-DAT.SG
'about whom it is known that they come to the reward'

b. 118.8
pet-it se statim a Domin-o custod-iri
ask.PRS-3SG REFL.ACC.SG at_once by lord-ABL.SG keep.PRS-INF.PASS
просит꙯ себе[19] абїе ѿ г͠а
pros-itъ sebe abïe ō(t) g̃-a
ask.PRS-3SG REFL.ACC at_once by lord-GEN.SG

---

19 Here a dative form себѣ (*sebě*) with graphic confusion between е (*e*) and ѣ (*ě*) cannot be totally excluded.

сохранену   быти
soxranen-u   by-ti
keep.PTCP.PST.PASS-DAT.SG   be-INF
'he requests to be immediately kept by the Lord'

c. Gospel of Nikodemus 4 (Haderka 1964: 528)
non   omn-is   multitudo   vult   eum   mor-i
NEG   all-NOM.SG   mass.NOM.SG   want.PRS.3SG   he.ACC.SG   die.PRS-INF
не   все   множьство   хоштетъ   иего
ne   vs-e   množьstv-o   xošt-etъ   jego
NEG   all-NOM.SG.N mass-NOM.SG   want.PRS-3SG   he.GEN/ACC.SG
оубиеноу   быти[20]
ubien-ou   by-ti
kill.PTCP.PST.PASS-DAT.SG   be-INF
'not the whole mass wants him to die'

6 Conclusions

Bruno's commented Psalter presents us a significant increase of infinitive and participle constructions, whose use diverges from the situation attested in earlier texts. Generally speaking, in the history of Church Slavonic translations, one observes a trend towards increasing literalism. While the first translations give evidence of syntactic independence from the Greek text (Bauer 1972 [1958]: 49), the influence of the Greek (in our case Latin) model considerably grows over time, as later translators tend to transfer quite mechanically syntactic patterns from the source to the target language. Interestingly, this is just the reverse of what happened in Western Europe. Here the cultural and linguistic superiority of the Latin (written) tradition was strongly felt "in the early days of the national literatures" (Blatt 1957: 47), whereas national idioms and vulgar languages underwent a gradual process of emancipation from Latin. For example, such constructions as the *accusativus cum infinitivo*, widely used at the beginning of the literary traditions, were almost totally lost in a later stage.

In section 2 we saw that the choice of the active form of the infinitive for the passive in the Latin text is without any doubt due to morphological and syntactical constraints, the passive form not fitting well into the Slavonic syntactic

---

[20] In other manuscripts the transitive-active readings оуморити (*umoriti*) and оубити (*ubiti*) are attested (Vaillant 1968: 18), which require a complement in the accusative.

system. Latin influence, instead, is clearly responsible for the large presence of subordinate clauses with the accusative case followed by the infinitive or the participle (with past time reference) in Bruno's commented Psalter. In addition, the overwhelming majority of infinitive constructions features the accusative case, and this, once again, is in contrast with the frequency and distribution of infinitive and participial constructions in Old Church Slavonic.

To sum up, translations, which take the lion's share of the entire corpus of Church Slavonic literature, offer us many perspectives and do not offer us any fewer problems to be tackled. On the one side, the comparison of the Slavonic text with its model, if properly identified, helps us in interpreting, understanding and analyzing the linguistic material. On the other side, however, we must be always very cautious about the translated text, taking into consideration the more or less strong influence of the original, especially in the case of religious and liturgical texts. In addition, we should never forget the particular circumstance that we usually deal with when tackling translations from extinct languages – in the sense that the language of these texts is very different from the still spoken register – into a written language with "changing" rules. Consequently, if we want to properly evaluate the various constructions, it is primarily necessary to work at more levels, taking into account at least four factors:

1) The force of the tradition, namely the possibility that some lexical or grammatical curious forms or constructions replicate old textual, not necessarily linguistic patterns.
2) Induced innovation, i.e. the impact of Latin models upon the linguistic behavior of the translator, the target language being somehow less important than the linguistic features of the text to be translated.
3) The character (genre) of the original text: hymnographic compositions, for example, being used in the celebration of the mass, are syntactically much simpler (but in no way easier) than a theological commentary intended for a monk's reading in his cell.
4) And, last but not least, the spoken language of the translator, which sometimes "pops up" in the translation and slightly transforms, or enriches, the syntactic rules of Church Slavonic.

However, a global approach, which should include original compositions as well as many more translations of Southern or Western origin, would help us identify some constants or regularities in the strategies employed in different Church Slavonic translations from Latin.

The fragmentary material we have presented here has hopefully made clear that, in order to properly understand the "mobile" syntax of Church Slavonic translations, we need a scrupulous, almost pedantic philological approach, further critically reliable bilingual text editions and, at the end of this preliminary work, a corpus which collects a sample of representative data from chronologically and territorially different textual traditions.

References

Barr, James. 1979. The Typology of Literalism in Ancient Biblical Translations. *Nachrichten der Akademie der Wissenschaften in Göttingen* 11. 279–325.

Bauer, Jaroslav. 1972 [1958]. Vliv řečtiny a latiny na vývoj syntaktické stavby slovanských jazyků [The influence of Latin on the syntactic development of the Slavonic languages]. In Jaroslav Bauer (ed.), *Syntactica slavica. Vybrané práce ze slovanské skladby*, 47–67. Brno: Universita J. E. Purkyně. [previously published in: *Československé přednášky pro IV. mezinárodní sjezd slavistů v Moskvě*. Praha: Nakladatelství Československé akademie věd, 1958, pp. 73–95].

Besters-Dilger, Juliane. 1992. Die Wiedergabe lateinischer syntaktischer Konstruktionen (Acc. cum inf., Part. coniunctum und Abl. absolutus) in Kurbskijs Damascenus-Übersetzung. *Anzeiger für slavische Philologie* 13. 1–24.

Besters-Dilger, Juliane (ed.). 1995. *Die Dogmatik des Johannes von Damaskus in der Übersetzung des Fürsten Andrej M. Kurbskij (1528–1583)*. Freiburg i. Br.: Weiher.

Birnbaum, Henrik. 1968. Obščeslavjanskoe nasledie i inojazyčnye obrazcy v strukturnyx raznovidnostjax staroslavjanskogo predloženija [Common Slavonic heritage and foreign patterns in structural varieties of the Old Church Slavonic sentence]. In Henry Kučera et al. (eds.), *American Contributions to the Sixth International Congress of Slavists (Prague, 1968, August 7–13)*, 29–63. The Hague & Paris: Mouton [Reprint Birnbaum 1974: 81–115].

Birnbaum, Henrik. 1971. Zum infiniten Ausdruck der Prädikation bei Johannes dem Exarchen. In Bohuslav Havránek (ed.), *Studia palaeoslovenica*, 37–47. Praha: Academia, nakladatelství Československé akademie věd. [Reprint Birnbaum 1974: 138–150].

Birnbaum, Henrik. 1974. *On Medieval and Renaissance Slavic Writing. Selected Essays*. The Hague & Paris: Mouton.

Blatt, Franz. 1957. Latin Influence on European Syntax. *Travaux du Cercle Linguistique de Copenhague* 11. 33–69.

Bulaxovskij, Leonid Arsen'evič. 1958. *Istoričeskij kommentarij k russkomu literaturnomu jazyku* [Historical commentary on the Russian literary language]. Pjatoe, dopolnennoe i pererabotannoe izdanie. Kiev: Gosudarstvennoe učebno-pedagogičeskoe izdatel'stvo "Radjans'ka škola".

Danylenko, Andrii. 2019. Do the parallels meet? On the origin of the accusative with infinitive construction in Slavic. *Belgian Journal of Linguistics* 33. 150–182.

Drinka, Bridget. 2011. The Sacral Stamp of Greek: Periphrastic Constructions in New Testament Translations of Latin, Gothic, and Old Church Slavonic. *Oslo Studies in Language* 3(3). 41–73.

Freidhof, Gerd. 1972. *Vergleichende sprachliche Studien zur Gennadius-Bibel (1499) und Ostroger Bibel (1580/81). Die Bücher Paralipomenon, Esra, Tobias, Judith, Sapientia und Makkabäer*. Frankfurt am Main: Athenäum.

Grković-Mejdžor [Grković-Major], Jasmina. 2010. O konstrukciji akuzativa s participom (tipološki i kognitivni aspekti) [On the construction 'accusative and participle' (typological and cognitive aspects)]. *Južnoslovenski filolog* 66. 187–204.

Haderka [Gaderka], Karel. 1964. Sočetanija sub''ekta, svjazannogo s infinitivom, v staroslavjanskix i cerkovnoslavjanskix pamjatnikax [The construction 'subject and infinitive' in Church Slavonic documents]. *Slavia* 33(4). 505–533.

Kappel, Guido. 1974. Die slavische Vituslegende und ihr lateinisches Original. *Wiener Slavistisches Jahrbuch* 20. 73–85.

Keipert, Helmut. 1988. Die slavische Übersetzung des Photius-Briefs an Boris-Michael von Bulgarien. In Hans-Bernd Harder & Hans Rothe (eds.), *Gattungen in den slavischen Literaturen. Festschrift für Alfred Rammelmeyer*, 89–113. Köln & Wien: Böhlau.

Keipert, Helmut. 1999. Die Kirchenslavisch-These des Cercle linguistique de Prague. In Ernst Hansack, Walter Koschmal & Norbert Nübler (eds.), *Festschrift für Klaus Trost zum 65. Geburtstag,* 123–133. München: Sagner.

Konzal, Václav. 1994. Latinské participium futuri v staroslověnském překladu (Responze latinské syntaxe v českosl. památkách I.) [The Latin future participle in the Old Church Slavonic translation. The answer to Latin Syntax in the Czech Church Slavonic documents]. *Slavia* 63(2). 193–205.

Konzal, Václav. 2006. *Čtyřicet homilií Řegoře Velikého na evangelia v českocírkevněslovanském překladu, díl druhý: homilie XXV-XL* [The forty homilies by Gregory the Great on the Gospel in Czech Church Slavonic translation, part II: homilies XXV-XL]. Praha: Slovanský ústav Akademie věd České republiky, Nakladatelství Euroslavica.

Kopylenko, Mojsej Michajlovič. 1957. Gipotaktičeskie konstrukcii slavjano-russkogo perevoda "Xroniki" Georgija Amartola [Hypotactic constructions in the Russian Church Slavonic translation of the "Chronicle" by George Hamartolos]. *Vizantijskij vremennik* (12). 232–241.

Kul'bakin, Stepan Michajlovič. 1921. Nekoliko reči o konstrukciji "da sa indikativom" mesto infinitiva u staroslovanskom prevodu Jevandjelija [Remarks on the construction "*da* with indicative" instead of an infinitive in the Old Slavonic translation of the Gospels]. In *Zbornik filoloških i livgvističkih studija A. Beliću povodom 25-godišnjice njegova naučnog rada posvećuju njegovi prijatelji i učenici*, 229–232. Beograd: Cvijanović.

Kurešević, Marina. 2006. Apsolutni dativ u srpskoj srednjovekovnoj pismenosti [The dative absolute in the medieval Serbian literature]. *Zbornik Matice srpske za filologiju i lingvistiku*. 49(1). 35–113.

Kurešević, Marina. 2018. The status and origin of the *accusativus cum infinitivo* construction in Old Church Slavonic. In Björn Hansen, Jasmina Grković-Major & Barbara Sonnenhauser (eds.), *Diachronic Slavic Syntax. The Interplay between Internal Development, Language Contact and Metalinguistic Factors*, 261–284. Berlin & Boston: de Gruyter Mouton.

Lunt, Horace G. 1987. On the Relationship of Old Church Slavonic to the Written Language of Early Rus'. *Russian Linguistics* 11(2–3). 133–162.

MacRobert, Catherine Mary. 1986. Foreign, Naturalized and Native Syntax in Old Church Slavonic. *Transactions of the Philological Society* 84(1). 142–166.

Mareš, František V. 1979. *An Anthology of Church Slavonic Texts of Western (Czech) Origin. With an Outline of Czech-Church Slavonic Language and Literature and with a Selected Bibliography*. München: Fink.

Mélanges linguistiques dédiés au premier Congrès des philologues slaves. 1929. Prague: Jednota československých matematiků a fysiků.

Mihaljević, Ana. 2018. *Sintaksa hrvatskoglagoljskih tekstova prevedenih s latinskoga* [The syntax of Croatian Glagolitic texts translated from Latin]. Zagreb: Sveučilište u Zagrebu, Filozofski fakultet dissertation.
Mrazek, Roman. 1963. K dativno-infinitivnym konstrukcijam v staroslavjanskom jazyke. [On the dative-and-infinitive-construction in Old Church Slavonic]. *Sborník prací filosofické fakulty Brněnské university* 12(11). 107–126.
Nimčuk, Vasyl' Vasyl'ovyč. 1983. *Kyjivs'ki hlaholyčni lystky. Najdavniša pam'jatka slov'jans'koji pysemnosti* [The Kiev Missal. The oldest document of Slavonic writing]. Kyjiv: Naukova dumka.
Pacnerová, Ludmila. 1958. K syntaxi infinitivu v staroslověnských evangelních kodexech [On the syntax of the infinitive in the Old Church Slavonic Gospel codices]. In Václav Machek (ed.), *Studie ze slovanské jazykovědy. Sborník k 70. narozeninám akademika Františka Trávníčka*, 263–270. Praha: Státní pedagogické nakladatelství.
Rothe, Hans. 1960. Unpersönliche Regentia mit dem Infinitiv im Altkirchenslavischen (Ein Beitrag zu der Diskussion über die sogenannte Kategorie des Zustandes). *Slovo* 9(10). 105–128.
Růžička, Rudolf. 1963. *Das syntaktische System der altslavischen Partizipien und sein Verhältnis zum Griechischen*. Berlin: Akademie-Verlag.
Růžička, Rudolf. 1966. O ponjatii «zaimstvovannyj sintaksis» v svete teorii transformacionnoj grammatiki [On the concept "borrowed syntax" against the background of the theory of transformational syntax]. *Voprosy jazykoznanija* 2006(4). 80–96.
Ščepkin, Vjačeslav Nikolaevič. 1899. Licevoj sbornik Imperatorskogo rossijskogo istoričeskogo muzeja. *Sbornik otdelenija russkogo jazyka i slovesnosti Imperatorskoj Akademii Nauk* 4(4). 1345–1385.
Steiner, Peter. 1982. *The Prague School. Selected Writings, 1929–1946*. Austin: University of Texas Press.
Tomelleri, Vittorio S. 2004. *Il Salterio commentato di Brunone di Würzburg in area slavo-orientale. Fra traduzione e tradizione (Con un'appendice di testi)*. München: Sagner.
Tomelleri, Vittorio S. 2013. O nekotoryx osobennostjax Tolkovoj Psaltiri Brunona (1535). Datel'nyj samostojatel'nyj, infinitivnye i pričastnye konstrukcii, gerundij i gerundiv [On some features of Bruno's commented Psalter. The dative absolute, infinitive and participle constructions, gerund and gerundive]. In *Lingvističeskoe istočnikovedenie i istorija russkogo jazyka 2012–2013*. 196–225. Moskva: Drevlechranilišče.
Uspenskij, Boris Andreevič. 2002. *Istorija russkogo literaturnogo jazyka (XI–XVII vv.)*. [The history of the Russian literary language (XI–XVII c.]. Izdanie 3-e, ispravlennoe i dopolnennoe. Moskva: Agent Press.
Vaillant, André. 1968. *L'Evangile de Nicodème. Texte slave et texte latin*. Genève & Paris: Droz.
Večerka, Radoslav. 1971. Vliv řečtiny na staroslověnštinu [The influence of Greek on Old Church Slavonic]. *Listy filologické* 94(2). 129–151.
Večerka, Radoslav. 1996. *Altkirchenslavische (altbulgarische) Syntax. Bd 3: Die Satztypen: Der einfache Satz*. Freiburg i. Br.: Weiher.
Večerka, Radoslav. 2002. *Altkirchenslavische (altbulgarische) Syntax. Bd 4: Die Satztypen: Der zusammengesetzte Satz*. Freiburg i. Br.: Weiher.
Xodova, Kapitolina Ivanovna. 1980. *Prostoe predloženie v staroslavjanskom jazyke* [The simple sentence in Old Church Slavonic]. Moskva: Nauka.
Živov, Viktor Markovič. 2017. *Istorija jazyka russkoj pis'mennosti* [The history of the language of Russian writing]. Tom 1. Moskva: Universitet Dmitrija Požarskogo.

Ana Šimić
Non-strict negative concord proper and languages in contact. Translating Latin into Croatian Church Slavonic and Greek into Old Church Slavonic

Abstract: Negative concord proper, as the most common negative concord variety, is the co-occurrence of negative indefinites with predicate negation. Non-strict negative concord proper refers to the word order ruled negative concord: it is obligatory with a postverbal negative pronoun/adverb and optional or not allowed at all with a preverbal negative pronoun/adverb. Croatian Church Slavonic is a non-strict negative concord proper language. The same goes for Old Church Slavonic and Greek. But Latin, as the source language of many Croatian Church Slavonic texts, does not exhibit negative concord at all.

The aim of this paper is to further the analysis of the relation between Latin and Croatian Church Slavonic with respect to non-strict negative concord proper. The analysis was conducted on the first part of the *Second Beram breviary*, the Croatian Church Slavonic manuscript from the 15th century containing texts translated from Latin or revised according to the Latin source texts. Quantitative data shows that the majority of sentences with a preverbal negative pronoun/adverb do not exhibit negative concord proper. In comparison, applied negative concord proper is the favoured option in *Codex Marianus*, an Old Church Slavonic manuscript translated from Greek.

These data confirm that the influence of a non-negative concord language (Latin) cannot change the essence of such a distinctive typological parameter like negative concord. It can however, where possible, have an impact on the choice of one of the two equally valid options. In contact linguistics, such a syntactic change is known as narrowing.

Keywords: syntactic change, negative concord, Church Slavonic, Latin, Greek

---

Ana Šimić, Staroslavenski institut, Zagreb, e-mail: ana.simic@stin.hr

https://doi.org/10.1515/9783110651331-011

1 Negative concord

Negative concord is a widespread language phenomenon in which a single instance of semantic negation is expressed by two or more different negative items. The following example is from (contemporary) Croatian:

(1) *Nikada neću zaboraviti Salzburg.*
    never not-will forget Salzburg
    'I will never forget Salzburg.'

It is differentiated from the so-called *negative doubling* (Zeijlstra 2004: 52; Polleto 2008) or *split negation* (Pfau 2008: 41),[1] which refers to the obligatory use of double negative particles/adverbs. This phenomenon is found in, for example, French (*Nous **ne** sommes **pas** fatigués* 'We are not tired').

Although absent from the contemporary language, negative doubling was indeed attested in the history of Croatian. So far, the only known confirmation is from a juridical Glagolitic manuscript dating from the 17th century:

(2) *ako ... ne bi Jakov ale nega redi ne*
    if NEG would Jacob or his heirs NEG
    plaćali ...[2]
    pay
    'If Jacob or his heirs wouldn't pay ...'
    (Kovačević 2016: 34)

Unlike negative doubling, negative concord is a widespread language phenomenon, found in the majority of the world's languages (Haspelmath 2013). In Europe, Slavonic languages are recognizable negative concord languages. Considering the other two major European language branches, Germanic and Romance, they also exhibit negative concord – to a certain extent – or they had at least exhibited it in the past.[3]

---

[1] Pfau (2008: 41) uses terms *split negation* and *negative concord* as synonyms.
[2] This form of negative doubling is similar to the one found in Afrikaans, where the same negative particle is repeated twice (e.g. *Ons is **nie** moeg **nie*** 'We are not tired'). Cf. Zeijlstra 2004: 52; Willis, Lucas and Breitbarth 2013: 15.
[3] Probably Germanic languages might seem least prone to exhibit negative concord. However, one doesn't have to be a linguist to notice negative concord in the contemporary *lingua franca*, the English language – *In baseball, you don't know **nothing*** (Yogi Berra), *I ain't **never** gonna shut you out* (Beyoncé), *I don't really trust them **no** more* (Cardi B). Apart from these non-standard

2 Negative concord proper

Negative concord proper (Giannakidou 2000: 458) is a negative concord variety illustrated in (1). It is the co-occurrence of predicate (sentential) negation and negative pronouns or adverbs (negative indefinites, n-words).

Throughout the history of Croatian, starting with Croatian Church Slavonic, negative concord proper includes not only co-occurrence of predicate negation and negative pronouns (Kovačević 2013: 503–504; Kovačević 2016: 243–245), but also co-occurrence of predicate negation and conjunction/particle *ni* 'and not, nor, neither, not even' (Kovačević 2016: 243–245). The example for the latter in contemporary Croatian is as follows:

(3) *Nisam ga ni ja vidjela.*
    not.AUX him neither I see
    'I didn't see him either.'

In both negative concord proper varieties, (1) and (3), apart from predicate negation there is the same negative item, once as a negative prefix (**ni**kada) and the other time as a negative conjunction/particle *ni*.

In this paper only the first negative concord proper variety, i.e. the one with predicate negation and negative pronoun/adverb will be examined.

2.1 Strict and non-strict negative concord proper

There is a difference between strict and non-strict negative concord proper (cf. Giannakidou 2000). What makes that difference is word order. Strict negative concord proper is in general always applied, regardless of word order. Like any other contemporary Slavonic language (Brown 2002: 166; Willis 2013: 369), contemporary Croatian is also a strict negative concord proper language (Zovko Dinković 2013: 232; Kovačević 2013: 503; Kovačević 2016: 259).[4]

Whether non-strict negative concord proper will be applied or not depends on the positioning of a negative pronoun/adverb and a predicate. If a predicate

---

varieties of English, it is well-known that negative concord was used in the history of English (Wallage 2012). Negative concord can be found in German dialects as well, e.g. in Southern Bavarian – *I hob **koan** Schnaps **net** bschtellt* 'I didn't order Schnapps' (Pfau 2008: 41).
4 Given that contemporary Croatian is a strict negative concord proper language, the rephrased example (1) with a different word order exhibits negative concord too: Neću *zaboraviti Salzburg* nikada.

precedes a negative pronoun/adverb, negative concord proper is obligatory. If a negative pronoun/adverb precedes a predicate, negative concord proper can be optional or it may not be applied at all. Some contemporary Romance languages, e.g. Spanish, are examples of the latter:

(4) a. *(No) vino nadie.
      NEG came n.person
      'Nobody came.'
    b. Nadie (*no) vino.
       n.person NEG came
       'Nobody came.'
       (Willis, Lucas, Breitbarth 2013: 34)[5]

Examples of the former are Catalan and certain dialects of Southern American English (Brown 2002). So are the two languages in the focus of this paper: the oldest attested Slavonic language and the first Slavonic literary language, Old Church Slavonic (Willis 2013: 370),[6] and the first Croatian literary language, Croatian Church Slavonic (Kovačević 2013: 503; 2016: 238–239).[7]

---

[5] Cf. Kovačević (2013: 505). Non-strict negative concord proper is attested in some non-standard varieties of English (Tubau Muntañá 2008) as well, but also in pre-modern stages of English (Ingham 2013).

[6] As summed up in Kovačević (2016: 235), see also Kovačević (2016: 51–66), the Old Church Slavonic word order rule concerning non-strict negative concord proper is referred to in the grammars by W. Vondrák (1912: 606), A. Vaillant (1948: 254) and G. A. Xaburgaev (1974: 402), without the terms used in this paper (i. e. non-strict negative concord proper). The same goes for the Old Church Slavonic negative concord proper descriptions in Zlatanova (1991: 383–384), Večerka (1989: 126–128; 1996: 137–138). For further discussion of Old Church Slavonic negative concord proper see, for example, Křižková (1968), Brown (2002), Dočekal (2009) and Kovačević (2016: 234–236).

[7] Croatian Church Slavonic or Croatian redaction of Church Slavonic (cf. Mihaljević, Reinhart 2013; Mihaljević 2014; Šimić 2014), is based on Old Church Slavonic but created under strong influence of the Croatian Chakavian vernacular. It was used from the end of the 11th until the 16th century. CCS texts are both liturgical (like Bible books and readings) and non-liturgical (like legends, visions, apocrypha, sermons, songs, legal documents and others). Most of them were translated from Latin or revised according to the Latin source texts. The ones that originated from Greek were actually mediated through common Church Slavonic heritage. Croatian Church Slavonic was written in Glagolitic script, since the Croats were the only people among the Slavs who long continued using Glagolitic script, changing its original round, circular forms into angular ones.

3 Non-strict negative concord proper in Croatian Church Slavonic

The Croatian Church Slavonic norm was at its strongest in liturgical books, breviaries and missals, especially in Bible readings.[8] The following examples of non-strict negative concord proper – (5a) with a postverbal negative pronoun/adverb and (6a$_1$/a$_2$) with a preverbal negative pronoun/adverb – are precisely these:

(5) a. ⰕⰏⰉ   ⰐⰡⰔⰕⰜ   ⰂⰟ   ⰐⰅⰏⰜ   ⰐⰋⰅⰄⰋⰐⰑⰅⰆⰅ[9]
    ... tmi   něst'   v   nem'   niedinoeže
    darkness not_be in him none
    'there is not any darkness in him'
    (BrVO 291c; 1 Jn. 1.5)

b. σκοτία   ἐν   αὐτῷ   οὐκ   ἔστιν   οὐδεμία
   skotia   en   autō   ouk   estin   oudemia
   darkness in himself NEG be none
   'there is not any darkness in him'

c. ... tenebrae in eo non sunt ullae
   darkness in he NEG be any
   'there is not any darkness in him'

(6) a$_1$. ⰐⰉⰝⰅⰔⰑⰆⰅ   ⰾⰹ   ⰐⰅ   ⰑⰕⰂⰡⱄⰀⰅⰞⰉ
    ničesože   li   ne   otveŝaeši
    nothing   Q   NEG   answer
    'Nothing do you say?'
    (MVat$_4$ 81a; Mk. 15.4)

a$_2$. ⰐⰉⰝⰅⰔⰑⰆⰅ   ⰾⰹ   ⰑⰕⰂⰡⱄⰀⰂⰀⰅⰞⰉ
    ničesože   li   otveŝavaeši
    nothing   Q   answer
    'Nothing do you say?'
    (MNov 81d)

b. οὐκ   ἀποκρίνῃ   οὐδέν
   ouk   apokrinē   ouden
   NEG   answer   nothing
   'Don't you answer anything?'

---

[8] Latin and Greek Bible reading varieties throughout the paper were derived from BibleWorks 8.
[9] The Glagolitic version does not fully correspond to the original due to *scriptura continua* and the usage of ligatures in the Croatian Glagolitic manuscripts.

c. *non respondes quicquam*
   NEG answer   anything
   'Don't you answer anything?'

The Greek and Latin versions of examples (5) and (6), i.e. (5b) and (5c) and (6b) and (6c), show that Greek exhibits negative concord proper while Latin, a non-negative-concord language, does not.

When a negative pronoun/adverb precedes a predicate, sentences with negative concord proper prevail in Croatian Church Slavonic (Kovačević 2016: 239).[10] However, Kovačević (2016: 214) noticed that sentences without negative concord proper prevail to some extent in those Croatian Church Slavonic texts with the Latin source texts, most often liturgical ones (breviaries and missals). On the other hand, those kinds of sentences are also found in Croatian Church Slavonic texts that were inherited from the earlier Old Church Slavonic literature (in which they were translated from Greek) as well as in those translations whose source texts have not been discovered yet. Furthermore, non-applied negative concord proper is attested in non-liturgical texts, i.e. in those with a weaker Croatian Church Slavonic norm. In the history of Croatian, non-strict negative concord proper was exhibited until the 19th century (Kovačević 2013: 503–504; 2016: 242).[11] Following those premises, together with the notion of the overall six varieties of negative concord in Croatian Church Slavonic,[12] Kovačević (2013: 504–505; 2016: 241–243) concludes that the question of Latin influence should be explained in

---

10 The research in Kovačević (2016) was conducted on the representative and referential corpus containing Latin and Greek source texts aligned to the respective Croatian Church Slavonic translations and containing 62 Croatian Glagolitic sources, both manuscripts and incunabula. The corpus was originally made for the purpose of the compilation of the *Dictionary of the Croatian redaction of Church Slavonic*, but it is widely used for different research projects. It is available as a paper card-file at the Old Church Slavonic Institute in Zagreb (Croatia). For more on the corpus, see Vukoja (2012; 2014).

11 E. g., a couple of the examples cited in Kovačević (2016: 242) in which negative concord proper is not exhibited in vernacular Croatian are: *u ničemur utihe najti mogoh* 'In nothing could I find any comfort' (Z. Planinić, *Planine*, 1569.), *Priko volje nigdar dobro more biti* 'It can never be good against one's will' (I. Zadranin, *Historija od Filomene*, 17–18th ct.).

12 Different combinations of Croatian Church Slavonic negative items – *ne* 'no, not', *ni* 'and not, nor, neither, not even', negative pronouns and adverbs (*nitkože, nikotore, niedinь, nikogdaže* ...), *bez* 'without' and *neže* 'than' – form six types of negative concord (Kovačević 2016: 236–255). Those are: 1. *ne* + negative pronoun/adverb, 2. *ne* + *ni*, 3. *ni* + negative pronoun/adverb, 4. negative pronoun/adverb + negative pronoun/adverb, 5. *bez* + negative pronoun/adverb, 6. *neže* + negative pronoun/adverb. The six Croatian Church Slavonic negative concord varieties emerged from the contrastive analysis between Croatian Church Slavonic translation and Latin source texts.

terms of encouraging one of two equally valid options when a negative pronoun or adverb precedes a predicate.[13]

Whether negative concord will be applied (6a$_1$) or not (6a$_2$) in the sentences with preverbal negative pronoun or adverb in the same text/manuscript or written by the same scribe is still to be described in terms of randomness or arbitrariness. A pattern in the choice, if there is any at all, has yet to be discovered.[14]

4 Non-strict negative concord proper in the *Second Beram breviary*

The data presented in Kovačević (2013) and Kovačević 2016 concerning non-strict negative concord proper in Croatian Church Slavonic are the results of an approximate estimation. The rest of this paper will further the analysis of the relation between Latin and Croatian Church Slavonic with respect to the non-strict negative concord proper by providing analytic data. In addition, a comparison will be made with the analogous relation between the Greek source text and the Old Church Slavonic translation.

---

[13] In the literature concerning historical aspects of the Croatian syntax (e.g. Maretić 1916; Kuzmić, Kuzmić 2009) the lack of predicate negation in sentences with negative pronouns/adverbs is attributed solely to the influence of Latin or even the Italian language, without any awareness of the word order rule or the fact that in the Old Church Slavonic texts, as translations from the non-Italic, negative concord language (Greek), predicate negation in sentences with preverbal negative pronoun/adverb can be omitted as well (Kovačević 2013: 503–505; 2016: 242–243).

[14] A reviewer suggested that concerning negative concord proper a potential role of the Vendlerian aspects (Vendler 1957) should be checked. Given that the Vendlerian aspects are lexical (semantical) in nature, examples such as – *mrtvi bo protivu n(a)m' ničtože ne g(lago)ljut'* 'Hence, the dead are speaking nothing against us' (BrBer$_2$ 190b) and *niktože g(lago)laše emu s(love)se* 'nobody was speaking a word to him' (BrBer$_2$ 240a, Job 2,13) – bring forward the same verbal lexical item (*glagolati* 'speak') with negative concord being both applied and not applied. Such examples speak in favour of the probability that the Vendlerian aspects are not the key factor in resolving the optionality of negative concord proper in sentences with preverbal negative pronoun/adverb. However, it is a matter that requires further analysis which goes beyond this paper's topic. In addition, with Croatian Church Slavonic being a historical language, such an analysis depends on a thorough semantic description of the Croatian Church Slavonic vocabulary, which is currently lacking. The ongoing *Dictionary of the Croatian redaction of Church Slavonic* is completed up to the letter *i* (Klenovar, Ribarova & Vela 2018).

4.1 The *Second Beram breviary*

Concerning the title of this paragraph, the first and most common negative concord variety – negative concord proper – will be examined in one particular medieval manuscript – the *Second Beram breviary*,[15] sometimes known also as the *Second Ljubljana Breviary* (named for the place where it is now kept). It is a Croatian Church Slavonic manuscript written in angular Glagolitic script in the 15th century. It was used in the town of Beram, situated in the centre of the Croatian coastal region of Istria.

As any other Roman breviary this one consists of two main parts, the temporale (Proper of seasons) and the sanctorale (Proper of saints). The former contains the Office of all Sundays and movable feasts while the latter contains the Office of (fixed) feasts of the saints. Both include texts like lessons, Bible readings, antiphons, responsories, psalms and rubrics. Rubrics with (liturgical) instructions are particularly interesting from a linguistic perspective because they are written in vernacular, unlike the rest of the breviary, which we may then consider to be a proper representation of the literary language norm.

The *Second Beram breviary* was transliterated into Latin script within *The Scientific centre of excellence for Croatian Glagolitism*, a project of the Old Church Slavonic Institute in Zagreb.[16] In this paper a thorough analysis of the first part of the breviary (the temporale), with 264 parchment sheets, was conducted.

The majority of its content is in the form of Bible readings, i. e. Bible texts, and homiletic readings from the most prominent Church Fathers and writers like Ambrose, Venerable Bede, Augustine of Hippo, Origen, Pope Leo the Great, Jerome, Thomas Aquinas and others.

4.2 Word order: What negative item comes first?

In the *Second Beram breviary* the vast majority of sentences with negative pronoun/adverb have a postponed predicate. In other words, in the context of negative concord proper negative pronouns/adverbs mostly precede a predicate, i. e. they are preverbal. Table 1 shows the total numbers and percentages (in brackets) of sentences with preceding negative pronouns/adverbs and those with preceding predicates:

---

[15] Cf. Mihaljević (2011); Šimić (2014: 42).
[16] Available at: https://beram.stin.hr/hr/transliteration/53/1 (the temporale and the sanctorale). The first part, i.e. the temporale is available as facsimile and transliterated edition in Mihaljević (2018).

Table 1: Word order in sentences with negative pronouns/adverbs in the *Second Beram breviary*.

Preceding negative pronoun/adverb	Preceding predicate
250 (88%)	34 (12%)

Regarding word order, the Croatian Church Slavonic translation most often follows its Latin source texts, e.g. *niktože ne čudit se* (BrBer₂ 73a) / *Nemo miretur* 'Nobody wonders'.[17] There are 16 exceptions, however. Shifts in word order have been attested in both directions:

(7) a.   ⰰ   ⰲⱄⰰⰽⱁⰵ   ⰴⱁⰱⱃⱁ   ⱀⰻⰽⱁⰾⰻⰶⰵ   ⱀⰵ   ⱆⰿⰰⱀⱽⰽⰰⰵⱅⱽ
      i   *v'sakoe*   *dobro*   *nikoliže*   *ne*   *uman'kaet'*
      and   every   good   never   NEG   lack
      'and all goodness is never missing'
      (BrBer₂ 105d/106a)
   b. *et*   *omne*   *bonum*   *non*   *deesse*   *umquam*   *poterit*
      and   all   good   NEG   be away   ever   can
      'and all goodness can never be away'

(8) a.   ⰲⰰ   ⰿⱽⱀⱑ   ⱀⰵ   ⰻⰿⰰⱅⱽ   ⱀⰻⱍⰵⱄⱁⰶⰵ
      va   *m'ně*   *ne*   *imat'*   *ničesože*
      in   me   NEG   have   nothing
      'in me he comes up with nothing'
      (BrBer₂ 138d)
   b. *in*   *me*   *nihil*   *inveniet*
      in   I   nothing   find
      'in me nothing does he find'

There is a preceding Croatian Church Slavonic negative pronoun in (7) for a preceding Latin predicate. The translator changes the word order and decides to apply negative concord proper. There are ten changes in word order similar to this one in the corpus, but negative concord proper is applied only twice.[18]

---

[17] The Latin versions are derived from the referential Croatian Church Slavonic corpus, see note 10.
[18] Seven of them are direct citations or paraphrases for John 1.3 in different parts of the manuscript (*sine ipso factum est nihil* 'without him nothing was made').

In (8) Latin has a preverbal negative adverb while Croatian Church Slavonic has a preceding predicate. As expected, because of the world order rule, negative concord proper is applied. The same goes with the other four similar sentences with word order shift in regard to the Latin source text.

4.3 Negative concord proper

Overall results concerning negative concord proper being applied or not are shown in Table 2. Sentences with no negative concord proper prevail over the ones with applied negative concord proper.

Table 2: Negative concord proper in the *Second Beram breviary*.

Negative concord proper applied	Negative concord proper not applied
103 (36%)	181 (64%)

4.3.1 Negative concord proper in sentences with a preceding predicate

In spite of the word order rule, not all sentences with a preceding predicate exhibit negative concord proper (Table 3).

Table 3: Negative concord proper in sentences with a preceding predicate.

Negative concord proper applied	Negative concord proper not applied
32 (94%)	2 (6%)

The first one (9a), when compared to another Croatian Glagolitic manuscript (9b) and Latin original (9c), is an obvious scribe's mistake. In other words, the second predicate was omitted:

(9) a. * aŝe ljube sebi sie tvoriši ničtože .
　　　 (BrBer₂ 118d)
　　 b. aŝe ljube sebe sie tvoriši ničtože tvoriši
　　　 if love oneself this make nothing make
　　　 'If from love for yourself you do this, you do nothing.'
　　　 (BrVat₅ 88b)

c. *Si amore tui   id facis, nihil   facis.*
   if love yours it do nothing do
   'If from love for yourself you do it, you do nothing.'

The second example with a preceding predicate and no negative concord proper cannot be explained like the previous one:

(10) a. ⱂⱃⱏ ⱆⱇⰵ ⰴⰰⰵ ⰽⱅⱁ ⰻⱄⱂⱁⰲⱑⰴⰰⰵⱅⱐ ⱄⰵ ⱅⰵⰱⱑ ·
     va   ade   že   kto   ispovest'   se   t(e)bě.
     in   hell   but   who   confess   REFL   you
     ⰵⰶⰵ ⰵ   ⱀⰻⰵⰴⰻⱀⱐ ·
     eže   e(stь)   niedin'.
     it   be   no-one
     'In hell, however, who confesses to you? It is no-one.'
     (BrBer₂ 106b)
   b. *In inferno autem quis confitebitur   tibi. Id est nullus.*
     in   hell   but   who   acknowledge   you   it   be   none
     'In hell, however, who acknowledges you? It is no-one.'

There is no negative concord proper, although the word order requires it. Three more prominent Croatian Glagolitic breviaries do not apply negative concord proper here either (BrVO 160b, BrVat₅ 78c, BrN₂ 77b).

It is not easy to address the question of why there is no negative concord proper in the cited example. More similar cases would maybe make it possible to offer a plausible hypothesis explaining the phenomenon. For now, we should content ourselves with mere recognition of its occurrence.

4.3.2 Negative concord proper in sentences with a preverbal negative pronoun/adverb

With a preverbal negative pronoun/adverb negative concord proper is optional. Table 4 shows how that optionality is resolved in favour of not applied negative concord proper in the *Second Beram breviary*:

Table 4: Negative concord proper in sentences with a preverbal negative pronoun/adverb (*Second Beram breviary*).

Negative concord proper applied	Negative concord proper not applied
71 (28%)	179 (72%)

There are more than double the number of sentences without negative concord proper in comparison to the ones with negative concord proper.

There is even one example (out of an overall of 12 sentences with negative pronouns/adverbs) of negative concord proper not being applied in vernacular rubrics, cf. ex. (11). This suggests that negative concord proper is generally avoided even in parts of the Breviary that are written in vernacular Croatian.

(11) ⰝⰈⰅⰐⰟⰓⰀ ⰀⰓⰀ   ⰕⰓⰑⰂⰏⰅ ⰕⰉⰐⰟ ⰔⰅ ⰔⰒⰑⰏⰅⰐⰖⰕⰉⰅ ⰑⰕ ⰇⰅⰓⰠⰅ
     nied'no ino   vrime   čini   se spomenut(i)e ot ferie
     no-one   other time   do   REFL mention   of feast (day)
     'There is no mention of a feast day in any other time.'
     (BrBer₂ 263b)

The overall data from the *Second Beram breviary* show that negative concord proper applied is a noticeable minority. That is not in concordance with the previously mentioned overall Croatian Church Slavonic data (see Section 3). The fact that the breviary represents the norm of the literary language at its strongest is one of the reasons for such a discrepancy. The other is that Latin is the language of the source text, as previously mentioned.

Within the Croatian Church Slavonic corpus, Mihaljević (2007) brings analytic data regarding negative concord proper in fragments (12th–13th c.) translated from Latin or Greek sources. In fragments from Greek sources there are four sentences with negative concord proper and three without it. In fragments from Latin sources, on the other hand, there is only one sentence (out of an overall of nine) with negative concord proper applied.

Bigger data for comparison can be found regarding a similar literary language – Old Church Slavonic – which was translated exclusively from Greek. Unlike Latin, Greek is a negative concord language (Muchnová 2016; Giannakidou 2006).

5 Non-strict negative concord proper in the Old Church Slavonic *Codex Marianus*

Applied negative concord proper prevails in the two known Old Church Slavonic fourfold Gospels: *Codex Marianus* and *Codex Zographensis* (Cakalidi 1981: 53–54; Večerka 1989: 127 and Večerka 1996: 137, cf. Kovačević 2016: 235).

Regarding the *Codex Marianus* only, Kovačević (2016: 235–236) gives percentages and a ratio concerning negative concord proper. In the *Codex Marianus* the ratio between sentences with and those without negative concord proper applied is 3:1. Sentences with preverbal negative pronouns/adverbs are a majority in the *Codex Marianus* (72%) with 65% of them being accompanied by a negated predicate.

The following absolute and relative data bring a revised analysis of the *Codex Marianus* in regard to negative concord proper.[19]

5.1 Word order

As shown in Table 5, in the *Codex Marianus* the negative pronouns/adverbs precede the predicate more often than not.

Table 5: Word order in sentences with negative pronouns/adverbs in *Codex Marianus*.

Preceding negative pronoun/adverb	Preceding predicate
133 (75%)	44 (25%)

Regarding word order, the Old Church Slavonic translation most often follows its Greek source texts. There are 18 exceptions, however. Shifts in word order have been attested in both directions: seven in favour of a preceding negative pronoun/adverb (12) and 11 in favour of a preceding predicate (13):

(12) a. bež   nego   ničьtože ne   bystъ eže   bystъ
        without he   nothing   NEG   be   which be
        'Without him nothing was made that was made.'
        (John 1.3)
     b. χωρὶς   αὐτοῦ ἐγένετο   οὐδὲ ἕν   ὃ   γέγονεν
        chōris   autou egeneto   oude hen   ho   genonen
        without he   become   NEG   one   which become
        'Without him became nothing that became.'

(13) a. obnoštь vьsǫ   troždьše sę   ne   jęsomъ ničesože
        night   all   labour   REFL NEG   catch   nothing
        'All night they labored (and) caught nothing.'
        (Lk. 5.5)

---

19 Jagić's edition of the *Codex Marianus* (Jagić1960 [1883]) was used for this analysis.

b. ὅλης   νυκτὸς   κοπιάσαντες   οὐδὲν   ἐλάβομεν
   holēs   nuktos   kopiasantes   ouden   elabomen
   whole   night   labour   nothing   receive
   'All night they laboured (and) nothing did they catch.'

5.2 Negative concord proper

Table 6 shows that sentences with applied negative concord proper occur more than three times as often as the ones with no negative concord proper.

Table 6: Negative concord proper in *Codex Marianus*.

Negative concord proper applied	Negative concord proper not applied
134 (76%)	43 (24%)

In concordance with the word order rule, all sentences with a preceding predicate exhibit negative concord proper in *Codex Marianus*.

With a preverbal negative pronoun/adverb, there are more than twice as many negative concord-sentences as those without negative concord, as shown in Table 7:

Table 7: Negative concord proper in sentences with a preverbal negative pronoun/adverb (*Codex Marianus*).

Negative concord proper applied	Negative concord proper not applied
90 (68%)	43 (32%)

5.2.1 Negative concord proper in the Greek Gospel texts

As previously stated, Greek is a negative concord proper language. However, it exhibits negative concord proper differently than Old Church Slavonic does. Gospel examples confirm Muchnová's conclusions (2016) on negative concord in Ancient Greek. Negative concord proper is more common with a preceding predicate, although it is not obligatory in that position. On the other hand, if a negative pronoun/adverb precedes a predicate, negative concord proper is allowed but it is very rare.

The analysis of sentences with potential negative concord proper in the *Codex Marianus* aligned with its Greek source showed that there is only one sentence in the Greek version with a preceding negative pronoun/adverb together with a negative predicate, i.e., with negative concord proper:

(14) καὶ   οὐδὲν   ὑμᾶς   οὐ   μὴ   ἀδικήσει
    kai   ouden   humas   ou   mē   adikēsei
    and   nothing you   NEG   NEG   harm
    'and nothing shall harm you'
    (Lk. 10.19)

With a preceding predicate, however, it is more likely that negative concord proper will be applied. In 26 out of 36 sentences with a preceding predicate, there is negative concord proper:[20]

(15) ὑμεῖς   οὐκ   οἴδατε   οὐδέν
    humeis   ouk   oidate   ouden
    you   NEG   know   nothing
    'You know nothing'
    (Jn. 11.49)

6 Data comparison: Negative concord proper in Croatian Church Slavonic and Old Church Slavonic

Negative concord proper is exhibited more often in the *Codex Marianus* than in the *Second Beram breviary*. Sentences with a preverbal negative pronoun/adverb are the ones that make a difference, because both idioms, in both Croatian Church Slavonic and Old Church Slavonic, require negative concord proper with a preceding predicate. Moreover, a preverbal negative pronoun/adverb is the preferred word order, especially in the *Second Beram breviary*.

Table 8 sums up the results previously shown in Tables 4 and 7:

---

20 As expected, the translation is not literal: that is why there are 44 sentences with a preceding predicate in Old Church Slavonic and not 36 as in the source text.

Table 8: Negative concord proper in sentences with a preverbal pronoun/adverb.

	Negative concord proper applied	Negative concord proper not applied
Second Beram breviary	71 (28%)	179 (72%)
Codex Marianus	90 (68%)	43 (32%)

There is a distinguishable difference between these two manuscripts regarding negative concord proper in sentences with a preverbal negative pronoun/adverb. The *Second Beram Breviary* greatly favours negative concord not being applied. The *Codex Marianus*, on the contrary, mostly opts for applied negative concord proper.

7 Conclusion

Both Croatian Church Slavonic and Old Church Slavonic are non-strict negative concord proper languages. In both languages non-strict negative concord proper refers to the rule that negative concord proper is obligatory with a postverbal negative pronoun/adverb and optional with a preverbal negative pronoun/adverb. The presented data emerged from a comparative quantitative study of a Croatian Church Slavonic manuscript translated from Latin (*Second Beram breviary*) and an Old Church Slavonic manuscript translated from Greek (*Codex Marianus*). Concerning the sentences with optional negative concord proper, i.e. the ones with a preverbal negative pronoun/adverb, it has been shown that the Croatian Church Slavonic text opted for negative concord proper almost 2.5 times less than the Old Church Slavonic one. One of the reasons for such a dissimilarity is obviously due to there being a different source language: Unlike Greek, Latin is a non-negative concord language.

However, it should be noted that the high rate of sentences with a preverbal negative pronoun/adverb and applied negative concord proper in the *Codex Marianus* is not encouraged by the source text; Greek favours negative concord with a preceding predicate.

Nevertheless, the sheer fact that Greek is a negative concord language probably did boost the translator's choices in favour of negative concord proper being applied, even when there was no similarity between the source text and its translation.

Regarding the Croatian Church Slavonic translation in the *Second Beram breviary* some aspects of its sociolinguistic situation make the analysed data more understandable: "Among the Slavic medieval cultures the Croatian glagolitism was specific as it emerged and developed in the bosom of the Roman church.

Therefore, it has always been torn between its Cyrillomethodian heritage and the need to conform to the demands of the Western church, i.e. the aspiration for legitimacy in the Western Church." (Mihaljević and Reinhart 2005: 31).

Although they were allowed to use a non-Latin language and a non-Latin script in liturgy long before the Second Vatican council (20th century), Croatian translators probably tried to match the target language with the Latin source language as much as possible, both consciously and unconsciously – even more so, because Latin was a prestigious language of scholarship and liturgy in medieval Western Europe. In addition, breviary and missal are the two most important liturgical books in the Western church. This made the translators and scribes of the *Second Beram breviary* more prone to adjusting their language to the Latin source text, without, however, violating the norms of the target language.

In terms of contact linguistics, this kind of adjustment can be ascribed to so-called narrowing, "whereby a pattern associated with a range of different optional uses comes to be restricted to one particular use because that use corresponds immediately to an equivalent use pattern in the model language, which does not offer such options" (Heine and Kuteva 2005: 61). An example of this is the preferred word order in Kadiwéu-Portuguese bilingual speakers in Brazil. Although Kadiwéu is a language with (relatively) free word order, Kadiwéu-Portuguese bilinguals "tend to prefer SVO word order, which matches Portuguese" (Heine and Kuteva 2005: 61).

The conducted quantitative and comparative analysis confirmed the previously stated conclusion (Kovačević 2013: 503–505 and Kovačević 2016: 243) that Latin could not change the essence of such a distinctive typological parameter like negative concord proper. Latin did, however, where possible (in sentences with a preverbal negative pronoun/adverb in Croatian Church Slavonic), influence the narrowing of the negative concord proper optionality by favouring the option which was more aligned to it.

Croatian Church Slavonic manuscripts abbreviations

BrBer$_2$ *The Second Beram breviary*, 15th century.
BrVat$_5$ *Breviary Illirico 5*, middle 14th century.
BrN$_2$ *The Second Novi breviary* (1495.)
BrVO   *Breviary of Vid Omišljanin*, 1396.
MNov   *Missal of duke Novak*, 1368.
MVat$_4$ *Missal Illirico 4*, early 14th century.

References

Brown, Sue. 2002. A minimalist approach to negation in Old Church Slavonic: a look at the Codex Marianus. In Wayles Browne, Ji-YungKim, Barbara Partee & Robert Rothstein (eds.), *Proceedings of Formal approaches to Slavic linguistics 11: The Amherst meeting*, 159–178. Ann Arbor: Michigan Slavic Publications.

Cakalidi, Tat'jana G. 1981. Obščeotricatel'nye konstrukcii v drevnebolgarskix tekstax evangelija-tetra X–XI vv [Negative constructions in the Old Bulgarian fourfold Gospel texts from the 10th–11th century]. *Paleobulgarica* 5(1). 48–54.

Dočekal, Mojmir. 2009. Negative Concord: From Old Church Slavonic to Contemporary Czech. In Björn Hansen & Jasmina Grković-Major (eds.), *Diachronic Slavonic Syntax: Gradual Changes in Focus*, 29–41. München, Berlin & Wien: Kubon & Sagner.

Heine, Bernd & Tania Kuteva. 2005. *Language Contact and Grammatical Change*. New York: Cambridge University Press.

Giannakidou, Anastasia. 2000. Negative . . . Concord? *Natural Language and Linguistic Theory* 18(3). 457–523.

Haspelmath, Martin. 2013. Negative Indefinite Pronouns and Predicate Negation. In Matthew S. Dryer & Martin Haspelmath (eds.), *The World Atlas of Language Structures Online*, Munich: Max Planck Digital Library. http://wals.info/chapter/115 (accessed 25 March 2018).

Ingham, Richard. 2013. Negation in the history of English. In David Willis, Christopher Lucas & Anne Breitbarth (eds.), *The History of Negation in the Languages of Europe and the Mediterranean. Volume I: Case Studies*, 119–150. Oxford: Oxford University Press.

Jagić, Vatroslav. 1960 [1883]. *Quattuor evangeliorum versionis paleoslovenicae Codex Marianus glagoliticus characteribus cyrillicis transcriptum*, 2nd edn. Graz: Akademische Druck- u.Verlagsanstalt.

Klenovar Maja, Zdenka Ribarova & Jozo Vela (eds.). 2018. *Rječnik crkvenoslavenskoga jezika hrvatske redakcije. 22. sveščić: zemlьnь – i* [Dictionary of the Croatian redaction of Church Slavonic. 22nd fascicle: *zemlьnь – i*]. Zagreb: Staroslavenski institut.

Kovačević, Ana. 2013. Red riječi i negacija u hrvatskome crkvenoslavenskome jeziku [Word order and negation in Croatian Church Slavonic]. *Rasprave: Časopis Instituta za hrvatski jezik i jezikoslovlje* 39(2). 497–508.

Kovačević, Ana. 2016. *Negacija od čestice do teksta. Usporedna i povijesna raščlamba negacije u hrvatskoglagoljskoj pismenosti* [Negation from particle to text. Comparative and historical analysis of negation in Croatian Glagolitic literacy]. Zagreb: Staroslavenski institut.

Kuzmić, Boris & Martina Kuzmić. 2009. Sintaktička obilježja Zoranićevih *Planina* [The syntactic characteristics of Zoranić's *Planine*]. In Divna Mrdeža Antonina (ed.), *Zadarski filološki dani II. Zbornik radova*, 205–214. Zadar: Sveučilište u Zadru.

Křižková, Helena. 1968. K voprosu o tak nazyvaemoj dvojnoj negacii v slavjanskix jazykax [On the question of the so-called double negation in Slavonic languages]. *Slavia* 37. 21–39.

Maretić, Tomo. 1916. Jezik dalmatinskih pisaca XVIII. vijeka. Drugi prilogistoričkoj gramatici našega jezika [Language of the writers from Dalmatia in the 18th century. The second addition to the historical grammar of our language]. *Rad JAZU* 211. 1–92.

Mihaljević, Milan & Johannes Reinhart. 2005. The Croatian Redaction: Language and Literature. *Incontri Linguistici* 28. 31–82.

Mihaljević, Milan. 2007. Sintaktička svojstva najstarijih hrvatskoglagoljskih tekstova [Syntactic characteristics of the oldest Croatian-Glagolitic texts]. In Lora Taseva, Roland Marti & Marija Jovčeva (eds.), *Mnogokratnite prevodi v južnoslavjanskoto srednovekovie*, 223–238. Sofija: Goreks Pres.

Mihaljević, Milan. 2011. Bilješke o jeziku Drugoga beramskog brevijara [Notes on the language of the *Second Beram breviary*]. *Tabula* 9. 126–139.

Mihaljević, Milan. 2014. Uvod [Introduction]. In Milan Mihaljević & Anita Šikić (eds.), *Hrvatski crkvenoslavenski jezik*, 9–22. Zagreb: Hrvatska sveučilišna naklada & Staroslavenski institut.

Mihaljević, Milan. 2018. *Drugi beramski brevijar. Hrvatskoglagoljski rukopis 15. stoljeća. I. Dio. Faksimil i transliteracija* [The Second Beram breviary. Croatian-Glagolitic manuscript from the 15th century. I. Part. Fascimile and transliteration]. Zagreb: Staroslavenski institut.

Muchnová, Dagmar. 2016. Negation in Ancient Greek: a typological approach. *Graeco-Latina Brunensia* 21(2). 183–200.

Pfau, Roland. 2008. The grammar of headshake: a typological perspective on German sign language negation. *Linguistics in Amsterdam* 1. 37–74.

Polleto, Cecilia. 2008. On negative doubling. *Quaderni di Lavoro ASIt* 8. 57–84. http://asit.maldura.unipd.it/documenti/ql8/poletto_2008.pdf (accessed 30 May 2018.)

Šimić, Marinka. 2014. Spomenici [Monuments]. In Milan Mihaljević & Anita Šikić (eds.), *Hrvatski crkvenoslavenski jezik*, 23–47. Zagreb: Hrvatska sveučilišna naklada & Staroslavenski institut.

Tubau Muntañá, Susagna. 2008. *Negative Concord in English and Romance: Syntax-morphology Interface Conditions on the Expression of Negation*. University of Amsterdam dissertation. Utrecht: LOT.https://www.lotpublications.nl/Documents/187_fulltext.pdf (accessed 10 August 2018.)

Vaillant, André. 1948. *Manuel du vieux slave*. Paris: Institut d' études slaves.

Večerka, Radoslav. 1989. *Altkirchenslavische (Altbulgarische) Syntax. I. Die lineare Satzorganisation*. Freiburg i. Br.: Weiher.

Večerka, Radoslav. 1996. *Altkirchenslavische (Altbulgarische) Syntax. III. Die Satztypen: Der einfache Satz*. Freiburg: Weiher.

Vendler, Zeno. 1957. Verbs and Times. *The Philosophical Review* 66(2). 143–160.

Vondrák, Wenzel. 1912. *Altkirchenslavische Grammatik*. Berlin: Weidmannsche Buchhandlung.

Vukoja, Vida. 2012. O korpusu Rječnika crkvenoslavenskoga jezika hrvatske redakcije i njegovu odnosu prema korpusima hrvatskoga jezika [On the corpus of the Dictionary of Croatian redaction of Church Slavonic and its relation towards the Croatian language corpora]. *Filologija* 59. 207–229.

Vukoja, Vida. 2014. The corpus of the Croatian Church Slavonic texts and the current state of affairs concerning the Dictionary of the Croatian redaction of Church Slavonic compiling. In Andrea Abel, Chiara Vettori & Natascia Ralli (eds.), *Proceedings of the XVI EURALEX International Congress: The User in Focus. 15–19 July 2014*, 1221–1235. Bolzano/Bozen: EURAC research.

Wallage, Phillip. 2012. Negative inversion, negative concord and sentential negation in the history of English. *English language and linguistics* 16(1). 3–33.

Willis, David. 2013. Negation in the history of the Slavonic languages. In David Willis, Christopher Lucas & Anne Breitbarth (eds.), *The History of Negation in the Languages of Europe and the Mediterranean. Volume I: Case Studies*, 341–398. Oxford: Oxford University Press.

Willis, David, Christopher Lucas & Anne Breitbarth. 2013. Comparing diachronies of negation. In David Willis, Christopher Lucas & Anne Breitbarth (eds.), *The History of Negation in the Languages of Europe and the Mediterranean. Volume I: Case Studies*, 1–50. Oxford: Oxford University Press.

Xaburgaev, Georgij A. 1986. *Staroslavjanskij jazyk* [The Old Church Slavonic language]. Moskva: Prosveščenie.

Zeijlstra, Hedde. 2004. Sentential negation and negative concord. University of Amsterdam dissertation. Utrecht: LOT Publications. https://www.lotpublications.nl/Documents/101_fulltext.pdf (accessed 8 December 2017).

Zlatanova, Rumjana. 1991. Prosto izrečenie [The simple sentence]. In Ivan Duridanov, Ekaterina Domagradžieva & Angelina Minčeva (eds.), *Gramatika na starobălgarskija ezik* [Old Bulgarian grammar], 361–427. Sofia: Izdatelstvo na Bălgarskata akademija na naukite.

Zovko Dinković, Irena. 2013. *Negacija u jeziku: Kontrastivna analiza negacije u engleskome i hrvatskome jeziku* [Negation in language: Contrastive analysis of negation in English and Croatian]. Zagreb: Hrvatska sveučilišna naklada.

Part IV: **In lieu of a conclusion**

Hanne Martine Eckhoff
First attestations. An Old Church Slavonic sampler

Abstract: Corpus linguistics and computational approaches to language constitute an important trend in today's linguistics, and Slavic historical linguistics is no exception. This chapter serves as an empirical touchstone for the entire volume. Using parallel Greek and Old Church Slavonic data from the PROIEL/ TOROT treebanks, the first attested state of the phenomena covered in the volume is explored, including their relationship to the Greek sources. The chapter covers accusatives with infinitives (Gavrančić this volume, Tomelleri this volume), absolute constructions (Mihaljević 2017), deverbal nouns (Tomelleri this volume), prepositional phrase connectors (Kisiel & Sobotka this volume), numeral syntax (Słoboda this volume), the ordering of pronominal clitics (Kosek, Čech & Navrátilová this volume), tense use in performative declaratives (Dekker this volume) and relative clauses (Sonnenhauser & Eberle this volume; Podtergera 2020). The chapter presents corpus statistics on each of the phenomena, and a brief discussion of the possibility of influence from Greek. The chapters that provide their own studies of Old Church Slavonic data (Fuchsbauer this volume on "mock" articles, Pichkhadze this volume on syntactic blocking and Šimić this volume on negative concord), are not replicated, but brought into the discussion when relevant.

Keywords: rule borrowing, infinitives, participles, clitics, numerals, performatives, tense, relative clauses, discourse connectors, Old Church Slavonic

This volume covers a wide range of Slavonic contact phenomena in syntax, the majority of them taking place in relatively well-documented historical times. Yet the very first attestation of Slavonic, Old Church Slavonic (OCS), is almost entirely found in translations from Koiné and Byzantine Greek, and its syntax seems almost inextricable from the syntax of its Greek source texts. Old Church Slavonic, which we can obviously know only as a written language, was devised as a literary language precisely for the purpose of translating overwhelmingly Greek Biblical, liturgical and other religious sources such as lives of saints. Its subsequent influence on later varieties of Slavonic, especially those linked to the Orthodox church, can hardly be overestimated.

Hanne Martine Eckhoff, University of Oxford, e-mail: hanne.eckhoff@mod-langs.ox.ac.uk

https://doi.org/10.1515/9783110651331-012

Greek and OCS are both typical old Indo-European languages, with a lot of structural similarities. The task of teasing Greek and Slavonic native syntax apart is a challenging one, and a good number of the contact phenomena covered in this volume are also ones that may be or certainly are influenced by Greek in the earliest sources (see e.g. the account of the problem in MacRobert 1986, which touches on several of the constructions discussed in this volume). We are, however, in the fortunate situation that more and more digital corpus resources are available for OCS and other early stages of Slavonic. Instead of providing a summary of this volume I will therefore look at the phenomena covered in the various articles in this book and use Greek and OCS treebank data from the PROIEL/TOROT treebanks,[1] using the Codex Marianus and its Greek parallel.[2] My aim will be to assess the state of the relevant phenomenon in the Marianus dataset. Does it exist at all, and if so, how Slavonic does it seem to be? I will look carefully at the sources of a potential Greek loan, and make a survey of how the OCS translation deals with each of these structures. This immediately raises the difficult and much discussed issue of how to distinguish between contact-induced and internally motivated change. Can a linguistic rule or syntactic pattern be borrowed at all, and how can we determine that it has? Thomason (2006: 674) suggests that an indisputable example of rule borrowing must involve no lexical transfer, and should result in an identical rule in the source language and in the receiving language, which is also completely new to the receiving language. We are quite rarely in this position with OCS, since it is hard to conclusively prove that any rule was completely absent in Slavonic before the hugely influential translations from Greek in the OCS text canon.

Three of the articles in this volume include their own studies of OCS data: Fuchsbauer's article "The article-like usage of the relative pronoun *iže* as an indicator of early Slavonic grammatical thinking, Pichkhadze's "Blocking of syntactic constructions without Greek counterparts in Church Slavonic", and Šimić's "Non-strict negative concord proper and languages in contact: translating Latin and Old Greek into Church Slavonic". For obvious reasons I have not tried to replicate their studies, but I will refer to them when their work proves relevant to the other topics. Tomelleri's article raises a wide range of syntactic issues. I will look

---

1 All datasets and scripts to process them are available at https://doi.org/10.18710/J572YW
2 The Greek New Testament text used in the PROIEL treebank is Tischendorf 1869–1872. This is, naturally, not the source text of the Codex Marianus, and that fact will necessarily create some noise in the data. I will therefore refer to manuscript variants in the Gospels in cases where I deem it necessary, especially in cases of very low-frequency deviations between the Greek and OCS texts.

at only one of them in depth (the use of productive deverbal nouns), but will refer to his article elsewhere when relevant.

As the title suggests, this chapter is intended as a sampler, not as a set of fully worked-out studies of the phenomena in question. The statistical analyses are sometimes quite simple, often due to a scarcity of data, and I do not pretend to supply a full literature survey for each topic; I cite researchers whose ideas I would like to acknowledge, often just a few representatives from a much larger body of literature.

1 Accusative with infinitive

The accusative with infinitive (AcI) is a rarity in OCS, but relatively frequent in Greek. Gavrančić's study of the Croatian AcI in this volume naturally takes Latin as the point of comparison, since Croatia belonged to the West church and translated its religious texts primarily from Latin, albeit with traces of the Cyrillo-Methodian translations in the Old Croatian sources. In Tomelleri's article we can see that this type of influence can be found in 16th century Russian Church Slavonic translations from Latin as well. As Gavrančić points out, the AcI was used less in the Vulgate than in Classical Latin, but it is still fairly well attested, and not much less used than in the Greek New Testament, which must be the point of departure for any study of the OCS AcI.[3]

A quick look at the Codex Marianus data immediately shows us that the majority of OCS examples corresponding to a Greek accusative with infinitive do *not* have an accusative with infinitive, or indeed any infinitive construction at all. We are therefore faced with the task of determining which contexts could be rendered with an AcI, which contexts with a dative with infinitive (DcI), and which contexts had to be rendered with various other means. It is easy to dismiss the OCS AcI as an outright loan, and essentially ungrammatical (see e.g. Večerka 1971: 140), but such as it was, it was clearly not used uncritically, but under very restricted conditions, largely when the Greek AcI is a 'true' complement of a typical complement-taking verb (communicative and cognitive). The usage of the

---

[3] In the PROIEL corpus (query performed June 2019) we find 577 constructions with accusative subjects in the Greek New Testament, 408 in the Vulgate. The number of complement infinitives is much more similar: 581 in the GNT and 620 in the Vulgate. Neither of these measures get us the exact number of AcIs, since not all accusative subjects belong in AcIs, not all AcIs have an overt subject, and not all AcI infinitives are direct complements – as we shall see, they are often nominalised with an article in the Greek.

AcI in OCS was thus considerably narrower that that observed by Gavrančić in 16th–19th century Croatian texts and by Tomelleri in 16th century Russian Church Slavonic.

For this study I extracted all Old Church Slavonic items which were aligned with a Greek nominal in the accusative case with the relation label SUB which depended on an infinitive (1).[4]

(1) a. πῶς λέγουσιν τὸν Χριστὸν εἶναι Δαυεὶδ υἱόν
pōs legousin ton Christon einai Daueid huion
how say.PRS.3PL the Christ.ACC be.INF.PRS David.INDECL son.ACC

b. како глѭтъ єдини х̅а бъіти
kako gljǫtъ[5] edini xa byti
how say.PRS.3PL some.NOM.PL Christ.GEN/ACC be.INF
с̅на д̅ва.
sna dva
son.GEN/ACC David-ov.M.SG.GEN/ACC

'How can they say that the Christ is David's son?' (Lk. 20.41, 48564, 41281)[6]

We find 170 examples of Greek infinitives with an accusative deemed to be the subject, which also have an aligned OCS translation in the Codex Marianus.[7] Looking at the Greek examples, we see that there are three main syntactic types. The AcI may be tagged COMP (112 examples),[8] which means that it is either considered a straight complement clause (as in (1) above) or a clausal argument which may correspond to either a subject or an object (2).

---

[4] Note that this yields quite a different set of examples from that found in Kurešević (2018), where constructions with transitive verbs of movement (*posъlati* 'send') followed by an accusative object and an infinitive of purpose are taken to be AcIs. In the PROIEL/TOROT treebanks such infinitives are seen as adverbial modifiers rather than a part of an AcI in both OCS and Greek. Kurešević also takes accusatives and infinitives depending on verbs like *tvoriti* 'make' to be AcIs, see further discussion of this point below.

[5] Underlined characters in the Latin transliteration indicate characters under a titlo in the manuscript.

[6] All examples are given with sentence IDs from PROIEL/TOROT for easy access.

[7] The criterion was that the Greek accusative subject must be aligned with something in the OCS translation. This means that in cases of coordinated accusative objects, each will be considered a data point. Only two example sentences are affected by this.

[8] One of these examples (Lk. 17.1, 21276) has an article in the genitive, but is clearly perceived as the subject argument of the structure.

(2) a. εὐκοπώτερον γάρ ἐστιν κάμηλον διὰ τρήματος
    eukopōteron gar estin kamēlon dia trēmatos
    easier for be.PRS.3SG camel.ACC through hole.GEN
    βελόνης εἰσελθεῖν ἢ πλούσιον εἰς τὴν
    belonēs eiselthein ē plousion eis tēn
    needle.GEN enter.INF.AOR than rich.M.ACC.SG in the
    βασιλείαν τοῦ θεοῦ εἰσελθεῖν.
    basileian tou theou eiselthein
    kingdom.ACC the God.GEN enter.INF.AOR
  b. оудобѣе бо естъ вельбѫдоу сквозѣ игьлинѣ
    udobĕe bo estъ velьbǫdu skvozĕ igьlinĕ
    easier for be.PRS.3SG camel.DAT through needle-*in*.F.ACC.DU
    оуши проити. неже богатоу въ
    uši proiti neže bogatu vъ
    ear.ACC.DU go_through.INF than rich.M.DAT.SG in
    ц҃срствие. вьнити.
    csrstvie vъniti
    kingdom.ACC enter.INF
    'For it is easier for a camel to go through the eye of a needle than for a rich person to enter the kingdom of God' (Lk. 18.25, 21376, 41113)

The AcI may be tagged PRED, which means that it is the predicate of a subordinate clause headed by a subjunction – either *hōste* (17 examples, 3) or *prin* (7 examples, 4).

(3) a. καὶ συνέρχεται πάλιν ὄχλος, ὥστε μὴ
    kai sunerchetai palin ochlos hōste mē
    and gather.PRS.3SG again crowd.NOM so_that not
    δύνασθαι αὐτοὺς μήτε ἄρτον φαγεῖν.
    dunasthai autous mēte arton fagein
    be_able.INF.PRS they.ACC even bread.ACC eat.INF.AOR
  b. и събърашѧ сѧ пакы народи. ѣко не
    i sъbъrašę sę paky narodi jako ne
    and gather.AOR.3PL REFL again people.NOM.PL that not
    мощи имъ ни хлѣба сънѣсти.
    mošti imъ ni xlĕba sъnĕsti
    be_able.INF they.DAT even bread.GEN eat.INF
    'and the crowd gathered again, so that they could not even eat'
    (Mk. 3.20, 6632, 36487)

(4) a. πρὶν   ἀλέκτορα   φωνῆσαι   δὶς   τρίς   με   ἀπαρνήσῃ.
       prin   alektora   fōnēsai   dis   tris   me   aparnēsēi
       before   rooster.ACC crow.INF.AOR   twice thrice I.ACC   deny.FUT.3SG
    b. прѣжде   даже   кокотъ   не   въꙁгласитъ   дъва
       prěžde   daže   kokotъ   ne   vъzglasitъ   dъva
       before   than   rooster.NOM   not   crow.PRS.3PL   two.ACC
       краты.   отъвръжеши   сѧ   мене   три   краты.
       kraty   otъvrъžeši   sę   mene   tri   kraty
       time.ACC.PL   deny.PRS.2SG   REFL   I.GEN   three.ACC time.ACC.PL
    'Before the rooster crows twice, you will deny me three times'
    (Mk. 14.72, 56965, 37276)

Finally, the infinitive may be nominalised and have a definite article. In 28 out of 33 examples, such nominalised infinitives are headed by a preposition, most frequently *en* 'in' (5).

(5) a. καὶ   ἐγένετο   ἐν   τῷ   ὑπάγειν   αὐτοὺς
       kai   egeneto   en   tōi   hupagein   autous
       and   happen.AOR.3SG in   the.DAT go_away.INF.PRS they.ACC
       ἐκαθαρίσθησαν.
       ekatharisthēsan
       cleanse.AOR.3PL.PASS
    b. и   бꙑстъ   идѫштемъ   имь.   иштистишѧ
       i   bystъ   idǫštemъ   imь   ištistišę
       and   be.AOR.3SG   go.PTCP.PRS.M.DAT.PL   they.DAT cleanse.AOR.3PL
       сѧ.
       sę
       REFL
    'And it came to pass that, as they went, they were cleansed'
    (Lk. 17.14, 21298, 41043)

Examples 1–5 also show us a number of the available OCS translation strategies. While example (1) does indeed have an AcI in the OCS translation, examples (2) and (3) have the much more common DcI. Example (4) has a subordinate clause with a finite head verb, while (5) has a dative absolute. An overview of the translation strategies is seen in Table 1.

Table 1: OCS translation of three main types of Greek AcI.

	AcI is predicate	AcI has article	AcI is complement clause or clausal argument
Finite clause	15	16	6[9]
AcI	0	0	9
DcI	8	0	10
Complement/predicate infinitive with no subject	1	0	1
Dative absolute	0	10	2
Purpose infinitive	0	2	1
Argument infinitive	0	0	67
Accusative with participle	0		4
Imperative	0	0	4
Other	0	5	8

To take the last group first, an infinitive can hardly be nominalised in OCS except with the help of the "article" usage of *iže* (see Fuchsbauer this volume). Nominalised AcIs are not normally translated as infinitive constructions, and not at all as AcIs or DcIs.[10] Instead we find ten examples of dative absolutes (5), all rendering nominalised infinitives in the dative case, headed by the preposition *en* 'in'.[11] The other main strategy (16 examples) is to translate the infinitive into a finite verb, typically in an adverbial clause, such as an *egda* clause (6).

(6) a. Ἐγένετο   δὲ   ἐν   τῷ   ὑποστρέφειν   τὸν
       Egeneto   de   en   tōi   hupostrephein   ton
       happen.AOR.3SG PTCL   in   the.DAT   return.INF.PRS   the
       Ἰησοῦν   ἀπεδέξατο   αὐτὸν   ὁ   ὄχλος·
       Iēsoun   apedexato   auton   ho   ochlos
       Jesus.ACC   praise.AOR.3SG he.ACC   the   crowd.NOM
    b. бъістъ   же   єгда   възврати   са   и҃съ
       bystъ   že   egda   vъzvrati   sę   isъ
       be.AOR.3SG   PTCL   when   return.AOR.3SG   REFL   Jesus.NOM

---

9 Including one *l*-participle which is treated as finite here, 36723.
10 The only two examples where the Greek nominalised infinitive is rendered with an infinitive have had the infinitives reinterpreted as purpose infinitives in the OCS translation (Lk. 2.27, 40031; Lk 5.17, 40183).
11 For further discussion, see the next section.

> ПРИѨТЪІ И НАРОДЪ.
> prijęty i narodъ
> receive.AOR.3SG he.ACC people.NOM
> 'And it came to pass that, when Jesus returned, the people received him'
> (Lk. 8.40, 48405, 40443)

In the second group, the Greek AcI serves as a predicate in a *hōste* or *prin* clause. Again we find no AcI renditions in the OCS translation. All of the seven *prin* clauses are rendered with a *prěžde* clause in the OCS dataset, and all of these examples have a finite predicate, as in (4). The *hōste* clauses are all rendered by *jako* clauses in OCS, eight with a finite predicate (7) and nine with an infinitive predicate (3). Eight out of nine infinitive predicates have dative subjects (3), and the final example has no subject, but a voice mismatch with the Greek, so that the Greek subject is aligned with the OCS object (8). For a discussion of the tendency in OCS to translate Greek passive infinitives as active ones under certain circumstances, see Tomelleri (this volume).

> (7) a. καὶ [...] ἐξῆλθεν ἔμπροσθεν πάντων, ὥστε
> kai [...] exēlthen emprosthen pantōn hōste
> and go_out.AOR.3SG before all.GEN.PL so_that
> ἐξίστασθαι πάντας
> existasthai pantas
> be_amazed.INF.AOR all.ACC.PL
>
> b. и изиде прѣдъ вьсѣми. ѣко дивлѣахѫ
> i izide prědъ vьsěmi jako divljaaxǫ
> and go_out.AOR.3SG before all.INS.PL so_that wonder.IMPERF.3PL
> сѧ вьси
> sę vьsi
> REFL all.NOM.PL
> 'and he went out before them all, so that they were all amazed'
> (Mk. 2.12, 6578, 50245)

> (8) a. καὶ δώσουσιν σημεῖα μεγάλα καὶ
> kai dōsousin sēmeia megala kai
> and give.FUT.3PL sign.N.ACC.PL great.N.ACC.PL and
> τέρατα, ὥστε πλανηθῆναι, εἰ
> terata hōste planēthēnai ei
> miracle.N.ACC.PL so_that deceive.INF.AOR.PASS if

　　　　δυνατόν,　　　　　καὶ　　　τοὺς　ἐκλεκτούς.
　　　　dunaton　　　　　　kai　　　tous　eklektous
　　　　possible.N.NOM.SG　even　　the　　chosen.M.ACC.PL
　b.　и　　　　дадѧтъ　　　знамениѣ　　велиѣ　　　　и
　　　　i　　　dadętъ　　　　znamenija　velija　　　　i
　　　　and　　give.PRS.3PL　sign.N.ACC.PL　great.N.ACC.PL　and
　　　　чюдеса.　　　　ѣко　　　прѣльстити.　аште　естъ
　　　　čjudesa　　　　jako　　prělьstiti　　ašte　estъ
　　　　miracle.N.ACC.PL　so_that　deceive.INF　if　be.PRS.3SG
　　　　въꙁможъно　　　иꙁбъранꙑѩ.
　　　　vъzmožъno　　　izbъranyję
　　　　possible.N.NOM.SG　chosen.M.ACC.PL
　　　　'and they will perform signs and miracles in order for even the chosen
　　　　ones to be mislead, if possible' (Mt. 24.24, 15901, 39480)

The first syntactic type is where we find the only examples of OCS AcIs, namely in translations of Greek AcIs tagged COMP. As demonstrated in example (2), not all of these are plain complements of the typical selection of complement-taking verbs – instead they may be clausal subject-like arguments of copular, existential or modal verbs. There are 58 such examples in the Marianus dataset, where the OCS verb translates a Greek AcI headed by the verbs *gignomai* 'become', *eimi* 'be', *exesti* 'be possible', *endekhomai* 'be possible' or *dei* 'be necessary'. Only 8 of the OCS translations have been analysed as containing a COMP infinitive construction, for example (9), none of them with an accusative subject.

(9)　a.　Ἐγένετο　　　　δὲ　　ἐν　　ἑτέρῳ　　σαββάτῳ
　　　　Egeneto　　　　de　　en　　heterōi　　sabbatōi
　　　　happen.AOR.3SG　PTCL　in　　other.SG.DAT　Sabbath.DAT
　　　　εἰσελθεῖν　　αὐτὸν　εἰς　τὴν　συναγωγὴν　καὶ　διδάσκειν.
　　　　eiselthein　　auton　　eis　tēn　sunagōgēn　　kai　didaskein
　　　　enter.INF.AOR　he.ACC　in　the　synagogue.ACC　and　teach.INF.PRS
　b.　Бъістъ　　　же　　и　　въ　　дроугѫѭ　　соботѫ.
　　　　Bystь　　　　že　　i　　vъ　　drugǫjǫ　　sobotǫ
　　　　be.AOR.3SG　PTCL　also　in　other.ACC.SG　Sabbath.ACC
　　　　вънити　　　емоу　въ　съньмиште　　и　　оучити.
　　　　vъniti　　　　emu　　vъ　sъnьmište　　　i　　učiti
　　　　enter.INF　he.DAT　in　synagogue.ACC　and　teach.INF
　　　　'And it came to pass also on another sabbath that he entered into the
　　　　synagogue and taught' (Lk. 6.6, 20453, 40228)

This does not mean that the remaining 50 examples do not contain infinitives and potential dative subjects – most of them do. But in most cases it is possible to analyse the dative argument as an argument or adverbial dependent of the head verb rather than the subject of the infinitive. This is the case in 37 of the examples, such as (2), where the camel is taken to be an adverbial dependent on *estъ* 'is', and (10), where the dative is taken to be the oblique argument of *podobati* 'be suitable'.[12]

(10) a. δεῖ ὑμᾶς γεννηθῆναι ἄνωθεν.
dei humas gennēthēnai anōthen
be_necessary.PRS.3SG you.ACC.PL give_birth.INF.AOR.PASS from_above

b. подобаатъ вамъ родити са съ въіше.
podobaatъ vamъ roditi sę sъ vyše
be_suitable.PRS.3SG you.DAT.PL give_birth.INF REFL from higher
'you must be born from above' (Jn. 3.7, 22011, 41716)

The same case could clearly be made for *dei* 'be necessary', but different annotation choices were made for OCS and Greek. In Greek it was deemed useful to find all the potential AcIs. OCS, on the other hand, has a large number of verbs that take a dative argument and an infinitive, and verbs like *podobati* were grouped with them. In this group, only examples such as (9) can be considered clear-cut examples of DcI, and there are no OCS AcI translations. There are, however, two dative absolutes.

This ambiguity is even clearer when we look at Greek COMP AcIs headed by the causative or jussive (and related) verbs *katakrinō* 'judge, deem', *keleuō* 'order', *kōluō* 'hinder', *poieō* 'make', *axioō* 'deem worthy', *aphiemi* 'allow', *eaō* 'allow', *erōtaō* 'ask' and *ōpheleō* 'profit' (26 examples). Here, the AcI cannot be considered a clausal subject of the head verb, but it is clearly possible to see the accusative as an argument of the main verb rather than the subject of the infinitive. Again, the latter analysis was chosen in OCS, where all the corresponding accusative or dative nominals are considered arguments of their head verb, as in (11) and (12), and are listed under argument infinitives in Table 1.

(11) a. καὶ τοὺς κωφοὺς ποιεῖ ἀκούειν καὶ
kai tous kōphous poiei akouein kai
even the deaf.M.ACC.PL make.PRS.3SG hear.INF.PRS and

---

[12] In all of these examples, the infinitive is headed by *podobati* 'be suitable', *dostojati* 'be worthy' or *byti* 'be'. They are included in Table 1 as argument infinitives.

        ἀλάλους λαλεῖν.
        alalous lalein
        dumb.M.ACC.PL speak.INF.PRS

  b. глоухꙑѩ творитъ слꙑшати і нѣмꙑѩ
      gluxyję tvoritъ slyšati i němyję
      deaf.M.ACC.PL make.PRS.3SG hear.INF and dumb.M.ACC.PL
      глати
      glati
      speak.INF
      'He even makes the deaf hear and the mute speak' (Mk. 7.37, 6896, 50377)

(12) a. κέλευσόν με ἐλθεῖν πρὸς σὲ ἐπὶ
        keleuson me elthein pros se epi
        order.IMP.2SG.AOR I.ACC come.INF.AOR to self.ACC on
        τὰ ὕδατα·
        ta hudata
        the water.ACC.PL

  b. повели ми прити къ тебѣ по водамъ.
      poveli mi priti kъ tebě po vodamъ
      order.IMP.2SG I.DAT come.INF to you.DAT along water.DAT.PL
      'command me to come to you on the water' (Mt. 14.28, 15318, 50862)

Thus, there are no clear-cut examples of AcIs or DcIs in this group.

The place to look for "real" OCS AcIs and DcIs therefore turns out to be the group of Greek AcIs tagged as COMPs that do not belong to any of the two above-mentioned groups. There are 28 such examples (Table 2). They are headed by speech, perception and thought verbs, primarily *legō* 'say' (14 examples), and in none of the 28 examples is there an alternative syntactic analysis available for the Greek accusative subject.

Table 2: OCS renditions of Greek AcI complements of speech and thought verbs.

Finite clause	6
AcI	9
DcI	3
Complement infinitive without subject	1
Argument infinitive	1
Accusative with participle	4
Other	4

In this group, the most common rendition is actually the AcI (Table 2). However, eight of the nine examples are extremely similar to example (1), as we can see in (13). Seven of these examples are headed by *legō* 'say' (one has *pepьševati* 'think, consider'), and the infinitive is *einai/byti* in all of them.

(13) a. τίνα   με   λέγουσιν   οἱ   ἄνθρωποι   εἶναι;
        tina   me   legousin   hoi   anthrōpoi   einai
        who.ACC   I.ACC   say.PRS.3PL   the   man.NOM.PL   be.INF.PRS
     b. кого   мѧ   глѭтъ   ч҃лвци   быти.
        kogo   mę   gljǫtъ   člvci   byti
        who.GEN/ACC   I.ACC   say.PRS.3PL   man.NOM.PL   be.INF
        'Who do people say I am?' (Mk. 8.27, 6946, 36789)

The exception is (14).

(14) a. καὶ   Πειλᾶτος   ἐπέκρινεν   γενέσθαι   τὸ
        kai   Peilatos   epekrinen   genesthai   to
        and   Pilate.NOM   judge.AOR.3SG become.INF.AOR   the
        αἴτημα   αὐτῶν·
        aitēma   autōn
        demand.ACC.SG   they.GEN.PL
     b. Пилатъ   же   посѫди   быти   прошениѥ   ихъ.
        Pilatъ   že   posǫdi   byti   prošenie   ixъ
        Pilate.NOM   PTCL   judge.AOR.3PL be.INF   demand.ACC   they.GEN.PL
        "and Pilate pronounced sentence that their demand be granted"
        (Lk. 23.24, 21760, 41483)

We only find three clear examples of the DcI in this group, all variations of (15):

(15) a. Καὶ   ἔρχονται   Σαδδουκαῖοι   πρὸς   αὐτόν,
        Kai   erchontai   Saddoukaioi   pros   auton
        and   come.PRS.3PL Sadducee.NOM.PL   to   he.ACC
        οἵτινες   λέγουσιν   ἀνάστασιν   μὴ   εἶναι
        hoitines   legousin   anastasin   mē   einai
        who.NOM   say.PRS.3PL   resurrection.ACC   not   be.INF.PRS
     b. и   придѫ   садоукеи   къ   немоу   иже
        i   pridǫ   sadukei   kъ   nemu   iže
        and   come.AOR.3PL Sadducee.NOM.PL   to   he.DAT   who.NOM.PL

	ГЛАГЛѪТЪ	НЄ	БЪІТИ	ВЬСКРѢШЕНИЮ
	glj̇otъ	ne	byti	vъskrěšeniju
	say.PRS.3PL	not	be.INF	resurrection.DAT

'And Sadducees came to him, who say that there is no resurrection' (Mk. 12.18, 7228, 37058)

We also find four examples of accusative + participle constructions, which (Kurešević 2018) considers important support for the AcI pattern in OCS (see also Večerka 2002: 447–449 and Tomelleri this volume). This is regularly found with perception verbs in OCS and Greek. In (16), the head verb is actually a perception verb in both languages, but Greek uses an AcI, while OCS has the regular accusative + participle.

(16) a. ὅτι   ἤκουσαν   τοῦτο   αὐτὸν   πεποιηκέναι
         hoti   ēkousan   touto   auton   pepoiēkenai
         because   hear.AOR.3PL this.N.ACC.SG   he.ACC.SG   do.INF.PERF
         τὸ   σημεῖον.
         to   sēmeion
         the sign.ACC

   b. ѣко   слъішашѧ   и   сътворьшь   се
       jako   slyšašę   i   sъtvorьšь   se
       because hear.AOR.3PL   he.ACC   do.PTCP.PST.M.ACC.SG   this.N.ACC.SG
       знамение
       znamenie
       sign.ACC

       'because they had heard that he had performed this sign'
       (Jn. 12.18, 22825, 42492)

Two of the examples are headed by thought verbs, which not infrequently pattern with perception verbs in this respect in OCS (17).

(17) a. ὅτι   ᾔδεισαν   τὸν Χριστὸν   αὐτὸν   εἶναι.
         hoti   ēideisan   ton Christon   auton   einai
         because   know.PLUPRF.3PL   the Christ.ACC   he.ACC   be.INF.PRS

   b. ѣко   вѣдѣахѫ   х҃а   самого
       jako   věděaxǫ   xa   samogo
       because know.IMPERF.3PL   Christ.GEN/ACC   self.M.GEN/ACC.SG
       сѫшта.
       sǫšta
       be.PTCP.PRS.M.GEN/ACC.SG

       'because they knew that he was the Christ' (Lk. 4.41, 20373, 40151)

But there is also a single example where *glagolati* 'say' takes an accusative + participle construction.

(18) a. ὅτι λέγετε ἐν Βεελζεβοὺλ ἐκβάλλειν
hoti legete en Beelzeboul ekballein
for say.PRS.2PL in Beelzebul.INDECL throw_out.INF.PRS
με τὰ δαιμόνια.
me ta daimonia
I.ACC the demon.ACC.PL

b. ѣко г҃лте о вельзѣвоулѣ изгонѧщъ
jako glte o velьdzěvulě izgonęštь
for say.PRS.2PL by Beelzebul.LOC drive_out.PTCP.PRS.M.ACC.SG
мѧ бѣсы.
mę běsy
I.ACC demon.ACC.PL

'For you say that I cast out demons by Beelzebul' (Lk. 11.18, 20917, 40671)

The rest of the examples either have finite complement clauses (19, 20) or various types of rephrasing.

(19) a. καὶ εἶπεν φωνηθῆναι αὐτῷ τοὺς
kai eipen phōnēthēnai autōi tous
and say.AOR.3SG call.INF.AOR.PASS he.DAT the.M.ACC.PL
δούλους τούτους
doulous toutous
servant.ACC.PL that.M.ACC.PL

b. и рече да пригласѧтъ емоу рабы
i reče da priglasętь emu raby
and say.AOR.3SG that summon.PRS.3PL he.DAT servant.ACC.PL
ты.
ty
that.M.ACC.PL

'he ordered these servants to be called to him' (Lk. 19.15, 21427, 41161)

(20) a, πεπεισμένος γάρ ἐστιν Ἰωάννην
pepeismenos gar estin Iōannēn
convince.PTCP.PRF.PASS.M.NOM.SG for be.PRS.3SG John.ACC
προφήτην εἶναι.
prophētēn einai
prophet.ACC be.INF.PRS

b. ізвѣстъно   бо   бѣ   людемъ.   ѣко
    izvěstъno   bo   bě   ljudemъ   jako
    known.N.NOM.SG for be.IMPERF.3SG people.DAT.PL that
    иоанъ   пркъ   бѣ.
    ioanъ   prkъ   bě
    John.NOM   prophet.NOM   be.IMPERF.3SG
    'for they are convinced that John was a prophet' (Lk. 20.6, 21491, 51655)

To conclude, we see that the translation of Greek AcIs is remarkably free in the Marianus dataset, with a wide range of constructions used for various purposes. OCS only responds with an AcI translation in a very small and restricted group of examples, namely in cases where the Greek AcI is a 'true' complement of a typical complement-taking verb. This may potentially be due to the support from accusative with participle constructions.

The use of unambiguous DcIs is also very limited – we see very few examples rendering 'true' complement AcIs. There are a few examples rendering Greek AcIs in the *egeneto* 'it came to pass' construction, and also some examples where the DcI serves as the predicate in a *jako* clause. There is, however, a large number of examples where the structure is ambiguous: the dative could be an argument of the head verb or the subject of a DcI. This is also the case for the accusative in many of the Greek AcI examples.

In quite a few cases, however, the OCS translation avoids an infinitive construction altogether. It will often render the AcIs as finite adverbial or complement clauses, and quite systematically opts for the dative absolute in cases where the Greek has a nominalised AcI dependent on the preposition *en*.

What we see, then, is that the usage of the AcI in OCS was considerably narrower than that observed by Gavrančić in 16th–19th century Croatian texts and by Tomelleri in 16th century Russian Church Slavonic, even in a situation with similar influence from a language rich in AcIs.

2 Dative absolute

Mihaljević's (2017) study of the dative absolute in the 15th century Croatian Glagolitic Second Beram Breviary shows us the construction at a stage where it was obsolete in the vernacular and susceptible to contact influence from Latin, yielding instrumental absolutes. As Mihaljević points out, the situation was very different in OCS.[13]

When we look at the status of the dative absolute in the Marianus dataset, we find that it is very different from that of the accusative with infinitive. The overall frequency of the Greek genitive absolute is similar to the frequency of (potential) Greek AcIs. We find 153 aligned examples where either OCS, Greek or both have an absolute construction. However, in as many as 124 of these cases there is a match, as in (21), where Greek has a genitive absolute which is translated by a dative absolute in the Marianus.

(21) a. ἔρχεται   ὁ   Ἰησοῦς   τῶν   θυρῶν
       erchetai   ho   Iēsous   tōn   thurōn
       come.PRS.3SG   the   Jesus.NOM   the   door.GEN.PL
       κεκλεισμένων,   καὶ   ἔστη   εἰς   τὸ   μέσον
       kekleismenōn   kai   estē   eis   to   meson
       shut.PTCP.PRF.PASS.F.GEN.PL and stand.AOR.3SG in the middle.ACC
   b. Приде   ӣс   двьремь   затворенамъ.
       Pride   is   dvьremь   zatvorenamъ
       come.AOR.3PL   Jesus.NOM   door.DAT.PL   shut.PTCP.PST.PASS.F.DAT.PL
       ι   ста   по   срѣдѣ
       i   sta   po   srědě
       and   stand.AOR.3SG   at   middle.DAT
       'Though the doors were locked, Jesus came and stood among them'
       (Jn. 20.26, 23359, 52175)

These matching examples are quite uniform. The subject part of speech is the same in all examples. The order of participle and subject is generally the same (ten exceptions, see (22)).

(22) a. Ταῦτα   αὐτοῦ   λαλοῦντος   πολλοὶ
       Tauta   autou   lalountos   polloi
       this.ACC.PL   he.GEN   say.PTCP.PRS.M.GEN.SG many.M.NOM.PL
       ἐπίστευσαν   εἰς   αὐτόν.
       episteusan   eis   auton
       believe.AOR.3PL   in   he.ACC

---

[13] See also Tomelleri's discussion of "contaminated" dative absolutes with overt subordinators (this volume).

b. си   глѭштю   емоу   мъноsи
   si   gljǫštju   emu   mъnodzi
   this.ACC.PL say.PTCP.PRS.M.DAT.SG he.DAT many.M.NOM.PL
   вѣроваша   въ   него
   věrovašę   vъ   nego
   believe.AOR.3PL in he.GEN/ACC
   'As he was saying these things, many believed in him' (Jn. 8.30, 22495, 42174)

The tense/aspect of the participle also largely follows the Greek (as is generally the case, see Eckhoff & Haug 2015). OCS has no perfect participle that can be used for this type of construction, but renders all six Greek examples with past participles (21). Apart from that, aorist participles are rendered with past participles (36 examples) and present participles with present participles (78 examples).[14]

Given the homogeneous nature of these examples, it is interesting to see that there are also mismatches in both directions: There are OCS dative absolutes that are not translations of Greek genitive absolutes (22 examples), and Greek genitive absolutes that are not translated into OCS dative absolutes.

In the first group we see two main types. The OCS dative absolute may, as we have already seen, translate an AcI, typically a nominalised one in an *en*+DAT PP (5). There are 13 such examples, two of which do not occur in *en*+DAT PPs but as subject-like arguments in *egeneto* constructions (23).[15]

(23) a. καὶ   γίνεται   κατακεῖσθαι   αὐτὸν   ἐν
        kai   ginetai   katakeisthai   auton   en
        and   happen.PRS.3SG   lie_at_table.INF.AOR   he.ACC in
        τῇ   οἰκίᾳ   αὐτοῦ
        tēi   oikiai   autou
        the   house.DAT he.GEN

---

[14] There is one apparent example of an aorist participle rendered by a present participle, but that is due to a textual mismatch (Lk. 11.53). There are also three examples of Greek present participles rendered by past participles, two of which are renditions of the Greek present participle *ginomenou* 'becoming', where OCS has no exact counterpart. The third example is in Lk. 2.42 and has the present participle *anabainontōn* 'going down' rendered by the past participle *vъšedъšemъ* 'having entered'.
[15] The Byzantine majority text has an *en*+DAT PP here, but not in the second example of the same type, Mk 2.23.

b. ι   вꙑстъ   въꙁлежѧштю   ємоу   въ
    i   bystъ   vъzležęštju   emu   vъ
    and   happen.AOR.3SG   lie_at_table.PTCP.PRS.M.DAT.SG he.DAT   in
    домоу   єго.
    domu   ego.
    house.LOC   he.GEN
    'And it happened that He was reclining at the table in his house'
    (Mk. 2.15, 6584, 50249)

The second main type is OCS dative absolutes rendering Greek adverbial participle constructions in the dative (five examples) or accusative (two examples). As we can see in example (24), these examples do have participles that pick up the case of an argument of the main verb, with which they are coreferential, but they are very like absolute constructions in that they seem to have their own subject. Such constructions are analysed as absolute constructions in the PROIEL annotation of the Greek text – the first *autōi* is analysed as the subject of *katabanti*, while the second *autōi* is the oblique argument of *ēkolouthēsan*. In the OCS translation there is no case match between *emu* and *ego*.

(24) a. Καταβάντι   δὲ   αὐτῷ   ἀπὸ   τοῦ   ὄρους
         Katabanti   de   autōi   apo   tou   orous
         go_down.PTCP.AOR.M.DAT.SG PTCL   he.DAT   from   the   mountain.GEN
         ἠκολούθησαν   αὐτῷ   ὄχλοι   πολλοί.
         ēkolouthēsan   autōi   ochloi   polloi
         follow.AOR3PL   he.DAT   crowd.NOM.PL   many.M.NOM.PL
     b. Съшедъшоу   же   ємоу   съ   горꙑ.
         Sъšedъšu   že   emu   sъ   gory
         go_down.PTCP.PST.M.DAT.SG   PTCL   he.DAT   from   mountain.GEN
         вь   слѣдъ   єго   идѫ   народи   мъноѕи.
         vь   slědъ   ego   idǫ   narodi   mъnodzi
         in   track.ACC   he.GEN   go.AOR.3PL   crowd.NOM.PL   many.M.NOM.PL
         'When he came down from the mountain, great crowds followed him'
         (Mt. 8.1, 14908, 38496)

Example (25) is very similar, but with an accusative participle construction.

(25) a. ἐξελθόντα   δὲ   αὐτὸν   εἰς   τὸν   πυλῶνα,
         exelthonta   de   auton   eis   ton   pulōna
         go_out.PTCP.AOR.M.ACC.SG   PTCL   he.ACC   in   the   gate.ACC

	εἶδεν	αὐτὸν	ἄλλη		
	eiden	auton	allē		
	see.AOR.3SG	he.ACC	other.F.NOM.SG		

b.
шьдъшоу		же	емоу	въ	врата.
išьdъšu		že	emu	vъ	vrata
go_out.PTCP.PST.M.DAT.SG		PTCL	he.DAT	in	gate.ACC.PL

оузьрѣ	и	дроугаѣ
uzьrě	i	drugaja
see.AOR.3SG	he.ACC	other.F.NOM.SG

'And when he went out to the entrance, another (servant girl) saw him' (Mt. 26.71, 16129, 51169)

In addition, there are two examples (Jh 2.3 and Mk 4.6) where Greek finite adverbial clauses are seemingly translated into dative absolutes. However, in both cases multiple text variants, including the Byzantine majority text, deviate from Tischendorf and have genitive absolutes.

There are seven apparent examples of Greek genitive absolutes that are not rendered as OCS dative absolutes. On closer inspection, though, there are only two examples that seem reasonably reliable, (26) and the similar Lk. 14.29. Both of them translate a genitive absolute into an *egda* adverbial clause with a finite predicate.

(26) a.
Καὶ	ἐλθόντος		αὐτοῦ	εἰς	τὸ	ἱερὸν
kai	elthontos		autou	eis	to	hieron
and	come.PTCP.AOR.M.GEN.SG		he.GEN	in	the	temple.ACC

προσῆλθον	αὐτῷ	διδάσκοντι
prosēlthon	autōi	didaskonti
approach.AOR.3PL	he.DAT	teach.PTCP.PRS.M.DAT.SG

οἱ	ἀρχιερεῖς
hoi	archiereis
the	chief_priest.NOM.PL

b.
ι	егда	приде	въ	црквъ.	пристѫпишѧ
i	egda	pride	vъ	crkvъ	pristǫpišę
and	when	come.AOR.3SG	in	temple.ACC	approach.AOR.3PL

къ	немоу	оучащю.		архиереи
kъ	nemu	učaštju		arxierei
to	he.DAT	teach.PTCP.PRS.M.DAT.SG		chief_priest.NOM.PL

'And when he entered the temple, the chief priests came up to him as he was teaching' (Mt. 21.23, 15697, 39280)

The rest of the examples either lack genitive absolutes in multiple text variants including the Byzantine majority text (Mt. 17.26, Lk. 23.24), really do have dative absolutes which are difficult to capture in queries (Jh. 6.23, Jh. 21.11) or translate a Greek construction that would be difficult to render directly (27).

(27) a. Ἤδη   δὲ   τῆς   ἑορτῆς   μεσούσης
       Hēdē   de   tēs   heortēs   mesousēs
       now   PTCL   the   feast.GEN be_in_middle.F.GEN.SG
       ἀνέβη   Ἰησοῦς   εἰς τὸ   ἱερὸν   καὶ
       anebē   Iēsous   eis to   hieron   kai
       go_up.AOR.3SG Jesus.NOM in   the temple.ACC and
       ἐδίδασκεν
       edidasken
       teach.IMPERF.3SG
   b. Абие   же   въ   прѣполовление   праздьника.
       Abie   že   vъ   prěpolovlenie   prasdьnika
       now   PTCL   in   middle.ACC   feast.GEN
       вьзиде   и҃с   въ   ц҃ркъ   и
       vьzide   is   vъ   crkъ   i
       go_up.AOR.3SG   Jesus.NOM   in   temple.ACC and
       оучааше.
       učaaše
       teach.IMPERF.3SG
       'About the middle of the feast Jesus went up into the temple and began teaching' (Jn. 7.14, 22344, 42043)

It seems likely that the translator had difficulty finding an OCS verb matching the Greek *mesoō* 'be in the middle', and chose a solution with a prepositional phrase instead.

To conclude, we see that OCS largely follows the Greek and translates genitive absolutes (and other absolute constructions) as dative absolutes. There is also evidence of systematic use of dative absolutes to render Greek AcIs, certainly when the AcI is nominalised and occurs in an adverbial PP. The status of the dative absolute is thus clearly very different from that of the AcI, which is only marginally used in a very narrow set of contexts. The dative absolute, on the other hand, is almost always acceptable when the Greek has a genitive absolute. This evidence supports the position that the dative absolute was a native Slavonic construction, but that the AcI was not. It is also clear that a substantial change must have taken place from the time of the translation of the Codex Marianus to Mihaljević's 15th century Croatian source.

3 Deverbal nouns

As we have already seen, Tomelleri's study brings up a number of syntactic topics, but the one I will concentrate on here is an interesting usage of deverbal nouns in a 16th-century Russian Church Slavonic translation from Latin (Bruno's commented Psalter). In this text, as in a number of other earlier and later translations from Latin into several of the Church Slavonic recensions, productive verbal nouns in *-(en)ije* regularly translate Latin gerundive purpose constructions; in Tomelleri's example (2a; this volume), *kъ prolitiju krovi* translates *ad effundendum sanguinem* '(in order) to shed blood'.

Deverbal nouns are very common in the Marianus dataset as well, and may easily be found since the PROIEL treebank has dedicated tagging for relational nouns. Looking at this tagging alone, there are 1070 occurrences of deverbal nouns with a Greek alignment in the dataset, 460 of which belong to a lemma ending in *-ije*. This formation is predictable and type frequent enough for Lunt (2001) to include it in all his OCS verbal paradigms (listed as "verbal substantive"), but as he points out, they often take on new, often resultative meanings, and may deserve their own entries in dictionaries (Lunt 2001:172). The great majority of these productive deverbal nouns (421 occurrences) are translations of Greek common nouns, most of them transparently deverbal, but derived with a variety of different suffixes, such as *anastasis* 'resurrection' (*-is*), *baptisma* 'baptism' (*-ma*), *epithumia* 'desire' (*-ia*) and many others. They occur in a wide range of constructions and environments, most frequently as subjects and objects of verbs or complements of prepositions, and overwhelmingly follow the Greek syntax. The nouns in these examples often have meanings other than pure process meanings (28), though the latter are also found (29).

(28) a. καὶ ἐγένετο ὡς ἤκουσεν τὸν ἀσπασμὸν
kai egeneto hōs ēkousen ton aspasmon
and happen.AOR.3SG when hear.AOR.3SG the greeting.ACC
τῆς Μαρίας ἡ Ἐλισάβετ, ἐσκίρτησεν
tēs Marias hē Elisabet eskirtēsen
the Mary.GEN the Elizabeth.NOM leap.AOR.3SG
τὸ βρέφος ἐν τῇ κοιλίᾳ αὐτῆς.
to brephos en tēi koiliai autēs
the infant.NOM in the womb.DAT she.GEN

b. ι бысть ѣко оуслыша єлисаветь
i bystь jako uslyša elisavetь
and be.AOR.3SG when hear.AOR.3SG Elizabeth.NOM

	цѣловани€	мариино		вьзигра	сѧ
	cělovanie	mariino		vъzigra	sę
	greeting.ACC	Mary_in.N.NOM.SG		play.AOR.3SG	REFL
	младьнєць	въ	ѹрѣвѣ	ѥıѩ	
	mladъnecь	vъ	črěvě	eję	
	infant.NOM	in	womb.LOC	she.GEN	

'When Elizabeth heard Mary's greeting, the baby leaped in her womb' (Lk. 1.41 20195, 39966)

(29) a.
καὶ	αὐτοὶ	ἐξηγοῦντο	τὰ		ἐν	τῇ	ὁδῷ
kai	autoi	exēgounto	ta		en	tēi	hodōi
and	they	tell.IMPERF.3PL	the.ACC		in	the	way.DAT
καὶ	ὡς	ἐγνώσθη		αὐτοῖς	ἐν	τῇ	κλάσει
kai	hōs	egnōsthē		autois	en	tēi	klasei
and	how	recognise.AOR.3SG.PASS		they.DAT	in	the	breaking.DAT
τοῦ	ἄρτου						
tou	artou						
the	bread.GEN						

b.
и	та		повѣдаашете	ѥже		
i	ta		povědaašete	jaže		
and	they.NOM.DU		tell.IMPERF.3DU	which.N.ACC.PL		
бышѧ	на	пѫти	и	ѣко	сѧ	позна
byšę	na	pǫti	i	jako	sę	pozna
be.AOR.3PL	on	way.LOC	and	that	REFL	recognise.AOR.3SG
има	въ	прѣломлении	хлѣба			
ima	vъ	prělomlenii	xlěba			
they.INS.DU	in	breaking.LOC	bread.GEN			

'Then the two told what had happened on the way, and how Jesus was recognized by them when he broke the bread' (Lk. 24.35, 21848, 41570)

There are also 11 occurrences where the OCS deverbal noun translates an adjective. These are all cases of nominalised adjectives in Greek, and thus resemble the noun-to-noun translations very much.

The really interesting group are the 28 occurrences of deverbal nouns translating a Greek verb, and primarily the 16 occurrences that translate Greek infinitives, since they are more likely to tell us something about the independent functions of the OCS deverbal noun. 14 out of 16 such occurrences render Greek prepositional phrases with a nominalised infinitive complement as a prepositional phrase with the deverbal noun as the complement. The semantics depends on the choice of preposition; there are seven occurrences with temporal semantics (30), six occurrences with purpose semantics (three of which can be seen in 31), and a single example with causal semantics (32).

(30) a. μετὰ   δὲ   τὸ   ἐγερθῆναί   με   προάξω
        meta   de   to   egerthēnai   me   prosaxō
        after   PTCL the.ACC rise.INF.AOR.PASS   I.ACC   go_before.PRS.1SG
        ὑμᾶς   εἰς   τὴν   Γαλιλαίαν
        humas   eis   tēn   Galilaian
        you.ACC.PL   in   the   Galilee.ACC

  b.   по   въск[р]ьсновени   же   моемь   варѣѭ
        po   vъsk[r]ьsnoveni   že   moemь   varějǫ
        after resurrection.LOC   PTCL   my.N.LOC.SG   go_before.PRS.1SG
        вы   въ   галилеи
        vy   vъ   galilei
        you.ACC in Galilee.LOC
        'But after I have risen, I will go ahead of you into Galilee'
        (Mt. 26.32, 16050, 39627)

(31) a. καὶ   παραδώσουσιν   αὐτὸν   τοῖς   ἔθνεσιν   εἰς   τὸ
        kai   paradōsousin   auton   tois   ethnesin   eis   to
        and   deliver.FUT.3SG he.ACC   the   Gentiles.DAT   in   the.ACC
        ἐμπαῖξαι   καὶ   μαστιγῶσαι   καὶ   σταυρῶσαι
        empaixai   kai   mastigōsai   kai   staurōsai
        mock.INF.AOR   and   flog.INF.AOR   and   crucify.INF.AOR

  b.   ι   прѣдадатъ   i   на   порѫгание
        i   prědadętъ   i   na   porǫganie
        and   deliver.PRS.3SG he.ACC   on   mocking.ACC
        ѩзкмъ   ι   биение   и   пропѧтье
        jęzkmъ   i   bienie   i   propętьe
        tribes.DAT   and   beating.ACC   and   crucifixion.ACC
        'and they will deliver him over to the Gentiles to be mocked and flogged and crucified' (Mt. 20.19, 15632, 39215)

(32) a. καὶ   διὰ   τὸ   πληθυνθῆναι   τὴν   ἀνομίαν
        kai   dia   to   plēthunthēnai   tēn   anomian
        and   through   the.ACC   increase.INF.AOR.PASS   the   lawlessness.ACC
        ψυγήσεται   ἡ   ἀγάπη   τῶν   πολλῶν
        psugēsetai   hē   agapē   tōn   pollōn
        chill.FUT.3SG.PASS   the   love.NOM   the   many.GEN

b. ї   за   оумъножение   безакониѣ   їсякнетъ
    i   za   umъnoženie   bezakonija   isęknetъ
    and   for   increase.ACC   lawlessness.GEN dry_out.PRS.3SG

    любы   мъногыхъ
    ljuby   mъnogyxъ
    love.NOM   many.GEN

'And because lawlessness will be increased, the love of many will grow cold.' (Mt. 24.12, 15890, 39469)

It is worth noting that both example (30) and (32) involve Greek accusatives with infinitives, both with passive infinitives, both of which are rarely directly translated from Greek even when they are not nominalised, as Tomelleri points out in his article in this volume.

There are also twelve occurrences of deverbal nouns translating Greek participles, but eleven of those can be disregarded, as they represent the noun *iměnije* translating the Greek participle *huparkhōn* in the sense 'possession'. The last one, however, is much more interesting, as it translates a genitive absolute: as already seen, in Jh. 7.14 (example 27 above) *tēs heortēs mesousēs* is rendered by *vъ prěpolovlenie prasdъnika*. As we saw previously, one of the independent functions of the dative absolute in OCS is to render precisely prepositional phrases with nominalised infinitive complements, and the existence of examples such as (27) serve as a nice bridging context between dative absolutes and constructions with productive deverbal nouns.

All in all there are strong indications that the use of deverbal nouns of the productive *-ije* type was not much influenced by Greek in the Marianus dataset. We find that they were used for a wide range of Greek deverbal noun formations, and have not specialised with a specific derivation type. We also see that they are quite frequently used to render Greek nominalised infinitives, usually in prepositional phrases, which suggests that they could have a very verbal character. It would therefore seem that the choice to render Latin gerundive constructions with such nouns in later texts is quite consistent with their distribution and semantics in canonical OCS.

4 PP connectors

Kisiel and Sobotka's study discusses the grammaticalization of prepositional phrases as linking particles. They note that this process is particularly common in West Slavonic, a fact that the authors partially ascribe to the influence of Latin.

The authors make the point that the Latin complex particle *ita-que* could more easily motivate a Slavonic PP rendition, while Greek had *oun* for the same function, which would lend itself better to be translated by a single discourse particle. When we look at the Marianus dataset, we see that this is true: all occurrences of Greek *oun* are translated into OCS discourse particles, predominantly *že* (167 out of 258 occurrences) and *ubo* (86 occurrences), but also scattered occurrences of *i* (3 occurrences), *bo* (one occurrence) and *da* (one occurrence). (33) and (34) are typical examples.

(33) a. λέγει   οὖν   ὁ   μαθητὴς   ἐκεῖνος
       legei   oun   ho   mathētēs   ekeinos
       say.PRS.3SG   PTCL the disciple.NOM that.M.NOM.SG
       ὃν   ἠγάπα   ὁ   Ἰησοῦς   τῷ
       hon   ēgapa   ho   Iēsous   tōi
       who.M.NOM.SG love.IMPERF.3SG the Jesus.NOM   the
       Πέτρῳ·
       Petrōi
       Peter.DAT

   b. гла   же   оученикъ   егоже
      gla   že   učenikъ   egože
      say.AOR.3SG   PTCL disciple.NOM who.M.GEN/ACC.SG
      любляше   исъ   петрови.
      ljubljaše   isъ   petrovi
      love.IMPERF.3SG Jesus.NOM   Peter.DAT
      'Then the disciple whom Jesus loved said to Peter' (Jh. 21.7, 23387, 43002)

(34) a. γρηγορεῖτε   οὖν, ὅτι   οὐκ   οἴδατε   τὴν
        grēgoreite   oun   hoti   ouk   oidate   tēn
        wake.IMP.2PL PTCL because not   know.PRF.2PL the
        ἡμέραν   οὐδὲ τὴν   ὥραν.
        hēmeran   oude tēn   hōran
        day.ACC   nor   the   hour.ACC

   b. бъдите   оубо ѣко   не   вѣсте   дьни
      bъdite   ubo   jako   ne   věste   dьni
      wake.IMP.2PL PTCL because not   know.PRS.2PL day.GEN
      ни   часа
      ni   časa
      nor hour.GEN
      'Watch therefore, for you know neither the day nor the hour'
      (Mt. 25.13, 15949, 39529)

Seemingly, the translator picks *že* when the inferential semantics is less clear: 'then', *ubo* when it is more clear: 'therefore'.

The authors also claim that combinations of prepositions and demonstratives with this type of content are rare in OCS. This is largely true, certainly there are no examples in the Marianus material of the three constructions in focus in their article: Russian *potomu* 'therefore', Czech *nadto* 'moreover' and Polish *zatym/ zatem* 'thus'. There are, however, two recurring PPs with similar semantics, which often render single Greek discourse particles: *kъ tomu* 'still' and *po tomь* 'then'.

The former PP consistently occurs with a negated verb to render Greek *ouketi* 'no longer' (14 examples) and *mēketi* 'no longer' (six examples), as shown in (35) and (36).

(35) a. οὐκέτι γὰρ ἐτόλμων ἐπερωτᾶν αὐτὸν
      ouketi gar etolmōn eperōtan auton
      no_longer PTCL dare.IMPERF.3PL ask.INF.PRS he.ACC
      οὐδέν.
      ouden
      nothing.ACC

   b. къ томоу же не съмѣахѫ его
      kъ tomu že ne sъmĕaxo ego
      to that.N.DAT.SG PTCL not dare.IMPERF.3PL he.GEN
      въпрашати ничьсоже.
      vъprašati ničьsože
      ask.INF nothing.GEN

And they no longer dared to ask him anything (Lk. 20.40, 21550, 41279)

(36) a. πορεύου καὶ μηκέτι ἁμάρτανε.
      poreuou kai mēketi hamartane
      go.IMP.2SG and no_longer sin.IMP.2SG

   b. иди и отъ селѣ не съгрѣшаи к томоу
      idi i otъ selĕ ne sъgrĕšai k tomu
      go.IMP.2SG and from now not sin.IMP.2SG to that.N.DAT.SG

Go and sin no more (Jn. 8.11, 22453, 42135)

The two Greek adverbs are both combinations of a negation (*ou, mē*) and *eti* 'still'. In the OCS expression the demonstrative pronoun *tъ* must at some point have referred back to a time specified in the previous context, but as it appears in the Marianus it seems quite grammaticalised, and can hardly be a calque of the Greek adverbs. Interestingly, the non-negated *eti* 'still' is consistently rendered as *ešte* 'still', not *kъ tomь*.[16]

The PP *po tomь* 'then' is semantically closer to the grammaticalised particles studied by the authors and is also interesting in that it translates a wider range of Greek structures. Its most common correspondence is Greek *eita* 'then' (eight out of 17 examples), as seen in (37), and the related *epeita* 'then' (one example).

(37) a. εἶτα πάλιν ἐπέθηκεν τὰς χεῖρας ἐπὶ τοὺς
eita palin epethēken tas cheiras epi tous
then again put.AOR.3SG the hand.ACC.PL on the
ὀφθαλμοὺς αὐτοῦ
ophthalmous autou
eye.ACC.PL he.GEN

b. по томь же пакы възложи рѫцѣ
po tomь že paky vъzloži rǫcě
after that.N.LOC.SG PTCL again put.AOR.3SG hand.ACC.DU
на очи его
na oči ego
on eye.ACC.DU he.GEN
'Then he laid his hands on his eyes again' (Mk. 8.25, 6941, 36784)

But it also translates the corresponding Greek PP *meta tauta* 'after this' (38) and various other combinations with *meta*, including one with a nominalised AcI (39). There are also combination examples (40).

(38) a. μετὰ ταῦτα εὑρίσκει αὐτὸν ὁ Ἰησοῦς ἐν τῷ
meta tauta heuriskei auton ho Iēsous en tōi
after this.ACC find.PRS.3SG he.ACC the Jesus.NOM in the
ἱερῷ
hierōi
temple.DAT

b. по томь же обрѣте и ӣс.
po tomь že obrěte i is
after this.LOC PTCL find.AOR.3SG he.ACC Jesus.NOM

---

16 There is a single exception in Lk. 16.2, but in that example the Greek has a negation elsewhere in the sentence, so the meaning is the same.

	въ	цркве.
	vъ	crkve
	in	church.LOC

'Afterward Jesus found him in the temple' (Jn. 5.14, 22169, 41871)

(39) a. ἀλλὰ μετὰ τὸ ἐγερθῆναί με προάξω
        alla meta to egerthēnai me proaxo
        but after the wake_up.INF.AOR.PASS I.ACC lead.FUT.1SG
        ὑμᾶς εἰς τὴν Γαλιλαίαν.
        humas eis tēn Galilaian
        you.ACC in the Galilee.ACC

   b. Нъ по томь егда въскръсnѫ варѭ
      Nъ po tomь egda vъskrъsnǫ varjǫ
      but after this.N.LOC.SG when rise.PRS.3SG go_ahead.PRS.3SG
      вы въ галилеи.
      vy vъ galilei
      you.ACC.PL in Galilee.LOC

'But after I am raised up, I will go before you to Galilee'
(Mk. 14.28, 7372, 37200)

(40) a. ἔπειτα μετὰ τοῦτο λέγει τοῖς μαθηταῖς·
        epeita meta touto legei tois mathētais
        then after this.N.ACC.SG say.PRS.3SG the disciples.DAT.PL

   b. по томь же гла оученикомъ
      po tomь že gla učenikomъ
      after this.N.LOC.SG PTCL say.AOR.3SG disciple.DAT.PL

'Then after this he said to the disciples' (Jn. 11.7, 22719, 42390)

We thus see that OCS seems to have a tendency to use PPs with demonstrative pronoun complements as linking devices in a relatively productive way. The two constructions we have looked at seem to be quite independent of the Greek ones, since they are primarily used when Greek has a simple adverb with no discernible structure. This type of device would thus seem to stem from Common Slavonic.

5 Numeral syntax

Słoboda's article suggests that language contact may have contributed to the restructuring of numeral syntax in Polish in particular and in Slavonic in general.

She puts forward three factors that may have conspired to achieve this. The fact that Latin has no dual might have weakened the dual in Old Polish. The fact that Latin numerals from 4 and up have adjectival syntax might have influenced the perception of the quantified element as the head of the quantified phrase. Finally, the Roman numeral notation in Old Polish is morphologically uninformative, and might have increased the temptation to case-mark the quantified noun at the expense of the numeral.

These potential sources of syntactic influence are all present in Greek as well. All numerals are indeclinable, and the quantified noun is the syntactic head of the phrase. There is no dual. We also see that there is a morphologically uninformative letter notation of numerals present in the Codex Marianus. However, in OCS there is no evident effect of these factors. The numeral system can be reduced to a combination of numeral syntactic type (adjective or noun) and the three-way number category (singular, dual, plural), and it seems entirely regular and is independent of the Greek.

Extracting all OCS correspondences of the Greek numeral *duo* 'two' in the Marianus dataset is instructive. There are 94 such examples. The OCS correspondences are the cardinal numeral *dъva* 'two' (76 occurrences), the collective numeral *dъvoi* 'two' (three occurrences) and *oba* 'both', which should perhaps be classified as a determiner (15 occurrences). 62 of the examples have the numeral in attributive position, as in (41), in the rest of the examples it stands alone with no quantified noun, sometimes with a quantifying PP as in (42).

(41) a. ἄνθρωπος εἶχεν τέκνα δύο
anthrōpos eichen tekna duo
man.NOM have.IMPERF.3SG child.ACC.PL two.INDECL

b. ч҃къ єтєръ имѣ дьвѣ
čkъ eterъ imě dьvě
man.NOM certain.M.NOM.SG have.AOR.3SG two.N.ACC.DU
чѧдѣ
čędě
child.ACC.DU
'A man had two sons' (Mt. 21.28, 15716, 39299)

(42) a. καὶ ἀποστέλλει δύο τῶν μαθητῶν αὐτοῦ
kai apostellei duo tōn mathētōn autou
and send.PRS.3SG two the disciple.GEN.PL he.GEN

b. ι посъла дъва отъ оученикъ
i posъla dъva otъ učenikъ
and send.AOR.3SG two.M.ACC.DU of disciple.GEN.PL

своихъ
svoixъ
REFL.POSS.PRON.M.GEN.PL
'And he sent two of his disciples' (Mk. 14.13, 7346, 37173)

As expected, we see no sign that the OCS syntax may be affected by the Greek in these two examples. The Greek numeral is always undeclined, and the case is always marked on the quantified noun. In (41) the form of the OCS quantified noun is unambiguously accusative dual, and we see that the numeral agrees with it in gender, case and number. In (42) the Greek has a partitive genitive dependent on the (still undeclined) *duo*, while OCS renders this with *otъ*+GEN, avoiding the case-governing pattern found with the OCS substantival numerals.

When the OCS numeral is in attributive position, the quantified noun is always in the dual. There are two apparent examples of plural quantified nouns, but on closer inspection they turn out to occur in sentences with coordinated numerals, such as (43).

(43) a. ἵνα ἐπὶ στόματος δύο μαρτύρων
hina epi stomatos duo marturōn
that on mouth.GEN two.INDECL witness.GEN.PL
ἢ τριῶν σταθῇ πᾶν
ē triōn stathēi pan
or three.GEN.PL stand.AOR.PASS.SBJV every.N.NOM.SG
ῥῆμα
rhēma
word.NOM

b. да въ оустѣхъ дъвою ли трии
da vъ ustěxъ dъvoju li trii
that in lip.LOC.PL two.GEN.DU or three.GEN.PL
съвѣдѣтель станетъ вьсѣкъ гл҃ъ
sъvědětelь stanetъ vьsjakъ glъ
witness.GEN.PL stand.PRS.3SG every.M.NOM.SG word.NOM
'that in the mouth of two or three witnesses every word may be established' (Mt. 18.16, 15520, 39103, KJV)

We see that the plural of the quantified noun *sъvědětelь* 'witnesses' is there because genitive dual *dъvoju* 'two' is coordinated with genitive plural *trii* 'three', which is closer to the quantified noun, and which agrees with it in case and number.

When the reflexes of *duo* occur in subject position, with or without a quantified noun head, we likewise see that the predicate agreement is consistently in the dual, as exemplified in (44), which also has a conjunct participle in the dual.

(44) a. ὕστερον   δὲ   προσελθόντες   δύο   εἶπον·
       husteron   de   proselthontes   duo   eipon
       finally   PTCL   approach.PTCP.AOR.M.NOM.PL two.INDECL   say.AOR.3PL

   b. Послѣдь   же   пристѫпьша   дъва
       Poslědь   že   pristǫpьša   dъva
       afterwards   PTCL   approach.PTCP.PST.M.NOM.DU   two.M.NOM.DU.
       лъжа   съвѣдѣтелѣ   рѣсте
       lъža   sъvědětelja   rěste
       false.M.NOM.DU   witness.NOM.DU   say.AOR.3DU
       'Finally two (false witnesses) came forward and said (Mt. 26.60, 16103, 39680)

There is only one apparent example of the plural, which again turns out to be due to coordination, in this case of multiple singular and dual subjects (45).

(45) a. ἦσαν   ὁμοῦ   Σίμων   Πέτρος   καὶ
       ēsan   homou   Simōn   Petros   kai
       be.IMPERF.3PL together   Simon.NOM   Peter.NOM   and
       Θωμᾶς [...]   καὶ οἱ   τοῦ   Ζεβεδαίου
       Thōmas [...] kai hoi   tou   Zebedaiou
       Thomas.NOM   and the.M.NOM.PL   the.M.GEN.SG Zebedee.GEN
       καὶ   ἄλλοι   ἐκ   τῶν   μαθητῶν   αὐτοῦ   δύο.
       kai   alloi   ek   tōn   mathētōn   autou   duo
       and   other.M.NOM.PL from   the   disciple.GEN.PL he.GEN two.INDECL

   b. бѣахѫ   въ коупѣ   симонъ   петръ   і
       běaxǫ   vъ kupě   simonъ   petrъ   i
       be.IMPERF.3PL together   Simon.NOM   Peter.NOM   and
       тома [...]   і   с͞на   зеведеова.
       toma [...]   i   sna   zebede-ova
       Thomas.NOM   and son.NOM.DU   Zebedee-ov.M.NOM.DU
       і   ина   дъва   отъ   оученикъ   его.
       i   ina   dъva   otъ   učenikъ   ego
       and other.M.NOM.DU two.M.NOM.DU   of   disciple.GEN.PL he.GEN
       'Simon Peter, Thomas [...], the sons of Zebedee, and two others of his disciples were together' (Jn. 21.2, 23372, 42988)

It should be noted that there are around 150 further indicative verbs in the dual in the Marianus material, with no explicit numeral in the subject. We must therefore conclude that the Slavonic dual is in excellent shape at this time of attestation.

For the numerals 3 and 4, Greek and OCS have exactly the same syntax: The numeral behaves like an adjective agreeing in case, gender and number with the quantified noun, which is the head of the phrase, as demonstrated in (46).

(46) a. δύναμαι καταλῦσαι τὸν ναὸν τοῦ θεοῦ
    dunamai katalusai ton naon tou theou
    be_able.PRS.1SG destroy.INF.AOR the temple.ACC the God.GEN
    καὶ διὰ τριῶν ἡμερῶν αὐτὸν οἰκοδομῆσαι.
    kai dia triōn hēmerōn auton oikodomēsai
    and through three.GEN.PL day.GEN.PL it.ACC build.INF.AOR
 b. могѫ разорити црькь бж҃ию.
    mogǫ razoriti crkvь bž-ijǫ
    be_able.PRS.1SG destroy.INF temple.ACC God-*ij*.F.ACC.SG
    и трьми дьньми соз꙯дати ѭ
    i trьmi dьnьmi sozъdati jǫ
    and three.INS.PL day.INS.PL build.INF it.ACC
    'I am able to destroy the temple of God and rebuild it in three days'
    (Mt. 26.61, 16105, 51163)

The most interesting differences can be observed in the numerals 5 and above. We will limit the discussion to the Greek numerals 5–9 and their OCS correspondences. While the Greek numerals *pente, hex, hepta, oktō* and *ennea* are all indeclinable and behave exactly like *duo*, we see that the OCS corresponding numerals behave like feminine i-stem nouns, in that they are inflected the same way and trigger feminine singular agreement in attributive adjectives. If there is an explicit quantified noun, it occurs in the genitive plural (47).

(47) a. ἴδε ἄλλα πέντε τάλαντα ἐκέρδησα.
    ide alla pente talanta ekerdēsa
    lo other.N.ACC.PL five.INDECL talent.ACC.PL gain.AOR.1SG
 b. се дроугѫѭ д҃ таланътъ приобрѣтъ ими
    se drugǫjǫ d̅ talanъtъ priobrětъ imi
    lo other.F.ACC.SG 5 talent.GEN.PL gain.AOR.1SG it.INS.PL
    'here, I have made five talents more' (Mt. 25.20, 47972, 51098)

In the OCS correspondences the numeral is always the head of the phrase, so the quantified noun will occur in the genitive plural regardless of the case of the numeral, as seen in (48).

(48) a. Καὶ μετὰ ἡμέρας ἓξ παραλαμβάνει ὁ
    Kai meta hēmeras hex paralambanei ho
    and after day.ACC.PL six.INDECL take_with.PRS.3SG the
    Ἰησοῦς τὸν Πέτρον
    Iēsous ton Petron [...]
    Jesus.NOM the Peter.ACC

b. ι по шєсти дєнъ поѩтъ и͠съ.
    i po šesti denъ pojętъ isъ
    and after six.LOC.SG day.GEN.PL take.AOR.3SG Jesus.NOM
    пєтра
    petra [...]
    Peter.GEN/ACC

'And after six days Jesus took Peter with him' (Mk. 9.2, 6967, 36809)

There is thus no sign that the Greek syntax affects OCS noun phrases with the numerals 5 and above either at this stage.

Finally, Słoboda suggests that numerals in opaque letter notation which does not provide any morphological information may be an environment that especially invites syntactic loans in order to disambiguate the syntactic role of the numeral phrase. We have already seen in (47) that the Marianus occasionally has letter notation of numerals. In a data set consisting of all the Marianus translations of the Greek numerals 2–9 (196 examples), we find 14 examples with letter notation. We find that there are no deviations from the expected OCS syntax in these examples. In (47) we see that the numeral *pętъ* 'five' has its expected syntax even though it is written in its conventional letter notation *d*. The quantified noun *talanъtъ* is in the genitive plural, and we see that the numeral triggers feminine accusative singular agreement in its adjectival modifier *drugǫjǫ*. In example (49) we see *dъva* 'two' written as *b* in letter notation. We see that the quantified noun still occurs in the dual even though the morphological signal from the numeral is invisible and the Greek has a plural.

(49) a. κύριε, δύο τάλαντά μοι παρέδωκας
    kurie duo talanta moi paredōkas
    lord.VOC two.INDECL talent.ACC.PL I.DAT hand_over.AOR.2SG

b. ГИ   Б̃   ТАЛАНЪТА   МИ   ЕСИ
   gi   b   talanъta   mi   esi
   lord.VOC 2   talent.ACC.DU I.DAT AUX.PRS.2SG
   ПРѢДАЛЪ
   prědalъ
   hand_over.LPTCP.M.NOM.SG
   'Master, you delivered to me two talents' (Mt. 25.22, 15961, 39541)

We can therefore conclude that even though the same conditions are in place in New Testament Greek as in the Latin source texts in Słoboda's study, the numeral syntax of the Marianus shows no sign of being influenced by the Greek system.

6 Pronominal clitics

Kosek, Čech and Navrátilová discuss pronominal clitic placement in early Czech bibles, and discuss the extent to which it may be influenced by the Latin original. Their survey covers the short pronominal forms *mi*, *sě*, *tě* 'I.DAT, REFL.ACC, you.ACC' dependent on a finite verb. For my mini-survey I have extracted the corresponding OCS items *mi*, *sę*, *tę* 'I.DAT, REFL.ACC, you.ACC' from the Codex Marianus, as well as the Greek source items, if any. As in the Czech Bible, there is rarely any correspondent for reflexive *sę*, since Greek middle and passive forms are largely synthetic, with inflectional affixes marking the voice of the verb. As we can see in Table 3, the opposite situation is found with *mi* and *tę*, which nearly always have a Greek correspondence. There are only four exceptions, three of which are down to voice differences between OCS and Greek.

Table 3: OCS short pronominals, existence of Greek corresponding expression.

	Greek source expression	no Greek source expression
mi	23	2
sę	18	831
tę	55	2

In their study, Kosek et al. observe that an Old Czech pronominal clitic may occur in four main positions: 1) Post-initial (Wackernagel) position, 2) preverbal contact position, 3) postverbal contact position and 4) isolated medial position, i.e. neither in contact with the head verb nor in post-initial position. To minimise manual annotation, I will look at distance from the head verb first.

Table 4: OCS short pronominals, position relative to verb (positive number: precedes verb, negative number: follows verb).

	3		2		1		-1		-2		-3	
mi	0	0%	4	16%	5	20%	16	64%	0	0%	0	0%
tę	0	0%	1	1.8%	15	26.3%	41	71.9%	0	0%	0	0%
sę	2	0.2%	6	0.7%	21	2.5%	775	91.2%	43	5.1%	2	0.2%

Table 4 shows us that contact position is hugely preferred for all our three short pronominal forms – 84%, 98.2% and 93.7% respectively are found in immediate contact position in the Marianus dataset. Out of these, the postverbal contact position is strongly preferred, especially for *sę* (91.2%). This is illustrated in examples (50) and (51).

(50) a. θυγάτερ,   ἡ   πίστις   σου   σέσωκέν   σε
         thugater   hē   pistis   sou   sesōken   se
         daughter.VOC the faith.NOM   you.GEN   save.PRF.3SG you.ACC
   b. дъшти   вѣра   твоѣ   спасе   тѧ
       dъšti   věra   tvoja   spase   tę
       daughter.VOC faith.NOM   your.F.NOM.SG   save.AOR.3SG you.ACC
       'Daughter, your faith has healed you' (Lk. 8.48, 20689, 51384)

(51) a. ὅπου   τὸ   σῶμα,   ἐκεῖ   καὶ   οἱ   ἀετοὶ
         hopou   to   sōma   ekei   kai   hoi   aetoi
         where   the   body.NOM   there   also   the   vulture.NOM.PL
         ἐπισυναχθήσονται
         episunachthēsontai
         gather.FUT.3PL.PASS
   b. идеже   тѣло   тоу   орьли   сънемлѭтъ   сѧ
       ideže   tělo   tu   orьli   sъnemljǫtъ   sę
       where   body.NOM   there   eagle.NOM.PL   gather.PRS.3PL   REFL
       'Where the corpse is, there the vultures will gather' (Lk. 17.36, 21334, 51588)

However, an item in contact position may simultaneously be in post-initial position: 32 out of the 39 short pronouns in absolute second position are either immediately postverbal (29 examples, 52) or immediately preverbal (three examples, 53).

(52) a. οἴδαμέν   σε   τίς   εἶ
       oidamen   se   tis   ei
       know.PRS.1PL you.ACC   who.NOM   be.PRS.2SG
   b. вѣмь   тѧ   кто   еси
       věmь   tę   kto   esi
       know.PRS.1PL you.ACC   who.NOM   be.PRS.2SG
       'I know you, who you are' (Mk. 1.24, 47274, 50226)

(53) a. τί   δοκεῖ   ὑμῖν,   ὅτι   οὐ   μὴ
       ti   dokei   humin   hoti   ou   mē
       what.NOM   seem.PRS.3SG you.DAT.PL   that   not   not
       ἔλθῃ   εἰς   τὴν   ἑορτήν;
       elthēi   eis   tēn   heortēn
       come.SBJV.AOR.3SG   in   the   feast.ACC
   b. что   сѧ   мьнитъ   вамъ.   ѣко   не
       čto   sę   mьnitъ   vamъ   jako   ne
       what.NOM   REFL   seem.PRS.3SG you.DAT.PL   that   not
       иматъ   ли   прити   въ   праздьникъ.
       imatъ   li   priti   vъ   prazdьnikъ
       have.PRS.3SG PTCL   come.INF   in   feast.ACC
       'What do you think? That he will not come to the feast at all?'
       (Jn. 11.56, 22804, 42472)

A good number of short pronouns in absolute third position must also be considered post-initial since the first word in the sentence is either a vocative (and thus intonationally separate from the rest of the sentence) or a proclitic (*ne* 'not', *ni* 'not even', *a* 'and, but', *i* 'and', *da* 'and, so that', *to* 'then', *nъ* 'but' and all mono- and disyllabic prepositions, cf. Večerka 1989: 33–40). We find that this is the case for 76 out of 147 short pronominal forms in absolute third position, and that all of them are in contact position (five preverbal (54), 71 postverbal (55)).

(54) a. γύναι,   τί   κλαίεις;
       gunai   ti   klaieis
       woman.VOC   what.ACC   cry.PRS.2SG
   b. жено   что   сѧ   плачеши
       ženo   čto   sę   plačeši
       woman.VOC   what.ACC   REFL   cry.PRS.2SG
       'Woman, why are you crying?' (Jn. 20.15, 23328, 52167)

(55) a. ἐδάκρυσεν   ὁ   Ἰησοῦς.
       edakrusen   ho   Iēsous
       weep.AOR.3SG   the   Jesus.NOM
    b. и   прослъзи   сѧ   Исъ
       i   proslъzi   sę   isъ
       and   weep.AOR.3SG   REFL   Jesus.NOM
       'Jesus wept' (Jn. 11.35, 22768, 42438)

There may be more pronouns beyond absolute second position that are actually in post-initial position (for instance, they may follow another clitic or the sentence could be introduced by multiple or complex vocatives). Nonetheless, this quick investigation clearly demonstrates that short pronouns are rarely found in post-initial position if they are not simultaneously in contact position.

We noted above that there were seven examples of short pronouns in absolute second position, but not in contact position. Interestingly, these examples are remarkably homogeneous: the pronouns are all in position 2 from the verb, with only one intervening element, and the intervening element is in all seven examples a pronoun dependent on the verb and in contact position with the verb (56, 57).

(56) a. Τί   ὑμῖν   δοκεῖ;
       Ti   humin   dokei
       what.NOM   you.DAT.PL   seem.PRS.3SG
    b. чъто   сѧ   вамъ   мьнитъ
       čъto   sę   vamъ   mьnitъ
       what.NOM   REFL   you.DAT.PL   seem.PRS.3SG
       'What do you think?' (Mt. 18.12, 15514, 50912)[17]

(57) a. ἐὰν   με   δέῃ   συναποθανεῖν
       ean   me   deēi   sunapothanein
       if   I.ACC   be_necessary.PRS.3SG.SBJV   with_die.INF.AOR
       σοι,   οὐ   μή   σε   ἀπαρνήσωμαι
       soi   ou   mē   se   aparnēsōmai
       not   you.DAT   not   you.ACC   deny.PRS.1SG
    b. аште   ми   сѧ   ключитъ   съ   тобоѭ
       ašte   mi   sę   ključitъ   sъ   tobojǫ
       if   I.DAT   REFL   happen.PRS.3SG   with   you.INS

---

17 Mt. 22.42 and Mt. 26.66 have exactly the same construction.

оумьрѣти.	не	отъврьгѫ	сѧ	тебе
umьrěti	ne	otъvrъgǫ	sę	tebe
die.INF	not	reject.PRS.1SG	REFL	you.GEN

'Even if I have to die with you, I will not deny you!'
(Mk. 14.31, 7378, 37206)[18]

As we can see in Table 4, the largest group of clear exceptions from the contact positions are examples of *sę* in second and even third postverbal position. However, when we look at these examples, we find that the short pronoun is always separated from the verb by one or more Wackernagel clitics (*bo*, *že*) and/or other short pronouns, typically in post-initial position (58, 59).

(58) a.
ἀφέωνταί	σου	αἱ	ἁμαρτίαι
apheōntai	sou	hai	hamartiai
forgive.PRF.3PL.PASS	you.GEN.SG	the	sin.NOM.PL

b.
отъпоуштаѭтъ	ти	сѧ	грѣси.
otъpuštajǫtъ	ti	sę	grěsi
forgive.PRS.3PL	you.DAT	REFL	sin.NOM.PL

'Your sins are forgiven' (Lk. 7.48, 20607, 51351)

(59) a.
οὐκέτι	ἀνταποδοθήσεται	δέ	σοι	ἐν	τῇ
ouketi	antapodothēsetai	de	soi	en	tēi
no_longer	repay.FUT.3SG.PASS	PTCL	you.DAT	in	the

ἀναστάσει	τῶν	δικαίων
anastasei	tōn	dikaiōn
resurrection.DAT	the.GEN.PL	just.GEN.PL

b.
въздастъ	бо	ти	сѧ	во	вьскрѣшение
vъzdastъ	bo	ti	sę	vo	vъskrěšenie
return.PRS.3SG	PTCL	you.DAT	REFL	in	resurrection.ACC

праведъныхъ
pravedъnyxъ
just.GEN.PL

'For you will be repaid at the resurrection of the just' (Lk. 14.14, 21135, 40883)

---

18 Mt. 26.35 has exactly the same construction. The two final examples, Jn. 8.22 and Jn. 8.53, have *sę* in absolute second position and *samъ* '(one)self' in third position.

The only real exception to this is (60), where *sę* appears to be a real direct object and not a reflexive marker, and has a proclitic *i* 'even' attached to it.[19] This strongly suggests that this particular occurrence was actually stressed.

(60) a. σωσάτω   ἑαυτόν,   εἰ   οὗτός   ἐστιν
        sōsatō   heauton   ei   houtos   estin
        save.IMP.AOR.3SG self.M.ACC.SG if this.M.NOM.SG be.PRS.3SG
        ὁ   Χριστὸς   τοῦ θεοῦ   ὁ   ἐκλεκτός
        ho   Christos tou theou   ho   eklektos
        the Christ.NOM the god.GEN the chosen.M.NOM.SG
     b. да   сп͞стъ   и   сѧ.   аште сь
        da   spstъ   i   sę   ašte sь
        let save.PRS.3SG even REFL.ACC if this.M.NOM.SG
        естъ х͞ъ   с͞нъ   бж҃ии.   і҃збранъі
        estъ xъ   snъ   bž-ii   izbъrany
        be.PRS.3SG Christ.NOM son.NOM god-*ij*.M.NOM.SG chosen.M.NOM.SG
        'let him save himself, if he is the Christ of God, his Chosen One!'
        (Lk. 23.35, 48594, 51738)

From these investigations we can conclude that contact position is very strongly preferred for our three short pronouns. We see that they are often *also* in post-initial position, and that clitic behaviour in post-initial position is often responsible for the few examples of non-contact position that can be found in our dataset. However, there is little to suggest that these three short pronouns can be placed in post-initial position if the contact between head verb and short pronoun is broken by items that are not particles or pronouns.

We can now turn to the question of potential Greek influence. As we already observed in Table 4, *sę* mostly lacks a Greek correspondence (as seen in examples 51 and 53–59), while *mi* and *tę* almost always corresponds to a Greek pronoun (45, 47). There are 96 examples where the short pronoun has a correspondence, and as we can see in Table 5, the position relative to the verb is the same in Greek and OCS in 74 (77%) of the examples. All of these 74 examples have the pronoun in contact position (58 postverbal, 16 preverbal), as illustrated in (50) and (52).

---

[19] There are three further apparent examples that are due to a technicality in the annotation.

Table 5: Position of short pronoun relative to verb compared to Greek equivalent's position.

	same position	per cent	different position	per cent
mi	14	60.9	9	39.1
tę	49	89.1	6	10.9
sę	11	61.1	7	38.9

Three of the mismatch occurrences are due to alignment technicalities, but the remaining 19 all show up real mismatches. In (57), the OCS pronoun is split off from the verb by a reflexive *sę*. Four examples, including (60), have a direct object usage of *sę*, which we may suspect of having individual stress, while the Greek has *heauton* 'himself'. Two examples have the OCS short pronoun in contact position with the auxiliary rather than the main verb, while the Greek has no auxiliary (49). In the remaining 11 examples there is no obvious reason for the mismatch, as in (61).

(61) a. καὶ   ὅστις   σε   ἀγγαρεύσει   μίλιον   ἕν,
       kai   hostis   se   aggareusei   milion   hen
       and   who.NOM   you.ACC   press.FUT.3SG mile.ACC one.N.ACC.SG
       ὕπαγε   μετ'   αὐτοῦ   δύο.
       hupage   met'   autou   duo.
       go.IMP.2SG   with   he.GEN   two.INDECL

   b. и   аще   къто
      i   ašte   kъto
      and   if   someone.NOM
      поиметъ   тѧ   по   силѣ.
      poimetъ   tę   po   silě.
      take.PRS.3SG   you.ACC   by   force.LOC
      попьрище   єдино.
      popьrište   edino.
      stadium.ACC   one.N.ACC.SG
      иди   съ   нимь
      idi   sъ   nimь
      go.IMP.2SG   with   he.INST
      дьвѣ
      dьvě
      two.N.ACC.DU
      'And if anyone forces you to go one mile, go with him two miles'
      (Mt. 5.41, 14813, 38399)

Given the large number of examples with no Greek correspondence, the relatively uniform behaviour of all the short pronouns, and the relatively common ordering mismatches between corresponding examples, it is hard to conclude from the evidence of the Marianus dataset alone that the Greek word order affects the placement of our three short pronoun forms.

Further comparison with non-translated text, as demonstrated in Pichkhadze (this volume), makes it possible to argue that Greek influence could suppress a native tendency to place reflexive *sę* in post-initial (Wackernagel) position (following Zaliznjak 2008). This is even more pertinent since many of the modern South Slavonic languages still have clitics and clitic clusters in Wackernagel position. The argument would then be that the translators identified *sę* with Greek middle and passive inflectional suffixes, and therefore placed them in postverbal contact position. Unlike in Kosek et al.'s Latin material, the Greek middle/passive forms are overwhelmingly synthetic, so there is little scope to mimic the position of an auxiliary verb. It is also worth noting that a fairly large share of the reflexive-marked verbs in the Marianus dataset correspond to Greek active verbs (283 examples, 270 without a corresponding Greek pronoun).

Table 6: OCS *sę* by Greek voice, no corresponding Greek pronoun, position relative to verb (positive number: precedes verb, negative number: follows verb).

	3		2		1		−1		−2		−3	
active	0	0%	3	1.1%	11	4.1%	241	89.3%	14	5.2%	1	0.4%
middle or passive	1	0.2%	2	0.4%	8	1.5%	505	92.8%	27	5.0%	1	0.2%
no voice	0	0%	0	0%	0	0%	16	94.1%	1	5.9%	0	0%

As seen in Table 6, the pattern found with these examples seems no different than the pattern found with translations of Greek middles and passives – they are overwhelmingly in postverbal contact position (of which quite a few are also in post-initial position). We can also note that none of the East Slavonic texts analysed by Zaliznjak display consistent post-initial placement, and it is easier to account for the data if we assume that both post-initial and contact position were allowed in the vernacular.

To conclude, if we compare the Marianus data to Kosek et al.'s Old Czech data, we see that even though the placement of pronominal clitics in both datasets is clearly strongly influenced by their Greek and Latin sources, the postinitial position is much rarer in the Marianus dataset. The preferred position is postverbal contact position. In the Old Czech data, Kosek et al. report a large number of examples of postinitial *sě* in cases where its only correspondence is a synthetic middle/passive verb form. In the Marianus dataset, we see that even these examples are predominantly in postverbal contact position. Data from non-translated Church Slavonic sources convincingly show a very different picture (Pichkhadze this volume), so it seems likely that the postinitial position was more prominent in the early South Slavonic vernacular than the Marianus data let on. However, it is difficult to account for the data if we assume that the postverbal contact position is an entirely non-Slavonic phenomenon.

7 Aorists and resultatives in performative formulae

Dekker's contribution looks at tense usage in performative formulae in Novgorodian birchbark letters, and observes a tendency for the aorist to replace the resultative in such constructions at a stage when the aorist was almost certainly no longer in use in the vernacular. He argues that this use of the aorist has models both in Ancient Greek and (Old) Church Slavonic. As he points out, OCS resultatives (*l*-forms) and Greek perfects are clearly not semantically equivalent. While the tense usage in the Marianus dataset largely follows the tense usage in Greek, the relationship between perfect and resultatives are a clear deviation. This can be seen in Table 7.

Table 7: OCS tense and Greek tense, all indicative aligned verb forms in the Codex Marianus.

	Greek aorist	Greek future	Greek imperfect	Greek pluperfect	Greek present	Greek perfect
OCS aorist	2955	6	79	13	393	**171**
OCS future	0	121	0	0	15	0
OCS imperfect	43	0	901	32	19	1
OCS present	17	727	3	1	2272	123
OCS resultative	**89**	1	27	13	7	18

OCS resultatives are usually translations of Greek aorists, while Greek perfects are normally translated as OCS aorists (62).[20] This constitutes the strongest piece of evidence that Greek tense was not slavishly transferred to OCS, and makes it seem unlikely that that OCS borrowed the use of the resultative or aorist in assertive declaratives from Greek.

---

[20] The number of present-tense translations also seems large, but 102 out of 123 occurrences are examples of Greek *oida* 'know', which irregularly uses the perfect tense in present meaning.

(62) a. οὔπω   γὰρ   ἀναβέβηκα   πρὸς   τὸν   πατέρα
       oupō   gar   anabebēka   pros   ton   patera
       not_yet   for   ascend.PRF.1SG to   the   father.ACC
    b. не   оу   бо   вьзидъ   къ   ѿцю   моемоу
       ne   u   bo   vьzidъ   kъ   otcju   moemu
       not   yet   for   ascend.AOR.1SG to   father.DAT my.M.DAT.SG
       'I have not yet ascended to the Father' (Jn. 20.17, 23338, 42955)

How, then, are assertive declaratives expressed in the Marianus dataset? While a full scrutiny of all potential candidates is beyond the scope of this brief survey, one way of looking for at least some of them is to extract sentences with first-person finite verb forms and the interjection *se* 'lo, behold', which is often found in Dekker's birchbark examples as well. There are 29 such examples in the Marianus dataset, twelve of which appear to be reasonably clear examples of assertive declaratives, such as (63).

(63) a. ἰδοὺ   τὰ   ἡμίσειά   μου   τῶν   ὑπαρχόντων,
       idou   ta   hēmiseia   mou   tōn   huparchontōn
       behold   the   half.ACC.PL   me.GEN   the   possession.GEN.PL
       κύριε,   τοῖς   πτωχοῖς   δίδωμι
       kurie,   tois   ptōchois   didōmi
       lord.VOC   the   poor.DAT.PL give.PRS.3SG
    b. се   полъ   имениѣ   моего   ги
       se   polъ   iměnija   moego   gi
       behold   half.ACC   property.GEN   my.N.GEN.SG   lord.VOC
       дамъ   ништиимъ
       damъ   ništiimъ
       give.PRS.3SG   poor.DAT.PL
       'Behold, Lord, the half of my goods I give to the poor'
       (Lk. 19.8, 21417, 41151)

Eleven of the examples, such as (63), have an OCS present-tense form, and ten of the examples have a present tense form in Greek too. Six of the OCS present-tense verbs are perfective-looking, such as (63), the rest of them look imperfective (*posylajǫ* vs. *sъljǫ*, *damъ* vs. *dajǫ*, for instance), cf. the interesting discussion on the ideal form for performatives in Dekker 2016. One example has a present-tense form (of an imperfective-looking verb) rendering a Greek perfect (64), and another has an aorist rendering a Greek aorist (65).

(64) a. ἰδοὺ   δέδωκα   ὑμῖν   τὴν   ἐξουσίαν   τοῦ
       idou   dedōka   humin   tēn   exousian   tou
       behold   give.PRF.1SG you.DAT   the   power.ACC   the.GEN
       πατεῖν   ἐπάνω   ὄφεων
       patein   epanō   opheōn
       trample.INF.PRS   on   snake.GEN.PL

   b. Се   даѭ   вамь   власть   настѫпати
      Se   dajǫ   vamъ   vlastь   nastǫpati
      behold give.PRS.1SG   you.DAT   power.ACC   step_on.INF
      на   змиѩ
      na   zmiję
      on   snake.ACC.PL
      'Behold, I give you the authority to tread upon serpents'
      (Lk. 10.19, 20838, 40596)

(65) a. καὶ   ἰδοὺ   ἐγὼ   ἐνώπιον   ὑμῶν
        kai   idou   egō   enōpion   humōn
        and   behold I.NOM   before   you.GEN.PL
        ἀνακρίνας   οὐθὲν   εὗρον   ἐν   τῷ
        anakrinas   outhen   heuron   en   tōi
        examine.PTCP.AOR.M.NOM.SG   nothing.ACC   find.AOR.1SG in   the
        ἀνθρώπῳ   τούτῳ   αἴτιον,
        anthrōpōi   toutōi   aition
        man.DAT   this.M.DAT.SG guilt.ACC

   a. ι   се   азъ   истѧзавъ
      i   se   azъ   istęzavъ
      and   behold   I.NOM   examine.PTCP.PST.M.NOM.SG
      обрѣтъ   прѣдъ   вами.   не   ни   единоѩ
      obrětъ   prědъ   vami.   ne   ni   edinoję
      find.AOR.3SG before   you.INS.PL   not   not   one.F.GEN.SG
      же   о   ч҃лвцѣ   семь   вины
      že   o   člvcě   semь   viny
      PTCL   about   man.LOC   this.M.LOC.SG   guilt.GEN
      'and behold, having examined Him before you, I have found no guilt
      in this man' (Lk. 23.14, 21745, 58769)

This is not much material, but it suggests that the present tense was a common choice in assertive declarations both in OCS and Greek, but also that the perfect and the aorist were possible choices in Greek.

8 Relative clauses

In their contribution to this volume, Sonnenhauser and Eberle explore the origins of the relativising function of the originally interrogative pronoun of the type 'which of two' in North Slavonic, such as Russian *kotoryj*, Polish *który* and Czech *který*, whereas Podtergera (2017) discusses the possibility that the introduction of Russian *kotoryj* in relative clauses was a contact-induced change. In the Marianus dataset, the situation is very simple: There are eight occurrences of *kotoryi*, and all of them have a clear interrogative function. They all have modifiers denoting 'of a certain group', but there is only one example where the group consists of only two individuals (66). None of the examples seem to be potential bridging constructions for future relative clauses, as hypothesised by Večerka (2002: 179).

(66) a. τίς   οὖν   αὐτῶν   πλεῖον   ἀγαπήσει   αὐτόν;
         tis   oun   autōn   pleion   agapēsei   auton
         who.M.NOM.SG   PTCL   he.GEN.PL   more   love.FUT.3SG he.ACC
         котории   оубо   ею   паче   възлюбитъ   и.
         kotory   ubo   eju   pače   vъzljubity   i
         which.M.NOM.SG PTCL   he.GEN.DU   more   love.PRS.3SG he.ACC
         'Now which of them will love him more?' (Lk. 7.42, 20591, 40362)

As in (66), they all correspond to Greek *tis* 'what, who', which is the general Greek interrogative pronoun 'who', and which does not come with any explicit contrastive semantics. There are 379 examples of Greek interrogative *tis* with an OCS correspondence in the material. The most common translations are, unsurprisingly, *čьto* 'what' (214 occurrences) and *kъto* 'who' (95 occurrences). The choice of *kotoryi* thus seems entirely independent of the Greek.

Podtergera also discusses the use of *čto* as a relative pronoun in colloquial Russian. The situation in the Marianus dataset is similar to that of *kotoryi*: of all the 242 occurrences of *čьto*, none are analysed as relative pronouns in the Marianus dataset. Instead, they can all comfortably be analysed as interrogative pronouns in direct or indirect questions (67) or as indefinite pronouns (68).

(67) a. μὴ   γνώτω   ἡ   ἀριστερά   σου
         mē   gnōtō   hē   aristera   sou
         not   know.IMP.AOR.3SG   the   left.F.NOM.SG   you.GEN
         τί   ποιεῖ   ἡ   δεξιά   σου
         ti   poiei   hē   dexia   sou
         what.N.ACC.SG   do.PRS.3SG   the   right.F.NOM.SG you.GEN

b. да   не   чюетъ   шюица   твоѣ.
    da   ne   čjuetъ   šjuica   tvoja
    may   not notice.PRS.3SG left_hand.NOM your.F.NOM.SG
    чьто   творитъ   десʼница   твоѣ.
    čьto   tvoritъ   desʼnica   tvoja
    what.ACC   do.PRS.3SG right_hand.NOM your.F.NOM.SG
    'do not let your left hand know what your right hand is doing'
    (Mt. 6.3, 14826, 38412)

(68) a. ἐπηρώτα   αὐτόν,   εἴ τι   βλέπει;
        epērōta   auton   ei ti   blepei
        ask.IMPERF.3SG he.ACC   if something.ACC see.PRS.3SG
     b. въпрашааше   и   аште   чьто   видитъ.
        vъprašaaše   i   ašte   čьto   viditъ
        ask.IMPERF.3SG   he.ACC   if   something.ACC   see.PRS.3SG
        'he asked him if he could see anything' (Mk. 8.23, 6938, 36781)

The standard relative pronoun in OCS is, as Podtergera points out, *iže* 'who, which'. There are 541 occurrences of relative *iže* in the Marianus dataset, 465 of which are aligned with the standard Greek relative pronoun *hos*. The translation is thus not mechanical. A further 50 examples are translations of the Greek indefinite relative pronoun *hostis* 'whoever, whatever, someone who, something which'. Interestingly, only five of these examples have the particle *ašte* to indicate indefiniteness. The remaining examples are translations of various other relative expressions, as well as a range of non-relative pronouns. Note that *iže* translations of Greek nominalised prepositional phrases (see Fuchsbauer this volume) are taken to be elliptic relative clauses in the PROIEL/TOROT analysis, so they are included in this count. In the Greek source text there are 480 occurrences of *hos* that are aligned with some OCS item. As we already know, 465 of them are translated into *iže*. The 15 remaining occurrences are rendered by a diverse range of relative expressions (*eliko, elikože, ideže*) and regular pronouns (*i, tъ, ovъ, onъ*). The usage of *iže* thus seems to be wider than that of *hos*, which does not suggest strong Greek influence on this particular syntactic pattern.

9 Conclusion

In this article I have made an attempt at linking the studies in this volume up with the situation in canonical Church Slavonic, as attested in the Codex Marianus, and its source text, the Greek Gospels. The results fall into two rough types. On the one hand we have syntactic phenomena that appear to have been influenced by the Greek source text, as well as by the the source language in the later study, but not necessarily to the same extent. This is clearly the case for the accusative with infinitive (Gavrančić and Tomelleri) and the placement of pronoun clitics (Kosek et al.): the Greek source text exerted the same type of influence on the language of the Marianus as Latin source texts exerted on 16th–19th century Croatian, Russian Church Slavonic and on Old Czech. The same can potentially be said for the dative absolute (Mihaljević 2017), but whatever one may think about the status of the dative absolute in canonical Church Slavonic, it must be considered much less artificial than the instrumental absolute found in 15th century Croatian. The problem we encounter is that raised in the introduction – it is difficult to know for certain exactly which patterns existed in Common Slavonic before the first contact with Greek.

The rest of the studies, except those directly dealing with Old Church Slavonic data, all deal with potentially contact-induced changes that happened after the time of canonical Old Church Slavonic. In some of the cases it seems clear that the Greek source text *could* have influenced the language of the Marianus in a similar way, but that it did not. This is especially clear in the case of numeral syntax. Even though we find exactly the same patterns in the Greek Gospels as in the Latin texts in Słoboda's study, the numeral syntax of the Marianus shows no sign of being influenced by the Greek system. Kisiel and Sobotka's PP-based linking devices are not in evidence in the Marianus dataset, but we do find other PP-based linking devices that seemingly are completely independent from the Greek. Similarly, Sonnenhauser and Eberle (this volume) and Podtergera (2017) look at relative clause patterns that were not yet around in the Marianus dataset. To the extent that we were able to examine tense usage in assertive declaratives (Dekker this volume), we found that it was not obvious that it was influenced by the Greek source text.

This survey is, naturally, relatively superficial and based on a limited empirical material, but it is my hope that it can spark further discussions and interpretations of the data at hand.

References

Dekker, Simeon. 2016. *Old Russian birchbark letters: A pragmatic approach*. PhD dissertation, University of Leiden. https://openaccess.leidenuniv.nl/handle/1887/43413

Eckhoff, Hanne & Dag Haug. 2015. Aspect and prefixation in Old Church Slavonic. *Diachronica* 32(2). 186–230.

Kurešević, Marina. 2018. The status and origin of the *accusativus cum infinitivo* construction in Old Church Slavonic. In Jasmina Grković-Major, Björn Hansen and Barbara Sonnenhauser (eds.), *Diachronic Slavonic syntax: The interplay between internal development, language contact and metalinguistic factors*, 261–283. Berlin: De Gruyter Mouton.

Lunt, Horace. 2001. *Old Church Slavonic Grammar*. 7th revised edition. Berlin: Mouton de Gruyter.

MacRobert, Catherine Mary. 1986. Foreign, naturalized and native syntax in Old Church Slavonic. *Transactions of the Philological Society* 84(1). 142–166.

Mihaljević, Milan. 2017. Absolute Constructions in the Second Beram (Ljubljana) Breviary. Paper presented at the workshop Diachronic Slavonic Syntax 3: Traces of Latin, Greek and Old Church Slavonic in Slavonic syntax, University of Salzburg, 3–4 November.

Podtergera, Irina. 2020. Otnositel'nye predloženija v russko-cerkovnoslavjanskom perevode „latinskix" knig Gennadievskoj biblii (na primere 1-oj knigi Paralipomenon [Relative clauses in the Russian Church Slavonic translation of the „Latin" books of the Gennadius Bible (The case of 1 Chronicle)]. *Trudy Instituta russkogo jazyka im. V. V. Vinogradova. Vypusk 23. Grammatičeskie processy i sistemy v diachronii. Pamjati Andreja Anatel'eviča Zaliznjaka*. 240–278.

Thomason, Sarah. 2006. Rule borrowing. In Keith Brown (ed.), *Encyclopedia of Language and Linguistics*, vol. 10, 671–677. 2nd edn. Oxford: Elsevier.

Tischendorf, Constantin von. 1869–1872. *Novum Testamentum Graece*. 8th edn. Leipzig: Hinrichs.

Večerka, Radoslav. 1971. Vliv řečtiny na staroslověnštinu. *Listy filologické* 94(2). 129–151.

Večerka, Radoslav. 1998. *Altkirchenslavische (altbulgarische) Syntax. I. Die Satztypen: Der zusammengesetzte Satz*. Freiburg: U.W.Weiher.

Večerka, Radoslav. 2002. *Altkirchenslavische (altbulgarische) Syntax. IV. Die lineare Satzorganisation*. Freiburg: U.W.Weiher.

Zaliznjak, Andrej A. 2008. *Drevnerusskie enklitiki* [Old Russian enclitics]. Moscow: Jazyki slavjanskich kul'tur.

Index

accusative with participle 219, 261, 265, 269
accusative with infinitive (AcI) 6, 81–82, 84–90, 93–94, 96–97, 100–103, 201, 213, 215, 217, 219, 221, 227, 257–267, 269–271, 274, 281, 301
adverbial 145, 147, 149, 258, 261, 264, 269, 273–274
adverbial clause 149, 261, 269, 273
adverbial participle 147, 272
agreement 37, 40–43, 45–47, 49–50, 118, 285–287
aorist 7, 179–180, 186–192, 271, 296–298

Baltic 137, 145–147
bilingualism 2, 5, 37–39, 43, 50, 82–84, 101–102, 123, 229, 249
birchbark letters 155, 159, 179–184, 186, 190–195, 296–297
Bulgarian 56, 165–166

Čakavian 88–90
cardinal number 39–46, 48–50, 283
Church Slavonic 1–7, 133–134, 139, 146, 148–149, 153, 155, 158–159, 163–164, 166, 179–180, 189, 194, 201–202, 204–205, 211, 213, 220, 226–228, 233, 236, 256, 275, 295, 300–301
code-switching 43–44, 50
Codex Assemanianus 25, 163–165, 167–169, 171–175
Codex Marianus 159, 165, 169, 171–172, 174, 212, 233, 244–248, 256–258, 263, 269–270, 274–275, 278–280, 283, 286–289, 294–297, 299–301
Codex Zographensis 134, 164–165, 169, 244
complement clause 86, 93–94, 146, 149, 258, 261, 268–269
conjunction 11–15, 25–27, 29–30, 32, 63, 85, 134, 147, 151, 153, 209, 210, 217, 235
'contact' word order 53, 60
Croatian 4, 6, 17, 56, 81–82, 84–85, 87–90, 93–94, 97, 100–102, 113, 159, 207, 234–236, 238, 240, 244, 248–249, 257–258, 269, 274, 301

Croatian Church Slavonic 5, 7, 84–85, 90, 233, 235–242, 244, 247–249
Czech 4, 6, 15, 17, 24, 25, 27, 29, 32, 37, 47, 53–57, 62, 66–67, 73–74, 82, 85, 102, 107, 123, 280, 288, 299

dative absolute 174, 208–209, 211, 260–261, 264, 269–274, 278, 301
dative with infinitive (DcI) 212–213, 219, 226, 257, 260–261, 264–266, 269
definite article 18, 31, 163, 260
definiteness 21, 32, 123, 146, 164

East Slavonic 4–5, 11, 15, 25, 31–32, 108, 124, 158, 194, 295
enclitic 53–64, 72, 75, 77, 133, 158
external factors 37–38, 201

face-to-face contact 2, 5, 124–125

genitive absolute 270–271, 273–274, 278
German 4–5, 37, 50, 89, 108, 123–126, 142, 184, 224, 235
Germanic 4, 20, 234
glagolitic 169, 203, 234, 236–238, 240, 242–243, 269
grammatical replication 101
grammaticalization 6, 11, 14–15, 25, 29, 31–32, 102, 159, 278
Greek 1–7, 11, 15, 31–32, 50, 64, 84–86, 133, 142, 147–149, 153, 155, 158–159, 163–177, 179–181, 188–189, 193, 196, 202–206, 208–209, 211, 213, 218, 219–220, 227, 233, 236–239, 244–248, 255–258, 261–265, 267, 269–276, 278–284, 286–288, 293–301
Greek influence 6, 101, 159–160, 163, 190, 293, 295, 300

indefiniteness 21, 111, 137–138, 146, 299–300
infinite construction 133–134, 153
infinitive 56, 85–86, 90, 93–94, 148–149, 151, 153, 164, 169, 173–177, 201–202,

204, 206, 211, 213, 215– 219, 221, 227–228, 255, 257–270, 276, 278, 301
infinitive clause 93, 97, 133, 148–149, 151, 211, 216
internal factors 37, 89, 103
interrogative pronoun 107, 123, 134, 299
Italian 87, 89, 94, 123, 239

Kajkavian 6, 88–90, 107–108, 112–116, 121, 123–126

language contact 1–3, 6, 50, 83–85, 88, 101, 107, 124, 282
language of distance 7, 179, 180, 184, 186, 196
Latin influence 2, 5–6, 11, 54, 69, 74, 76–77, 82, 122, 124–126, 221, 228, 238
light verb 133, 153, 158
linking particle 11, 13–15, 25–27, 30, 32, 278
literacy 5, 37, 82–84, 88, 107, 125–126, 163, 179, 181–182, 184, 190–194
literacy contact 1–6
literacy interference 1–2
Lithuanian 134–135, 142

matrix clause 55, 117, 149, 153, 213, 219
matrix verb 81, 84–85, 90, 93–94, 97, 101

non-standard(ised) 116, 126, 234, 236
North Slavonic 6, 11, 15, 25, 31, 107, 112, 299
numeral 6, 37–41, 43, 45–47, 49–50, 164, 255, 282–284, 286–288, 301

Old Church Slavonic (OCS) 3–5, 7, 15, 24, 31, 50, 64, 85, 101, 138, 153, 158, 163–165, 168–169, 174, 179–180, 189–190, 201–204, 211, 219, 221, 228, 233, 236, 238–240, 244–248, 255–258, 260–265, 267, 269–276, 278–280, 282–284, 286–289, 293–301
Old Czech 5–6, 46, 53–55, 58–60, 63–65, 67–77, 135, 288, 295, 301
Old Polish 6, 13, 31, 37–40, 46, 49–50, 108, 135, 283
Old Russian (OR) 7, 15, 26, 31, 116, 135, 137, 140, 142–144, 146–147, 149, 151, 179–180, 182–183, 186, 188–191, 194–196

participial construction 201, 221–222, 225, 228
pattern replication 81, 87, 89
perception verb 85, 94, 102–103, 267
perfect 71, 179–180, 183, 185–191, 271, 296–298
performative 7, 179–180, 182–183, 186–191, 194, 196, 255, 296–297
Polish 1, 4, 6, 11–13, 15, 17–18, 20–25, 27, 29, 31–32, 37–41, 43–50, 82, 85, 90, 94, 102, 111, 117, 119, 123–124, 280, 282–283, 299
pragmaticalization 11, 15

relative clause (RC) 18, 22, 107–110, 112–114, 117, 120–123, 126, 135, 145, 166, 168–170, 172, 174, 255, 299–301
relative pronoun 7, 21–22, 108–109, 111, 117–118, 125, 135, 137, 163, 165–166, 168, 172–173, 176, 256, 299–300
relativisation marker 112, 124
replication 81, 83–87, 89–90, 101
Romance 4, 86–87, 89, 94, 234, 236
Russian Church Slavonic 159, 166, 201, 269, 275, 301

Second Beram breviary 233, 239–244, 247–249, 269
second South Slavonic influence 166, 195
Serbian 85, 94, 103, 209
Slavia orthodoxa 3–5
Slavia romana 3–4
Slavonic languages 1, 4, 6, 11, 17, 20, 24, 27, 32, 37, 50, 56, 82, 85, 90, 123–124, 138, 146, 149, 153, 158–159, 160, 176, 234
Slovene 4–6, 107–112, 114–116, 121–126
sociolinguistic 81–82, 84, 102, 180, 194, 248
South Slavonic 3–6, 108, 126, 166, 295
standardisation 113
Štokavian 88–90, 113
structural borrowing 83
syntactic calque 101, 201, 204
syntactic change 1, 6, 37, 41, 50, 81, 83–84, 88, 94, 100, 102, 233

translation 2, 4–5, 7, 30–31, 37–39, 48, 50, 53–54, 58–60, 63–65, 68–69, 72–75, 77, 87–90, 93–94, 96, 101, 124, 134, 137, 141–144, 153, 156–159, 164–166, 168–170, 174–176, 179–180, 183, 189, 201, 203–207, 210–211, 213, 215, 220–222, 224–225, 227–228, 238–239, 241, 245, 247–248, 255–258, 260–264, 269, 271–272, 274–276, 287, 295–296, 299–300

verba dicendi 85–86

verba sentiendi 81, 86–87, 90, 93, 97, 101, 222

vernacular 1, 4–7, 41, 81–85, 88, 90, 96–97, 101–102, 108, 124, 179–180, 183, 186, 192, 195, 236, 238, 240, 244, 269, 295–296

Vulgate 6, 53, 59, 63–64, 68–69, 73–76, 89, 90, 170, 257

West Slavonic 3–5, 11, 15, 31–32, 278

word order 6, 53, 54–57, 59, 62–64, 71, 74–77, 87, 133, 158–159, 203, 233, 235–236, 239–243, 245–247, 249, 294

www.ingramcontent.com/pod-product-compliance
Lightning Source LLC
Chambersburg PA
CBHW031422150426
43191CB00006B/355